CUBA

MINING LAWS AND REGULATIONS HANDBOOK

VOLUME 1

STRATEGIC INFORMATION AND REGULATIONS

International Business Publications, USA
Washington DC, USA

CUBA
MINING LAWS AND REGULATIONS HANDBOOK
VOLUME 1 STRATEGIC INFORMATION AND REGULATIONS

UPDATED ANNUALLY

We express our sincere appreciation to all government agencies and international organizations which provided information and other materials for this handbook

Cover Design: **International Business Publications, USA**

2016 Updated Reprint International Business Publications, USA
ISBN 1-4330-7726-4

For customer service and information, please contact:

in the USA: **International Business Publications, USA**
P.O.Box 15343, Washington, DC 20003
Phone: (202) 546-2103, Fax: (202) 546-3275.
E-mail: rusric@erols.com

Printed in the USA

CUBA

MINING LAWS AND REGULATIONS HANDBOOK

VOLUME 1

STRATEGIC INFORMATION AND REGULATIONS

TABLE OF CONTENTS

STRATEGIC INFORMATION

Capital and largest city	Havana 23°8′N 82°23′W23.133°N 82.383°W
Official languages	Spanish
Ethnic groups	64.1% White 26.6% Mulatto / Mestizo 9.3% Black
Demonym	Cuban
Government	Single-party Marxist-Leninist state
- President	Raúl Castro
- First Vice President	Miguel Díaz-Canel
- President of the National Assembly	Esteban Lazo Hernández
Legislature	National Assembly
	Independence from Spain
- Ten Years' War	October 10, 1868 – 1878
- Republic declared	May 20, 1902
- Cuban Revolution	July 26, 1953 - January 1, 1959
- Current constitution	February 24, 1976
	Area
- Total	109,884 km^2 (106th) 42,426 sq mi
- Water (%)	negligible
	Population
- 2012 census	11,167,325
- Density	102/km^2 (106th) 264.0/sq mi
GDP (PPP)	2011 estimate
- Total	$212 billion (58th)
- Per capita	$18,796 (60th)
GDP (nominal)	2011 estimate
- Total	$68.233 billion (68th)
- Per capita	$6,051 (90th)
Gini	38.0 medium
HDI	0.815 very high · 44th
Currency	Peso (CUP) Convertible peso[a] (CUC)
Time zone	CST (UTC−5)
- Summer (DST)	CDT (UTC−4)
Drives on the	right
Calling code	+53
ISO 3166 code	CU
Internet TLD	.cu

Cuba, officially the **Republic of Cuba** is an island country in the Caribbean. The nation of Cuba comprises the main island of Cuba, the Isla de la Juventud, and several archipelagos. Havana is the capital of Cuba and its largest city. The second largest city is Santiago de Cuba. To the north of Cuba lies the United States (150 km or 93 mi away), the Bahamas and the Turks and Caicos Islands are to the northeast, Mexico is to the west (210 km or 130 mi away), the Cayman Islands and Jamaica are to the south, and Haiti and the Dominican Republic are to the southeast.

The island of Cuba was inhabited by numerous Mesoamerican tribes prior to the landing of explorer Christopher Columbus in 1492, who claimed it for the Kingdom of Spain. Cuba remained a colony of Spain until the Spanish–American War of 1898, after which it was briefly administered by the United States until gaining nominal independence in 1902. The fragile republic endured increasingly radical politics and social strife, and despite efforts to strengthen its democratic system, Cuba came under the dictatorship of former president Fulgencio Batista in 1952.

Growing unrest and instability led to Batista's ousting in January 1959 by the July 26 movement, which afterwards established a socialist government under the leadership of Fidel Castro. Since 1965, the country has been governed as a single-party state by the Communist Party.

Cuba is the largest island in the Caribbean, and with over 11 million inhabitants, is the second-most populous after Hispaniola, albeit with a much lower population density than most nations in the region. A multiethnic country, its people, culture, and customs derive from diverse origins, including the aboriginal Taíno and Ciboney peoples, the long period of Spanish colonialism, the introduction of African slaves, a close relationship with the Soviet Union during the Cold War, and proximity to the United States.

Cuba ranks high in metrics of health and education, with a very high Human Development Index of 0.815 as of 2014. According to data it presents to the United Nations, Cuba was the only nation in the world in 2006 that met the World Wide Fund for Nature's definition of sustainable development, with an ecological footprint of less than 1.8 hectares per capita, 1.5 hectares, and a Human Development Index of over 0.855

Background: Fidel CASTRO led a rebel army to victory in 1959, and his guiding vision has defined Cuba's Communist revolution while his iron will has held the country together for more than four decades. CASTRO brought Cuba onto the world stage by inviting Soviet support in the 1960s, inciting revolutionary movements throughout Latin America and Africa in the 1970s, and sending his army to fight in Angola in the 1980s. At home, Havana provided Cubans with high levels of healthcare, education, and social security while suppressing the Roman Catholic Church and arresting political dissidents. Cuba is slowly recovering from severe economic recession following the withdrawal of former-Soviet subsidies, worth $4billion-$6 billion per year, in 1990.

GEOGRAPHY

Location: Caribbean, island between the Caribbean Sea and the North Atlantic Ocean, south of Florida
Geographic coordinates: 21 30 N, 80 00 W
Map references: Central America and the Caribbean

Area:
total: 110,860 sq km
land: 110,860 sq km
water: 0 sq km

Area—comparative: slightly smaller than Pennsylvania

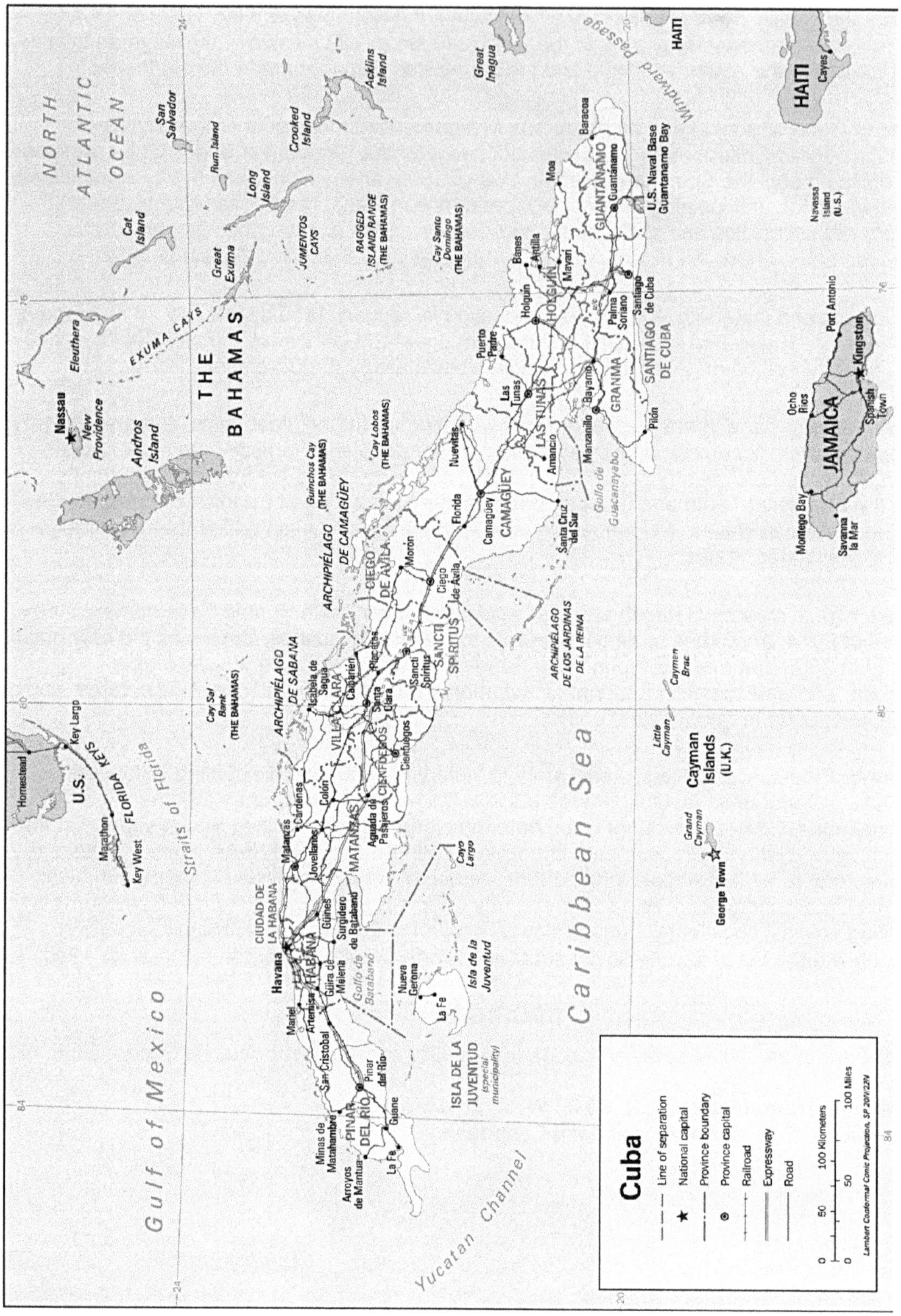

Land boundaries:
total: 29 km

border countries: US Naval Base at Guantanamo Bay 29 km
note: Guantanamo Naval Base is leased by the US and thus remains part of Cuba

Coastline: 3,735 km

Maritime claims:
exclusive economic zone: 200 nm
territorial sea: 12 nm

Climate: tropical; moderated by trade winds; dry season (November to April); rainy season (May to October)

Terrain: mostly flat to rolling plains, with rugged hills and mountains in the southeast

Elevation extremes:
lowest point: Caribbean Sea 0 m *highest point:* Pico Turquino 2,005 m

Natural resources: cobalt, nickel, iron ore, copper, manganese, salt, timber, silica, petroleum

Land use:
arable land: 24% *permanent crops:* 7% *permanent pastures:* 27%
forests and woodland: 24% *other:* 18%

Irrigated land: 9,100 sq km

Natural hazards: the east coast is subject to hurricanes from August to October (in general, the country averages about one hurricane every other year); droughts are common

Environment—current issues: pollution of Havana Bay; overhunting threatens wildlife populations; deforestation

Environment—international agreements:
party to: Antarctic Treaty, Biodiversity, Climate Change, Desertification, Endangered Species, Environmental Modification, Hazardous Wastes, Law of the Sea, Marine Dumping, Ozone Layer Protection, Ship Pollution
signed, but not ratified: Antarctic-Environmental Protocol, Marine Life Conservation

Geography—note: largest country in Caribbean

PEOPLE

Population: 11,096,395

Age structure:
0-14 years: 22% (male 1,236,899; female 1,172,560)
15-64 years: 69% (male 3,820,255; female 3,801,768)
65 years and over: 9% (male 496,772; female 568,141)

Population growth rate: 0.4%
Birth rate: 12.9 births/1,000 population
Death rate: 7.38 deaths/1,000 population

Net migration rate: -1.52 migrant(s)/1,000 population

Sex ratio:
at birth: 1.06 male(s)/female
under 15 years: 1.05 male(s)/female
15-64 years: 1 male(s)/female
65 years and over: 0.87 male(s)/female
total population: 1 male(s)/female

Infant mortality rate: 7.81 deaths/1,000 live births

Life expectancy at birth:
total population: 75.78 years
male: 73.41 years
female: 78.3 years

Total fertility rate: 1.58 children born/woman

Nationality:
noun: Cuban(s)
adjective: Cuban

Ethnic groups: mulatto 51%, white 37%, black 11%, Chinese 1%
Religions: nominally 85% Roman Catholic prior to CASTRO assuming power; Protestants, Jehovah's Witnesses, Jews, and Santeria are also represented

Languages: Spanish

Literacy:
definition: age 15 and over can read and write
total population: 95.7%
male: 96.2%
female: 95.3%

GOVERNMENT

Country name:
conventional long form:
Republic of Cuba
conventional short form:
Cuba
local long form:
Republica de Cuba
local short form:
Cuba

Government type:
Communist state

Capital:
name:
Havana
geographic coordinates:
23 07 N, 82 21 W
time difference:
UTC-5 (same time as Washington, DC, during Standard Time)
daylight saving time:
+1hr, begins second Sunday in March; ends first Sunday in November; note - Cuba has been known to alter the schedule of DST on short notice in an attempt to conserve electricity for lighting

Administrative divisions:
15 provinces (provincias, singular - provincia) and 1 special municipality* (municipio especial); Artemisa, Camaguey, Ciego de Avila, Cienfuegos, Granma, Guantanamo, Holguin, Isla de la Juventud*, La Habana, Las Tunas, Matanzas, Mayabeque, Pinar del Rio, Sancti Spiritus, Santiago de Cuba, Villa Clara

Independence:
20 May 1902 (from Spain 10 December 1898; administered by the US from 1898 to 1902); noacknowledged by the Cuban Government as a day of independence

National holiday:
Triumph of the Revolution, 1 January (1959)

Constitution:
several previous; latest adopted by referendum 15 February 1976, effective 24 February 1976; amended 1978, 1992, 2002 (2010)

Legal system:
civil law system based on Spanish civil code

International law organization participation:
has not submitted an ICJ jurisdiction declaration; non-party state to the ICCt

Suffrage:
16 years of age; universal

Executive branch:
chief of state:
President of the Council of State and President of the Council of Ministers Gen. Raul CASTRO Ruz (president since 24 February 2008); First Vice President of the Council of State and First Vice President of the Council of Ministers Miguel DIAZ-CANEL Bermudez (since 24 February 2013); note - the president is both chief of state and head of government
head of government:
President of the Council of State and President of the Council of Ministers Gen. Raul CASTRO Ruz (president since 24 February 2008); First Vice President of the Council of State and First Vice President of the Council of Ministers Miguel DIAZ-CANEL Bermudez (since 24 February 2013)
cabinet:
Council of Ministers proposed by the president of the Council of State, appointed by the National

Assembly or the 28-member Council of State, and elected by the assembly to act on its behalf when it is not in session

elections:

president and vice presidents elected by the National Assembly for a five-year term; election last held on 24 February 2013 (next to be held in 2018)

election results:

Gen. Raul CASTRO Ruz reelected president; percent of legislative vote - 100%; Miguel DIAZ-CANEL Bermudez elected vice president; percent of legislative vote - 100%

Legislative branch:

unicameral National Assembly of People's Power or Asamblea Nacional del Poder Popular (number of seats in the National Assembly is based on population and currently exceeds 600; members elected directly from slates approved by special candidacy commissions to serve five-year terms)

elections:

last held on 3 February 2013 (next to be held in 2018)

election results:

Cuba's Communist Party is the only legal party, and officially sanctioned candidates run unopposed

Judicial branch:

highest court(s):

People's Supreme Court (consists of court president, vice president, 41 professional justices, and NA lay judges; organized into the "Whole," State Council, and criminal, civil, administrative, labor, crimes against the state, and military courts)

judge selection and term of office:

professional judges elected by the National Assembly to serve 2.5-year terms; lay judges nominated by workplace collectives and neighborhood associations and elected by municipal or provincial assemblies; lay judges appointed for 5-year terms and serve up to 30 days per year

subordinate courts:

People's Provincial Courts; People's Regional Courts; People's Courts

Political parties and leaders:

Cuban Communist Party or PCC [Raul CASTRO Ruz, first secretary]

Political pressure groups and leaders:

Damas de Blanco
National Association of Small Farmers
Patriotic Union of Cuba
political dissidents and bloggers
The Cuban Commission for Human Rights and National Reconciliation

International organization participation:

ACP, ALBA, AOSIS, CELAC, FAO, G-77, IAEA, ICAO, ICC (national committees), ICRM, IFAD, IFRCS, IHO, ILO, IMO, IMSO, Interpol, IOC, IOM (observer), IPU, ISO, ITSO, ITU, LAES, LAIA, NAM, OAS (excluded from formal participation since 1962), OPANAL, OPCW, PCA, Petrocaribe, UN, UNCTAD, UNESCO, UNIDO, Union Latina, UNWTO, UPU, WCO, WFTU (NGOs), WHO, WIPO, WMO, WTO

Diplomatic representation in the US:

none; note - the Cuban Interests Section of the Embassy of Switzerland is headed by Jose R. CABANAS Rodriguez (since October 2012); address: Cuban Interests Section, Swiss

Embassy, 2630 16th Street NW, Washington, DC 20009; telephone: (202) 797-8518; FAX: (202) 986-7283

Diplomatic representation from the US:
none; note - the United States Interests Section of the Embassy of Switzerland is headed by John P. CAULFIELD (since September 2011); address: USINT, Swiss Embassy, Calzada between L and M Streets, Vedado, Havana; telephone: [53] (7) 839-4100; FAX: [53] (7) 839-4247; protecting power in Cuba is Switzerland

Flag description:
five equal horizontal bands of blue (top, center, and bottom) alternating with white; a red equilateral triangle based on the hoist side bears a white, five-pointed star in the center; the blue bands refer to the three old divisions of the island: central, occidental, and oriental; the white bands describe the purity of the independence ideal; the triangle symbolizes liberty, equality, and fraternity, while the red color stands for the blood shed in the independence struggle; the white star, called La Estrella Solitaria (the Lone Star) lights the way to freedom and was taken from the flag of Texas
note:design similar to the Puerto Rican flag, with the colors of the bands and triangle reversed

National anthem:
name:
"La Bayamesa" (The Bayamo Song)

ECONOMY

The government continues to balance the need for loosening its socialist economic system against a desire for firm political control. The government in April 2011 held the first Cuban Communist Party Congress in almost 13 years, during which leaders approved a plan for wide-ranging economic changes. Since then, the Cuban government has slowly and incrementally implemented limited economic reforms, including allowing Cubans to buy electronic appliances and cell phones, stay in hotels, and buy and sell used cars.

The Cuban government also opened up some retail services to "self-employment," leading to the rise of so-called "cuentapropistas" or entrepreneurs. Recent moves include permitting the private ownership and sale of real estate and new vehicles, allowing private farmers to sell agricultural goods directly to hotels, and expanding categories of self-employment. Despite these reforms, the average Cuban's standard of living remains at a lower level than before the collapse of the Soviet Union and the resulting downturn of the 1990s. Since late 2000, Venezuela has been providing oil on preferential terms, and it currently supplies over 100,000 barrels per day of petroleum products. Cuba has been paying for the oil, in part, with the services of Cuban personnel in Venezuela, including some 30,000 medical professionals.

GDP (purchasing power parity):
$121 billion (2012 est.)
country comparison to the world: 68
$117.3 billion (2011 est.)
$114.1 billion (2010 est.)
note:data are in 2012 US dollars

GDP (official exchange rate):
$72.3 billion (2012 est.)

GDP - real growth rate:
3.1% (2012 est.)
country comparison to the world: 112
2.8% (2011 est.)
2.4% (2010 est.)

GDP - per capita (PPP):
$10,200 (2010 est.)
country comparison to the world: 118
$10,000 (2009 est.)
$10,000 (2008 est.)
note:data are in 2010 US dollars

Gross national saving:
13.4% of GDP (2013 est.)
country comparison to the world: 118
11.1% of GDP (2012 est.)
11.7% of GDP (2011 est.)

GDP - composition, by end use:
household consumption:
52.1%
government consumption:
34.4%
investment in fixed capital:
10%
investment in inventories:
-3.4%
exports of goods and services:
26%
imports of goods and services:
-19.2%
(2013 est.)

GDP - composition, by sector of origin:
agriculture:
3.8%
industry:
22.3%
services:
73.9% (2013 est.)

Agriculture - products:
sugar, tobacco, citrus, coffee, rice, potatoes, beans; livestock

Industries:
petroleum, nickel, cobalt, pharmaceuticals, tobacco, construction, steel, cement, agricultural machinery, sugar

Industrial production growth rate:

2.6% (2013 est.)
country comparison to the world: 114

Labor force:
5.233 million
country comparison to the world: 72
note:state sector 72.3%, non-state sector 27.7% (2013 est.)

Labor force - by occupation:
agriculture:
19.7%
industry:
17.1%
services:
63.2% (2011)

Unemployment rate:
4.3% (2013 est.)
country comparison to the world: 39
3.8% (2012 est.)
note:these are official rates; unofficial estimates are about double the official figures

Population below poverty line:
NA%

Household income or consumption by percentage share:
lowest 10%:
NA%
highest 10%:
NA%

Budget:
revenues:
$47.62 billion
expenditures:
$50.29 billion (2013 est.)

Taxes and other revenues:
65.9% of GDP (2013 est.)
country comparison to the world: 2

Budget surplus (+) or deficit (-):
-3.7% of GDP (2013 est.)
country comparison to the world: 140

Public debt:
35.9% of GDP (2013 est.)
country comparison to the world: 105
35.8% of GDP (2012 est.)

Fiscal year:
calendar year

Inflation rate (consumer prices):
6% (2013 est.)
country comparison to the world: 172
5.5% (2012 est.)

Central bank discount rate:
NA%

Commercial bank prime lending rate:
NA%

Stock of narrow money:
$11.21 billion (31 December 2013 est.)
country comparison to the world: 74
$10.97 billion (31 December 2012 est.)

Stock of broad money:
$24.63 billion (31 December 2013 est.)
country comparison to the world: 78
$24.08 billion (31 December 2012 est.)

Stock of domestic credit:
$NA

Current account balance:
$289.8 million (2013 est.)
country comparison to the world: 55
-$134.4 million (2012 est.)

Exports:
$6.252 billion (2013 est.)
country comparison to the world: 107
$5.972 billion (2012 est.)

Exports - commodities:
petroleum, nickel, medical products, sugar, tobacco, fish, citrus, coffee

Exports - partners:
Canada 17.7%, China 16.9%, Venezuela 12.5%, Netherlands 9%, Spain 5.9% (2012)

Imports:
$13.6 billion (2013 est.)
country comparison to the world: 89
$13.72 billion (2012 est.)

Imports - commodities:

petroleum, food, machinery and equipment, chemicals

Imports - partners:
Venezuela 38.3%, China 10.8%, Spain 8.9%, Brazil 5.2%, US 4.3% (2012)

Reserves of foreign exchange and gold:
$4.993 billion (31 December 2013 est.)
country comparison to the world: 96
$4.693 billion (31 December 2012 est.)

Debt - external:
$23.44 billion (31 December 2013 est.)
country comparison to the world: 78
$22.51 billion (31 December 2012 est.)

Stock of direct foreign investment - at home:
$NA

Stock of direct foreign investment - abroad:
$4.138 billion (2006 est.)
country comparison to the world: 63

Exchange rates:
Cuban pesos (CUP) per US dollar -
1 (2013 est.)
1 (2012 est.)
0.9259 (2010 est.)
0.9259 (2009)
0.9259 (2008)

ENERGY

Electricity - production:
17.8 billion kWh
country comparison to the world: 77

Electricity - consumption:
13.64 billion kWh
country comparison to the world: 80

Electricity - exports:
0 kWh
country comparison to the world: 124

Electricity - imports:
0 kWh
country comparison to the world: 132

Electricity - installed generating capacity:

5.914 million kW
country comparison to the world: 72

Electricity - from fossil fuels:
99.3% of total installed capacity
country comparison to the world: 51

Electricity - from nuclear fuels:
0% of total installed capacity
country comparison to the world: 71

Electricity - from hydroelectric plants:
0.6% of total installed capacity
country comparison to the world: 143

Electricity - from other renewable sources:
0.1% of total installed capacity
country comparison to the world: 103

Crude oil - production:
50,800 bbl/day
country comparison to the world: 61

Crude oil - exports:
83,000 bbl/day
country comparison to the world: 41

Crude oil - imports:
165,000 bbl/day
country comparison to the world: 36

Crude oil - proved reserves:
124 million bbl
country comparison to the world: 69

Refined petroleum products - production:
100,600 bbl/day
country comparison to the world: 73

Refined petroleum products - consumption:
150,200 bbl/day
country comparison to the world: 66

Refined petroleum products - exports:
11,320 bbl/day

country comparison to the world: 83

Refined petroleum products - imports:
4,877 bbl/day
country comparison to the world: 151

Natural gas - production:
1.03 billion cu m
country comparison to the world: 64

Natural gas - consumption:
1.03 billion cu m
country comparison to the world: 88

Natural gas - exports:
0 cu m
country comparison to the world: 85

Natural gas - imports:
0 cu m
country comparison to the world: 180

Natural gas - proved reserves:
70.79 billion cu m
country comparison to the world: 59

Carbon dioxide emissions from consumption of energy:
28.41 million Mt

COMMUNICATIONS

Telephones - main lines in use:
1.217 million
country comparison to the world: 68

Telephones - mobile cellular:
1.682 million
country comparison to the world: 149

Telephone system:
general assessment:
greater investment beginning in 1994 and the establishment of a new Ministry of Information Technology and Communications in 2000 has resulted in improvements in the system; national fiber-optic system under development; 95% of switches digitized by end of 2006; mobile-cellular telephone service is expensive and must be paid in convertible pesos; cell phones in Cuba number around 2 million; state communications started service of email to cell phones through nauta.cu accounts; Cuban Government has opened Internet cafes around the island, which are expensive and offer slow-speed connections
domestic:

fixed-line density remains low at 10 per 100 inhabitants; mobile-cellular service expanding but remains only about 10 per 100 persons
international:
country code - 53; the ALBA-1 fiber-optic submarine cable links Cuba, Jamaica, and Venezuela; fiber-optic cable laid to but not linked to US network; satellite earth station - 1 Intersputnik (Atlantic Ocean region)

Broadcast media:
government owns and controls all broadcast media with private ownership of electronic media prohibited; government operates 4 national TV networks and many local TV stations; government operates 6 national radio networks, an international station, and many local radio stations; Radio-TV Marti is beamed from the US

Internet country code:
.cu

Internet hosts:
3,244
country comparison to the world: 154

Internet users:
1.606 million
country comparison to the world: 79
note:private citizens are prohibited from buying computers or accessing the Internet without special authorization; foreigners may access the Internet in large hotels but are subject to firewalls; some Cubans buy illegal passwords on the black market or take advantage of public outlets to access limited email and the government-controlled "intranet"

TRANSPORTATION

Airports:
133
country comparison to the world: 42

Airports - with paved runways:
total:
64
over 3,047 m:
7
2,438 to 3,047 m:
10
1,524 to 2,437 m:
16
914 to 1,523 m:
4
under 914 m:
27

Airports - with unpaved runways:
total:
69
914 to 1,523 m:

11
under 914 m:
58

Pipelines:
gas 41 km; oil 230 km

Railways:
total:
8,203 km
country comparison to the world: 25
standard gauge:
8,134 km 1.435-m gauge (124 km electrified)
narrow gauge:
69 km 1.000-m gauge
note:48 km of standard gauge track is not for public use

Roadways:
total:
60,858 km
country comparison to the world: 69
paved:
29,820 km (includes 639 km of expressways)
unpaved:
31,038 km

Waterways:
240 km (almost all navigable inland waterways are near the mouths of rivers) (2011)
country comparison to the world: 95

Merchant marine:
total:
3
country comparison to the world: 136
by type:
cargo 1, passenger 1, refrigerated cargo 1
registered in other countries:
5 (Curacao 1, Panama 2, unknown 2) (2010)

Ports and terminals:
major seaport(s):
Antilla, Cienfuegos, Guantanamo, Havana, Matanzas, Mariel, Nuevitas Bay, Santiago de Cuba

MILITARY

Military branches:
Revolutionary Armed Forces (Fuerzas Armadas Revolucionarias, FAR): Revolutionary Army (Ejercito Revolucionario, ER, includes Territorial Militia Troops (Milicia de Tropas de Territoriales, MTT)); Revolutionary Navy (Marina de Guerra Revolucionaria, MGR, includes Marine Corps); Revolutionary Air and Air Defense Forces (Defensas Anti-Aereas y Fuerza Aerea Revolucionaria, DAAFAR), Youth Labor Army (Ejercito Juvenil del Trabajo, EJT)

Military service age and obligation:
17-28 years of age for compulsory military service; 2-year service obligation; both sexes subject to military service

Manpower available for military service:
males age 16-49: 2,998,201
females age 16-49: 2,919,107

Manpower fit for military service:
males age 16-49: 2,446,131
females age 16-49: 2,375,590

Manpower reaching militarily significant age annually:
male: 72,823
female: 69,108

Military - note:
the collapse of the Soviet Union deprived the Cuban military of its major economic and logistic support and had a significant impact on the state of Cuban equipment; the army remains well trained and professional in nature; the lack of replacement parts for its existing equipment has increasingly affected operational capabilities

TRANSNATIONAL ISSUES

Disputes - international:
US Naval Base at Guantanamo Bay is leased to US and only mutual agreement or US abandonment of the facility can terminate the lease

Trafficking in persons:
current situation: Cuba is a source country for adults and children subjected to forced labor and sex trafficking; child prostitution and child sex tourism reportedly occurs in Cuba, and laws do not appear to penalize the prostitution of children between the ages of 16 and 18; allegations have been made of Cubans being subjected to forced labor, particularly with Cuban work missions abroad; the scope of trafficking within Cuba is particularly difficult to gauge due to the closed nature of the government and sparse non-governmental or independent reporting
tier rating: Tier 3 - Cuba does not fully comply with the minimum standards for the elimination of trafficking and is not making significant efforts to do so; the government has not publicized information about government measures to address human trafficking through prosecution, protection, or prevention efforts but did share information about its general approach to protection for children and youth; the government has a network of shelters for victims of domestic violence and child abuse but has not verified if trafficking victims receive care in those centers

Illicit drugs:
territorial waters and air space serve as transshipment zone for US- and European-bound drugs; established the death penalty for certain drug-related crimes in 1999 (2008)

IMPORTANT INFORMATION FOR UNDERSTANDING CUBA

PROFILE

OFFICIAL NAME: Republic of Cuba

Geography
Area: 110,860 sq. km. (44,200 sq. mi.); about the size of Pennsylvania.
Cities: *Capital*--Havana (pop. 2 million). *Other major cities*--Santiago de Cuba, Camaguey, Santa Clara, Holguin, Guantanamo, Matanzas, Cienfuegos, Pinar del Rio.
Terrain: Flat or gently rolling plains, hills; mountains up to 2,000 meters (6,000 ft.) in the southeast.
Climate: Tropical, moderated by trade winds; dry season (November-April); rainy season (May-October).

People
Population: 11 million; 70% urban, 30% rural.
Ethnic groups: 51% mulatto, 37% white, 11% black, 1% Chinese (according to Cuban census data).
Language: Spanish. *Literacy*--97% (according to Cuban government sources).
Work force (4.6 million): *Government and services*--30%; *industry*--22%; *agriculture*--24%; *commerce*--11%; *construction*--11%; *transportation and communications*--6%.

Government
Type: Totalitarian Communist state; current government assumed power by force January 1, 1959.
Independence: May 20, 1902.
Political party: Cuban Communist Party (PCC); only one party allowed.
Administrative subdivisions: 14 provinces, including the city of Havana, and one special municipality (Isle of Youth).

Economy
Natural resources: Nickel, cobalt, iron ore, copper, manganese, salt, timber, oil, natural gas.
Agriculture: *Products*--sugar, citrus and tropical fruits, tobacco, coffee, rice, beans, meat, vegetables.
Industry: *Types*--sugar and food processing, oil refining, cement, electric power, light consumer and industrial products, pharmaceutical and biotech products.
Trade: *Exports*--$1.999 billion f.o.b. (2005): nickel/cobalt, pharmaceutical and biotech products, sugar and its byproducts, tobacco, seafood, citrus, tropical fruits, coffee. *Major markets* (2005)--Netherlands $599.7 million (30%); Canada $437.9 (22%); Venezuela $241 million (12%); Spain $161.2 million (8%); China $99.6 million (5%); Russia $57.6 million (3%); France $49.3 million (2%); others $352.5 million (18%). *Imports* --$7.528 billion f.o.b. (2005): petroleum, food, machinery, chemicals. *Major suppliers* (2005)--Venezuela $1.859 billion (25%); China $885.4 million (12%); Spain $653.3 (9%); United States $470.3 (9%); Canada $327.9 million (4%); Brazil $312.4 million (4%); Germany $309.3 million (4%); Italy $292 million (4%); Mexico (4%); Vietnam $251.8 (3%); others (25%).
Official exchange rate: Convertible pesos per U.S.$1 = 0.93.
Cuba has two currencies in circulation: the Cuban peso (CUP), and the convertible peso (CUC). In April 2005, the official exchange rate changed from $1 per CUC to $1.08 per CUC (0.93 CUC per $1), both for individuals and enterprises. Individuals can buy 24 Cuban pesos (CUP) for each

CUC sold, or sell 25 Cuban pesos for each CUC bought; enterprises, however, must exchange CUP and CUC at a 1:1 ratio. It is also important to note that the Cuban regime taxes and receives approximately 10% of each conversion of U.S. dollars into CUCs.

PEOPLE AND RELIGION

Cuba is a multiracial society with a population of mainly Spanish and African origins. The largest organized religion is the Roman Catholic Church, but evangelical protestant denominations continue to grow rapidly. Afro-Cuban religions, a blend of native African religions and Roman Catholicism, are widely practiced in Cuba. Officially, Cuba has been an atheist state for most of the Castro era. In 1962, the government of Fidel Castro seized and shut down more than 400 Catholic schools, charging that they spread dangerous beliefs among the people. In 1991, however, the Communist Party lifted its prohibition against religious believers seeking membership, and a year later the constitution was amended to characterize the state as secular instead of atheist.

While the Cuban constitution recognizes the right of citizens to freedom of religion, the government de facto restricts that freedom. Twenty-two denominations, including Presbyterians, Episcopalians, and Methodists, are members of the Cuban Council of Churches (CCC). Most CCC members are officially recognized by the State, though several, including the Evangelical Lutheran Church, are not registered and are recognized only through their membership in the CCC. Another 31 officially recognized denominations, including Jehovah's Witnesses and the small Jewish community, do not belong to the CCC. The government does not favor any one particular religion or church; however, the government appears to be most tolerant of those churches that maintain close relations to the State through the CCC. Unregistered religious groups experience various degrees of official interference, harassment, and repression. The Ministry of Interior engages in active efforts to control and monitor the country's religious institutions, including through surveillance, infiltration and harassment of religious professionals and practitioners. The most independent religious organizations--including the Catholic Church, the largest independent institution in Cuba today--continue to operate under significant restrictions and pressure imposed on them by the Cuban regime. The Cuban Government continues to refuse to allow the church to have independent printing press capabilities; full access to the media; to train enough priests for its needs or allow adequate numbers of foreign priests to work in the country; or to establish socially useful institutions, including schools and universities, hospitals and clinics, and nursing homes. All registered denominations must report to the Ministry of Interior's Office of Religious Affairs.

The visit of Pope John Paul II in January 1998 was seen as an important, positive event for bringing a message of hope and the need for respect of human rights. Unfortunately, these improvements did not continue once the Pope left the island. While some visas were issued for additional priests to enter Cuba around the time of the visit, the regime has again sharply restricted issuance of visas. Moreover, despite explicit regime guarantees and repeated follow-up requests, the regime has refused to permit the Catholic Church to establish Internet connections or an intranet among dioceses on the Island. In a pastoral letter entitled "There is No Country Without Virtue" ("No Hay Patria Sin Virtud"), the Cuban Conference of Catholic Bishops in February 2003 openly criticized the government's strict control over the activities of the Catholic Church, especially state restrictions on religious education and Church access to mass media, as well as the increasingly amoral and irreligious character of Cuban society under Communist rule.

Other Cuban religious groups--including evangelical Christians, whose numbers continue to grow rapidly--also have benefited from the relative relaxation of official restrictions on religious organizations and activities. Although particularly hard hit by emigration, Cuba's small Jewish community continues to hold services in Havana and has members in Santiago, Camaguey, and other parts of the island. See also the Department's report on international religious freedom for further information.

HISTORY

Spanish settlers established the raising of cattle, sugarcane, and tobacco as Cuba's primary economic pursuits. As the native Indian population died out, African slaves were imported to work the ranches and plantations. Slavery was abolished in 1886.

Cuba was the last major Spanish colony to gain independence, following a lengthy struggle begun in 1868. Jose Marti, Cuba's national hero, helped initiate the final push for independence in 1895. In 1898, the United States entered the conflict after the USS Maine sank in Havana Harbor on February 15 due to an explosion of undetermined origin. In December of that year, Spain relinquished control of Cuba to the United States with the Treaty of Paris. On May 20, 1902, the United States granted Cuba its independence but retained the right to intervene to preserve Cuban independence and stability in accordance with the Platt Amendment. In 1934, the Platt Amendment was repealed. The United States and Cuba concluded a Treaty of Relations in 1934 which, among other things, continued the 1903 agreements that leased the Guantanamo Bay naval base to the United States.

Independent Cuba was often ruled by authoritarian political and military figures who either obtained or remained in power by force. Fulgencio Batista, an army sergeant, organized a non-commissioned officer revolt in September 1933 and wielded significant power behind the scenes until he was elected president in 1940. Batista was voted out of office in 1944 and did not run in 1948. Both those elections were won by civilian political figures with the support of party organizations. Running for president again in 1952, Batista seized power in a bloodless coup 3 months before the election was to take place, suspended the balloting, and began ruling by decree. Many political figures and movements that wanted a return to the government according to the Constitution of 1940 disputed Batista's undemocratic rule.

On July 26, 1953, Fidel Castro, who had been involved in increasingly violent political activity before Batista's coup, led a failed attack on the Moncada army barracks in Santiago de Cuba in which more than 100 died. After defending himself in a trial open to national and international media, he was convicted and jailed, and subsequently was freed in an act of clemency, before going into exile in Mexico. There he organized the "26th of July Movement" with the goal of overthrowing Batista, and the group sailed to Cuba on board the yacht Granma, landing in the eastern part of the island in December 1956.

Batista's dictatorial rule fueled increasing popular discontent and the rise of many active urban and rural resistance groups, a fertile political environment for Castro's 26th of July Movement. Faced with a corrupt and ineffective military--itself dispirited by a U.S. Government embargo on weapons sales to Cuba--and public indignation and revulsion at his brutality toward opponents, Batista fled on January 1, 1959. Although he had promised a return to constitutional rule and democratic elections along with social reforms, Castro used his control of the military to consolidate his power by repressing all dissent from his decisions, marginalizing other resistance figures, and imprisoning or executing thousands of opponents. An estimated 3,200 people were executed by the Castro regime between 1959-62 alone. As the revolution became more radical, hundreds of thousands of Cubans fled the island.

Castro declared Cuba a socialist state on April 16, 1961. For the next 30 years, Castro pursued close relations with the Soviet Union and worked in concert with the geopolitical goals of Soviet communism, funding and fomenting violent subversive and insurrectional activities, as well as military adventurism, until the demise of the U.S.S.R. in 1991.

Relations between the United States and Cuba deteriorated rapidly as the Cuban regime expropriated U.S. properties and moved toward adoption of a one-party communist system. In response, the United States imposed an embargo on Cuba in October 1960, and, in response to Castro's provocations, broke diplomatic relations on January 3, 1961. Tensions between the two governments peaked during the October 1962 missile crisis.

GOVERNMENT

Cuba is a totalitarian state controlled by Fidel Castro, who is chief of state, head of government, First Secretary of the PCC, and commander in chief of the armed forces. Castro seeks to control most aspects of Cuban life through the Communist Party and its affiliated mass organizations, the government bureaucracy, and the state security apparatus. In March 2003, Castro announced his intention to remain in power for life. The Ministry of Interior is the principal organ of state security and control.

According to the Soviet-style Cuban constitution of 1976, the National Assembly of People's Power, and its Council of State when the body is not in session, has supreme authority in the Cuban system. Since the National Assembly meets only twice a year for a few days each time, the 31-member Council of State wields power. The Council of Ministers, through its 9-member executive committee, handles the administration of the economy, which is state-controlled except for a tiny and shriveling open-market sector. Fidel Castro is President of the Council of State and Council of Ministers and his brother Raul serves as First Vice President of both bodies as well as Minister of Defense.

Although the constitution theoretically provides for independent courts, it explicitly subordinates them to the National Assembly and to the Council of State. The People's Supreme Court is the highest judicial body. Due process is routinely denied to Cuban citizens, particularly in cases involving political offenses. The constitution states that all legally recognized civil liberties can be denied to anyone who opposes the "decision of the Cuban people to build socialism." Citizens can be and are jailed for terms of 3 years or more for simply criticizing the communist system or Fidel Castro.

The Communist Party is constitutionally recognized as Cuba's only legal political party. The party monopolizes all government positions, including judicial offices. Though not a formal requirement, party membership is a de facto prerequisite for high-level official positions and professional advancement in most areas, although a tiny number of non-party members have on extremely rare occasions been permitted by the controlling Communist authorities to serve in the National Assembly. The Communist Party or one of its front organizations approves candidates for any elected office. Citizens do not have the right to change their government. In March 2003, the government carried out one of the most brutal crackdowns on peaceful opposition in the history of Cuba when it arrested 75 human rights activists, independent journalists and opposition figures on various charges, including aiding a foreign power and violating national security laws. Authorities subjected the detainees to summary trials and sentenced them to prison terms ranging from 6 to 28 years. Amnesty International identified all 75 as "prisoners of conscience." The European Union (EU) condemned their arrests and in June 2003, it announced its decision to implement the following actions: limit bilateral high-level governmental visits, reduce the profile of member states' participation in cultural events, reduce economic assistance and invite Cuban dissidents to national-day celebrations. See also the Department's Country Report on Human Rights Practices for Cuba.

Although the constitution allows legislative proposals backed by at least 10,000 citizens to be submitted directly to the National Assembly, in 2002 the government rejected a petition known as the Varela Project, supporters of which submitted 11,000 signatures calling for a national referendum on political and economic reforms. Many of the 75 activists arrested in March 2003 participated in the Varela Project. In October 2003, Project Varela organizers submitted a second petition to the National Assembly with an additional 14,000 signatures. Since April 2004, some prisoners of conscience have been released, seven of whom were in the group of 75; all suffered from moderate to severe medical conditions and many of them continue to be harassed by state security even after their release from prison. Moreover, in response to a planned protest by activists at the French Embassy in Havana in late July 2005, Cuban security forces detained 33 opposition members, three of whom had been released on medical grounds. At least 16 other activists were either arrested or sentenced to prison since 2004 for opposing the Cuban Government. There has also been a resurgence of harassment of various activist groups, most notably the "Damas en Blanca," a group of wives of political prisoners.

On July 31, 2006 the Castro regime announced a "temporary" transfer of power from Fidel Castro to his brother Raul, who until that time served as head of the Cuban armed forces and second-in-command of the government and the Communist Party. It was the first time in the 47 years of Fidel Castro's rule that power had been transferred. The transfer took place due to intestinal surgery of an undetermined nature.

Government Leaders

MEMBERS OF THE COUNCIL OF MINISTERS

Raúl Castro Ruz President of the Councils of State and Ministers. First Secretary of the Central Committee of the CCP. Army General. Graduated from Higher Military Training. Birthdate: June 3, 1931
José Ramón Machado Ventura Second Secretary of the Central Committee of the CCP. Politburo member of the PCC. MD. Birthdate: October 26, 1930
Days-Canel Bermúdez Miguel First Deputy Cabinet Member of the Political Bureau of the CPC. electronics engineer. Birthdate: April 20, 1960
Ramiro Valdés Menéndez Vice President of the Councils of State and Ministers. Commander of the Revolution. Politburo member of the PCC. Council Member State. Deputy to the National Assembly of People's Power. Graduated from Higher Military Training.

Birthdate: April 28, 1932
Ricardo Cabrisas Ruiz . Vice President of the Cabinet and its Executive Committee . Bachelor of Political Science Date of Birth: January 21, 1937
Ulises Rosales del Toro Vice President of Council of Ministers and its Executive Committee. Member of the Central Committee of the CCP. Deputy to the National Assembly of People's Power. Graduated from Higher Military Training. Birthdate: March 8, 1942
Antonio Enrique Lussón Battle Vice Cabinet. Member of the Central Committee of the CCP. Division General.
Marino Alberto Murillo Jorge Vice President of the Council of Ministers and member of the State Council. Politburo member of the PCC. Bachelor in Economics. Birthdate: February 19, 1961
Adel Yzquierdo Onofre Rodriguez Minister of Economy and Planning. Vice President of Council of Ministers. Politburo member of the PCC. Mechanical Engineer. Birthdate: June 12, 1945
Abelardo Colome Ibarra Secretary. Vice President of the State Council. Politburo member of the PCC. Corps General. Graduated from Higher Military Training. Birthdate: September 13, 1939
Gustavo Rodríguez Rollero Minister of Agriculture. Agronomist. Birthdate: June 21, 1963
Mary Blanca Ortega Barredo Minister of Domestic Trade. Bachelor in Economics and a Masters in Business Administration. Birthdate: November 17, 1962
René Mesa Villafana

Minister of Construction. Civil Engineer. Birthdate: April 7, 1958
Julian Gonzalez Toledo Minister of Culture.
Ena Elsa Velázquez Cobiella Minister of Education. Deputy of the National Assembly of People's Power. Degree in Chemistry. Birthdate: April 19, 1956
Rodolfo Alarcón Ortiz Minister of Higher Education.
Leopoldo Cintra Frias minister of the Revolutionary Armed Forces. Politburo member of CPC Central Committee and the State Council. Corps General. Bachelor of Political and Social Sciences. Birthdate: July 17, 1941
Lina Olinda Pedraza Rodríguez Minister of Finance and Prices. Member of the Central Committee of the CCP. Deputy of the National Assembly of People's Power. Bachelor of Economic Control. Birthdate: September 16, 1955
Maimir Mesa Ramos . Minister of Communications . regular academic graduate course specializing in Communications at the Academy of FAR Communications Engineer. Birthdate: November 25, 1962
María del Carmen Concepción González Minister of the Food Industry. Member of the Central Committee of the CCP. Deputy of the National Assembly of People's Power. Graduated in History and Social Sciences. Birthdate: September 15, 1957
Salvador Pardo Cruz Industries Minister Engineer technician. Birthdate: December 20, 1947
María Esther Reus González Minister of Justice. Bachelor of Law.

Birthdate: May 23, 1962
Bruno Eduardo Rodriguez Parrilla, Minister for Foreign Affairs. Member of the Central Committee of the CCP. Bachelor in Law Date of Birth: January 22, 1958
Roberto Morales Ojeda. Minister of Public Health. Member of the Central Committee of the CCP. Graduated Medicine. Masters in Public Health. Birthdate: June 15, 1967
Margarita Marlene González Fernández Minister of Labour and Social Security. Industrial Engineering and Master in Human Resources Management. Birthdate: July 20, 1964
Cesar Ignacio Arocha Masid Minister of Transport. Brig. Graduated from Higher Military Training. engineer Railways. Birthdate: February 1, 1959
Manuel Marrero Cruz Tourism Minister. Architect. Birthdate: July 11, 1963
Rodrigo Malmierca Minister of Foreign Trade and Foreign Investment. Member of the Central Committee of the CCP. Bachelor in Economics. Birthdate: October 14, 1956
Ernesto Medina Villaveirán President of Banco Central de Cuba. Member of the Central Committee of the CCP. Bachelor in Economics. Birthdate: July 22, 1955
Elba Rosa Perez Montoya Minister of Science, Technology and Environment.
Alfredo López Valdés Minister of Energy and Mines. Automation Electrical Engineer. Birthdate: April 19, 1945
Ines Maria Chapman Waugh

. President of the National Institute of Hydraulic Resources . Committee Member of the CPC Hydraulic Engineering Date of Birth: September 9, 1965
Julio Christian Jiménez Molina President, National Institute of Sports, Physical Education and Recreation. Bachelor in Political Science. Birthdate: November 12, 1951
Danylo Sirio López president of the Cuban Institute of Radio and Television. director of TV programs. Birthdate: December 24, 1950

PROVINCIAL GOVERNMENT BODIES

Ernesto Barreto Castillo President of the Provincial Assembly of People's Power of Pinar del Río. Deputy to the National Assembly of People's Power. Mechanical Engineer. Birthdate: April 16, 1960
Raul Rodriguez Cartaya President of the Provincial Assembly of People's Power of Artemis. Deputy to the National Assembly of People's Power. standard level Superior. Birthdate: May 22, 1965
David González Yero President of the Provincial Assembly of People's Power Mayabeque.
Marta Hernández Romero . President of the Provincial Assembly of Popular Power in Havana . Deputy of the National Assembly of People's Power . Master of Education Date of Birth: March 19, 1958
Tania Leon Silveira President of the Provincial Assembly of People's Power of Matanzas. Council Member State. Deputy of the National Assembly of People's Power. Agronomist. Birthdate: July 19, 1964
Pestana jorgelina Mederos President of the Provincial Assembly of People's Power of Villa Clara. Deputy of the National Assembly of People's Power.

Bachelor of Law. Birthdate: October 30, 1964
Pernia Mairelis Cordero President of the Provincial Assembly of People's Power of Cienfuegos. Deputy of the National Assembly of People's Power.
Teresita Romero Rodriguez President of the Provincial Assembly of People's Power of Sancti Spiritus. Deputy of the National Assembly of People's Power. Bachelor in Economics and a Masters in Accounting and Finance. Birthdate: May 20, 1965
Victorio Carmenate Raúl Pérez President of the Provincial Assembly of People's Power of Ciego de Ávila. Deputy to the National Assembly of Popular Power BA in Economics. Birthdate: May 21, 1961
Isabel Gonzalez Cardenas President of the Provincial Assembly of People's Power of Camagüey. Deputy of the National Assembly of People's Power
Lilian González Rodríguez President of the Provincial Assembly of People's Power of Las Tunas. Deputy of the National Assembly of People's Power Architect. Birthdate: March 4, 1962
Tellez C. Tamayo Susel the President of the Provincial Assembly of Popular Power in Havana. Deputy of the National Assembly of People's Power
Santiago Manuel Sobrino Martinez President of the Provincial Assembly of People's Power of Granma. Deputy to the National Assembly of People's Power. Industrial Engineer. Birthdate: June 25, 1971
Reinaldo Garcia Zapata President of the Provincial Assembly of People's Power of Cuba Santiago. Deputy to the National Assembly of People's Power. engineer. Birthdate: March 9, 1968
Nancy Acosta Hernández President of the Provincial Assembly of People's Power of Guantánamo. Deputy of the National Assembly of People's Power. Bachelor of Education and Doctor of Pedagogical Sciences.

Birthdate: January 15, 1965
Arelys Casañola Quintana President of the People's Assembly of the Municipality Special Isla de la Juventud. Deputy of the National Assembly of People's Power.

NATIONAL SECURITY

Under Castro, Cuba is a highly militarized society. From 1975 until the late 1980s, massive Soviet military assistance enabled Cuba to upgrade its military capabilities and project power abroad. The tonnage of Soviet military deliveries to Cuba throughout most of the 1980s exceeded deliveries in any year since the military build-up during the 1962 missile crisis.

With the loss of Soviet-era subsidies in the early 1990s, Cuba's armed forces have shrunk considerably, both in terms of numbers and assets. Combined active duty troop strength for all three services is estimated at 50,000 to 55,000 personnel (compared to some 235,000 on active duty 10 years ago) and much of Cuba's weaponry appears to be in storage. Cuba's air force, once considered among the best equipped in Latin America, no longer merits that distinction, though it still possesses advanced aircraft and weapons systems; the navy has become primarily a coastal defense force with no blue water capability. The Cuban army is still one of the region's more formidable, but it also is much reduced and no longer has the considerable resources necessary to project power abroad.

The military plays a growing role in the economy and manages a number of hotels in the tourist sector. The country's two paramilitary organizations, the Territorial Militia Troops and the Youth Labor Army, have a reduced training capability. Cuba also adopted a "war of the people" strategy that highlights the defensive nature of its capabilities. The government continues to maintain a large state security apparatus under the Ministry of Interior to repress dissent within Cuba, and in the last decade has formed special forces units to confront indications of popular unrest.

ECONOMY

Rank	95th
Currency	Cuban peso (CUP) = 100 centavos and Cuban Convertible Peso (CUC) = 24 CUP
Fiscal year	yes
	Statistics
GDP	$72.3 billion $121 billion (PPP)
GDP growth	2.7%
GDP per capita	$10,200 (PPP)
GDP by sector	Agriculture: 4.3%, industry: 21.6%, services: 74%
Inflation (CPI)	1.5% (2009 est.)
Population below poverty line	1.5%
Labor force	5.159 million (Public sector: 78%, Personal sector: 22%)
Labor force by occupation	Agriculture: 20%, industry: 19.4%, services: 60.6%
Unemployment	3.8%
Main industries	Sugar, petroleum, tobacco, construction, nickel, steel, cement, agricultural machinery, pharmaceuticals
	External

Exports	$2.458 billion f.o.b.
Export goods	sugar, medical products, nickel, tobacco, shellfish, citrus, coffee
Main export partners	Canada 17.3% China 16.6% Venezuela 12.7% Netherlands 8.8% Spain 5.8%
Imports	$8.963 billion f.o.b.
Import goods	petroleum, food, machinery and equipment, chemicals
Main import partners	Venezuela 36.4% China 10.5% Spain 8.7% Brazil 5.1% United States 4.2%
Public finances	
Public debt	$19.44 billion (31 December 2009 est.); another $20.8 billion owed to Russia, $0.9 billion owed to Romania and $0.2 billion owed to Hungary
Revenues	$35.01 billion
Expenses	$36.73 billion
Economic aid	$87.8 million

The **economy of Cuba** is a largely centrally planned economy dominated by state-run enterprises overseen by the Cuban government, though there remains significant foreign investment and personal enterprise in Cuba. Most of the means of production are owned and run by the government, and most of the labor force is employed by the state, although in recent years, the formation of cooperatives and self-employment has been encouraged by the Communist Party.

In the year 2000, public sector employment was 76% and private sector, mainly composed by personal property, employment was 23% compared to the 1981 ratio of 91% to 8%. Capital investment is restricted and requires approval by the government. The Cuban government sets most prices and rations goods to citizens. In 2009, Cuba ranked 51st out of 182 with an HDI of 0.863; remarkably high considering its GDP per capita only places it 95th. Public services and transport in Cuba, however, are second-rate compared to more developed counterparts on the mainland. The country's public debt in 2012 was measured at 35.3% of GDP. At the same time, inflation (CDP) was ranked at 5.5%. Furthermore, in the same year, the economy encountered a 3% growth in GDP.

In the 1950s, Cuba had a vibrant but extremely unequal economy, with large capital outflows to foreign investors. The country compared favourably with Spain and Portugal on socioeconomic measures. Furthermore, its income in 1929 was reportedly 41% of the US, thus higher than in some Southern states of the US, such as Mississippi and South Carolina The country has made significant progress towards a more even distribution of income since the Revolution and being placed under economic embargo by the United States. Following the collapse of the Soviet Union, Cuba's GDP declined by 33% between 1990 and 1993, partially due to loss of Soviet subsidies, and partly due to a crash in sugar prices in the early 1990s. Yet Cuba has managed to retain high levels of healthcare and education.

Cubans receive low housing and transportation costs, free education, and health care and food subsidies. Corruption is common, though allegedly lower than in most other countries in Latin

America. However, in their book, *Corruption in Cuba*, Sergio Diaz-Briquets and Jorge F. Pérez-López Servando state that Cuba has "institutionalized" corruption and that state-run monopolies, cronyism, and lack of accountability have made Cuba one of the world's most corrupt states".

The Cuban Government continues to adhere to socialist principles in organizing its state-controlled economy. Most of the means of production are owned and run by the government and, according to Cuban Government statistics, about 75% of the labor force is employed by the state. The actual figure is closer to 93%, with some 150,000 small farmers and another 150,000 "cuentapropistas," or holders of licenses for self-employment, representing a mere 2.1% of the nearly 4.7 million-person workforce.

The Cuban economy is still recovering from a decline in gross domestic product of at least 35% between 1989 and 1993 as the loss of Soviet subsidies laid bare the economy's fundamental weaknesses. To alleviate the economic crisis, in 1993 and 1994 the government introduced a few market-oriented reforms, including opening to tourism, allowing foreign investment, legalizing the dollar, and authorizing self-employment for some 150 occupations. These measures resulted in modest economic growth; the official statistics, however, are deficient and as a result provide an incomplete measure of Cuba's real economic situation. Living conditions at the end of the decade remained well below the 1989 level. Lower sugar and nickel prices, increases in petroleum costs, a post-September 11, 2001 decline in tourism, devastating hurricanes in November 2001 and August 2004, and a major drought in the eastern half of the island caused severe economic disruptions. Growth rates continued to stagnate in 2002 and 2003, while 2004 and 2005 showed some renewed growth. Moreover, the gap in the standard of living has widened between those with access to dollars and those without. Jobs that can earn dollar salaries or tips from foreign businesses and tourists have become highly desirable. It is not uncommon to see doctors, engineers, scientists, and other professionals working in restaurants or as taxi drivers.

Castro's regime has pulled back on earlier market reforms and is seeking tighter state control over the economy. The Cuban Government is aggressively pursuing a policy of recentralization, making it increasingly difficult for foreigners to conduct business on the island. Likewise, Cuban citizens are adversely affected by reversion to a peso economy.

Prolonged austerity and the state-controlled economy's inefficiency in providing adequate goods and services have created conditions for a flourishing informal economy in Cuba. As the variety and amount of goods available in state-run peso stores has declined, Cubans have turned increasingly to the black market to obtain needed food, clothing, and household items. Pilferage of items from the work place to sell on the black market or illegally offering services on the sidelines of official employment is common, and Cuban companies regularly figure 15% in losses into their production plans to cover this. Recognizing that Cubans must engage in such activity to make ends meet and that attempts to shut the informal economy down would be futile, the government concentrates its control efforts on ideological appeals against theft and shutting down large organized operations. A report by an independent economist and opposition leader speculates that more than 40% of the Cuban economy operates in the informal sector. Since 2005, the government has carried out a large anti-corruption campaign as it continues efforts to recentralize much of the economy under the regime's control.

Sugar, which has been the mainstay of the island's economy for most of its history, has fallen upon troubled times. In 1989, production was more than 8 million tons, but by the mid-1990s, it had fallen to around 3.5 million tons. Inefficient planting and cultivation methods, poor management, shortages of spare parts, and poor transportation infrastructure combined to deter the recovery of the sector. In June 2002, the government announced its intention to implement a "comprehensive transformation" of this declining sector. Almost half the existing sugar mills were closed, and more than 100,000 workers were laid off. The government has promised that these workers will be "retrained" in other fields, though it is unlikely they will find new jobs in Cuba's stagnant economy. Moreover, despite such efforts, the sugar harvest continued to decline, falling to 2.1 million tons in 2003, the smallest since 1933. The harvest was not much better in 2004, with 2.3 million tons, and even worse in 2005, with 1.3 million tons.

In the mid-1990s, tourism surpassed sugar as the primary source of foreign exchange. Tourism figures prominently in the Cuban Government's plans for development, and a top official cast it as at the "heart of the economy." Havana devotes significant resources to building new tourist facilities and renovating historic structures for use in the tourism sector. Roughly 1.7 million tourists visited Cuba in 2001, generating about $1.85 billion in gross revenues; in 2003, the number rose to 1.9 million tourists, predominantly from Canada and the European Union, generating revenue of $2.1 billion. The number of tourists to Cuba in 2004 crossed the 2 million mark (2.05 million), including the so-called "medical tourists" from other Latin American countries seeking free medical treatment at Cuban facilities. In 2005 the number of tourists increased to 2.32 million.

Nickel is now the biggest earner among Cuba's goods exports. The nickel industry has been operating close to full capacity and therefore currently stagnant, but it is benefiting from unprecedented increases in world market prices. Revenues have more than doubled from $450 million in 2001 to $1 billion in 2005. The government is making attempts to increase extraction capacity.

Remittances also play a large role in Cuba's economy. Cuba does not publish accurate economic statistics, but academic sources estimate that remittances total from $600 million to $1 billion per year, with most coming from families in the United States. U.S. regulation changes announced in June 2004 allow remittances to be sent only to the remitter's immediate family; they cannot be remitted to certain Cuban Government officials and members of the Cuban Communist party; and the total amount of family remittances that an authorized traveler may carry to Cuba is now $300, reduced from $3,000. (See also the Commission on Assistance to a Free Cuba report at www.cafc.gov, cited below.) The Cuban Government captures these dollar remittances by allowing Cuban citizens to shop in state-run "dollar stores," which sell food, household, and clothing items at a high mark-up averaging over 240% of face value.

Beginning in November 2004, Castro mandated that U.S. dollars be exchanged for "convertible pesos"--a local currency that can be used in special shops on the island but has no value internationally--for a 10% charge. The 10% conversion fee disproportionately affects Cubans who receive remittances from relatives in the U.S.

To help keep the economy afloat, Cuba has actively courted foreign investment, which often takes the form of joint ventures with the Cuban Government holding half of the equity, management contracts for tourism facilities, or financing for the sugar harvest. A new legal framework laid out in 1995 allowed for majority foreign ownership in joint ventures with the Cuban Government. In practice, majority ownership by the foreign partner is nonexistent. Of the 540 joint ventures formed since the Cuban Government issued the first legislation on foreign investment in 1982, 397 remained at the end of 2002, and 287 at the close of 2005. Due in large part to Castro's recentralization efforts, it is estimated that one joint venture and two small cooperative production ventures have closed each week since 2000. Responding to this decline in the number of joint ventures, a spokesperson for the Ministry of Foreign Investment explained that foreign investment is not a pillar of development in and of itself. Moreover, the hostile investment climate, characterized by inefficient and overpriced labor imposed by the communist government, dense regulations, and an impenetrable bureaucracy, continue to deter foreign investment. Foreign direct investment flows decreased from $448 million in 2000 to $39 million in 2001 and were at zero in 2002. In July 2002, the European Union, through its embassies in Havana, transmitted to the Cuban Government a document that outlined the problems encountered in operating joint ventures in Cuba. Titled "The Legal and Administrative Framework for Foreign Trade and Investment by European Companies in Cuba," the paper noted the difficulty in obtaining such basic necessities as work and residence permits for foreign employees--even exit visas and drivers licenses. It complained that the Government of Cuba gave EU joint venture partners little or no say in hiring Cuban staff, often forced the joint venture to contract employees who were not professionally suitable, and yet reserved to itself the right to fire any worker at any time without cause. It noted administrative difficulties in securing financing and warned that "the difficulties of state firms in meeting their payment obligations are seriously threatening some firms and increasing the risk premium which all operators have to pay for their operations with Cuba." The Cuban Government offered no response.

Investors are also constrained by the U.S.-Cuban Liberty and Democratic Solidarity (Libertad) Act that provides sanctions for those who "traffic" in property expropriated from U.S. citizens. More than a dozen companies have pulled out of Cuba or altered their plans to invest there due to the threat of action under the Libertad Act.

In an attempt to provide jobs for workers laid off due to the economic crisis and bring some forms of black market activity into more controllable channels, the Cuban Government in 1993 legalized self-employment for some 150 occupations. This small private sector is tightly controlled and regulated. Set monthly fees must be paid regardless of income earned, and frequent inspections yield stiff fines when any of the many self-employment regulations are violated. Rather than expanding private sector opportunities, in recent years, the government has been attempting to squeeze more of these private sector entrepreneurs out of business and back to the public sector. Many have opted to enter the informal economy or black market, and others have closed. These measures have reduced private sector employment from a peak of 209,000 to less than 100,000 now. Moreover, a large number of those people who nominally are self-employed in reality are well-connected fronts for military officials. No recent figures have been made available, but the Government of Cuba reported at the end of 2001 that tax receipts from the self-employed fell 8.1% due to the decrease in the number of these taxpayers. Since October 1, 2004, the Cuban Government no longer issues new licenses for 40 of the approximately 150 categories of self-employment, including for the most popular ones, such as private restaurants.

In June 2005, 2,000 more licenses were revoked from self-employed workers as a means to reassert government control over the economy and to stem growing inequalities associated with self-employment. The licenses for self-employed workers were typically for service-oriented work, allowing the Cuban people to eke out a small living in an otherwise impoverished state. Moreover, workers in Cuba's tourist sector--at resorts where native Cubans are prohibited unless they are on the job--have been prohibited by a Ministry of Tourism regulation from accepting gifts, tips, or even food from foreigners, in a further attempt at increasing the tourist apartheid that exists on the island.

A 2004 UN Economic Commission on Latin America and the Caribbean (ECLAC) report recommends that Cuba "redesign the parameters of competition in the public, private and cooperative sectors [and] redefine the role of the state in the economy." It recommends more flexibility in self-employment regulations, property diversification, economic decentralization, and a role for the market. The Cuban Government, however, is today reversing the economic liberalization of the 90s and re-centralizing its economy. Evidence of this is found in the decline in the number of firms participating in the *perfeccionamiento empresarial*, or entrepreneurial improvement (EI), program, which is based on capitalist management techniques. EI was instituted in the 1980s as a military-led pilot project, and in 1998, the Cuban Government extended it from military to civilian "parastatals," reportedly to foster capitalist competitiveness. At first, the government highlighted participating companies' achievements in cutting costs and boosting profitability and quality and suggested that the increased autonomy of state managers under EI was producing an efficient form of socialism with a strong link between pay and performance. However, many in the Communist Party, even Castro himself, resisted EI. Many of the original participants have since left the program and participating firms have seen little growth in revenue. The EI program has fallen far short of expectations and the Cuban Government no longer heralds its successes or its future prospects. In 2003 the Cuban Government also tightened foreign exchange controls, requiring that state companies hold money in convertible pesos and obtain special authorization from the central bank before making hard currency transactions. Practically speaking, this restricted companies from using the dollar for internal trade. Following this, in 2004 the government announced that all state entities must stop charging in U.S. dollars and charge only in pesos for any products and services not considered a part of a company's "fundamental social objective." It also recently implemented new requirements to channel imports through monopolistic Soviet-style wholesale distribution companies.

Cuba's precarious economic position is complicated by the high price it must pay for foreign financing. The Cuban Government defaulted on most of its international debt in 1986 and does not have access to credit from international financial institutions like the World Bank, which means Havana must rely heavily on short-term loans to finance imports, chiefly food and fuel. Because of its poor credit rating, an $11 billion hard currency debt, and the risks associated with Cuban investment, interest rates have reportedly been as high as 22%. In 2002, citing chronic delinquencies and mounting short-term debts, Moody's lowered Cuba's credit rating to Caa1 -- "speculative grade, very poor." Dunn and Bradstreet rate Cuba as one of the riskiest economies in the world.

HUMAN RIGHTS

Cuba is an authoritarian state led by Raul Castro, who is president of the council of state and council of ministers, Communist Party (CP) first secretary, and commander in chief of security forces. The constitution recognizes the CP as the only legal party and "the superior leading force of society and of the state." A CP candidacy commission preapproved all candidates for the February 2013 uncontested National Assembly elections, which were neither free nor fair. The national leadership, including members of the military, maintained effective control over the security forces.

The principal human rights abuses included those involving the abridgement of the ability of citizens to change the government and the use of government threats, extrajudicial physical assault, intimidation, violent government-organized counter-protests against peaceful dissent, and harassment and detentions to prevent free expression and peaceful assembly.

The following additional abuses continued: short-term, arbitrary unlawful detentions and arrests, harsh prison conditions, selective prosecution, denial of fair trial, and travel restrictions. Authorities interfered with privacy, engaging in pervasive monitoring of private communications. The government did not respect freedom of speech and press, restricted internet access, maintained a monopoly on media outlets, circumscribed academic freedom, and maintained some restrictions on the ability of religious groups to meet and worship. The government refused to recognize independent human rights groups or permit them to function legally. In addition the government continued to prevent workers from forming independent unions and otherwise exercising their labor rights.

Most human rights abuses were committed by officials at the direction of the government. Impunity for the perpetrators remained widespread.

FOREIGN RELATIONS

Cuba's once-ambitious foreign policy has been scaled back and redirected as a result of economic hardship and the end of the Cold War. Cuba aims to find new sources of trade, aid, and foreign investment and to promote opposition to U.S. policy, especially the trade embargo and the 1996 Libertad Act. Cuba has relations with over 160 countries and has civilian assistance workers--principally physicians and nurses--in more than 20 nations.

Since the end of Soviet backing, Cuba appears to have largely abandoned monetary support for guerrilla movements that typified its involvement in regional politics in Latin America and Africa, though it maintains relations with several guerrilla and terrorist groups and provides refuge for some of their members in Cuba. Cuba's support for Latin guerrilla movements, its Marxist-Leninist government, and its alignment with the U.S.S.R. led to its isolation in the hemisphere. Cuba is a member of the Organization of American States (OAS), although its present government has been excluded from participation since 1962 for incompatibility with the principles of the inter-American system. Cuba hosted the Non-Aligned Movement (NAM) summit in September 2006 and will hold the NAM presidency until 2009. In the context of the NAM and its ordinary diplomacy, Cuba has developed friendly relations with Iran, North Korea and other rogue states.

Throughout the 1970s and 1980s, Cuba expanded its military presence abroad, spending millions of dollars in exporting revolutions; deployments reached 50,000 troops in Angola, 24,000 in Ethiopia, 1,500 in Nicaragua, and hundreds more elsewhere. In Angola, Cuban troops, supported logistically by the U.S.S.R., backed the Popular Movement for the Liberation of Angola (MPLA) in its effort to take power after Portugal granted Angola its independence. Cuban forces played a key role in Ethiopia's war against Somalia and remained there in substantial numbers as a garrison force for a decade. Cubans served in a non-combat advisory role in Mozambique and the Congo. Cuba also used the Congo as a logistical support center for Cuba's Angola mission. In the late 1980s, Cuba began to pull back militarily. Cuba unilaterally removed its forces from Ethiopia, met the timetable of the 1988 Angola-Namibia accords by completing the withdrawal of its forces from Angola before July 1991, and ended military assistance to Nicaragua following the Sandinistas' 1990 electoral defeat.

EU-Cuban diplomatic relations have suffered as a result of the March 2003 crackdown on dissidents. In June 2004, EU members imposed restrictive measures on Cuba including inviting dissidents to national day celebrations and suspending high-level meetings between EU members and the Cuban Government. In January 2005, though, the restrictions were suspended in an effort to re-engage the regime as a means of advancing the EU's policy of encouraging reform while preparing for the transition.

Spain is among the most important foreign investors in Cuba. The ruling Zapatero government continues Spain's longstanding policy of encouraging further investment and trade with Cuba. Cuba imports more goods from Spain (almost 13% of total imports) than from any other country. Spanish economic involvement with Cuba is exclusively centered on joint venture enterprises that provide financial benefit to the Cuban Government through state-owned firms. Spain's desire to provide support to its business community often impedes its willingness to pressure the Cuban Government on political reform and human rights issues.

Cuba's bilateral relationship with Venezuela has helped keep the Cuban economy afloat. The "Integral Cooperation Accord" signed by Fidel Castro and Venezuelan President Hugo Chavez in October 2000 laid the groundwork for a quasi-barter exchange of Venezuelan oil for Cuban goods and services that has since become a lifeline for Cuba. For Cuba, the benefits of the cooperation accord are subsidized petroleum and increased hard currency flows. The original agreement allowed for the sale, at market prices, of up to 53,000 barrels per day of crude oil and derivatives (diesel, gasoline, jet fuel, etc.) by PDVSA, Venezuela's state-owned petroleum company, to its Cuban counterpart, CUPET. The number of barrels of oil Venezuela began selling to Cuba has risen to over 90,000 barrels daily. Under the accord, PDVSA extended preferential payment terms to CUPET, including 90-day short-term financing instead of the 30 days offered to its other customers and, in lieu of a standard letter of credit backed by an international bank, PDVSA accepted IOUs from Cuba's Banco Nacional, the central banking entity responsible for servicing Havana's foreign debt. In August 2001, Venezuelan President Hugo Chavez amended the 2000 accord to allow Venezuela to compensate the Cuban Government in hard currency for any and all Cuban products and services originally intended as in-kind payment for Venezuelan oil. As a result, Cuban exports of goods and services to Venezuela climbed from $34 million in 2001 to more than $150 million in 2003. Venezuelan ministries are contracting with Cuba for everything from generic pharmaceuticals to pre-fabricated housing and dismantled sugar mill equipment. On April 28, 2005, Chavez and Castro signed 49 economic agreements in Havana, covering areas as diverse as oil, nickel, agriculture, furniture, shoes, textiles, toys, lingerie, tires, construction materials, electricity, transportation, health, and education. Venezuela is also committed to sending more than $400 million in various products duty free to Cuba and plans to open an office of state-owned commercial Venezuelan Industrial Bank (BIV) in Havana to finance imports and exports between the two countries, while Cuba will open an official Banco Exterior de Cuba in Caracas. Increased economic engagement along with the rapid growth in Cuban sales to Caracas has established Venezuela as one of the island's largest export markets.

A series of recent economic agreements between Cuba and China have strengthened trade between the two countries. Sino-Cuban trade totaled more than $525 million in 2004, according to China Customs statistics. This represents an increase of more than 47% over 2003. Most of China's aid involves in-kind supply of goods or technical assistance. During President Hu-Jintao's visit to Cuba in November 2004, China signed investment-related memorandums of understanding (MOUs) estimated at more than $500 million, according to press reports. If these MOUs are fully realized, they would represent a sharp increase in known Chinese investments in Cuba. In addition to these MOUs, a number of commercial accords were signed at the first-ever Cuba-China Investment and Trade Forum. China also plans to invest approximately $500 million in a nickel operation in Moa in the eastern province of Holguin. According to the MOU, Cuba will own 51% of the enterprise and Chinese-owned Minmetals the remaining 49%. Chinese and Venezuelan economic support, including investment and direct aid, have given Cuba the space to eliminate many of the tentative open market reforms Cuba put in place during the depth of its mid-1990s economic crisis.

The Russian prime minister visited Cuba in October 2006, signaling a new effort to expand trade and investment, albeit financed by Russian credit. Russia set aside, for the moment, more than USD 20 billion in Soviet-era debt, restructured post-1991 debt, and extended a new credit line to Cuba. The new credit line is for USD 355 million repayable over 10 years at an interest rate of five percent. The new credit is conditioned in that it must be used to purchase Russian cars, trucks, planes, as well as to finance Cuban energy and transport infrastructure projects, including air navigation systems. Russia further agreed to restructure USD 166 million in debt accumulated since 1993. Both nations also signed an agreement on military equipment and technical services.

U.S.-CUBAN RELATIONS

Cuba and the United States restored diplomatic relations on July 20, 2015, which had been severed in 1961 during the Cold War. U.S. diplomatic representation in Cuba is handled by the United States Embassy in Havana, and there is a similar Cuban Embassy in Washington, D.C.. The United States, however, continues to maintain its commercial, economic, and financial embargo, which makes it illegal for U.S. corporations to do business with Cuba, although the U.S. President, Barack Obama, has called for the ending of the embargo but U.S. law requires congressional approval to end the embargo.

As the sway of the Spanish Empire over its possessions in the Americas was crushed in the 1820s as a result of the Spanish American wars of independence, only Cuba and Puerto Rico remained under Spanish rule until the Spanish–American War (1898) that resulted from the Cuban War of Independence. Under the Treaty of Paris, Cuba became a U.S. protectorate; the U.S. gained a position of economic and political dominance over the island, that persisted after it became formally independent in 1902.

Following the Cuban Revolution of 1959, bilateral relations deteriorated substantially. In 1961, the U.S. severed diplomatic ties with Cuba and began pursuing covert operations to topple the Communist regime. Moreover, the U.S. imposed and subsequently tightened a comprehensive set of restrictions and bans vis-à-vis the Cuban regime as retaliation for the nationalization of U.S. corporations' property by Cuba. Meanwhile, several organizations, including a nearly unanimous UN General Assembly, have called for "an end to the United States' decades-long economic, commercial and financial embargo against Cuba."

On December 17, 2014, U.S. President Barack Obama and Cuban President Raúl Castro announced the beginning of a process of normalizing relations between Cuba and the U.S., which media sources have named "the Cuban Thaw." Negotiated in secret in Canada and the Vatican City over preceding months, and with the assistance of Pope Francis, the agreement led to the lifting of some U.S. travel restrictions, fewer restrictions on remittances, U.S. banks access to the Cuban financial system, and the establishment of a U.S. embassy in Havana, which closed after Cuba became closely allied with the USSR in 1961. The countries' respective "interests sections" in one another's capitals were upgraded to embassies on July 20, 2015

AFTER THE COLD WAR

The Cold War ended with the collapse of the Soviet Union in the late 1980s and early 1990s, leaving Cuba without its major international sponsor. The ensuing years were marked by economic difficulty in Cuba, a time known as the Special Period. U.S. law allowed private humanitarian aid to Cuba for part of this time. However, the long standing U.S. embargo was reinforced in October 1992 by the Cuban Democracy Act (the "Torricelli Law") and in 1996 by the Cuban Liberty and Democracy Solidarity Act (known as the Helms-Burton Act). The 1992 act prohibited foreign-based subsidiaries of U.S. companies from trading with Cuba, travel to Cuba by U.S. citizens, and family remittances to Cuba. Sanctions could also be applied to non-U.S. companies trading with Cuba. As a result, multinational companies had to choose between Cuba and the U.S., the latter being a much larger market.

On February 24, 1996, two unarmed Cessna 337s flown by the group "Brothers to the Rescue" were shot down by Cuban Air Force MiG-29, killing three Cuban-Americans and one Cuban U.S. resident. The Cuban government claimed that the planes had entered into Cuban airspace.

Some veterans of CIA's 1961 Bay of Pigs invasion, while no longer being sponsored by the CIA, are still active, though they are now in their seventies or older. Members of Alpha 66, an anti-Castro paramilitary organization, continue to practice their AK-47 skills in a camp in South Florida.

In January 1999, U.S. President Bill Clinton eased travel restrictions to Cuba in an effort to increase cultural exchanges between the two nations. The Clinton administration approved a two-game exhibition series between the Baltimore Orioles and Cuban national baseball team, marking the first time a Major League Baseball team played in Cuba since 1959.

At the United Nations Millennium Summit in September 2000, Castro and Clinton spoke briefly at a group photo session and shook hands. U.N. Secretary-General Kofi Annan commented afterwards, "For a U.S. president and a Cuban president to shake hands for the first time in over 40 years—I think it is a major symbolic achievement". While Castro said it was a gesture of "dignity and courtesy," the White House denied the encounter was of any significance. In November 2001, U.S. companies began selling food to the country for the first time since Washington imposed the trade embargo after the revolution. In 2002, former U.S. President Jimmy Carter became the first former or sitting U.S. president to visit Cuba since 1928.

TIGHTENING EMBARGO

Relations deteriorated again following the election of George W. Bush. During his campaign Bush appealed for the support of Cuban-Americans by emphasizing his opposition to the government of Fidel Castro and supporting tighter embargo restrictions Cuban Americans, who until 2008 tended to vote Republican, expected effective policies and greater participation in the formation of policies regarding Cuba-U.S. relations. Approximately three months after his inauguration, the Bush administration began expanding travel restrictions. The United States Department of the Treasury issued greater efforts to deter American citizens from illegally traveling to the island.

Also in 2001, five Cuban agents were convicted on 26 counts of espionage, conspiracy to commit murder, and other illegal activities in the United States. On June 15, 2009, the U.S. Supreme Court denied review of their case. Tensions heightened as the Under Secretary of State for Arms Control and International Security Affairs, John R. Bolton, accused Cuba of maintaining a biological weapons program. Many in the United States, including ex-president Carter, expressed doubts about the claim. Later, Bolton was criticized for pressuring subordinates who questioned the quality of the intelligence John Bolton had used as the basis for the assertion. Bolton identified the Castro government as part of America's "axis of evil," highlighting the fact that the Cuban leader visited several U.S. foes, including Libya, Iran and Syria.

Following his 2004 reelection, Bush declared Cuba to be one of the few "outposts of tyranny" remaining in the world.

Cuban propaganda poster in Havana featuring a Cuban soldier addressing a threatening Uncle Sam. The translation reads: "Imperialist sirs, we have absolutely no fear of you!"

In January 2006, United States Interests Section in Havana began, in an attempt to break Cuba's "information blockade", displaying messages, including quotes from the Universal Declaration of Human Rights, on a scrolling "electronic billboard" in the windows of their top floor. Following a protest march organized by the Cuban government, the government erected a large number of poles, carrying black flags with single white stars, obscuring the messages.

On September 8, 2006, it was revealed that at least ten South Florida journalists received regular payments from the U.S. government for programs on Radio Martí and TV Martí, two broadcasters that support an opening of Cuban society and multi-party elections in Cuba. The payments totaled thousands of dollars over several years. Those who were paid the most were veteran reporters and a freelance contributor for El Nuevo Herald, the Spanish-language newspaper published by the corporate parent of The Miami Herald. The Cuban government has long contended that some South Florida Spanish-language journalists were on the federal payroll.

On September 12, 2006, the United States announced that it had created five inter-agency working groups to monitor Cuba. The groups were set up after the July 31 announcement that the ailing Cuban leader had temporarily ceded power to a collective leadership headed by his brother Raúl. U.S. officials say three of the newly created groups are headed by the State Department: diplomatic actions; strategic communications and democratic promotion. Another that coordinated humanitarian aid to Cuba is run by the Commerce Department, and a fifth, on migration issues, is run jointly by the National Security Council and the Department of Homeland Security.

On October 10, 2006, the United States announced the creation of a task force made up of officials from several U.S. agencies to pursue more aggressively American violators of the U.S. trade embargo against Cuba, with penalties as severe as 10 years of prison and hundreds of thousands of dollars in fines for violators of the embargo.

In November 2006, U.S. Congressional auditors accused the development agency USAID of failing properly to administer its program to for promoting democracy in Cuba. They said USAID had channeled tens of millions of dollars through exile groups in Miami, which were sometimes wasteful or kept questionable accounts. The report said the organizations had sent items such as chocolate and cashmere jerseys to Cuba. Their report concludes that 30% of the exile groups who received USAID grants showed questionable expenditures.

After Fidel Castro's announcement of resignation in 2008, U.S. Deputy Secretary of State John Negroponte said that the United States would maintain its embargo.

VISION FOR "DEMOCRATIC TRANSITION

In 2003, the United States Commission for Assistance to a Free Cuba was formed to "explore ways the U.S. can help hasten and ease a democratic transition in Cuba." The commission immediately announced a series of measures that included a tightening of the travel embargo to the island, a crackdown on illegal cash transfers, and a more robust information campaign aimed at Cuba. Castro insisted that, in spite of the formation of the Commission, Cuba is itself "in transition: to socialism [and] to communism" and that it was "ridiculous for the U.S. to threaten Cuba now".

In a 2004 meeting with members of the Commission for Assistance to a Free Cuba, President Bush stated, "We're not waiting for the day of Cuban freedom; we are working for the day of freedom in Cuba." The President reaffirmed his commitment to Cuban-Americans just in time for his 2004 reelection with promises to "work" rather than wait for freedom in Cuba.

In April 2006, the Bush administration appointed Caleb McCarry "transition coordinator" for Cuba, providing a budget of $59 million, with the task of promoting the governmental shift to democracy after Castro's death. Official Cuban news service Granma alleges that these transition plans were created at the behest of Cuban exile groups in Miami, and that McCarry was responsible for engineering the overthrow of the Aristide government in Haiti.

In 2006, the Commission for Assistance to a Free Cuba released a 93-page report. The report included a plan that suggested the United States spend $80 million to ensure that Cuba's communist system does not continue after the death of Fidel Castro. The plan also includes a classified annex that Cuban officials claim could be a plot to assassinate Fidel Castro or a United States military invasion of Cuba, though they have provided no evidence to support this claim.

CONTEMPORARY RELATIONS

Main article: Cuban Thaw

Relations between Cuba and the United States remain tenuous, but since Fidel Castro stepped down from official leadership of the Cuban state and Barack Obama became president of the United States, they have improved.

In April 2009, Obama, who had received nearly half of the Cuban-American vote in the 2008 presidential election, began implementing a less strict policy towards Cuba. Obama stated that he was open to dialogue with Cuba, but that he would only lift the trade embargo if Cuba underwent political change. In March 2009, Obama signed into law a congressional spending bill which eased some economic sanctions on Cuba and eased travel restrictions on Cuban-Americans (defined as persons with a relative "who is no more than three generations removed from that person") traveling to Cuba. The April executive decision further removed time limits on Cuban-American travel to the island. Another restriction loosened in April 2009 was in the realm of telecommunications, which would allow quicker and easier access to the internet for Cuba.

The loosening of restrictions is likely to help nonprofits and scientists from both countries who work together on issues of mutual concern, such as destruction of shared biodiversity and diseases that affect both populations. At the 2009 5th Summit of the Americas, President Obama signaled the opening of a new beginning with Cuba.

Obama's overtures were reciprocated, to some degree, by new Cuban President Raúl Castro. On July 27, 2012, Raúl Castro said that the Government of Cuba is willing to hold talks with the United States government to "discuss anything".On December 10, 2013, at a state memorial service for Nelson Mandela, Barack Obama and Raúl Castro shook hands, with Castro saying in English: "Mr. President, I am Castro." Though both sides played down the handshake (much like the Clinton handshake of 2000), an adviser to Obama said that Obama wanted to improve relations with Cuba, yet had concerns about human rights on the island.

Beginning in 2013, Cuban and U.S. officials held secret talks brokered in part by Pope Francis and hosted in Canada and Vatican City to start the process of restoring diplomatic relations between Cuba and the United States. On December 17, 2014, the framework of an agreement to normalize relations and eventually end the longstanding embargo was announced by Castro in Cuba and Obama in the United States. Cuba and the United States pledged to start official negotiations with the aim of reopening their respective embassies in Havana and Washington.

As part of the agreement, aid worker Alan Gross and an unnamed Cuban national working as a U.S intelligence asset were released by the Cuban government, which also promised to free an unspecified number of Cuban nationals from a list of political prisoners earlier submitted by the United States. For its part, the U.S. government released the last three remaining members of the Cuban Five. Reaction to this change in policy within the Cuban-American community was mixed, and Cuban-American senators Bob Menendez (D-NJ), Marco Rubio (R-FL), and Ted Cruz (R-TX) all condemned the Obama administration's change in policy. However, opinion polls indicated the thaw in relations was broadly popular with the American public.

High-level diplomats from Cuba and the United States met in Havana in January 2015. While the talks did not produce a significant breakthrough, both sides described them as "productive", and Cuban Foreign Ministry official Josefina Vidal said further talks would be scheduled.

Under new rules implemented by the Obama administration, restrictions on travel by Americans to Cuba are significantly relaxed as of January 16, 2015, and the limited import of items like

Cuban cigars and rum to the United States is allowed, as is the export of American computer and telecommunications technology to Cuba.

On April 14, 2015, the Obama administration announced that Cuba would be removed from the United States "Terrorist Sponsor" list. The House and Senate had 45 days from April 14, 2015 to review and possibly block this action, but this did not occur, and on May 29, 2015, the 45 days lapsed, therefore officially removing Cuba from the United States' list of state sponsors of terrorism. This move by President Obama further departs the United States from the Cold War conflict and its strain on Cuba-United States relations. On July 1, 2015, President Barack Obama announced that formal diplomatic relations between Cuba and the United States would resume, and embassies would be opened in Washington and Havana. Relations between Cuba and the United States have been formally re-established on July 20, 2015, with the opening of the Cuban embassy in Washington and the U.S. embassy in Havana.

TRADE RELATIONS

Under the Trade Sanctions Reform and Enhancement Act of 2000, exports from the United States to Cuba in the industries of food and medical products are permitted with the proper licensing and permissions from the U.S. Department of Commerce and the United States Department of the Treasury.

The Obama administration eased specific travel and other restrictions on Cuba in January 2011.

A delegation from the United States Congress called on Cuban president Raúl Castro on February 24, 2012 to discuss bilateral relations. The Congress delegation included Patrick Leahy, Democratic Senator from the state of Vermont and chairman of the Senate Committee on the Judiciary, and Richard Shelby, Republican Senator from the state of Alabama and ranking member of the Committee of Banking, Housing and Urban Matters; they went to Cuba as part of a delegation of Senators and Representatives of the Congress of United States.

Travel and import restrictions levied by the United States were further relaxed by executive action in January 2015 as part of the Cuban Thaw

The United States established diplomatic relations with the Republic of Cuba in 1902, opening the first U.S. Embassy in Havana in 1923. The Embassy was closed in 1961 when the United States severed diplomatic relations. During President Carter's administration in 1977, the United States and Cuba signed an agreement establishing the U.S. Interests Section (USINT) in Havana, and the Cuban Interests Section in Washington, DC. Under the formal protection of the Embassy of Switzerland, USINT operated out of the former U.S. Embassy building, which first opened in 1953. On December 17, 2014, President Obama announced the intention to re-establish diplomatic relations with Cuba. After six months of negotiations, the two nations officially renewed diplomatic relations on July 20, 2015, and USINT became U.S. Embassy Havana.

The functions of U.S. Embassy are similar to those of any U.S. government presence abroad: consular services, a political and economic reporting section, a public diplomacy program, law enforcement liaisons through the Regional Security Office and U.S. Coast Guard, a management and administrative office, and other programs to promote coordination with the Cuban government on a growing number of topics of mutual interest.

U.S. Embassy Havana key officers:

Chargé D'affaires: Ambassador Jeffrey DeLaurentis
Deputy Chief of Mission: Scott Hamilton
Political/Economic Chief: Dana Brown
Consul General: Brendan Mullarkey
Management Officer: Jennifer Johnson
Public Affairs Officer: Bruce Kleiner

The U.S. Embassy Havana is located at Calzada between L & M Streets, Vedado, Havana, switchboard: (53-7) 33-3551-3559, fax/general: 33-3700. U.S. Information Service: 33-3967 fax: 33-3869, hours: 8:30 a.m. to 5:00 p.m. Emergencies/after hours: 33-3026.

REFUGEE APPLICATION PROCESS

If a person believes he/she meets the eligibility criteria, that person can apply for refugee status through the Havana Refugee Section.

To apply, an individual person must complete a Preliminary Questionnaire, which can be downloaded from this site, or requested in writing. The written request can be placed in a drop-box located at the gate of the Refugee Section, located at Malecón and J, faxed to (537) 834-4515, or mailed to:

Embajada de los Estados Unidos
Sección de Refugiados
Calzada e L y M
Vedado, La Habana

The application steps are as follows:

Submission of Preliminary Questionnaire
The applicant must submit a completed Preliminary Questionnaire to the Havana Refugee Section. The questionnaire must state the refugee applicant's claim and may include spouse and unmarried children under 21. Individuals over 21 or married must complete their own preliminary questionnaire.

Receipt of Active Case Letter
An individual who appears to meet eligibility criteria will be scheduled for a pre-screen interview in the future. Those who do not qualify will receive a letter informing them that they are not eligible for the program. Applicants are requested not to call or write to check on the status of their application. However, they should inform the Refugee Section by telephone of any change in address or telephone number.

Pre-Screen Interview
When the time has arrived for a pre-screening interview, the applicant will be called or sent a letter asking them to schedule the interview. The purpose of the pre-screening interview is to determine whether an individual meets eligibility criteria. Cases that qualify will have a second interview with a United States Citizenship & Immigration Services (USCIS) officer.

USCIS Interview
A USCIS officer interviews the applicant(s) and makes a determination of refugee status under Section 101(A)(42) of the Immigration and Nationality Act (INA).
For more information about USCIS interviews, please, see the website: http://www.uscis.gov/portal/site/uscis.

For information about requests for reconsideration by USCIS, see the website: http://www.uscis.gov/portal/site/uscis/menuitem.5af9bb95919f35e66f614176543f6d1a/?vgnextoid=c26164337c77e210VgnVCM100000082ca60aRCRD&vgnextchannel=385d3e4d77d73210VgnVCM100000082ca60aRCRD

Security Clearance
Refugee candidates must undergo a security clearance review by U.S. law enforcement agencies.

Departure Documents
Refugee candidates must obtain documents from Cuban officials needed to depart Cuba and enter the United States, including a passport and a medical examination certification.

Flight Departure
Once all security clearances and documents are in order, the Refugee Section will contact the approved refugee to schedule travel.

The Refugee Section will arrange a flight for the refugee(s) from Cuba to the United States. The refugees are required to sign a loan repayment note and pay back transportation costs after arrival in the United States.

TRAVEL AND BUSINESS INFORMATION

The U.S. Department of State's Consular Information Program advises Americans traveling and residing abroad through Consular Information Sheets, Public Announcements, and Travel Warnings. **Consular Information Sheets** exist for all countries and include information on entry and exit requirements, currency regulations, health conditions, safety and security, crime, political disturbances, and the addresses of the U.S. embassies and consulates abroad. **Public Announcements** are issued to disseminate information quickly about terrorist threats and other relatively short-term conditions overseas that pose significant risks to the security of American travelers.

Travel Warnings are issued when the State Department recommends that Americans avoid travel to a certain country because the situation is dangerous or unstable.

For the latest security information, Americans living and traveling abroad should regularly monitor the Department's Bureau of Consular Affairs Internet web site at http://www.travel.state.gov, where the current Worldwide Caution, Public Announcements, and Travel Warnings can be found. Consular Affairs Publications, which contain information on obtaining passports and planning a safe trip abroad, are also available at http://www.travel.state.gov. For additional information on international travel, see http://www.usa.gov/Citizen/Topics/Travel/International.shtml.

The Department of State encourages all U.S citizens traveling or residing abroad to register via the State Department's travel registration website or at the nearest U.S. embassy or consulate abroad. Registration will make your presence and whereabouts known in case it is necessary to contact you in an emergency and will enable you to receive up-to-date information on security conditions.

Emergency information concerning Americans traveling abroad may be obtained by calling 1-888-407-4747 toll free in the U.S. and Canada or the regular toll line 1-202-501-4444 for callers outside the U.S. and Canada.

The National Passport Information Center (NPIC) is the U.S. Department of State's single, centralized public contact center for U.S. passport information. Telephone: 1-877-4USA-PPT (1-877-487-2778). Customer service representatives and operators for TDD/TTY are available Monday-Friday, 7:00 a.m. to 12:00 midnight, Eastern Time, excluding federal holidays.

Travelers can check the latest health information with the U.S. Centers for Disease Control and Prevention in Atlanta, Georgia. A hotline at 877-FYI-TRIP (877-394-8747) and a web site at http://www.cdc.gov/travel/index.htm give the most recent health advisories, immunization recommendations or requirements, and advice on food and drinking water safety for regions and countries. A booklet entitled "Health Information for International Travel" (HHS publication number CDC-95-8280) is available from the U.S. Government Printing Office, Washington, DC 20402, tel. (202) 512-1800.

With the April 2009 directives, the Obama administration removed all travel restrictions for Cuban-Americans to visit and send money to family members in Cuba. However, for those Americans who are not of Cuban descent or have no family in Cuba, there are still ways to travel to Cuba. According to the Cuban Assets Control Regulations, individuals who are subject to U.S. jurisdiction (even if traveling through a third country) must first obtain a license before engaging in travel to, from, and within Cuba.

General licenses are given to certain kinds of travelers including those who are visiting a close relative who is a national of Cuba (including third-country nationals residing in Cuba), journalists and supporting personnel, government officials on official business, members of international organizations (of which the U.S. is a member) traveling on official business, full-time professionals traveling for non-commercial research, full-time professionals traveling for a professional non-commercial meeting or conference organized by an international organization, employees or representative of a U.S. telecommunications services provider, and individuals regularly employed by a producer or distributor of agricultural commodities or medicine.

For those individuals who do not fall under the scope of the general licenses, they may be eligible to obtain a specific license from OFAC. Specific OFAC licenses are given to those who wish to visit a close relative in Cuba who is not a Cuban national, to educational institutions, religious organizations, and other specific licenses are approved on a case-by-case basis.

To apply for a specific license, individuals need to send a letter requesting the specific license and with the details of the potential visit. Academic institutions must send a similar letter and include proof that the institution is accredited by an appropriate association. Religious organizations must send the detailed letter as well and include examples of religious activities they will host in Cuba. The letters must be sent to: Licensing Division, Office of Foreign Assets Control, U.S. Department of Treasury, 1500 Pennsylvania Ave, NW, Washington, DC 20220. More specific guidelines can be found at http://www.treas.gov/offices/enforcement/ofac/programs/cuba/cuba_tr_app.pdf

Once a proper license has been obtained the traveler must have a valid passport and visa. American citizens are issued visas (tourist cards) upon arrival to Cuba or can attain a visa from the Cuban Interest Section in Washington D.C., however make sure to have received the appropriate type of visa for your visit. Additionally, as of May 2010 Cuba requires that all visitors be covered by a non-U.S. medical insurance. Cuba will sell a temporary policy to visitors who do not have a non-U.S. insurer.

Also, keep in mind that credit cards issued by U.S. banks cannot be used in Cuba and the U.S. dollar has not been accepted for commercial transactions since November of 2004. However, there are specially designated Cuban banks that accept major U.S. travelers checks and U.S. dollars can be converted to convertible or non-convertible Cuban pesos (the effective exchange rate including the 10 percent fee for exchanging US dollars to convertible Cuban pesos results in 1 USD = 0.80 CUC) Additionally, keep in mind that there will be a $20 Cuban departure tax that must be paid before leaving the country. The maximum Per Diem rate, or max that can be spent per day of travel in Cuba is $179. Some general and specific licenses, such as for journalists, allow for a higher rate depending on the necessary equipment.

CUBA MINING SECTOR: STRATEGIC INFORMATION

THE MINERAL INDUSTRY OF CUBA

Nickel was the most important mineral commodity to the Cuban economy, followed by cobalt, which was produced as a byproduct of the mining of nickel. Other minerals produced in the country included asphalt, bentonite, cement, chromite, clay, crushed stone, feldspar, gypsum, iron ore, lime, limestone, marble, salt, sand, steel, sulfuric acid, volcanic ash, and zeolite. Cuba also produced ammonia, natural gas, petroleum, petroleum products, and sulfur as a byproduct of the refining of petroleum. The Ministerio de la Industria Básica was the Government entity responsible for the mineral and petroleum sectors. Unión Geológico Minera S.A. was the company in charge of prospecting for, exploring for, and mining all metallic and nonmetallic minerals with the exception of cobalt and nickel, which were overseen by Unión del Níquel S.A. Cubapetróleo S.A. was the company in charge of petroleum prospecting, exploration, marketing, and refining.

PRODUCTION

Production of most mineral commodities, with the exception of asphalt, bentonite, feldspar, limestone, marble, salt, sulfuric acid, volcanic ash, and zeolites, decreased during 2009. Mineral commodities for which production decreased by more than 10% included gypsum, nitrogen, all petroleum refinery products (except naphtha), silica sand, and steel. Data on mineral production are in table 1; production of cobalt and nickel were estimated.

STRUCTURE OF THE MINERAL INDUSTRY

Table 2 is a list of major mineral industry facilities. More-extensive coverage of the mineral industry of Cuba can be found in the 2008 U.S. Geological Survey Minerals Yearbook, volume III, Area reports—International—Latin America and Canada, which is available on the World Wide Web at http://minerals.usgs.gov/minerals/pubs/country.

IMPORTANT DEVELOPMENTS

In recent years the government of the Republic of Cuba has sought to exploit and expand the mining of Nickel and Cobalt, especially in the Eastern region of their island. This action has raised several concerns that directly, or indirectly effect both the actual physical enviorment of Cuba, as well as the social/political scene, including the issue of Human Rights. Furthermore, the issue of trade is also involved in this scenario as a result of the United States trade embargo against Cuba, as codified in the Helms-Burton Legislation. These U.S. actions have infuriated Canada--whose firms lead the ranks of foreign investors in Cuba. Canada has initiated a complaint against the United States under the North American Free Trade Agreement.

At present the economy of Cuba is in a severe state of crisis. With the dissolution of the Soviet Union Cuba now finds herself in a situation where its traditional main export (sugar) will not save the country from further economic difficulties. Thus, the Cuban government has sought mesures in which it can diversify its stagnent economy. Cuba has established 211 joint ventures with foreigners and attracted some $5 billion in foreign investment deals, mostly in tourism, communications, mining, petroleum and agriculture. Havana is eager to attract new investment in biotechnology and assembly plants in Cuba's new free-trade zones. This has included everything to increasing and improving the facilities related to the tourism sector. It has also included reviving and expanding the mining of Nickel and Cobalt.

The mining of these materials has a long history in Cuba. During the 1950's the mines suppled the American government with the majority of the nickel and cobalt needed to fight the war in Korea. After the Castro revolution the mines were nationalized without compensation given to their American owners and the mines then went on to serve Cuba's new ally, the Soviet Union. However, the collaspe of the Soviet Union has not only ment the collaspe of another market it has also ment the withdrawl of Soviet aid and technical support for the mining industry. Furthemore, years of a centrally planned economy has taken its toll on the condition and efficiency of these mines.

Hence, the Cuban government has once again sought foriegn investment in the mining sector. Investment has come from a variety of contries however, it is Canada (currently Cuba's largest overall investor) that has provided most of the investment capital. Canada, which has nickel and cobalt resources of its own, is well tooled with the knowlege it takes to run such an industy. Furthermore, companies such as Toronto based Sherritt International seek to be a controling power in the production of nickel and cobalt.

Therefore the Cuban government which is desperate for foreign investment to keep it's economy afloat has changed its past stand on foreign investment. It now permits and invites foreign companies to invest jointly with the Cuban government on selected projects. Foreign investors are now able to own up to 49% of selected opperations. This arrangement is hoped to provide favourable profits for both the foreign investor, and the Cuban government. Furthermore, these arrangments permit the Cuban government to maintain control over a situation that exists more out of financial nesssity, then out of their own personal want. Thus, since 1990 Sherritt International has invested over a half billion dollars in the production of nickel and cobalt in the Eastern region of Cuba near the town of Moa. The Moa mines with their 1950's American machinary still in working order and heaps of nickel-cobalt littering the slopes around it, was said to be a tresure trove. Evidently this has proved true when by 1995 production at Moa sored by 80%.

Therefore, according to Sherritt, Cuba has proven to be an excellent investment opportunity. However, part of the reason why Cuba is such a wonderfull investment opportunity lies in Cuba's laxed attitude toward enviormental protection. Officially of course, Cuba mantains a strong stand on the protection of the enviroment. Their new laws relating to foreign investment also contain clauses dealing with eviormental protection. Article 54 of the new investment code states that 'foreign investment is conceived and stimulated in the context of the country's sustainable development, which implies that during the course of that investment, enviormental conservation and the rational use of natural resources shall be carefully undertaken". Article 56 states "the person or company responsible for the damage or harm is obliged to reestabish the previous enviormental situation, repair the material damage and indemnify the injured people"(Oro 25).

However, it is well known that money talks especially in poor nations eager to develop. Cuba is a country that has a government set on maintaining it's power. Thus, the level to which these laws are actually enforced is dependent on that knowlege. Furthermore, Cuba is in many ways the subservant partner in these investment programmes. Again without foreign investment the Cuban economy will continue to spiral into an even more problelmatic situation. Henceforth, the Castro government would fall deeper into choas to the point where social frustrations could condition a movement for a coup d'etat. Another reason why these laws are poorly enforced lies in the nature of the Cuban state itself. Cuba is a repressive state that does not permit its citizens to organize freely without the fear of repression. Thus, with a strong reactionary civil society absent from the picture, it would seem unlikely that the public would risk protesting government policy, even though they are the indirect victims of such.

Thus according to the Cuban American National Foundation's report on the status of Human Rights in Cuba presented in Geneva in 1998, it was argued that "as a result of Sherritt's mining operations in Moa, local residents are now suffering from a high rate of diseases of the skin, and other illnesses associated with the respiratory system. Additionally Moa Bay shows clear evidence of contamination from the raw pollutants that are being irresponsibly cast into its water (p. 4 text).

Jose Oro author of The Poisoning of Paridise: The Enviormental Crisis in Cuba, examines the mining industries nagative enviormental effect even closer. He argues that the Nickel factory "Che Guevara" at Moa omits large amounts of smoke, soot, NH3, noise and vibrations. He also notes that the dust level in the quarries are at unhealthy levels as well. Oro states that this factory alone produces two and 1/2 million tons of waste each year. Their is also a serious potential of NH3 discharge. The ecological impact of the pollution on the local level is seen by the significant damage done in the town of Punta Brava, as waste runs directly through the town (via the Punta Gorda river) and then eventually out to sea. Thus increasing the chances of enviormental damage to sea life as well (Oro 81).

Furthermore, the "Pedro Soto Alba" nickel instalation also in Moa launches large quantities of H2S into the atmosphere. Again a huge amount of dust exists in the quarries and nearly two million tons of waste is produced each year. In this case Oro argues the local, national, and potentially international impact is great. Notably the amount of H2S launched into the atmosphere is capable of generating acid rain in the Eastern region of Cuba and possibly beyond Cuba itself. Moa bay is again a concern as waste from this facility is also frequently dumped there. Finally, as a result of this dumping the coral reef barrier in this region has suffered greatly. If present conditions are not changed it is likely that the reef will be completly destroyed in ten years time.(Oro p.82)

Moving on to Human Rights (other then having an enviorment free from dangerous waste) we note that the Cuban government and those companies who invest jointly with that government (in this case study Sherritt) are thus involved directly, or indirectly with the violation of workers Human Rights. Many of these violations are actually seen by companies like Sherritt, as an advatage to investing in Cuba. They include (as to be explained) low wage payment of workers, and the ability to have a labour force free from unions. Begining with the payment of workers we note that the only employer in Cuba is the Cuban government. Thus the nature of a joint venture where the Cuban government hold marjority control over oppporations ensures, the government that tiltle of sole employer. Thus, Sherritt does not actually pay their Cuban labour force directly, instead Sherritt pays the Cuban government in hard currency (IE US$) in turn the Cuban government pays the workers in nonconveratable Cuban pesos. (Once must note that in present day Cuba those who have dollars are able to buy the products that the state is longer able to supply, those who do not have acess to dollars are therefore condemed to suffer the hardships of everyday life in Cuba) Thus Sherritt pays the Cuban government $US 9.500 dollars per year per worker hired. In turn, the goverment pays workers the equivalent of $US 120 dollars per year in Cuban pesos! In other words, the government appropriates 98.7% of each workers wages. Meanwhile, the Castro government which is a serverly repressive one, is able to stay affloat as a result of their ability to live off the spoils of their workers. Another aspect that must be noted in this relationship is that in Cuba their is one union that is controlled by the Cuban state. It is not one that is democratically elected rather, it is an arm of the repressive Cuban state. In Cuba today the notion of stikes do not exist, as they are officially illegal. Those who wish to partake in a strike are then entitled to a state founded housing allowence in one of Cuba's prisons. Thus Sherritt benefits, and henceforth takes advantage of a labour force that is compliant and technically free from inserrection.

Moving on to trade, and the implications involved in this case we must note the role of the US law: Helms-Burton. Helms-Burton is the latest edition of the US trade embargo toward Cuba which was first put into effect in 1961, as a consequence of the Castro's government decision to nationalized all US owned property without compensation. Helms-Burton replaces all pervious US embargo legislation, and is unique due to its international implications (to be explained as it relates to Sherritt/mines).

Helms-Burton provides that the following must take place for the embargo to be lifted: Legalization of all political activity, public Commitments to free and fair elections, the exclusion of Fidel Castro and his brother Raul Castro from the government, respect for internationally recognized Human Rights, and finally, commitments and progress assuring the return, or compensation for, properties taken from present day US Nationals. Thus, under Helms-Burton, the United States embargo for the first time affects non-US companies. More specifically, Helms-Burton provides that foreign companies can be sued in US courts if they engage in business with Cuba (or involving) property that was previously owned by a US citizen (including those persons who obtained US citizenship through naturalization--ie the majority of Cuban-Americans today).

Therefore, Sherritt like many other non-US corporations that have invested in Cuba falls into the catogory where under US law it can be prosecuted for traficing in stolen US property. This is possible because the mines Sherritt invested in, were formally owned (until they were expropriated by the Cuban government) by Moa Bay Mining Corp., now known as Freeport-McMoRan Inc. based in New Orleans (Worsnip).

However, as for now, Helms-Burton is US law, but the President has yet to fully impliment the law. This is primarly due to the large upset this law has created with many of America's major trading partners including Canada. So far the only real action that has been taken against Sherritt is that some employes of that corporation and their families have been restricted from entering US territory. Furthermore, Sherritt has not been able to invest in the United States as any investment they do make can under Helms-Burton be conficated, and taken as payment for the loss incured by the before mentioned US company. Finally, as the embargo agaist Cuba does not permit any product that is totally or partially of Cuban origin from entering the United States. This means that the nickel and cobalt that is mines in Cuba and then further processed in Canada is bared from the United States. Canada which is the US's largest trading partner and NAFTA member has threated action. This has inculded Canada joining with the European Union in the WTO in an effort to fight the US law there. It has also caused Canada to take up the US at the United Nations as well. Interestingly enough the vote in the United Nations totally favoured Canada and other Cuba investors with only Isreal and Usbeckastan (both of which trade with Cuba) favouring the United States.

Canada has also passed their own version of Helms-Burton. Their version argues that those Canadians who are decendent of the United Empire Loyaltists who fled to Canada after the American revolution have the right to sue Americans that are using "their" property. It should be know that recent examinations have found that many city centres are built on such property, including New York's Wall street. However, all in all this measure taken by the Canadian parliment is largly to show how absurd the US law is and is not intented to be acted upon. In many respects it would seem that Helms-Burton itself falls into the same category as the Clinton admistration seems to understand how much tension it would cause amongst major US trading partners. However, with that said it must be known that the law has not be repealed rather it has only been suspended for 6 mounths. Therefore, the threat of US action still shadows the sitaution. Such a shadow has thus made many potential Cuba investors including Sherritt causios about new investments. At the same time a large consenus believes that the threat is only that and should not deter furtue investments in Cuba.

In conclusion the minning of nickel and cobalt in Eastern Cuba has raised serveral issues. Namely, due to the servere economic crisis the repressive Cuban dictatorship has sought foreign investment capital in the form of joint ventures to secure their government's furture rule. This investment as seen by are study of Sherritt has noted that the Cuban government is so desperate for investment that they are willing to overlook enviormental concerns. Futhermore, the Cubans who are the true victims are unable to express their anger at Sherritt/governments actions as a reslut of the repressive nature of that government. In relation to rights we see how foreign firms abuse the already a bad situation of their workers. This is especially noted in the fact that independent unions and strikes are illegal in Cuba. Furthermore, the fact that the Cuban government steals most of the mine workers wages is just another Human Rights violation. Finally, the issue of trade and sanctions is bought in on two main levels involving these mines. First off, the product of these mines are officially banned from the United States as a result of the US emabargo against that country. Additionally, due to the international nature of the US embargo as codified in Helms-Burton Sherritt has been prosecutly (to a degree (although if the law is fully implimented they can be completly prosecuted) as a result of being accused of traficking in stolen US property. Thus the issue of mining in Cuba is a complex one that needs serious attention from many different perspectives.

Cuba has seen a history of mining extending over a period of three hundred years. During the period 1900 to 2002 mining has been a permanent activity and, during WWII, the mining of manganese, some copper, and nickel was most important, particularly nickel from the extensive literates that are considered among the largest reserves in the world. Cuba ranks with Canada, Russia, Australia and New Caledonia among the world's principal producers.

Cuba is an important nickel and cobalt producer and ranks sixth in the world in terms of nickel and accounts for 8% of the world's cobalt production. Cuban mineral production is state controlled, although the government has made steps to amend the mineral laws and legislation, which will hopefully change the industry's structure. In 1993, Geominera was formed as a private company that ut8ilised state funds. Geominera focus on gold and base metal exploration, whilst foreign investors are currently developing nickel/cobalt and gold resources.

In recent years the government of the Republic of Cuba has sought to exploit and expand the mining of Nickel and Cobalt, especially in the Eastern region of their island. This action has raised several concerns that directly, or indirectly effect both the actual physical environment of Cuba, as well as the social/political scene, including the issue of Human Rights. Furthermore, the issue of trade is also involved in this scenario as a result of the United States trade embargo against Cuba, as codified in the Helms-Burton Legislation. These U.S. actions have infuriated Canada--whose firms lead the ranks of foreign investors in Cuba. Canada has initiated a complaint against the United States under the North American Free Trade Agreement.

At present the economy of Cuba is in a severe state of crisis. With the dissolution of the Soviet Union Cuba now finds herself in a situation where its traditional main export (sugar) will not save the country from further economic difficulties. Thus, the Cuban government has sought measures in which it can diversify its stagnant economy. Cuba has established 211 joint ventures with foreigners and attracted some $5 billion in foreign investment deals, mostly in tourism, communications, mining, petroleum and agriculture. Havana is eager to attract new investment in biotechnology and assembly plants in Cuba's new free-trade zones. This has included everything to increasing and improving the facilities related to the tourism sector. It has also included reviving and expanding the mining of Nickel and Cobalt.

The mining of these materials has a long history in Cuba. During the 1950's the mines supplied the American government with the majority of the nickel and cobalt needed to fight the war in Korea. After the Castro revolution the mines were nationalized without compensation given to their American owners and the mines then went on to serve Cuba's new ally, the Soviet Union. However, the collapse of the Soviet Union has not only mint the collapse of another market it has also mint the withdrawal of Soviet aid and technical support for the mining industry. Furthermore, years of a centrally planned economy has taken its toll on the condition and efficiency of these mines.

Hence, the Cuban government has once again sought foreign investment in the mining sector. Investment has come from a variety of countries however; it is Canada (currently Cuba's largest overall investor) that has provided most of the investment capital. Canada, which has nickel and cobalt resources of its own, is well tooled with the knowledge it takes to run such an industry. Furthermore, companies such as Toronto based Sherritt International seek to be a controlling power in the production of nickel and cobalt.

Therefore the Cuban government which is desperate for foreign investment to keep it's economy afloat has changed its past stand on foreign investment. It now permits and invites foreign companies to invest jointly with the Cuban government on selected projects. Foreign investors are now able to own up to 49% of selected operations. This arrangement is hoped to provide favorable profits for both the foreign investor, and the Cuban government. Furthermore, these arrangements permit the Cuban government to maintain control over a situation that exists more out of financial necessity, then out of their own personal want. Thus, since 1990 Sherritt International has invested over a half billion dollars in the production of nickel and cobalt in the Eastern region of Cuba near the town of Moa. The Moa mines with their 1950's American machinery still in working order and heaps of nickel-cobalt littering the slopes around it, was said to be a treasure trove. Evidently this has proved true when by 1995 production at Moa soared by 80%.

Therefore, according to Sherritt, Cuba has proven to be an excellent investment opportunity. However, part of the reason why Cuba is such a wonderful investment opportunity lies in Cuba's relaxed attitude toward environmental protection. Officially of course, Cuba maintains a strong stand on the protection of the environment. Their new laws relating to foreign investment also contain clauses dealing with environmental protection. Article 54 of the new investment code states that 'foreign investment is conceived and stimulated in the context of the country's sustainable development, which implies that during the course of that investment, environmental conservation and the rational use of natural resources shall be carefully undertaken".

Article 56 states "the person or company responsible for the damage or harm is obliged to reestablish the previous environmental situation, repair the material damage and indemnify the injured people"(Oro 25).

However, it is well known that money talks especially in poor nations eager to develop. Cuba is a country that has a government set on maintaining it's power. Thus, the level to which these laws are actually enforced is dependent on that knowledge. Furthermore, Cuba is in many ways the sub servant partner in these investment programmers. Again without foreign investment the Cuban economy will continue to spiral into an even more problematic situation. Henceforth, the Castro government would fall deeper into chaos to the point where social frustrations could condition a movement for a coup d'etat. Another reason why these laws are poorly enforced lies in the nature of the Cuban state itself. Cuba is a repressive state that does not permit its citizens to organize freely without the fear of repression. Thus, with a strong reactionary civil society absent from the picture, it would seem unlikely that the public would risk protesting government policy, even though they are the indirect victims of such.

Thus according to the Cuban American National Foundation's report on the status of Human Rights in Cuba presented in Geneva in 1998, it was argued that "as a result of Sherritt's mining operations in Moa, local residents are now suffering from a high rate of diseases of the skin, and other illnesses associated with the respiratory system. Additionally Moa Bay shows clear evidence of contamination from the raw pollutants that are being irresponsibly cast into its water

Jose Oro author of The Poisoning of Paridise: The Environmental Crisis in Cuba examines the mining industries negative environmental effect even closer. He argues that the Nickel factory "Che Guevara" at Moa omits large amounts of smoke, soot, NH_3, noise and vibrations. He also notes that the dust level in the quarries are at unhealthy levels as well. Oro states that this factory alone produces two and 1/2 million tons of waste each year. Their is also a serious potential of NH_3 discharge. The ecological impact of the pollution on the local level is seen by the significant damage done in the town of Punta Brava, as waste runs directly through the town (via the Punta Gorda river) and then eventually out to sea. Thus increasing the chances of environmental damage to sea life as well

Furthermore, the "Pedro Soto Alba" nickel installation also in Moa launches large quantities of H_2S into the atmosphere. Again a huge amount of dust exists in the quarries and nearly two million tons of waste is produced each year. In this case Oro argues the local, national, and potentially international impact is great. Notably the amount of H_2S launched into the atmosphere is capable of generating acid rain in the Eastern region of Cuba and possibly beyond Cuba itself. Moa bay is again a concern as waste from this facility is also frequently dumped there. Finally, as a result of this dumping the coral reef barrier in this region has suffered greatly. If present conditions are not changed it is likely that the reef will be completely destroyed in ten years time.(Oro p.82)

Moving on to Human Rights (other then having an environment free from dangerous waste) we note that the Cuban government and those companies who invest jointly with that government (in this case study Sherritt) are thus involved directly, or indirectly with the violation of workers Human Rights. Many of these violations are actually seen by companies like Sherritt, as an advantage to investing in Cuba.

They include (as to be explained) low wage payment of workers, and the ability to have a labor force free from unions. Beginning with the payment of workers we note that the only employer in Cuba is the Cuban government. Thus the nature of a joint venture where the Cuban government hold majority control over apportions ensures, the government that title of sole employer. Thus, Sherritt does not actually pay their Cuban labor force directly, instead Sherritt pays the Cuban government in hard currency (IE US$) in turn the Cuban government pays the workers in nonconvertible Cuban pesos. (Once must note that in present day Cuba those who have dollars are able to buy the products that the state is longer able to supply, those who do not have access to dollars are therefore condemned to suffer the hardships of everyday life in Cuba) Thus Sherritt pays the Cuban government $US 9.500 dollars per year per worker hired. In turn, the government pays workers the equivalent of $US 120 dollars per year in Cuban pesos! In other words, the government appropriates 98.7% of each workers wages. Meanwhile, the Castro government which is a severely repressive one, is able to stay afloat as a result of their ability to live off the spoils of their workers.

Another aspect that must be noted in this relationship is that in Cuba their is one union that is controlled by the Cuban state. It is not one that is democratically elected rather, it is an arm of the repressive Cuban state. In Cuba today the notion of stakes do not exist, as they are officially illegal. Those who wish to partake in a strike are then entitled to a state founded housing allowance in one of Cuba's prisons. Thus Sherritt benefits, and henceforth takes advantage of a labor force that is compliant and technically free from insurrection.

Moving on to trade, and the implications involved in this case we must note the role of the US law: Helms-Burton. Helms-Burton is the latest edition of the US trade embargo toward Cuba which was first put into effect in 1961, as a consequence of the Castro's government decision to

nationalized all US owned property without compensation. Helms-Burton replaces all pervious US embargo legislation, and is unique due to its international implications (to be explained as it relates to Sherritt/mines).
Helms-Burton provides that the following must take place for the embargo to be lifted: Legalization of all political activity, public Commitments to free and fair elections, the exclusion of Fidel Castro and his brother Raul Castro from the government, respect for internationally recognized Human Rights, and finally, commitments and progress assuring the return, or compensation for, properties taken from present day US Nationals. Thus, under Helms-Burton, the United States embargo for the first time affects non-US companies. More specifically, Helms-Burton provides that foreign companies can be sued in US courts if they engage in business with Cuba (or involving) property that was previously owned by a US citizen (including those persons who obtained US citizenship through naturalization--i.e. the majority of Cuban-Americans today). Therefore, Sherritt like many other non-US corporations that have invested in Cuba falls into the category where under US law it can be prosecuted for trafficking in stolen US property. This is possible because the mines Sherritt invested in, were formally owned (until they were expropriated by the Cuban government) by Moa Bay Mining Corp., now known as Freeport-McMoRan Inc. based in New Orleans (Worship).

However, as for now, Helms-Burton is US law, but the President has yet to fully implement the law. This is primarily due to the large upset this law has created with many of America's major trading partners including Canada. So far the only real action that has been taken against Sherritt is that some employees of that corporation and their families have been restricted from entering US territory. Furthermore, Sherritt has not been able to invest in the United States as any investment they do make can under Helms-Burton be confiscated, and taken as payment for the loss incurred by the before mentioned US company. Finally, as the embargo against Cuba does not permit any product that is totally or partially of Cuban origin from entering the United States. This means that the nickel and cobalt that is mines in Cuba and then further processed in Canada is bared from the United States. Canada which is the US's largest trading partner and NAFTA member has threaten action. This has included Canada joining with the European Union in the WTO in an effort to fight the US law there. It has also caused Canada to take up the US at the United Nations as well. Interestingly enough the vote in the United Nations totally favored Canada and other Cuba investors with only Israel and Uzbekistan (both of which trade with Cuba) favoring the United States.

Canada has also passed their own version of Helms-Burton. Their version argues that those Canadians who are descendent of the United Empire Loyalists who fled to Canada after the American Revolution have the right to sue Americans that are using "their" property. It should be know that recent examinations have found that many city centers are built on such property, including New York's Wall street. However, all in all this measure taken by the Canadian parliament is largely to show how absurd the US law is and is not indented to be acted upon. In many respects it would seem that Helms-Burton itself falls into the same category as the Clinton admistration seems to understand how much tension it would cause amongst major US trading partners. However, with that said it must be known that the law has not be repealed rather it has only been suspended for 6 months. Therefore, the threat of US action still shadows the situation. Such a shadow has thus made many potential Cuba investors including Sherritt causes about new investments. At the same time a large consensus believes that the threat is only that and should not deter future investments in Cuba.

In conclusion the mining of nickel and cobalt in Eastern Cuba has raised several issues. Namely, due to the severe economic crisis the repressive Cuban dictatorship has sought foreign investment capital in the form of joint ventures to secure their government's future rule. This investment as seen by are study of Sherritt has noted that the Cuban government is so desperate for investment that they are willing to overlook environmental concerns.

Furthermore, the Cubans who are the true victims are unable to express their anger at Sherritt/governments actions as a result of the repressive nature of that government. In relation to rights we see how foreign firms abuse the already a bad situation of their workers. This is especially noted in the fact that independent unions and strikes are illegal in Cuba. Furthermore, the fact that the Cuban government steals most of the mineworker's wages is just another Human Rights violation. Finally, the issue of trade and sanctions is bought in on two main levels involving these mines. First off, the product of these mines are officially banned from the United States as a result of the US embargo against that country. Additionally, due to the international nature of the US embargo as codified in Helms-Burton Sherritt has been prosecuted (to a degree (although if the law is fully implemented they can be completely prosecuted) as a result of being accused of trafficking in stolen US property. Thus the issue of mining in Cuba is a complex one that needs serious attention from many different perspectives.

COBALT SEA MINING (COBALT)

CASE NAME:Cobalt Sea Mining

A. IDENTIFICATION

1. The Issue

The issue in the Pacific Ocean Manganese and Cobalt mining case is the establishment of a precedent on how "the common heritage of mankind" will be exploited, who has rights to the economic benefits, and who will regulate resource depletion and other potential environmental damage. Since seabed mining is not yet commercially viable in the depths beyond national jurisdiction, the a priori approach taken in this case could act as a framework for future trade and environmental issues in multilateral forums, and will impact every state in the world.

2. Description

The discourse of the seabed provisions of the United Nations Convention on the Law of the Sea (the "Convention") have been contentious since "[i]n 1967, Arvid Pardo, the Ambassador of Malta to the United Nations, delivered a speech to the First Committee of the General Assembly, calling for an international regime to govern the deep seabed, mine the manganese nodules and distribute the profits from their sale to the neediest countries." This led to the establishment of UN Seabed Committees and laid the groundwork for the third and present Convention which concluded in 1982.

Even though Democratic and Republican administrations had been working on the establishment of an international law of the sea since 1958, the Reagan administration was so adamantly opposed to the anti-market provisions in the proposed seabed regime, that it refused to even sign the Convention, more less submit it for ratification. In the words of President Clinton's Deputy Assistant Secretary of State (Oceans) David Colson:

The basic flaws of that [1982] deep seabed mining regime are manifold. But stated simply, it failed to provide the US and other states with major economic interests a voice commensurate with those interests in decision making relating to the management of deep seabed resources and it was based on a highly interventionist, central economic planning model that was overly bureaucratic and would have preempted private investment in deep seabed mineral resource development, thus preventing the development of those resources when economic conditions warrant.

In 1990, the Bush administration started to explore the possibility of an amendment to the Convention which would make it amenable to US interests. The Clinton administration continued the process, and in July of 1994 announced that he would sign a new amendment, and in October sent it to the Senate for ratification. Now the Convention and its Amendments will be considered by the new Republican controlled Senate, and notably, overseen by Senate Foreign Relations Committee Chairman Sen. Jesse Helms (R-NC).

The ratification of the Convention would set a new standard for activities on and under the high seas. "The articles on the protection and preservation of the marine environment that finally emerged as part XII of the Convention represent the first attempt to set out a general framework for a legal regime that establishes on a global, conventional basis the obligations, responsibilities and powers of states in all matters of marine environmental protection."

The International Sea-Bed Authority will have responsibility for controlling pollution from activities on the deep seabed under Article 145, but the primary responsibility for adopting and enforcing laws and regulations remains with the states under Article 209. This responsibility will have doubtful effect when such activities do not damage the flag state's territory and contributes important resources to the national economy. The geographic region covered by the Convention is called the "Area" which means "the seabed and ocean floor and subsoil thereof, beyond the limits of national jurisdiction." This means any part of the ocean floor, world wide, that is not covered by any state's exclusive economic zone (EEZ).

The Habitat would include any plant and animal life found at the respective mining sites which average 12,000-20,000 feet in depth, and the plant and animal life affected by the enormous amount of sediment that can be stirred-up from the use of air lift mining vacuums and/or dredging equipment. The potential supply of manganese could be in the billions of tons. Manganese is used in the refining of steel and for scrubbing sulphur from stack gas, usually from coal burning plants. Manganese can also be refined to extract copper and cobalt.

Since the US is overwhelmingly the largest consumer of manganese (and will be for the foreseeable future), this issue is of special interest for the US, and to a certain degree Japan, Germany and other highly industrialized countries who have developed deep-sea mining technology and refine large quantities of steel. The economic viability and impact of this issue is unclear, but potentially could be a multi-billion dollar industry which could employ thousands of people.

The environmental impact of seabed mining would include biodiversity issues, ocean floor species and plant life loss, and pollution from activities such as drilling, dredging, excavation, waste disposal and related activities in the maintenance of mining installations. Scientists are just now learning more about the type of habitat that surrounds sites with high levels of mineral sulfides (which typically contain manganese, cobalt, copper, zinc, lead and iron; and sometimes silver and gold).

As little as 15 years ago, many scientists thought the deep seabed was like a desert, but recent deep sea exploration has found thriving communities of many species, some unknown elsewhere. "Such communities form around hydrothermal vents which produce warm water zones of tectonic activity such as the mid-ocean ridges as well as around cold jets of unusually salty water and places where hydrocarbons seep from the sea floor. The basis of life in these ecosystems is not photosynthesis but the activity of bacteria that use the substances coming out of the sea floor sulfides in the hot water, for example to produce organic compounds and energy." These autotrophy bacteria are the first links in very long food chains, in which 233 invertebrate species have already been found.

Some potential miners have proposed trying to collect minerals as they precipitate out of active vents, which would almost certainly cause great habitat and species loss. But the technology necessary to accomplish this feat is not available and may be unnecessarily complex. Research on the Escanaba Trough along the Gorda Ridge off California suggests that deposits which are formed within sediments efficiently trap and concentrate minerals as they leave volcanic domes.

Scientists assume that hydrothermal vents have life spans of less than fifty years, and once vents are no longer active, their fauna disappear leaving only the valuable crusts.

Therefore, future legislation could restrict mining to deposits on inactive vents to minimize the destruction of species and habitat.

3. Related Cases
4. Draft Author: David Bew
B. LEGAL Clusters

5. Discourse and Status: Agreement and IN Progress The Convention on the Law of the Sea entered into force on November 16, 1994 with the 60 parties necessary for the Convention to enter into force, but no major sea power or industrialized country, save for Iceland, has ratified the Convention. As of January 27, 1995, 72 countries were party to the amendment to the Convention addressing the "non-market"
mining provisions.
6. Forum and Scope: UN and Multilateral
7. Decision Breadth: 72

The Law of the Sea Treaty received the necessary 60 ratifications and entered into force November 16, 1994. Since Iceland was the only industrialized country to ratify the treaty, UN members have been amenable to the new amendment which addresses the reservations of the US and is expected to be ratified by virtually all countries. Even the countries not ratifying the treaty will be effected by its provisions since much of its contents are considered customary international law.

Number of parties affected: All states
8. Legal Standing:TREATY
C. GEOGRAPHIC Clusters
9. Geographic Locations
a. Geographic Domain: OCEAN
b. Geographic Site: OCEAN
c. Geographic Impact: MANY
10. Sub-National Factors: NO
11. Type of Habitat: OCEANS
The habitat in this case is the area at or near the ocean
floor in depths ranging from 12,000-20,000 feet.
12. Type of Measure: Licensing
13. Direct vs. Indirect Impacts: Direct
14. Relation of Measure to Environmental Impact

Licensing and regulation is direct as they cover the process of mining, and not the use of the manganese, cobalt, etc.

A. Directly Related: YES Mineral
b. Indirectly Related: NO
c. Not Related: NO
d. Process Related: YES Pollution Sea [POLS]
The environmental and trade impacts are directly related to the process of mining. Any mining conducted in the Area will be licensed and regulated by the Authority, which has responsibility for controlling the activities on the seabed.

15. Trade Product Identification: RAW, HARD MINERAL
16. Economic Data

The industry is only in its infancy; there are not yet any commercially viable mine sites.

17. Impact of Measure on Trade Competitiveness: HIGH
18. Industry Sector: Mineral
19. Exporters and Importers: MANY and MANY

EXPORTERS

The leading preliminary US consortium is led by Lockheed (plus two possible others may have site claims "grand fathered" into the Amendment); other site claims so far have come from Japan, France, Russia, India and China. Importers: Leading consumer of subject minerals is the US.

20. Environmental Problem Type:

Species Loss Sea [SPLS]
Species and habitat loss could extend to the 223 invertebrate species that have been identified near hydrothermal vents, most of which are endemic, differing considerably in separate geographical zones. The potential loss from the destruction of these seabed habitats could also have a direct human impact. "Some of the hot vent organisms can tolerate temperatures up to 250øC, a property unusual enough to make these bacteria valuable...in biotechnology to produce heat-resistant enzymes."

21. Name, Type, and Diversity of Species
Name:MANY
Type:MANY
Diversity:NA

As a beginning, 223 invertebrate species have been described living around hydrothermal vents in the deep seabed around Escanaba Trough. Most of these species are "mollusks, annelids, arthropods or members of Vestimentifera, the tube worms. The peracarides and echinoderms that dominate 'normal' seabed communities are only weakly represented. Most of the hydrothermal species are endemic, differing considerably between vents in separate geographical zones."

22. Resource Impact and Effect: HIGH and Regulatory
23. Urgency and Lifetime: LOW and 100s of years
24. Substitutes: Synthetics

F. OTHER Factors
25. Culture: YES
Much of the controversy surrounding the Law of the Sea Treaty is related to the expected profits generated by seabed mining. Many participants in the debate want land locked and poor countries to benefit from the development of the "common heritage of mankind" since the Area falls outside the jurisdiction of any country's EEZ.
27. Human Rights: NO
26. Trans-Border: NO
27. Rights: YES

The basic question is who owns these resources. The law does recognize the common heritage but assumes a first-come, first-serve attitude to exploitation.

28. Relevant Literature

The body of literature on this issue is extremely large and spans more than thirty years. The most important document is the UN Convention on the Law of the Sea, especially Part XI and Part XII. The applicable articles include the following.
art. 145 Protection of the Marine Environment
art. 186 Sea-Bed Disputes Chamber of the International Tribunal for the Law of the Sea
art. 187 Jurisdiction of the Sea-Bed Disputes Chamber
art. 208 Pollution from sea-bed activities
art. 209 Pollution from activities in the Area
art. 214 Enforcement with respect to pollution from sea-bed activities
ANNEX VI. art. 14 Sea-Bed Disputes Chamber
Carter, Barry and Phillip Trimble, International Law, Little, Brown and Company, Boston, 1991.
Dispatch, "UN Convention on the Law of the Sea," 5/22 (May, 1994) 359.

Dispatch, "US to sign Seabed Mining Agreement of the Law of the Sea Convention," 5/29 (December 1994) p.485.
Janis, Mark, An Introduction to International Law, Little, Brown and Company, Boston, 1993.
New Scientist, "A Strategy for the Sea Floor," October 12, 1991, 34.

Oceans, "Looking Toward Seabed Mining," 21/1 (January, 1988), 69. Oceans, "Prospecting Two Miles Down," 21/2 (February, 1988), 16.

SHERRITT - MOA BAY NICKEL

U.S. DEPARTMENT OF STATE BACKGROUND NOTES: CUBA PUBLISHED BY THE BUREAU OF PUBLIC AFFAIRS NOVEMBER 1994 Cuba was the last major Spanish colony to gain independence. In a movement which began in 1850, Cuban planters financed and led several expeditions against Spanish garrisons. In 1868, the 10-years' war for independence began under the leadership of Carlos Manuel de Cespedes, whom the Cubans consider to be the father of their country. Jose Marti, Cuba's greatest national hero, initiated plans for a general uprising 24 years later. In 1895, Marti announced the Grito de Baire ("Call to arms from Baire"), heralding the beginning of Cuba's final struggle for independence. Shortly after, he died in battle. The United States entered the conflict on the side of the revolutionaries when the U.S.S. Maine, anchored in Havana Harbor to provide protection for U.S. citizens, was sunk by an explosion of unknown origin on February 15, 1898.

On December 10, 1898, Spain signed the Treaty of Paris, ending the Spanish-American War and relinquishing control of Cuba to the United States. The United States administered the island for three years. Independence was proclaimed on May 20, 1902, although the United States retained the right to intervene to preserve Cuban independence and stability under the Platt Amendment, which established conditions mandated by Congress for the withdrawal of U.S. troops from Cuba. In 1934, the amendment was repealed in keeping with the Roosevelt Administration's "Good Neighbor" policy. Later the same year, the United States and Cuba reaffirmed by treaty the 1903 agreement which leased the Guantanamo Bay naval base to the United States. This agreement remains in force today and can only be terminated by mutual agreement or abandonment by the United States....Traditionally, Cuba's mining sector has accounted for a significant part of export earnings. The country's nickel reserves are the fourth-largest in the world. The ore is processed on the island in two formerly U.S.-owned plants at Nicaro and Moa Bay. Plants are also located at Punta Gorda and Las Camariocas.

Memorandum by the Deputy Assistant Secretary of State for Inter-American Affairs (Mann) to the Assistant Secretary of State for Inter-American Affairs (Cabot) **...**Freeport operated the plant under contract with the United States Government during World War II and until its closing in 1947 as an uneconomic enterprise. Freeport owns the nickel-ferrous ore deposits now used by the plant and receives a generous royalty from the present operator. Freeport itself did not compete in 1950 for the right to operate the rehabilitated plant, but American Smelting & Refining Company, an unsuccessful bidder, had made an arrangement with Freeport to give it a half non-controlling interest in the proposed operating company in lieu of royalties....The General Services Administration was given the responsibility in 1950 to rehabilitate and bring back into operation the Nicaro nickel plant in order to meet defense needs for this critical metal. In early 1951 it awarded the rehabilitation contract to the Frederick Snare Corporation and the operating contract to the Dutch Billiton company, which had in General Services' opinion submitted a better bid than the only other bidder, the American Smelting & Refining Company.....Freeport has indicated it now is itself interested in operating Nicaro, and would like to bid for the privilege on an equal basis with other interested parties. It is undoubtedly influenced by the increase in the market price of nickel, the continuing demand for defense requirements, including stockpiling, and the development by the United States Government of additional ore reserves in connection with a projected expansion of Nicaro with consequent reduced dependence upon Freeport ore.....Nicaro reached full production in July 1952 and is producing nickel oxide at the rate of 27.5 million pounds per annum. The operating company is committed to research in the further development of nickel production and the reclamation of cobalt. The United States Government invested 32 million dollars in the original plant and 12 million dollars in the rehabilitation, and for your confidential information, has in prospect an expansion program which would cost about 43 million dollars and would increase plant capacity by about 75 percent.....

The Batista Government like the Prio Government wants Nicaro to continue as a permanent Cuban industry. It is willing to grant tax exemptions and other privileges because Nicaro is a non-profit United States Government-financed industry, contributing to hemisphere and free world defense and to the Cuban economy. The Cuban group which purchased participation in the operating company was sponsored by the Prio Government, and its initial spokesman, Inocente Alvarez, was close to Prio and does not have the confidence of the Batista Government. The Batista Government informed us in July 1952 that it viewed the Prio letter as irregular and as having no validity, and that the United States Government need not feel obligated by it....The Freeport representatives may attack the General Services Administration for decisions disliked by Freeport. In commenting upon their statement, it is recommended you emphasize General Services' statutory authority and responsibility for Nicaro and stress the Department's limited interest and contribution. It may be advisable to affirm that the Department recommended that General Services consider the desirability of Cuban participation, because the Cuban Government strongly urged it and because the Department approved participation by Cuban nationals in principle. In such case, you should emphasize that the Department recommended no particular Cuban group.

Time Magazine Article 5/5/1958 "Plugged Nickel" Like a hot-blooded Don Juan, the Government makes some extravagant promises when it sorely wants something from industry. But once it gets what it wants, the Government often cools rapidly. To build up its nickel supply during World War II, the U.S. signed at least 28 long-term purchase contracts for nickel, now is trying to wiggle out of every one of them, because there is a nickel glut. The U.S. estimates that it has lost $31 million by paying premium prices for nickel, stands to lose $124 million if it honors all its contracts. Last week a House Government Operations subcommittee, investigating some of these nickel deals, wanted to know particularly why the U.S. cannot cut its nickel purchases and get out of the nickel business by selling its $87 million Nicaro nickel plant in eastern Cuba (current annual production: 52 million lbs., about 11% of the free world's supply). The big obstacle is that the U.S. has contracted to pay steep royalties to Freeport Sulphur Co. for the ore that the plant uses, is even now battling to renegotiate the contract and slash the royalties.

Few companies are willing to bid on the plant until peace is declared and a steady stream of ore is guaranteed at a good price. Price Fight. When the Government built the Nicaro plant in 1942, it badly needed ore to feed it. Freeport Sulphur Co. owned a rich ore body just four to eight miles away, and the Government lent $1,100,000 to Freeport to develop the ore. The Government promised to buy at least one-third of Nicaro's ore needs from Freeport through 1968, now gets all of Nicaro's ore from Freeport, pays a royalty of $1.73 per ton, and also pays the cost of extracting the ore. The Bureau of Mines contends that the Government, which operates the mine, should pay only 60¢ to 90¢. Last year Freeport offered to cut the price to $1.24 if the Government would sign an irrevocable contract to buy at least two-thirds of its Nicaro ore needs from Freeport through 1978. General Services Administrator Franklin Floete turned down the offer, called on Lawyer Ira D. Beynon, 62, to clean up the Nicaro dispute. Beynon attacked the chore with vigor. Testified Freeport Sulphur's President Langbourne Williams: "Mr. Beynon began to call us names, to threaten us with congressional investigations. He said, 'You reduce [the ore price] or I'll shut this plant down. We don't need your ore.

We've got all the ore we need.' " Then Freeport's Williams did something that widely irritated official Washington and raised many an eyebrow in business circles. He hired an ex-FBI investigator to question Beynon's old friends and associates about his private life as far back as 1926. Beynon testified that the inquisitor asked his friends such questions as "I'd like to know how Mr. Beynon made his money." Williams also checked police records on Beynon, but all he could dig up was a traffic violation. Explained Williams: "It's normal business practice for me to find out all I can about the man I'm dealing with." Yet he admitted that Freeport had never before hired a private eye to track a man. Tears & Profit. Last week Beynon wept openly as he told Congressmen how Freeport had pried into his personal life. Said he: "The contract under which we are buying ore from Freeport is unconscionable, and I am going to do everything I can do to remedy this situation.

These kinds of deals destroy confidence." In rebuttal, Freeport argued that it had opened up the ore supply, run the Nicaro plant for the U.S. in World War II, and developed many nickel-production techniques that the Government now uses. But it also profited. Freeport has collected $13.7 million in Nicaro royalties from the Government since 1952, now gets about $3,500,000 per year. More than that, the Government last year made it possible for Freeport to get financing for a huge $119 million nickel-and-cobalt operation, abuilding at Moa Bay, Cuba, near Nicaro. The U.S. did so by signing a contract, which the committee is also investigating, to buy up to 271 million lbs. of Freeport's Moa Bay nickel at 74¢ per lb. and 23,835,000 lbs. of cobalt at $2 per lb. Since then, the nickel market has suddenly softened. As for the Nicaro deal with Freeport, the Government next month will complete a 15-mile railroad from the Nicaro plant to a Government-owned mine that holds 43 million tons of nickel ore, enough to supply the nickel plant for 17 years.

Time Magazine Less Than Total War Apr. 14, 1958 n the week that was supposed to open Fidel Castro's battle for Cuba, his ragged rebel army showed clearly enough what it could and could not do against the well-armed troops of Dictator Fulgencio Batista....For most of the week, the army holed up in its fortified bases—Manzanillo, Bayamo and Santiago—and the rebels took over the countryside, cutting off Oriente from the rest of Cuba. Fidel's brother, Raul, led his 150 men out of the Sierra del Cristal, 100 miles northeast of the main rebel strongholds. One night at Moa Bay they held the Freeport Sulphur Co.'s $75 million nickel mining project for twelve hours before pulling out. With no traffic moving in or out of Santiago, residents began dipping into hoarded food supplies.

The rebels admitted that they were not yet ready to take Santiago by armed assault, and the army seemed in no mood to leave the cities and go hunting in rebel country. Death to Strikers. Castro hopes to turn this stalemate into victory by a general strike. Last week Batista served notice of just how bloody a strike would be. Using his emergency powers to govern by decree, he ruled that strikers would be fired, that employers who close shop would be jailed, and that loyal workers could carry arms. There would be no punishment, he decreed, for wounding or killing strikers. To make certain he has enough arms to pass around, Batista flew in 3,500 rifles from fellow Dictator Rafael Trujillo's Dominican Republic. The "Cristobal" rifles, manufactured in Trujilloland by refugee Hungarian gunsmiths, more than made up for a shipment of 1,950 Garands, bound from the U.S. last month under a mutual defense pact but embargoed at the last minute by the U.S. for the duration of hostilities.

Speech by Fidel Castro to United Nations 9/26/1960 "But in our country the land was not the only thing in the hands of the U.S. monopolies. The principal mines were also in the hands of the monopolies. For example, Cuba produces large amounts of nickel, and all the nickel was controlled by U.S. interests. Under the Batista dictatorship, a U.S. company called Moa Bay had obtained such a juicy concession that in a mere five years - mark my words, in a mere five years - it sought to amortize an investment of $120 million. A $120 million investment amortized in five years!. So the revolutionary government passed a mining law that obliged these monopolies to pay a 25 percent tax on the export of minerals."

Castro on Meet the Press - Havana, CMP Television Network, Sept. 30, 1960 - (Castro refers to UPI item saying that the U.S. Government will close the Nicaro Nickel Plant in Cuba because of the confiscatory taxes imposed on it.) The U.S. Government sent a note to our Labor Ministry informing him that it was thinking of closing down the nickel plant within 30 days of the communications. They have been exporting nickel without paying any taxes on it. In order not to paralyze the plant, we told them that we were disposed either to discuss the purchase of the plant, or to find some formula to solve the problem. We were discussing the matter with them. If the material is so strategic and if they need it so badly, let them pay the tax, which is a matter of 25 percent of the value of the export. They spend more than a million dollars in espionage; they spend more than 40 billion dollars in arms. Yet here they are exploiting our nickel mine and they will not pay anything for it. They say that a 25-percent tax is confiscatory. If they do not want to discuss the matter, if they do not want to pay the tax; if they wish to shut down the plant, well, let them do so. We wish to say to the Nicaro workers not to worry.

We also wish to tell them to careful. We want no sabotage; we want no damage to the machinery; we want no stealing of equipment. the workers must be careful that nothing happens to the plant. At any rate, today's note (from the U.S. Government?) said they were disposed to continue the discussions. Well, if they are, we are, too. Nickel is very important to the world. The Canadians also have nickel mines and now the Canadians are going to control the nickel market. We have good relations with the Canadians. We are ready to discuss the Nicaro matter with the United States--we are also a nickel power (words indistinct). *(estainlesssteel note - in a letter from Marvin Nichols to Secretary of Interior Douglas McKay, the Nicaro plant was "capable of producing 10% of the free world's nickel")*

Luxner News Cubaniquel seeks financing to expand nickel production CubaNews / February 2003 - "That's the word from Angel Roberto Hernández, director of state nickel monopoly Cubaniquel, in a Jan. 27 interview with the official business weekly Opciones. "We are not only going to modernize the industry to significantly reduce costs, but also expand production," said Hernández, whose entity operates two of three processing plants in Holguín province, 800 kms east of Havana. The two, both in Moa, are Pedro Soto Alba (formerly Moa

Nickel Co.), which began production in 1960, and Che Guevara, finished in 1986 with Soviet technology. Cubaniquel also owns 50%, along with Toronto-based Sherritt International Corp., of the René Ramos Latour plant, which began production in 1943 and was formerly known as Nicaro Nickel Co."

Cuba's potential eclipsed by U.S.-Castro feud - Nickel American Metal Market, August 6, 1996 by Martin Chase "For nearly 40 years, nickel mining activity in Cuba has taken a back seat to international intrigue, Cold War politics and the state monopoly and control of big business by Communist dictator Fidel Castro. Today the climate is beginning to warm in these post-Cold War days. Castro has opened the door to meaningful foreign investment in mining for the first time and a number of major Canadian, Australian, European and South African companies are poking around the hills of eastern Cuba looking for potential nickel and gold deposits. But Cuba remains off limits to U.S. investors, and the prospects for an end to the 36-year deep freeze in U.S.-Cuba relations appear dimmer than ever. Thanks to passage of the Helms-Burton amendment... "The U.S. really is becoming something of a laughing stock with this policy," said one Toronto-based mining executive. "Here are the world's largest nickel deposits sitting right on your doorstep and you're not allowed to have it. It's all kind of sad ... and strange."...Cuba's nickel resources are among the world's largest, representing roughly 37 percent of the world's proven reserves....Mining analysts in the United States and Canada estimate that production at Moa Bay rose by more than 50 percent last year to about 20,000 tons, representing nearly half of Cuba's total nickel output....."

David Atlee Phillips, Clay Shaw and Freeport Sulphur by Lisa Pease (This article first appeared in Probe magazine (Vol. 3, No. 3, March-April, 1996) and can now be found in The Assassination) "Nickel Mining in Cuba, Processing in New Orleans According to Cuban lawyer Mario Lazo, whose firm represented Freeport Sulphur in Cuba, the Nicaro project was conceived just two months after Pearl Harbor. The strange Cuban nickel-cobalt ore required a special extraction process. Freeport had developed a new chemical process-and Washington approved the financing-to aid the development of nickel (used in the manufacturing of steel) for the war effort. The Nicaro nickel plant cost American taxpayers $100,000,000. At one point, the plant produced nearly 10% of all the nickel in the free world. New Orleans became home to a special plant Freeport set up just outside the city to process the nickel-cobalt ore. When the Moa Bay Mining project was conceived, Freeport Nickel, a wholly owned Freeport Sulphur subsidiary, put up $19,000,000 of $119,000,000 to develop the Cuban nickel ore. The rest of the money came from a group of American steel companies and major automobile makers. (Freeport's pattern of putting in a small portion of total cost is a recurrent one.) $44,000,000 of the original funds went into Louisiana for the development of the New Orleans nickel processing facility at Port Nickel. Batista, Castro and the Moa Bay Mining Company In 1957, two things happened that allowed Freeport to develop nickel not just through the government-owned Nicaro nickel plant, but for itself. The first was a break on taxes, won through negotiations with Batista, for the proposed Moa Bay Mining Company. The second was a government contract in 1957 in which the U.S. Government committed itself to buying up to $248,000,000 worth of nickel.

Both of these would lead to public criticism of Freeport in the years to come. The tax break led to charges that the U.S. Ambassador to Cuba and Langbourne Williams of Freeport Sulphur made a special deal with Batista. The contract would eventually lead Freeport into a Senate investigation and a confrontation with President Kennedy over the issue of stockpiling...... *(Whitney, the Ambassador, and Batista's Tax Break for Freeport Sulphur In the September 12, 1960 issue of The New Republic, Professor Samuel Shapiro wrote an article about Cuba, Castro, and American business involvement. Shapiro wrote that the former U.S. Ambassador to Cuba, Earl E. T. Smith, owing his apppointment largely to the support of John Hay Whitney (by that time former Chairman of Freeport but still a large stockholder), negotiated a substantial tax reduction for the Moa Bay Mining Company with Cuban President Fulgencio Batista. Smith wrote a belligerent letter back, published in the October 3, 1960 issue, stating: This is a clear and grave charge that I employed my official position and influence as US Ambassador to Cuba for the private profit of the Moa Bay Mining Company. This is utterly untrue. Smith then went on to cite a State Department release from 1959 that had stated that: neither the State Department nor the American Embassy ever intervened during the negotiations of the new industry concessions granted by the Cuban Government to Moa Bay Mining Company in August 1957.*

Negotiations were completed in July 1957, before Ambassador Smith's arrival in Cuba, and the subsequent decree granting the concessions was published in August, 1957. One of Freeport's vice presidents, John C. Carrington, added: This tax treatment . . . came under a principle of law predating Batista and honored by Castro. . . . Ambassador Smith had nothing whatever to do with the matter and in fact did not even come to Cuba until July 1957. In his rebuttal also published in the October 3, 1960 issue, Shapiro responded: Sirs: Neither the Batista Government nor Moa Bay officials ever made public the details of the special tax treatment granted the company. In view of the extremely cordial relations that existed between Ambassadors Gardner and Smith and the dictatorship, documented at great length in such books as Jules Dubois' Fidel Castro, it is most difficult to believe that the subject was never brought up. As Mr. Carrington himself indicates, the tax reduction was held up for over a year, and though approved "in substance" in July, 1957, the month of Ambassador Smith's arrival in Havana, did not actually go into effect until some time later; furthermore, the tax cut could have been withdrawn at any time. The specific charge that Ambassador Smith used his influence on behalf of Moa Bay was made in a special number of Bohemia, something of a Cuban equivalent of Life, in January, 1959. Ambassador Smith resigned on January 10 after seeing an advance copy but before the issue went on sale. The statement Ambassador Smith and Mr. Carrington quote was thus made after Ambassador Smith's departure from Cuba. In my article I did not intend to single out the Freeport Sulphur Company as particularly reprehensible in its dealings with the dictatorship.

Every businessman in Cuba had to get along by the use of influence and bribes. If Moa Bay really got its tax reduction without political or diplomatic pressure, and without the distribution of money in the right places (and Carrington does not say that it did), this was an example of generosity almost without parallel in the history of Cuba. In his response to Shapiro's parenthetical comment, published a month later, Carrington wrote: I now state, for Mr. Shapiro's future reference, that Moa Bay obtained its new industry tax exemption without the distribution of money, and I repeat that it did so without political or diplomatic pressure. . . In sum, there is no ground for Mr. Shapiro's accusation-by-innuendo against our company. . . and I request that a proper retraction be made. Shapiro had the last word in his final response to Carrinton: I am happy to accept Mr. Carrington's assurance, but as both he and Ambassador Smith have denied that the Ambassador used political or diplomatic pressure to secure the grant of new-industry tax status to the Moa Bay operation, it may be pertinent to quote the notice that appeared in The New York Times on August 17, 1957: "Work on a project for mining and refining nickel and cobalt at Moa Bay in Oriente Province will start immediately, the Presidential Palace said today.

The announcement was made following talks by Earl E. T. Smith, United States Ambassador, L.M. Williams, President of Freeport Sulphur Company and other officials of the enterprise with President Fulgencio Batista. "About $75,000,000 will be invested in the Moa Bay project, officials said. The way was cleared for the start of construction when President Batista granted the project a classification as a new industry with tax exemption. Production is scheduled to begin within two years." [. . .] I believe it should be said that Mr. Smith showed poor judgement in interceding with the dictator on behalf of an American company seeking a tax concession. But then, Mr. Smith was a political appointee with no previous diplomatic experience. He had contributed $3,800 to the Republican campaign chest in 1956. . . . In 1956, John Hay Whitney, Freeport's then Chairman and significant investor as well as Ambassador Smith's promoter, was Chairman of the United Republican Finance Committee.) .....

The Seizing of the Moa Bay Mining Company by Castro Unfortunately for Freeport's board, the Moa Bay Mining company was short-lived in Cuba. With $75,000,000 invested in that operation, one can see how vital the special tax exemption leftover from Batista's reign was to Freeport's Moa Bay operation. And since the deal was negotiated under Batista's regime, one can also see how this must have stuck like a craw in the throat of Castro's revolutionaries as they took control of Cuba in 1959. The Castro government wanted to end the special tax exemption. Freeport wanted to keep it. By March of 1960, Freeport Nickel (parent of Moa Bay Mining, subsidiary of Freeport Sulphur) threatened the Cuban government with an ultimatum:

If their special tax status was revoked, the Moa Bay and Nicaro nickel facilities would be shut down. Freeport knew that Cuba needed the jobs and even partial income that Freeport's nickel operations provided. Freeport must have thought it could bluff this one through, largely due to the particular quality of the Moa Bay ore. The ore was an unusual combination of cobalt and nickel, elements which needed to be separated through a highly complex chemical process, handled at that time by Freeport's New Orleans processing plant. Industry observers were quoted as saying the best thing Cuba could do was to negotiate a compromise, because Cuba could not afford to build the kind of plant Freeport owned. Even the instructions for the process were not kept in Cuba. Deliberations with the new Cuban government fell apart in August of 1960. According to an "unimpeachable source" in the New York Times, the Cuban government felt negotiations should be suspended because of the tense situation between Cuba and the United States. Cuba performed what they characterized as an "intervention," a temporary measure of stepping in and taking control of the mining facility, rather than outright nationalization.

This was reported as Cuba trying to leave the door slightly open for some sort of negotiated settlement. But Freeport considered the takeover a battle cry and wanted to invoke international law to protect its rights to the plant. Cuba ended up retaining the plant, and the United States ending up attempting to invade Cuba under the ill-fated Bay of Pigs operation. One of the planners of the Bay of Pigs, as well as an advocate for assassinating Castro, was Admiral Arleigh Burke. Burke later become a director of Freeport Sulphur. Freeport versus Kennedy: The Stockpiling Investigation Already reeling from its losses over Castro's appropriation of the Moa Bay plant, Freeport found itself under attack from a new quarter: a Senate investigation into stockpiling surpluses, requested by President Kennedy himself. In 1962, President Kennedy asked Congress to look into the war-emergency stockpiling program, stating it was "a potential source of excessive and unconscionable profits." He said he was "astonished" to discover that the program had accumulated $7.7 billion worth of stockpiled material, exceeding projected needs by $3.4 billion. Kennedy also pledged full executive cooperation with the investigation, mentioning specifically $103 million in surplus nickel.

The Senate pursued an investigation into stockpiling surpluses. Special attention was paid to three companies in which the Rockefeller brothers had substantial holdings: Hannah Mining, International Nickel, and Freeport Sulphur. A December 18, 1962 headline in the New York Times read "U.S. Was Pushed into Buying Nickel, Senators Are Told." The article opened with this: A federal official told Senate stockpile investigators today that the U.S. Government got a bad deal in a 1957 nickel purchase contract with a potential $248,000,000 obligation. John Croston, a division director in the General Services Administration, testified that he had strongly opposed the contract with the Freeport Sulphur Company. But, he said, officials in the agency "knew that the contract was in the bag from the beginning." Pressure for it, he said, came from the Office of Defense Mobilization, then headed by Arthur S. Flemming. Dr. Arthur S. Flemming was regularly a part of the National Security Council under Eisenhower. Right after Ike's election, in November of 1952, Dr. Flemming served with Ike's brother Milton on the three-member President's Advisory Committee on Government Organization, headed by Nelson Rockefeller. Perhaps it was his friendship with Nelson that caused some to accuse Dr. Flemming of some arm-twisting on Freeport's behalf. The New York Times (12/19/62), reported: The subcommittee was told yesterday by officials of several Government agencies that they opposed the contract because they felt the need for nickel was exaggerated. These officials said, however, that Dr. Arthur S. Flemming, then head of the Office of Defense Mobilization, was determined that the contract be signed. One witness said Mr. Flemming had indicated that competition aginst the International Nickel Company, the giant in the field, should be encouraged.

But what Flemming apparently didn't know, or hadn't shared if he did, was that both Freeport and International Nickel Company (INCO) shared some of the very same investors: the Rockefellers. Croston said he had opposed the contract with Freeport from the beginning, stating "there was no real shortage of nickel at any time" and that cobalt "was running out of our ears." Freeport's earlier 1954 contract with the government caused the U.S. to spend $6,250,000 to help build that special Louisiana nickel-cobalt ore processing plant so necessary to the Cuban mining operations. Another contract obligated the government to buy up to 15,000,000 pounds of nickel at a premium price, as well as 15,000,000 pounds of cobalt. The committee's head, Senator Stuart Symington, reported that it was John Whitney who exerted his influence from Freeport's end to get the government contract for the nickel. Freeport's Chairman, Langbourne Williams, defended the contract, claiming the contract had saved the Treasury money, and had not been entered into for the purposes of stockpiling, but rather to increase nickel production capacity. He contended that the government ended up not having to purchase any nickel under the contract because Freeport had been able to sell to other buyers the nickel and cobalt produced at Moa Bay before Castro took it over. But the controversy flowed over into 1963, and Press Secretary Pierre Salinger stated that the Kennedy administration planned to make stockpiling an issue in the 1964 campaign. As we know, JFK didn't live long enough to fulfill that promise.......In August, 1959, Freeport Director and top engineer Forbes Wilson met with Jan van Gruisen, managing director of the East Borneo Company, a mining concern. Gruisen had just stumbled upon a dusty report first made in 1936 regarding a mountain called the "Ertsberg" ("Copper Mountain") in Dutch New Guinea, by Jean Jacques Dozy. Hidden away for years in a Netherlands library during Nazi attacks, the report had only recently resurfaced. Dozy reported a mountain heavy with copper ore. If true, this could justify a new Freeport diversification effort into copper. more
Canada Protests Controversial Bill Maclean's March 18, 1996 - "....

The once-stalled bill that Helms authored with Indiana Representative Dan Burton passed easily in the Senate by 74 to 22 votes, and by an even more lopsided 336 to 86 in the House the next day. The Feb. 24 downing of two civilian American airplanes by Cuban jet fighters has sparked outrage in the United States, and politicians are wary of appearing soft on Castro in an election year. President Bill Clinton, who had earlier threatened to veto the bill, was to sign it into law this week.....The provision that rankles is aimed at halting foreign joint ventures in Cuba. It allows Cuban-Americans to use U.S. courts to pursue international firms investing in property expropriated by the Castro regime following the 1959 revolution. Another clause bars executives of firms that have benefited from expropriated assets - and their families - from entering the United States. Toronto-based Sherritt International Corp., led by outspoken CEO Ian Delaney, is the largest Canadian target. Sherritt's nickel mine at Moa Bay was originally built by Freeport Sulphur Co. of New Orleans in 1959. It had only just started shipping nickel concentrate to Freeport's refinery in Louisiana when it was seized by Castro in the summer of 1960. Freeport, now called Freeport-McMoran, will not discuss the specifics of its claims against the property, but U.S. reports put the Moa Bay claim at $115 million. According to Sherritt, its deal with the Cubans indemnifies it for any damages. Still, the mere threat of litigation could not only discourage Sherritt's lenders and suppliers, but investors as well.....

Mother lode awaits change in political wind American Metal Market, Sept 1, 1998 by Martyn Chase "One-quarter of the world's nickel supplies lie in a stretch of land along the northeastern coast of Cuba, in a strip running 50 air miles or so along the coast from Mayan to Baracoa and extending about 15 miles inland....Oro cited five major deposits that are world class, by any measure: Mayan, Moa, Pinta Gorda, San Felipe and Cajalbana. "San Felipe has reserves to sustain 50,000 tons (of production) for 200 years," he said. "It's a monster deposit."....Moa Bay was owned and operated by two U.S. companies--Freeport-McMoRan and NL Industries--until Castro took over and nationalized the industry in 1960."

TAXATION OF CUBAN CONFISCATED ASSETS AFTER PROPERTY CLAIMS SETTLEMENTS: ISSUES FOR TAXPAYERS AND THE U.S. GOVERNMENT by Timothy Ashby and Tania Mastrapa Cuba in Transition ASCE 2005 "....The confiscated U.S. assets included 90 percent of all electricity generated on the island (Cuban Electric Company), the entire telephone system (ITT), most of the mining industry (Moa Bay Mining Company and Nicaro Nickel Company), and large tracts of high quality land (between 1.5 and 2 million acres)....A further example of the accounting and legal complexities that will be involved in Cuban settlements is the case of Moa Bay Mining Company, which claimed $88.3 million in confiscation losses. The company was wholly owned by Freeport Nickel Company, a subsidiary of Freeport Sulphur Corporation. Freeport Sulphur merged with McMoRan Oil & Gas, LLC in 1998 but remained a wholly owned subsidiary of the successor company McMoRan Exploration Co. ("McMoRan"). In 2002, McMoRan sold Freeport to a 50–50 joint venture between IMC Global Inc.—the world's largest purchaser and user of sulphur—and Savage Industries Inc., a major materials management and transportation systems company. The possible compensation for Moa Bay's Cuban assets should be of interest to IMC and Savage, as the current value of the confiscated nickel and cobalt mines is estimated at $5–7 billion. Since 1990, Canada's Sherritt International has invested over half a billion dollars in Freeport's former mines under a joint venture with the Cuban government, and China is negotiating a similar joint venture. Cuban nickel is considered to be Class II with an average 90 percent nickel plus content. Holguín Province, where the Moa Bay mines are located, is estimated to contain 34 percent of the world's known reserves of nickel, or some 800 million tons of proven nickel plus cobalt reserves, and another 2.2 billion tons of probable reserves."

(estainlesssteel note - These provisions are now in effect and, unlike the provisions of Title III, cannot be suspended by the U.S. President. One of the first companies notified under Title IV of the Helms-Burton Act was Toronto-based Sherritt International Corp. On July 10, 1996, Sherritt s officers were informed that company principals would be banned from the U.S. unless Sherritt pulled out of its Cuban nickel-cobalt operations within 45 days. They refused and they, their wives, and dependant children age 18 and younger, have been banned from entry to the US ever since)

On Feb 3, 1971, the US Foreign Claims Settlement Commission certified the Moa Bay Mining Company a $88,349,000 claim against the government of Cuba under Title V of the International Claims Settlement Act plus 6% interest per annum from August 19, 1960. Also, related to nickel assets on Cuba, the Commission awarded the Nicaro Nickel Company a claim of $22,494,708.62 on June 30, 1971 with 6% interest beginning from October 24, 1960. It denied a $68,071,000 claim by Cuban American Nickel Company, and likewise denied property claims by Freeport Sulphur Company stating finding the "claimant has failed to prove that its mining concessions had any value on the date of loss". (pdf of rulings) *(estainlesssteel note - Moa Bay Mining Company, who in 1960, was a subsidiary of the Cuban American Nickel Company, which in turn was a subsidiary of the Freeport Sulphur Company of New Orleans, Louisiana.)*

01-APR-02 IMC Global Inc. announced today that it has entered into a definitive agreement to acquire the sulphur transportation, marketing and terminaling assets of Freeport-McMoRan Sulphur LLC, a subsidiary of McMoRan Exploration Co. , through a 50-50 joint venture with Savage Industries Inc.

STRATEGIC AND ANALYTICAL MATERIALS

NICKEL METAL MINING INDUSTRY IN CUBA[1]

Nickel retained its first place among Cuban exports in 2006, its earnings boosted by unprecedented high prices on the international market, although output was lower than the government had hoped.

Over the past year, the price of nickel ore rose by 157 percent to today's market value of more than 30,000 dollars a ton. On Dec. 15, it was quoted at 34,800 dollars a ton on the London market.

However, experts are now warning that the predicted slow-down in the U.S. economy in 2007, and a temporary oversupply of nickel on the global market, may bring nickel prices down in the near future.

Nickel has been Cuba's top traditional export product since 2000, and in 2005 it was once again the country's top source of foreign exchange, along with services and the biotechnology sector.

However, Canadian firm Sherritt International announced an estimated shortfall of 3,000 tons at an ore-processing plant it operates in partnership with Cuba. This means that the national production target of 76,700 tons for this year, a modest increase over production in 2005, is unlikely to be met.

The Cuban-Canadian joint venture Moa-N□quel (formerly Pedro Soto Alba) S.A. said in its report for the first quarter of 2006 that it would have to readjust its planned output target of 33,000 tons for 2006 downwards to 30,000 tons, because of bottlenecks in the production process, apparently in the first quarter.

"So far, strong prices have compensated for the decline in production," a Cuban researcher who wished to remain anonymous told IPS. Total Cuban nickel production in 2005 amounted to 75,900 tons, similar to output for 2004, and a very modest increment of 1..1 percent was planned for 2006. Given the upward trend in international prices, which crossed the 20,000 dollar a ton mark in 2000, the Cuban government designed an ambitious plan for a gradual increase in production.

Last year, Cuba reached an agreement with Sherritt International for expanding production at the Moa-N□quel plant, and incorporating the latest technology at a Canadian cobalt-nickel refinery, financed with more than 500 million dollars contributed equally by both partners.

The expansion of the Moa-N□quel plant was intended to increase output by 16,000 tons year, or about 50 percent, by the end of 2008.

But Sherritt itself has now announced that the plans to increase Moa-N□quel's capacity will have to be reviewed, and are now forecasting staged production increases of 4,000 tons for 2008, 9,000 tons in 2009, and a further 3,000 tons by 2011.

---

[1] Patricia Grogg IPS

The Cuban-Canadian joint venture owns the processing plant at Moa, in the eastern Cuban province of Holgu□n, a refining facility at Fort Saskatchewan, in the western Canadian province of Alberta, and a trading corporation in the Bahamas.

Two other nickel processing plants, the Ren□ Ramos Latour and the Ernesto Che Guevara facilities, operated at full capacity in 2005, according to informed sources consulted by IPS. They are both owned and operated by the Cuban state Uni□n del N□quel company.

Cuba has substantial nickel and cobalt reserves located in Moa and Nicaro, in the province of Holgu□n.

Proven nickel reserves are estimated at 800 million metric tons, and probable reserves at two billion tons. Cuba's cobalt reserves, meanwhile, account for approximately 26 percent of the world's total reserves.

Official statistics indicate that the island's processing capacity is about 70,000 tons a year, including all three processing plants.

Expansion plans for the industry include building a ferronickel plant, a compound of iron and nickel used almost entirely in the manufacture of stainless steel. The plant will be built jointly with China, according to an agreement signed in 2005 during Chinese President Hu Jintao's state visit to Havana.

The ferronickel factory, also to be located in Moa, is expected to produce 68,000 tons a year of iron-nickel alloy. Conceived as a joint venture, Cuba will own 51 percent of the shares and the Chinese Minmetals group the remaining 49 percent.

There are plans for China to invest in a fifth processing plant, to be built close to the ore reserves at San Felipe in the eastern province of Camaguay, which would increase Cuban nickel production to 120,000 tons a year (up from its current 76,000 tons) in the future.

China is to invest over one billion dollars in the Cuban-Chinese San Felipe project, according to the agreements signed by Cuban President Fidel Castro and President Hu in Havana.

Without going into details, Venezuelan President Hugo Ch□vez said in Caracas on Dec. 14 that Venezuela and Cuba are planning to manufacture stainless steel with Cuban nickel and Venezuelan iron.

At present, it is estimated that China absorbs half of Cuba's total nickel output, and would be capable of buying up the other 50 percent, according to experts, because China is the world's top producer of steel, and its industry is still expanding.

Experts concur that until the day when oil starts gushing from the underwater reserves in the Cuban zone of the Gulf of Mexico—China is also involved in oil exploration there—nickel is important as collateral for the loans Beijing has given Havana in recent years.

China is now Cuba's second largest trading partner, after Venezuela. Trade between Cuba and China was worth more than one billion dollars in 2006, and the Asian giant is providing the Caribbean country with large amounts of soft credit. According to the U.S. Geological Survey, world nickel production stood at 1.5 million tons in 2005. Russia, the United States, Canada, Australia, Norway and Cuba are the world's foremost producers of nickel, a non-ferrous metal used in a large number of industrial processes. Stainless steel manufacturing uses about 60 percent of the total production of nickel, which is also employed in the chemical, petrochemical, electronic, aerospace and automobile industries.

CUBA MINING LAW

LEY DE MINAS

CHAPTER 1

OBJETIVOS Y ALCANCE DE LA LEY

ARTICULO 1.- La presente ley se denomina Ley de Minas y tiene como objetivos establecer la política minera y las regulaciones jurídicas de dicha actividad de manera tal que garanticen la protección, el desarrollo y el aprovechamiento racional de los recursos minerales en función de los intereses de la Nación, trazando directivas obligatorias controladas por los funcionarios del Gobierno vinculados con la actividad.

ARTICULO 2.- A los efectos de la presente Ley se entiende por recursos minerales todas las concentraciones de minerales sólidos y líquidos que existan en el suelo y en el subsuelo del territorio nacional, así como en el fondo marino y subsuelo de la zona económica de la República, en la extensión que fija la ley.

Los minerales radioactivos y los hidrocarburos líquidos y gaseosos se rigen por su legislación específica. Los minerales radioactivos que constituyan mena acompañante o de baja ley, se rigen además por la presente Ley.

ARTICULO 3.- A los efectos de la interpretación, cumplimiento y aplicación de los preceptos de esta Ley, se establecen las definiciones siguientes:

Acumulaciones Residuales: Acumulación de material sólido, o líquido no aprovechable en un proceso tecnológico determinado.

Canon: Cantidad que se paga por el disfrute de alguna propiedad del Estado.

Colas: Residuos no aprovechables de un determinado procesamiento, que aún contienen minerales.

Concentraciones de mineral: Acumulación natural de minerales.

Escombreras: Conjunto de sobrantes originados como consecuencia del laboreo minero que será aprovechable con el desarrollo de una tecnología consecuente.

Escoriales: Lugares de acumulación de los residuos desechables de un determinado proceso industrial metalúrgico; estos residuos pueden ser reutilizados mediante la aplicación de otros procesos industriales para extraer sus componentes.

Exploración: Conjunto de operaciones, trabajos y labores mineras que tienen como objetivo la determinación de la estructura del yacimiento, la morfología, dimensiones y condiciones de yacencia del cuerpo mineral, la tectónica de la zona que lo contiene, el contenido y calidad del o de los minerales existentes en el mismo, así como el cálculo de las reservas, incluyendo la evaluación económica del yacimiento y otros estudios que ayuden a su mejor explotación.

Explotación: Conjunto de operaciones, obras, trabajos y labores mineras destinado a la preparación y desarrollo del yacimiento y a la extracción y transportación de los minerales.

Fondo Marino: Lecho del mar.

Impacto Ambiente: Consecuencias degradantes para el medio ambiente que genera la acción del hombre u otro elemento ajeno a dicho medio.

Laboreos: Arte de explotar las minas, haciendo las labores o excavaciones necesarias, fortificándolas, disponiendo el tránsito por ellas y, extrayendo las menas aprovechables.

Ley del Mineral: Concentración de metal contenido en una mena.

Mena: Porción útil de un mineral metalífero.

Microlocalización: Selección en detalle del área del terreno objeto de la concesión.

Mina: Obra resultante del conjunto de excavaciones e instalaciones superficiales y subterráneas que se realizan para la investigación y la explotación de un yacimiento mineral.

Minería: Arte de laborar el conjunto de las minas y explotaciones mineras.

Mineral: Sustancia inorgánica que se halla en el suelo o en el subsuelo, y principalmente aquella cuya explotación ofrece interés económico.

Mineral Acompañante: Es aquel que no siendo el objeto principal de la acción minera se encuentra presente en un yacimiento, y puede tener o no determinado interés económico.

Mineral Principal: Es aquél que constituye el objeto básico de la actividad minera dentro de un yacimiento.

Mineral Radioactivo: Mineral que contiene, entre otros, elementos del las familias del uranio y del torio, que por su concentración generalmente puede ser aprovechado la industria.

Operaciones Mineras: Son las actividades que se realizan en la mina con la ayuda de instrumentos y equipos apropiados para la investigación y explotación del mineral.

Procesamiento: Tratamiento de los minerales explotados para elevar su calidad o contenido útil, separarlos, purificarlos, adecuarlos para el consumo o envasarlos, con vistas a su uso o comercialización.

Proceso Tecnológico del Recurso Mineral: Fases por las que atraviesan los minerales extraídos para su adecuado aprovechamiento.

Prospección: Conjunto de trabajos con empleo de técnicas y métodos que tienen como objetivo la búsqueda de indicios y concentraciones minerales que pudieran constituir yacimiento.

Reconocimiento: Realización de trabajos preliminares en determinadas áreas, definiendo zonas de interés para la prospección.

Registro Minero: Sistema de control en el que figuran, entre otros, los datos relativos a los derechos concedidos a personas naturales y jurídicas para realizar actividades mineras.

Reserva del Mineral: Cantidad de mineral con un determinado grado de evaluación geológica y pendiente de explotación mineral.

Roca de Caja o de Destape: Material rocoso y estéril que forma parte del yacimiento y que obstaculiza la extracción del mineral, por lo que en ocasiones tiene que ser removido.

Servidumbre: Es un gravamen impuesto sobre un inmueble en beneficio de otro, perteneciente a distinto dueño. El inmueble a cuyo favor esta constituida la servidumbre se llama predio dominante; el que la sufre, predio sirviente.

Subsuelo: Porción compuesta por rocas y minerales que se encuentra inmediatamente por debajo del suelo, sobre el cual las leyes establecen el dominio público, que puede ser otorgado mediante concesiones para la actividad minera.

Suelo: Capa superior de la superficie terrestre en las cuales están enraizadas las plantas, y que constituye un medio ecológico particular.

Terreno franco: Terreno libre y disponible para efectuar en éste cualquier actividad, incluyendo la minera.

Testigo Reducido de Perforación: Porción disminuida de una muestra de roca o mineral extraída por medio de la perforación y que se conserva con fines investigativos durante el tiempo que se determine.

Tratamiento de los Residuales: Proceso de descontaminación parcial o total de los remanentes o desperdicios del proceso tecnológico a que se somete el mineral.

Yacimiento: Cualquier acumulación natural de sustancias minerales en el suelo o en el subsuelo, que pueda ser utilizado y explotado como fuente de materia prima y como fuente de energía, y las concentraciones de piedras preciosas y semipreciosas y de cualquier otra sustancia mineral cuya explotación tenga importancia económica.

Zona de Interés: Lugar donde se han localizado anomalías, muestras o alteraciones geológicas que permiten presumir la existencia de minerales.

Zona Mineralizada: Es aquella extensión del suelo o subsuelo en la que se encuentran concentraciones de mineral de aprovechamiento económico.

CHAPTER II

DEL RÉGIMEN DE PROPIEDAD DE LOS RECURSOS MINERALES

ARTICULO 4.- Al Estado le corresponde el dominio inalienable e imprescriptible del subsuelo, las minas y todos los recursos minerales, donde quiera que éstos se encuentren, dentro de las regulaciones constitucionales.

CHAPTER III

DE LA EJECUCIÓN DE LA POLÍTICA MINERA

ARTICULO 5.- El Consejo de Ministros o su Comité Ejecutivo a través del Ministerio de la Industria Básica, controla el desarrollo, ejecución y aplicación de la política minera, sin perjuicio de lo establecido en el artículo 18 de la presente Ley.

ARTICULO 6.- Para el cumplimiento de lo que se dispone en el Artículo anterior, el Ministerio de la Industria Básica tiene las atribuciones siguientes:

a) asesorar a la Asamblea Nacional del Poder Popular y al Consejo de Estado en la elaboración de la Política minera;

b) proponer al Consejo de Ministros o su Comité Ejecutivo las declaratorias de áreas mineras reservadas;

e) controlar la política minera, mediante planes y programas de desarrollo y fomento minero a corto, mediano y largo plazo;

d) promover la investigación geológica en el país;

e) reglamentar y controlar la actividad minera, sin perjuicio de las competencias que la legislación les confiere a otros organismos de la Administración Central del Estado; y

f) las demás que se otorguen en la legislación vigente.

CHAPTER IV

DE LA ACTIVIDAD MINERA

SECCIÓN PRIMERA

Generalidades

ARTICULO 7.- Se entiende por actividad minera el conjunto de operaciones y acciones a que se refiere el artículo 12 de la presente Ley.

ARTICULO 8.- La actividad minera se compatibiliza con los intereses de la Defensa Nacional.

ARTICULO 9.- La ejecución de la actividad minera tiene en cuenta la competencia que la legislación le confiere al Ministerio de Ciencia, Tecnología y Medio Ambiente en asuntos ambientales.

ARTICULO 10.- Se declara de utilidad pública e interés social la actividad minera, la que goza de preferencia sobre cualquier otro uso o aprovechamiento del terreno, siempre que razones económicas o sociales lo hagan recomendable.

ARTICULO 11.- Para realizar la actividad minera los concesionarios pueden ser autorizados por el Consejo de Ministros o su Comité Ejecutivo a ocupar o utilizar bienes de propiedad estatal. En los casos de bienes de propiedad privada se aplica, cuando es posible, el régimen especial de las servidumbres mineras así como cualquiera otras alternativas de solución que no impliquen el desplazamiento o la afectación de posesión disfrutada por un tercero. Si dichas alternativas no tuvieran éxito debe aplicarse la expropiación forzosa la cual, en su caso, es promovida ante los tribunales por el Ministerio de la Industria Básica. Este procedimiento, que incluye la debida indemnización, es válido para el uso del suelo y de otros bienes indispensables a la ejecución de la actividad minera.

ARTICULO 12.- Para los efectos de aplicación de esta Ley, la actividad minera se divide en las siguientes fases:

a) Reconocimiento.

b) Investigación Geológica: que se divide en las subfases Prospección y Exploración.

c) Explotación.

d) Procesamiento.

e) Comercialización.

SECCIÓN SEGUNDA

De la Clasificación de los Minerales

ARTICULO 13.- Los recursos minerales se clasifican a los efectos de esta Ley en los grupos siguientes:

Grupo I. Minerales no metálicos, utilizados fundamentalmente como materiales de construcción o materia prima para la industria y otras ramas de la economía. En este grupo se incluyen las piedras preciosas y semipreciosas.

Grupo II. Minerales metálicos. Este grupo incluye los metales preciosos, los metales ferrosos y no ferrosos, así como los minerales acompañantes metálicos y no metálicos

Grupo III. Minerales portadores de energía.

Grupo IV. Aguas y fangos minero-medicinales. Comprende las aguas minero-industriales, minero-medicinales, minerales naturales, las termales y los fangos minero-medicinales.

Grupo V. Otras acumulaciones minerales. Este grupo incluye:

a) las acumulaciones constituidas por residuos de actividades mineras que resulten útiles para el aprovechamiento de algunos de sus componentes tales como colas, escombreras y escoriales; y:

b) todas las acumulaciones minerales y demás recursos geológicos que no están especificados en los anteriores grupos y puedan ser objeto de explotación.

CHAPTER V

DE LA AUTORIDAD MINERA

SECCIÓN PRIMERA

Funciones de la Autoridad Minera

ARTICULO 14.- Se crea la Oficina Nacional de Recursos Minerales, en lo adelante la Autoridad Minera, como institución con personalidad jurídica, adscrita al Ministerio de la Industria Básica, que es la entidad encargada de:

a) fiscalizar y controlar la actividad minera y uso racional de los recursos minerales según lo dispuesto en la presente Ley y demás disposiciones vigentes, asesorando al Ministerio de la Industria Básica en esta materia, y a los demás organismos de la Administración Central del Estado sin perjuicio de sus respectivas competencias.

b) aprobar, registrar y controlar las reservas minerales certificando el grado de preparación de los yacimientos para su asimilación industrial;

c) emitir los dictámenes técnicos sobre el otorgamiento, anulabilidad y extinción de concesiones mineras y

d) aprobar, de conformidad con esta Ley, los proyectos de explotación minera;

c) llevar el Registro Minero y mantener actualizadas las anotaciones sobre concesiones mineras, áreas mineras reservadas, yacimientos, manifestaciones minerales, áreas en investigación y minas en explotación o abandonadas;

f) constituirse en depositario de la información geológica y minera de la Nación;

g) ejercer la inspección estatal sobre las personas naturales y jurídicas que ejecuten la actividad minera, para comprobar el cumplimiento de los acuerdos y obligaciones a que se hayan comprometido dichas entidades, así como de las disposiciones legales vigentes que rijan la actividad que se inspecciona;

h) controlar la ejecución de los planes de preservación del medio ambiente y de las medidas para mitigar el impacto ambiental;

i) mantener actualizadas las estadísticas mineras del país; y

j) participar en el cierre de minas y controlar las medidas del programa de cierre que se ejecute.

SECCIÓN SEGUNDA

Del Registro Minero

ARTICULO 15.- Son inscribibles en el Registro Minero, además de las anotaciones previstas en el artículo 14, inciso e) de esta Ley, las siguientes:

a) título por el que se otorga la concesión;

b) modificaciones, prórrogas, nulidad, anulación y extinción de las concesiones;

c) transferencia de la concesión;

d) declaraciones judiciales que afecten el otorgamiento o disfrute de la concesión, y

e) servidumbres mineras.

ARTICULO 16.- El procedimiento para la inscripción en el Registro Minero es el establecido en el Reglamento de la presente Ley, previo el pago de los gravámenes que en el mismo y en la legislación tributaria general se establezcan.

CHAPTER VI

DE LAS CONCESIONES MINERAS

SECCIÓN PRIMERA

Generalidades

ARTICULO 17.- A los efectos de esta Ley se entiende por Concesión Minera, que en lo sucesivo se denomina genéricamente Concesión, la relación jurídica nacida de un acto gubernativo unilateral por el que se otorga temporalmente a una persona natural o jurídica el derecho de realizar actividades mineras, bajo las condiciones y con todos los derechos y obligaciones que esta Ley y su Reglamento determinan. Todos los recursos minerales que se relacionan en el artículo 13 de la presente Ley son concesibles, sin perjuicio de la declaración de reservas exclusivas de determinados minerales por parte del Estado.

ARTICULO 18.- El Consejo de Ministros o su Comité Ejecutivo otorga, o deniega las concesiones mineras y dispone también su anulación y extinción.

ARTICULO 19.- Las concesiones comprenden espacios en superficie y profundidad. Los límites en superficie se miden por hectáreas y están dados por el sistema de coordenadas nacionales de los vértices del polígono o de la figura geométrica que resulte y de la línea recta que una los vértices. Los límites en profundidad coinciden con los señalados en la superficie. No obstante la profundidad está dada por la localización de las reservas o el alcance de la técnica minera.

SECCIÓN SEGUNDA

De los Concesionarios

ARTICULO 20.- Son concesionarios, a los efectos de esta Ley, las personas naturales o jurídicas, debidamente autorizadas para el ejercicio de una o varias fases de la actividad minera por el correspondiente titulo.

ARTICULO 21.- Todos los concesionarios quedan sometidos a las leyes y demás disposiciones vigentes en la República de Cuba.

ARTICULO 22.- Las concesiones son de investigación geológica, de explotación o de procesamiento. Los trabajos de reconocimiento no requieren del otorgamiento de concesiones, siendo objeto de permisos por el Ministerio de la Industria Básica.

Los permisos de reconocimiento confieren a su titular la facultad de llevar a cabo trabajos preliminares para determinar zonas de interés para la prospección, en forma no exclusiva, durante el período de su vigencia, con relación a las clases de minerales especificados en el permiso y dentro de las áreas descritas en el mismo.

Las concesiones de investigación geológica dan derecho al concesionario para la ejecución de los trabajos relativos a las subfases de prospección y exploración, según se definen en el artículo 3 de este cuerpo legal.

Las concesiones de explotación dan derecho al concesionario para la ejecución de los trabajos definidos en el Artículo 3 de la presente Ley, a la apropiación de los minerales autorizadas y, en caso de incluirse expresamente en la concesión, a su procesamiento y comercialización.

Las concesiones de procesamiento dan derecho al concesionario para realizar los tratamientos definidos en el artículo 3 de esta Ley.

ARTICULO 23.- La duración de las concesiones de investigación geológica es de tres (3) años, prorrogables por dos (2) años más; contados a partir de la fecha del otorgamiento de la prórroga.

ARTICULO 24.- Las concesiones explotación y de procesamiento tienen un término máximo de veinticinco (25) años, contados a partir de la fecha de su otorgamiento. Dicho término puede ser prorrogado por períodos sucesivos, hasta otros veinticinco (25) años cuando el concesionario demuestre la posibilidad de continuar explotando los recursos minerales previstos en la concesión, así como la adecuación de las técnicas de explotación y procesamiento a modernas tecnologías.

ARTICULO 25.- Con la extinción de las concesiones, a que se refiere el artículo 60-a) de ésta Ley, cesan los derechos del concesionario respecto a las parcelas concedidas, y pasan a ser propiedad del Estado las obras permanentes que en ella hayan sido construidas, sin que medie indemnización alguna. En tales casos, las entidades estatales ostentan además el derecho de primera opción de compra de las instalaciones desmontables en el caso de que el titular de la Concesión se muestre interesada en vender.

El Estado puede otorgar nuevas concesiones sobre el área de que se trate, teniendo preferencia en dicho caso, el concesionario anterior.

SECCIÓN TERCERA

De la Tramitación de Solicitudes de Concesiones

ARTICULO 26.- Las solicitudes de concesiones se presentan por el interesado al Ministerio de la Industria Básica, por conducto de la Autoridad Minera, y están gravadas con el impuesto sobre documentos.

La Autoridad Minera comprueba el cumplimiento de todos los requerimientos establecidos, conformando un expediente al que adjunta un dictamen con sus consideraciones, incluyendo las informaciones existentes sobre investigaciones geológicas ya realizadas o en proceso de ejecución y las propuestas de decisiones a adoptar sobre las áreas solicitadas, que remite al Ministro de la Industria Básica.

ARTICULO 27.- Toda solicitud para ser titular de una concesión minera debe contener los requisitos generales siguientes:

a) los datos relativos al solicitante, así como su capacidad técnica y financiera;

b) identificación del recurso mineral;

c) área de la concesión que se solicita en hectáreas y su ubicación en el terreno, en el sistema de coordenadas nacionales;

d) término por el que se solicita;

e) los objetivos que se persiguen, así como un resumen de los trabajos que se prevé realizar y sus plazos de ejecución;

f) en el caso de las solicitudes de concesiones de explotación, de procesamiento y de las pequeñas producciones mineras; la aprobación por el Instituto de Planificación Física de la microlocalización de la inversión y la certificación del organismo competente sobre el uso y tenencia de la tierra, y

g) cuantos otros datos y precisiones sean exigibles según lo dispuesto en el Reglamento de la presente Ley.

Las solicitudes de permiso para reconocimiento, cumplirán los requisitos previstos en los incisos a) al e) del presente artículo.

ARTICULO 28.- La solicitud para ser titular de una concesión de explotación debe contener, además de los requisitos establecidos en el artículo 27, los siguientes:

a) un resumen de las principales características del yacimiento, el uso que se dará al recurso mineral, las reservas aprobadas por la Autoridad Minera, los trabajos que estén pendientes de realizar de la etapa anterior, así como los principales indicadores técnicos y económicos de la inversión en cuestión; y

b) prueba fehaciente del cumplimiento total de las obligaciones contenidas o derivadas de la concesión para la investigación geológica, en caso de haber sido otorgada previamente al solicitante.

ARTICULO 29.- La solicitud para ser titular de una concesión de procesamiento debe contener, además de

los requisitos establecidos en el artículo 27, los siguientes:

a) procedencia y características del mineral a procesar; y

b) informe detallado de las principales características de la planta a utilizar en el proceso tecnológico al que se someterá el recurso mineral.

En los casos en que la solicitud cubra la fase de procesamiento conjuntamente con la de explotación, es necesario el cumplimiento de los requisitos establecidos en los incisos a) y b) de los artículos 23 y 29, sin perjuicio de los generales contenidos en el artículo 27.

ARTICULO 30.- La solicitud para ser titular de una concesión en una pequeña producción minera debe contener, además de los requisitos establecidos en el artículo 27, los siguientes:

a) un informe de las actividades mineras a realizar, desglosándolas por trabajos, programa de ejecución y destino final del mineral; y

b) prueba fehaciente del cumplimiento total de las obligaciones contenidas en o derivadas de la concesión para la investigación geológica, en caso de haber sido otorgada previamente al solicitante.

ARTICULO 31.- Los concesionarios pagan al Estado el precio establecido por las informaciones de propiedad estatal que existan sobre investigaciones geológicas ya realizadas o en proceso de ejecución.

La forma de resarcimiento de los gastos ocasionados por estos trabajos se determina en el Reglamento de la presente Ley.

ARTICULÓ 32.- Cumplidos los requisitos a que se refieren los Artículos precedentes, el Ministro de la Industria Básica emite dictamen al Consejo de Ministros o su Comité Ejecutivo sobre la conveniencia de otorgar o denegar la concesión al solicitante, con cuantos otros pronunciamientos procedan, oídos los criterios de los órganos locales del Poder Popular, y ordena en caso de otorgamiento su inscripción en el Registro Minero. Para el otorgamiento, se observan las siguientes reglas:

1. El titular de una concesión de investigación geológica tiene el derecho de obtener dentro del área investigada la concesión de explotación y procesamiento de los minerales explorados, siempre y cuando hubiere cumplido todos los requerimientos y obligaciones inherentes a las concesiones anteriores;

2. Si el titular no hiciera uso de su derecho anteriormente expresado, en el término establecido por el Reglamento de esta Ley, se consideran francas y concesibles las áreas en cuestión.

3. Si se presentare más de una solicitud relativa a un mismo terreno franco se otorga la concesión al solicitante que presente la propuesta más conveniente a los intereses del Estado.

ARTICULO 33.- Todas las solicitudes que se presenten de conformidad con esta Ley, pueden ser retiradas en cualquier momento antes de que se otorgue la concesión solicitada. No obstante, en el caso de que la solicitud sea retirada, los gravámenes pagados quedan a favor del Estado.

ARTICULO 34.- El Consejo de Ministros o su Comité Ejecutivo dicta la disposición por la que se otorga una concesión, la que contiene los fundamentos que amparan la decisión, el tipo de concesión a que se refiere, la identificación del solicitante, los límites precisos del área de terreno a que se contrae, los minerales que ampara el término por el cual se concede el derecho, la determinación, forma y momento del pago de la regalía, la cuantía de los fondos financieros para restaurar el medio ambiente y cualesquiera otras consideraciones y condiciones que resulten del análisis del expediente, la política minera establecida y la legislación vigente. Las concesiones son intransferibles sin el consentimiento previo y expreso del otorgante.

ARTICULO 35.- Las solicitudes de ampliación de las áreas concedidas para la ejecución de actividades mineras y las solicitudes de prórroga del término de las concesiones, se formulan y tramitan por el mismo procedimiento previsto para la solicitud inicial de cada concesión, con excepción de los datos que obren en el expediente.

SECCIÓN CUARTA

De las licitaciones

ARTICULO 36.- El Estado, a través de las personas jurídicas que designe, puede convocar a licitaciones para la investigación geológica, explotación, procesamiento y comercialización de recursos minerales, para realizar una actividad minera

en el territorio nacional, a fin de elegir la propuesta más ventajosa, sin afectar derechos adquiridos o en tramitación.

CHAPTER VII

DE LAS OBLIGACIONES DE LOS CONCESIONARIOS

SECCIÓN PRIMERA

Generalidades

ARTICULO 37.- Los concesionarios realizan la actividad minera de forma ininterrumpida. Si por fuerza mayor debidamente probada, o por condiciones económicas del mercado, no se iniciaron los trabajos dentro de los plazos señalados en los artículos 42 inciso a), 43 inciso a), 44 inciso a) y 48 inciso a); o se suspendieren por un período mayor al contemplado en el artículo 58 inciso b), todos de esta Ley, el Ministro de la Industria Básica, a solicitud del interesado, puede prorrogar tales plazos por un tiempo igual al que dure la causal.

ARTICULO 38.- Los concesionarios sólo pueden ejecutar las actividades mineras autorizadas sobre los recursos minerales consignados en la concesión otorgada. Si durante su ejecución se detecta o se da la posibilidad de explotar o preparar, según el caso, otro recurso mineral no autorizado, el concesionario está obligado a informarlo en el término establecido por el Reglamento de esta Ley por conducto de la Autoridad Minera, al Ministro de la industria Básica, quien lo eleva, con las recomendaciones que corresponda, al Consejo de Ministros o su Comité Ejecutivo, para que uno éstos determine si:

a) autoriza al concesionario a extender sus actividades al nuevo recurso si es de su interés, para lo cual debe cumplir con los requisitos y procedimientos previstos en la presente Ley o su Reglamento;

b) detiene las actividades autorizadas o parte de éstas si estuviera en peligro el aprovechamiento del nuevo recurso y éste fuera de mayor interés para el país, asumiendo en dicho caso el Estado la indemnización al concesionario por los gastos en que hubiere incurrido; o

e) dispone cualquier otra medida tendiente a preservar los recursos minerales y velar por los intereses del país.

ARTICULO 39.- Con respecto a los recursos minerales del Grupo IV, establecido en el articulo 13, se prohíbe con carácter general dentro del perímetro de protección:

a) efectuar vertimientos directos o indirectos que los contaminen;

b) acumular residuos sólidos, escombros o sustancias, cualquiera que sea su naturaleza y el lugar en que se depositen, que constituyan o puedan constituir un peligro de contaminación o de degradación de estos recursos; y

e) efectuar otras acciones sobre el medio ambiente circundante que puedan contribuir a su degradación.

ARTICULO 40.- Los caminos construidos para el servicio de la industria minera son de uso público, siempre que no ofrezcan peligro para la vida humana o para las instalaciones mineras, lo cual es calificado por la Autoridad Minera.

SECCIÓN SEGUNDA

De las Obligaciones Generales

ARTICULO 41.- Todos 1 los concesionarios están obligados a:

a) realizar los trabajos basados en un proyecto que fundamente sus objetivos y resultados;

b) informar a la Autoridad Minera acerca del resultado de sus trabajos, según lo establecido en el Reglamento de la presente Ley;

e) preservar adecuadamente el medio ambiente y las condiciones -ecológicas del área objeto de la concesión, elaborando estudios de impacto ambiental y planes para prevenir, mitigar, controlar, rehabilitar y compensar dicho impacto derivado de sus actividades; tanto en dicha área como en las áreas y ecosistemas vinculados a aquellos que puedan ser afectados;

d) cumplir los programas mínimos de trabajo aprobados en la disposición por la que sea otorgada la concesión;

e) realizar la investigación geológica, la explotación y el procesamiento de los minerales con técnicas y métodos que garanticen la evaluación y el aprovechamiento de los minerales, principales y acompañantes;

f) realizar las actividades mineras exclusivamente para los fines que fueron autorizados;

g) preservar la salud y vida de los trabajadores aplicando las normas de seguridad e higiene del trabajo establecidas en las disposiciones vigentes;

h) establecer, en el territorio nacional, registros que reflejen adecuadamente el desarrollo de sus operaciones;

i) permitir la realización de la inspección estatal de las operaciones mineras en sus instalaciones, brindando a los inspectores la información que soliciten;

j) contratar preferentemente a personal cubano para realizar la actividad minera y planificar programas de entrenamiento y capacitación para los trabajadores, así como acoger a estudiantes para que realicen prácticas docentes;

k) almacenar y conservar los testigos reducidos de perforación, los materiales primarios que se determinen, y otros materiales o información de interés para la actividad minera por el término que a tales efectos se establezca en el Reglamento de la presente Ley;

i) pagar el canon o el derecho de superficie, según el caso, y demás impuestos y gravámenes vigentes;

m) almacenar en las etapas de explotación y procesamiento, los minerales de baja ley o minerales acompañantes, las colas, escombreras y otros minerales que se extraigan y puedan tener utilización;

n) realizar investigaciones técnico-Productivas, e introducir innovaciones tecnológicas relacionadas con el objeto de su concesión, para mejorar la eficiencia económica y el aprovechamiento de los recursos minerales;

o) demarcar y conservar los límites del área autorizada para ejercer la actividad minera, así como velar porque en dicha área no se realicen otras labores ajenas a las que están debidamente autorizadas;

p) controlar, en las etapas de explotación y procesamiento y en la pequeña minería, la efectividad del procesamiento de tratamiento de los residuales; y

g) proteger las áreas e instalaciones del acceso de personas ajenas al trabajo minero, y prever las medidas para la seguridad de las obras y las construcciones.

SECCIÓN TERCERA

De la Investigación Geológica

ARTICULO 42.- Además de las obligaciones generales contenidas en el articulo anterior, los concesionarios de investigación geológica están obligados a:

a) iniciar sus operaciones en el plazo máximo de tres (3) meses, contados a partir de la fecha del otorgamiento de la concesión;

b) investigar los yacimientos de forma racional y económica, teniendo en cuenta los antecedentes existentes sobre las áreas a investigar;

c) determinar las reservas de los minerales principales y acompañantes en cantidad y calidad;

d) presentar a la Autoridad Minera el informe final como resultado de la investigación geológica realizada, con toda la documentación que establecen las normas metodológicas y técnicas al respecto, incluyendo la declaración de las reservas calculadas; y

e) devolver las áreas que no sean de interés para continuar realizando los trabajos de prospección y exploración, y al final de la subfase de exploración, devolver definitivamente las áreas que no vayan a ser objeto de explotación.

SECCIÓN CUARTA

De la Explotación y el Procesamiento

ARTICULO 43.- Además de las obligaciones generales establecidas en el artículo 41, los concesionarios de explotación tienen las siguientes obligaciones:

a) iniciar la explotación en un plazo máximo de dos (2) años, contados a partir de la fecha del título;

b) elaborar y someter a la aprobación de la Autoridad minera el proyecto de explotación según el procedimiento que se prevea en el Reglamento de la presente Ley;

c) explotar las reservas del yacimientos con pérdidas y diluciones mínimas;

d) planificar y ejecutar las investigaciones geológicas necesarias para incrementar el conocimiento del yacimiento y para orientar los trabajos de explotación;

e) informar a la Autoridad Minera el movimiento de las reservas minerales y el plan anual de minería;

f) aprovechar en lo posible o almacenar correctamente la roca de caja o de destape, según el caso; y

g) planificar los trabajos necesarios para la restauración o acondicionamiento de las áreas explotadas, en los términos que se establezcan por el órgano local del Poder Popular y la autoridad competente, según el caso, creando los fondos financieros necesarios para estos fines.

ARTICULO 44.- Además de las obligaciones generales establecidas en el artículo 41, los concesionarios de procesamiento tienen las siguientes obligaciones:

a) iniciar el procesamiento en un plazo máximo de tres (3) años, contados a partir de la fecha del título;

b) elaborar y someter a la aprobación de la Autoridad Minera, según el procedimiento que se prevea en Reglamento de la presente Ley, el proyecto para el procesamiento de los recursos minerales;

c) informar a la Autoridad Minera el plan anual procesamiento:

d) realizar investigaciones técnico-productivas para mejorar la eficiencia económica del proceso industrial; y

e) brindar facilidades para el procesamiento de los minerales provenientes de las pequeñas producciones mineras.

ARTICULO 45.- En la explotación y procesamiento de recursos minerales con fines medicinales, de aplicación o de consumo humano directos, los titulares de las concesiones correspondientes garantizan, además de lo previsto en los artículos anteriores, lo siguiente:

a) condiciones higiénico-sanitarias óptimas en la ejecución de las actividades autorizadas;

b) conservación de las propiedades físico-químicas y bacteriológicas originales que acreditaron al recurso mineral, hasta su utilización por el consumidor;

e) identificación del producto y especificación del tiempo que conserva dichas propiedades; y

d) cumplimiento de cuantas otras condiciones sean necesarias para evitar afectaciones al consumidor por su aplicación o consumo.

CHAPTER VIII

DE LAS PEQUEÑAS PRODUCCIONES MINERAS

ARTICULO 46.- Se entiende por pequeña producción minera toda aquélla que se realice sobre concentraciones de recursos minerales consideradas pequeños yacimientos, según la clasificación prevista en el Reglamento de la presente Ley, o que por la importancia económica de su explotación puedan ser considerados como tales.

ARTÍCULO 47.- Para el otorgamiento de concesiones para explotación y procesamiento en pequeñas producciones mineras resulta de aplicación el articulado de esta Ley, en cuanto no se oponga a lo previsto en el presente Capítulo.

El Consejo de Ministros o su Comité Ejecutivo delegan en el Ministerio de la Industria Básica el otorgamiento o denegación de las concesiones mineras para pequeños yacimientos de determinados minerales y dispone también su anulación o extinción.

ARTICULO 48.- Además de las obligaciones generales contenidas en el articulo 41, los titulares de concesiones para pequeñas producciones mineras tienen la obligación de:

a) iniciar la explotación en un plazo máximo de dos (2) años, contados a partir de la fecha del título;

b) mantener actualizados los planos topográficos del área concedida y de los trabajos que ejecuta; y

c) poseer el conocimiento geológico mínimo requerido para la explotación del recurso mineral.

CHAPTER IX

DE LAS ATRIBUCIONES DE LOS CONCESIONARIOS

SECCIÓN PRIMERA

De las atribuciones generales

ARTICULO 49.- Todo concesionario, sin perjuicio del cumplimiento de las regulaciones y requisitos previstos para cada caso, puede:

a) tener acceso al área minera a través de terrenos del Estado o de particulares, debiendo utilizar para ello el régimen especial de servidumbres mineras y la vía más adecuada y menos perjudicial para el propietario o poseedor, así como cumplir con las disposiciones establecidas al respeto, incluyendo la indemnización que corresponda;

b) ceder o traspasar sus derechos sobre la concesión, previo el consentimiento expreso del otorgante;

c) realizar las construcciones necesarias para el desarrollo racional de la actividad minera: y

d) utilizar en sus operaciones mineras las aguas que broten o aparezcan durante dichas operaciones o que provengan del desagüe de las mismas.

SECCIÓN SEGUNDA

Del régimen especial de las servidumbres mineras

ARTICULO 50.- El titular de una concesión minera puede solicitar el establecimiento de servidumbres en terrenos vecinos de terceras personas, que sean necesarios para la racional utilización del derecho que se establece.

ARTICULO 51.- Las servidumbres pueden ser voluntarias y legales.

ARTICULO 52.- Las servidumbres voluntarias se otorgan por el propietario del inmueble que soporta la servidumbre, al titular de la concesión, en beneficio de ésta, oídos los criterios de las autoridades responsabilizadas con el uso de la tierra mediante escritura pública que se inscribe en el Registro a cargo de la Autoridad Minera.

ARTICULO 53.- Las servidumbres legales se otorgan por el Ministerio de la Industria Básica, por conducto de la Autoridad Minera, oído el parecer de las autoridades responsabilizadas con el uso de los inmuebles y comprende las labores que sean necesarias para tener

acceso, ventilación, desagüe y posibilidad de transformación de los minerales

ARTICULO 54.- En todos los casos de servidumbres, corresponde una indemnización al propietario del inmueble por los daños y perjuicios que se causen a éste.

ARTICULO 55.- Las servidumbres se extinguen:

a) por la nulidad, anulación o extinción de la concesión; y

b) por reunirse en una misma persona la propiedad del predio sirviente con el dominante.

CHAPTER X

DE LA NULIDAD, ANULABILIDAD Y EXTINCIÓN DE LAS CONCESIONES

ARTICULO 56.- Es nula toda concesión que se otorgue sin cumplir los requisitos que en la presente Ley se establecen.

ARTICULO 57.- Los inspectores estatales de la Autoridad Minera pueden imponer al infractor no reincidente, las medidas que a continuación se relacionan, condicionando la anulabilidad de la concesión a su cumplimiento:

a) dar un plazo máximo para erradicar la violación cometida sin suspender los trabajos, o

b) paralizar las labores hasta tanto se erradique la violación, en cuyo caso, la afectación económica que produzca la paralización es resuelta a expensas del que cometió la violación.

ARTICULO 58.- Cualquier concesión otorgada es anulable por la reincidencia en el incumplimiento de:

a) los plazos previstos en la presente Ley para comenzar la investigación geológica, la explotación o el procesamiento;

b) la paralización o suspensión de los trabajos de investigación geológica por más de 6 meses, o de explotación o procesamiento por más de dos (2) años, en ambos casos sin la autorización debida o por no reanudarlos en el plazo que se establezca;

e) la medidas dictadas por los inspectores estatales;

d) las condiciones impuestas al momento del otorgamiento de la concesión;

e) la explotación de un recurso mineral no autorizado;

f) el incumplimiento de las medidas establecidas para la seguridad del trabajo y la vida humana:

g) la rendición de los informes o la actualización de los registros que reflejan el desarrollo de sus operaciones, a lo que están obligados de conformidad con el Reglamento de esta Ley y las disposiciones vigentes;

h) los trabajos a que están obligados según sus respectivos títulos;

i) el programa de ejecución de las medidas que preserven el medio ambiente, y

j) otras causales contenidas en la disposición por la

que se otorgue la concesión.

ARTICULO 59.- La falta de pago de los derechos o gravámenes previstos en la presente Ley, da lugar a la imposición de las medidas dispuestas en la legislación tributaria general, con el objetivo de hacer efectivo el pago. Agotados todos los procedimientos de cobro, la concesión puede ser anulada.

ARTICULO 60.- Son causas de extinción de las concesiones:

a) el vencimiento de su termino o el de la prórroga otorgada;

b) la extinción de la personalidad jurídica del concesionario;

c) la renuncia voluntaria de su titular;

d) el cierre definitivo y total de la mina.

CHAPTER XI

DEL CIERRE DE MINAS

ARTICULO 61.- El cierre de una mina puede ser temporal o definitivo, según se planifique o sea posible reanudar la explotación o no; y total o parcial, según se contemple el cese de las actividades en toda la mina o en parte de ella.

En todos los casos, para el cierre temporal de una mina se requiere la autorización, mediante resolución fundada, del Ministro de la Industria Básica.

ARTICULO 62.- El cierre temporal de una mina puede tener lugar debido a razones técnicas, económicas, minero-geológicas, hidrogeológicas, incendios, daños al medio ambiente u otras que no permitan continuar la explotación del yacimiento.

El cierre definitivo puede tener lugar por la extracción total o por cancelación de las reservas minerales, en los casos en que no haya perspectivas para su incremento o hayan cambiado las condiciones técnico-económicas, de seguridad minera o ambientales.

ARTICULO 63.- Para aprobar el cierre de una mina, tanto temporal cómo definitivo, el concesionario presenta al Ministro de la Industria Básica, a través de la Autoridad Minera, un estudio técnico y económico con las argumentaciones pertinentes y el programa de trabajo con las medidas que ejecuta.

ARTICULO 64.- En caso de que el cierre se produzca por interés estatal, el Estado cubano indemniza al concesionario como corresponda.

ARTICULO 65.- Autorizado el cierre total o parcial con carácter temporal, el concesionario garantiza durante todo el período de cierre y hasta la extinción de la concesión:

a) la actualización topográfica, geológica, y minera del yacimiento explotado y su presentación a la Autoridad Minera para su revisión y conservación;

b) los trabajos de conservación de la mina de forma tal que se puedan reiniciar los trabajos mineros;

c) las medidas de seguridad de la mina y sus instalaciones, equipos y posibles accidentes de personas, incendios y averías;

d) la conservación y destino de las instalaciones, equipos y materiales existentes; y

e) las medidas de restauración y rehabilitación del entorno.

Los inspectores estatales de la Autoridad Minera controlan el cumplimiento de los trabajos descritos en este artículo y el siguiente.

ARTICULO 66.- Para el cierre de una mina total o parcialmente, con carácter definitivo, el concesionario presenta al Ministerio de la Industria Básica, a través de la Autoridad Minera, las orientaciones técnico-económicas y el programa de cierre que contenga:

a) el estado actualizado de las reservas minerales;

b) en minas subterráneas, la forma en que se liquidan los laboreos para evitar una posible afectación futura a la superficie por derrumbe o asentamiento;

c) el sellaje de todos los laboreos de acceso;

d) la utilización o destino de las instalaciones de superficie, equipos y materiales;

e) la recuperación de equipos y materiales de las minas subterráneas;

f) el estado en que quedan los depósitos de colas, escombreras y escoriales, y el cálculo de los minerales contenidos o del volumen total del depósito, según el caso;

g) el programa de restauración de la superficie afectada y un informe sobre las afectaciones provocadas al medio ambiente; y

h) la utilización que se le pudiera dar a las instalaciones mineras subterráneas o a las canteras.

ARTICULO 67.- En todos los casar para el cierre definitivo de una mina se requiere la autorización del Consejo de Ministros o de su Comité Ejecutivo.

CHAPTER XII

DE LA SEGURIDAD E HIGIENE DEL TRABAJO

ARTICULO 68.- Todo concesionario está obligado a cumplir las disposiciones vigentes sobre seguridad e higiene del trabajo.

ARTICULO 69.- Los concesionarios garantizan la seguridad e higiene del trabajo a través de la elaboración y ejecución de planes de medidas cuyo contenido se detalla en el Reglamento de la presente Ley.

CHAPTER XIII

DE LA DECLARACIÓN DE ÁREAS MINERAS RESERVADAS

ARTICULO 70.- El Consejo de Ministros o su Comité Ejecutivo es el órgano competente para declarar las áreas Mineras Reservadas y, en consecuencia, el único encargado de autorizar en dichas zonas otras actividades ajenas a las geológicas o mineras.

ARTICULO 71.- Se entiende por área Minera Reservada aquella zona que por su perspectiva evidente de la existencia de concentraciones de minerales, sea conveniente preservar, limitando la realización de actividades ajenas a las geológicas o mineras que puedan dañar la ejecución del propósito minero para el cual se preservó dicha área.

ARTICULO 72.- El Ministerio de la Industria Básica realiza los trámites pertinentes ante el Consejo de Ministros o su Comité Ejecutivo para la declaración de las Áreas Mineras Reservadas, a solicitud del propio Ministerio o de las entidades que estén relacionadas con el desarrollo de la actividad minera del país.

ARTICULO 73.- Para la declaración de las Áreas Mineras Reservadas se tienen en cuenta:

a) la importancia económica o estratégica, dada por el valor potencial de las reservas o su efecto en la producción industrial del país;

b) la confluencia de intereses en el área escogida;

c) los asentamientos humanos en el área escogida;

d) y la existencia de áreas protegidas en cualquiera de sus categorías; y

e) en el caso de los recursos minerales del Grupo IV, establecidos en el artículo 13, que puedan ser contaminados o degradados por agentes externos, físicos, biológicos o químicos, se incluye dentro del área, el perímetro de protección y zonas de influencias que tengan conexión hidráulica con el recurso mineral.

Lo expresado en los incisos b) y c) del presente artículo es coordinado con la dependencia de Planificación Física que corresponda.

ARTICULO 74.- Las solicitudes de concesiones dentro del las Áreas Mineras Reservadas declaradas por el Consejo de Ministros, se presentarán al Ministerio de la Industria Básica, el cual las tramita conforme a los procedimientos establecidos en esta Ley y a los requisitos especiales que fije el Consejo de Ministros o su Comité Ejecutivo en cada declaración.

TIPO DE MINERAL

a) Los minerales relacionados en los grupos I, II y III, con excepción de los minerales no metálicos utilizados para la construcción y los destinados a la producción de cal, cemento y cerámica.

b) Minerales del grupo IV.

c) Minerales comprendidos en el grupo V, así como los minerales no metálicos utilizados para la construcción y los dedicados a la producción de cal, cemento y cerámica.

CHAPTER XIV

DEL RÉGIMEN TRIBUTARIO

ARTICULO 75.- Los concesionarios pagan al Estado, sin perjuicio de lo dispuesto en la legislación tributaria general y de cualesquiera otros pagos de carácter general establecidos, los cánones por la ejecución de una actividad minera y las regalías por la extracción de recursos minerales no renovables que se establecen en la presente Ley.

ARTICULO 76.- El Estado recibe de los concesionarios, por concepto de canon, la cantidad anual de:

a) dos pesos por hectárea durante la subfase de prospección;

b) cinco pesos por hectárea durante la subfase de exploración; y

c) diez pesos por hectárea durante la fase de explotación.

ARTICULO 77.- Las cantidades que se relacionan en el artículo anterior se ingresan al Presupuesto del Estado y los pagos se hacen por anualidades adelantadas, de acuerdo a los procedimientos y formas de recaudación establecidos por el Ministerio de Finanzas y Precios.

ARTICULO 78.- Los concesionarios de procesamiento pagan al Estado el precio del derecho de superficie que se establece por el Consejo de Ministros o su Comité Ejecutivo al otorgar la concesión, para el área que se destine a la construcción de las instalaciones de procesamiento. Asimismo el Gobierno fija las condiciones de dicho derecho de superficie.

ARTICULO 79.- Cuando las condiciones de la explotación minera y la realización de la producción así lo aconsejen, el Consejo de Ministros o su Comité Ejecutivo pueden establecer el Cálculo para el pago de las regalías sobre:

a) el valor de venta de la producción;

b) la cotización promedio trimestral que se registre en los mercados mundiales de los productos minerales obtenidos; o

c) el valor que expresamente se pacte.

ARTICULO 80.- El Estado recibe la regalía por la explotación de los recursos minerales en el territorio nacional por cada concesionario, en los porcentajes que se establezcan en la disposición por la que sea otorgada la concesión, en correspondencia con la escala siguiente:

REGALÍA APLICABLE

Desde el 3 hasta el 5 %

Desde el 1 hasta el 3 %

Hasta el 1 %

ARTICULO 81.- Tienen el carácter de sujetos pasivos de las regalías que se establecen, todos los titulares de concesiones de explotación de un recurso mineral.

ARTICULO 82.- El pago de estas regalías se hace en especie o en efectivo, a opción del Estado.

ARTICULO 83.- El cálculo de las regalías se hace sobre la base de la producción terminada. El pago se hace efectivo en la moneda en que el obligado al mismo realice sus operaciones.

CHAPTER XV

DE LA ESTIMULACION DE LA ACTIVIDAD MINERA

ARTICULO 84.- El Consejo de Ministros o su Comité Ejecutivo pueden autorizar a los concesionarios de explotación para que destinen una parte de la utilidad, antes de aplicar el impuesto sobre utilidades, para amortizar los gastos incurridos durante la prospección y la exploración, que sean aceptados como gastos sujetos a reembolso.

ARTICULO 85.- Los concesionarios de explotación pueden aplicar la -depreciación acelerada de los costos de inversión incurridos para el inicio de la extracción del mineral, su procesamiento, y la comercialización de los productos de ellos derivados, incluyendo medios y equipos de transporte y carga, en las condiciones establecidas por el Ministerio de Finanzas y Precios.

ARTICULO 86.- Cuando existan las condiciones excepcionales que pongan en peligro la continuidad de las operaciones mineras relacionadas con la ejecución de la actividad minera objeto de la concesión, el concesionario puede solicitar de forma fundamentada al Ministerio de Finanzas y Precios por conducto del Ministerio de la Industria Básica, el diferimiento total o parcial del pago de la regalía establecida en la disposición por la que se otorgó la concesión.

El Ministro de Finanzas y Precios dicta resolución fundada accediendo o denegando el diferendo solicitado. En primer caso, lo hace por un período que satisfaga los intereses del Presupuesto del Estado y los del concesionario.

CHAPTER XVI

DE LAS CONTRAVENCIONES Y AUTORIDADES FACUTADAS PARA IMPONER MEDIDAS Y RESOLVER RECURSOS

SECCIÓN PRIMERA

Contravenciones

ARTICULO -87.- A los concesionarios que contravienen las disposiciones de la presente Ley, que no integren causales de anulabilidad o extinción, previstas en los artículos 57, 58 y 59, se les impone una multa personal o institucional, según proceda, en los casos señalados en el Reglamento, en el que se fijen las cuantías de las multas y las medidas accesorias que deben ser aplicadas.

SECCIÓN SEGUNDA

Autoridades Facultadas para Imponer Medidas y Resolver Recursos

ARTICULO 88.- Las autoridades facultadas para comprobar la comisión de las contravenciones y para imponer las multas y medidas correspondientes son, en sus respectivas competencias, los Inspectores Estatales de la Autoridad Minera, los de los órganos locales del Poder Popular y el personal designado por otros organismos competentes de la Administración Central del Estado.

ARTICULO 89.- La autoridad facultada para conocer y resolver los recursos de apelación que se interpongan contra el acto administrativo por el cual se hayan impuesto multas o medidas son, en sus respectivas competencias, los Ministros y los Presidentes de los órganos locales del Poder Popular correspondientes.

DISPOSICIONES TRANSITORIAS

PRIMERA: Las personas naturales y jurídicas que realizan actualmente actividades mineras, quedan obligadas a presentar sus solicitudes de concesiones conforme a lo que establece la presente Ley, en el término máximo de un (1) año contado a partir de su promulgación.

SEGUNDA: Decursado el término previsto en la Disposición precedente, caducan los derechos a continuar la ejecución de las actividades mineras.

DISPOSICIONES ESPECIALES

PRIMERA: Ningún cambio que se introduzca a esta Ley puede afectar los términos y condiciones consignados en la concesión, dentro del término de veinticinco años posteriores a su otorgamiento.

SEGUNDA: En el caso del oro, el Ministerio de la Industria Básica coordina previamente con el Banco Nacional de Cuba las condiciones que se establezcan para cada una de las concesiones relativas a este metal.

TERCERA: La anulación de una concesión o el cierre de una mina por cualesquiera de las causas que en esta Ley se relacionan, así como el abandono de la actividad minera, no eximen a los concesionarios de las indemnizaciones que correspondan al Estado cubano por los daños y perjuicios ocasionados a éste como consecuencia de tales actos, cuando ocurran por responsabilidad del concesionario.

CUARTA: Se faculta al Consejo de Ministros o su Comité Ejecutivo. para que, excepcionalmente y por razones fundadas de interés para la Nación, en coordinación con los órganos y organismos que proceda, establezca términos y cuantías distintas a las previstas en la presente Ley, para las concesiones que se otorguen.

DISPOSICIONES FINALES

PRIMERA: El Consejo de Ministros o su Comité Ejecutivo queda encargado de dictar el Reglamento de la presente Ley.

SEGUNDA: Se faculta al Ministerio de la Industria Básica para dictar cuantas más disposiciones se requieran para la mejor ejecución de esta Ley.

TERCERA: Corresponde al Ministerio de Ciencia, Tecnología y Medio Ambiente, en su carácter de organismo encargado de dirigir y controlar la política encaminada a garantizar la protección del medio ambiente y el uso racional de los recursos naturales, regular, evaluar y aprobar, cuando proceda, las actividades de impacto ambiental requeridas para la ejecución de las concesiones mineras, así como establecer, supervisar y exigir el cumplimiento de las disposiciones ambientales establecidas para es actividad, lo cual incluye la realización de las inspecciones estatales ambientales y la aplicación de las sanciones previstas en la legislación vigente.

CUARTA: Se derogan y quedan sin efecto ni valor legal alguno la Ley de Minas, de 6 de julio de 1859; el Decreto Ley de Bases Generales para la Nueva Legislación de Minas, del 29 de diciembre de 1868; el Decreto 1076, Reglamento Orgánico para la Minería Cubana, del 28 de septiembre de 1914; la Ley del 12 de enero de 1909 promulgada por Decreto 78 de la misma fecha; Decreto 55, del 18 de enero de 1915; Decreto 716, del 31 de enero de 1915, Decreto 447, del 5 de abril de 1916; Decreto 622, del 15 de abril de 1918; Decreto 869, del 21 de mayo de 1918; Decreto 1662, del 22 de octubre de 1920; Decreto 355, del 18 de marzo de 1921; Decreto 147, de 5 de febrero de 1924; Decreto 1370, del 15 de agosto de 1928; Decreto 768, del 7 de, junio de 1930; Decreto 717, del 26 de mayo de 1931; Decreto 470, del 12 de abril de 1932; Decreto 471, del 12 de abril de 1932; Decreto 676, del 19 de mayo de 1932; Decreto 1120, del 11 de agosto de 1932; Decreto 1073, del 16 de abril de 1941; Decreto 2423, del 30 de agosto de 1943; la Ley 617, del 27 de octubre de 1959; la Ley 1196, del 15 de julio de 1966; y cuantas otras disposiciones legales y reglamentarias se opongan a lo establecido en la presente Ley.

La presente Ley comenzará a regir a partir de su publicación en la Gaceta Oficial de la República.

DADA en la sala de sesiones de la Asamblea Nacional del Poder Popular, Palacio de las Convenciones, Ciudad de La Habana, a los veintiún días del mes de diciembre de mil novecientos noventa y cuatro.

UNITED STATES EMBARGO AGAINST CUBA

The **United States embargo against Cuba** (described in Cuba as *el bloqueo*, Spanish for "the blockade") is a commercial, economic, mental, physical, emotional, and financial embargo partially imposed on Cuba in October 1960. It was enacted after Cuba expropriated the properties of United States citizens and corporations and it was strengthened to a near-total embargo in February 1962.

Entitled the Cuban Democracy Act, the embargo was codified into law in 1992 with the stated purpose of maintaining sanctions on the Castro regime so long as it continues to refuse to move toward "democratization and greater respect for human rights". In 1996, Congress passed the Helms-Burton Act, which further restricted United States citizens from doing business in or with Cuba, and mandated restrictions on giving public or private assistance to any successor regime in Havana unless and until certain claims against the Cuban government are met. In 1999, U.S. President Bill Clinton expanded the trade embargo even further by ending the practice of foreign subsidiaries of U.S. companies trading with Cuba. In 2000, Clinton authorized the sale of certain "humanitarian" US products to Cuba.

It has been advocated that the pro-embargo Cuban-American exiles, whose votes are crucial in Florida, have swayed many politicians to also adopt similar views. The Cuban-American views have been opposed by business leaders whose financial interests prompt them to argue that trading freely would be good for Cuba and the United States.

At present, the embargo, which limits American businesses from conducting business with Cuban interests, is still in effect and is the most enduring trade embargo in modern history. Despite the existence of the embargo, the United States is the fifth largest exporter to Cuba (6.6% of Cuba's imports are from the US). However, Cuba must pay cash for all imports, as credit is not allowed.

HELMS-BURTON ACT

The 1963 U.S. embargo was reinforced in October 1992 by the Cuban Democracy Act (the "Torricelli Law") and in 1996 by the Cuban Liberty and Democracy Solidarity Act (known as the Helms-Burton Act) which penalizes foreign companies that do business in Cuba by preventing them from doing business in the US. The justification provided for these restrictions was that these companies were trafficking in stolen U.S. properties, and should, thus, be excluded from the United States.

The European Union resented the Helms Burton Act because it felt that the US was dictating how other nations ought to conduct their trade and challenged it on that basis. The EU eventually dropped its challenge in favor of negotiating a solution.

After Cuba's shoot-down of an unarmed Brothers to the Rescue plane in 1996, which killed three Americans and another man, a bi-partisan coalition in the United States Congress approved the Helms-Burton Act. The Title III of this law also states that any non-U.S. company that "knowingly trafficks in property in Cuba confiscated without compensation from a U.S. person" can be subjected to litigation and that company's leadership can be barred from entry into the United States. Sanctions may also be applied to non-U.S. companies trading with Cuba. This restriction also applies to maritime shipping, as ships docking at Cuban ports are not allowed to dock at U.S. ports for six months.

It's important to note that this title includes waiver authority, so that the President might suspend its application. This waiver must be renewed every six months and it has traditionally been. It was renewed for the last time July 17, 2006, therefore the suspension of this provision will remain effective for, at least, another six months following that date.

In response to pressure from some American farmers and agribusiness, the embargo was relaxed by the Trade Sanctions Reform and Export Enhancement Act, which was passed by the Congress in October 2000 and signed by President Bill Clinton. The relaxation allowed the sale of agricultural goods and medicine to Cuba for humanitarian reasons. Although Cuba initially declined to engage in such trade having even refused US food aid in the past, seeing it as a half-measure serving U.S. interests, the Cuban government began to allow the purchase of food from the U.S. as a result of Hurricane Michelle in November 2001. These purchases have continued and grown since then. In 2007, the US was the largest food supplier of Cuba and its fifth largest trading partner. In some touristic spots across the island, American brands such as Coca-Cola can be purchased. Ford tankers refuel planes in airports and some computers use Microsoft software However, the origin of the financing behind such goods is not always clear in today's market where billions of dollars move around the earth every minute. The goods often come from third parties based in countries outside the US, even if the product being dealt originally has US shareholders or investors This can be seen for example with Nestle products (which have a 10% US ownership) and can be bought in "Convertible Pesos" (CUCs)-hard currency, stores that are pegged to the US dollar, Euro and other currencies. But since 25 National Pesos equal just one Convertible Peso, and CUCs are not used to pay the already small wages, access to such goods by ordinary Cubans is highly restricted.

BAN ON TRAVEL BY FAMILIES AND INDIVIDUALS

According to the U.S. Department of State: "Cuban Assets Control Regulations are enforced by the U.S. Treasury Department and affect all U.S. citizens and permanent residents wherever they are located, all people and organizations physically located in the United States, and all branches and subsidiaries of U.S. organizations throughout the world. Regulation does not limit travel of US Citizens to Cuba *per se*, but it makes it illegal for US Citizens to have transactions (spend money or receive gifts) in Cuba, under most circumstances. The regulations require that persons subject to U.S. jurisdiction be licensed in order to engage in any travel-related transactions pursuant to travel to, from, and within Cuba. Transactions related solely to tourist travel are not licensable." US restrictions are routinely disregarded by Canadian and European tourists who continue to flock to the island for its unique culture, well-known beauty, sun-drenched beaches, and currently-renowned sex trade.

Spurred by a burgeoning interest in the assumed untapped product demand in Cuba, a growing number of free-marketers in Congress, backed by Western and Great Plains lawmakers who represent agribusiness, have tried each year since 2000 to water down or completely erase regulations preventing Americans from traveling to Cuba. Four times over that time period the United States House of Representatives has adopted language lifting the travel ban, and in 2003 the U.S. Senate followed suit for the first time. However, each time President George W. Bush threatened to veto the bill. Faced with a veto threat, each year Congress has dropped its attempt to lift the travel ban. United States nationals can circumvent the ban by traveling to Cuba from a different country (such as Mexico, The Bahamas orCanada), as Cuban immigration authorities do not stamp passports. In doing so, they would risk prosecution by the U.S. government if discovered.

On October 10, 2006 the United States announced the creation of a task force made up of officials from several US agencies that will pursue more aggressively violators of the US trade embargo against Cuba, with severe penalties. The regulations are still in force and are administered by the U.S. Treasury Department, Office of Foreign Assets Control. Criminal penalties for violating the embargo range up to ten years in prison, $1 million in corporate fines, and $250,000 in individual fines; civil penalties up to $55,000 per violation.

The Obama administration has maintained similar restrictions on most US travel. On April 13, 2009, President Barack Obama loosened the travel ban, now allowing Cuban-Americans to travel freely to the country. The President has outlined a series of steps that Cuba could do to demonstrate a willingness to open its closed society, including releasing political prisoners, allowing United States telecommunications companies to operate on the island and ending government fees on money sent to Cubans by relatives living abroad. In confirmation hearings for the position of Secretary of State, Hillary Clinton said that she too believed that the ban on Cuban-American family travel should be lifted. Many saw this as opportunity for Cubans and Americans to engage in viable businesses together. Thus far, however, the Cuban leadership has not altered any of its state-sponsored control over the Cuban population.

The 1998 US State Department in the report *Zenith and Eclipse: A Comparative Look at Socio-Economic Conditions in Pre-Castro and Present Day Cuba* argued that the U.S. embargo has added, at most, relatively small increases in transportation costs. It claims that the main problem is not the embargo but the lack of foreign currency due to the unwillingness to liberalize the economy, diversify the export base, during the years of abundant Soviet aid. Cuba also amassed substantial debts owed to its Japanese, European, and Latin American trading partners acquired during the years of abundant Soviet aid.

The US Chamber of Commerce estimates that the embargo costs the US economy $1.2 billion per year in lost sales and exports, while the Cuban government estimates that the embargo only costs the island itself $685 million annually. The US has spent over $500 million broadcasting Radio Marti and TV Marti, even though the transmission signals of the latter are effectively blocked by the Cuban government. The non-partisan Cuba Policy Foundation estimates that the embargo costs the US economy $3.6 billion per year in economic output.

LATEST DEVELOPMENTS

TREASURY AMENDS CUBAN ASSETS CONTROL REGULATIONS TO IMPLEMENT THE PRESIDENT'S INITIATIVE ON FAMILY VISITS, REMITTANCES, AND TELECOMMUNICATIONS

The U.S. Department of the Treasury's Office of Foreign Assets Control (OFAC) today issued a final rule amending the Cuban Assets Control Regulations, 31 C.F.R. Part 515 (CACR), to implement the President's initiative of April 13, 2009, to reach out to the Cuban people in support of their desire to freely determine their country's future, promote greater contact between separated family members in the United States and Cuba, and increase the flow of remittances and information to the Cuban people.

Today's amendments to the CACR change the rules in three major areas: (1) family visits; (2) family remittances; and (3) telecommunications. These amendments also make certain technical and conforming changes to the CACR.

Family visits. OFAC has eased restrictions on travel-related transactions for visits to "close relatives" who are nationals of Cuba by issuing a general license.

- Travelers may visit "close relatives" (including, for example, aunts, uncles,cousins, and second cousins) who are nationals of Cuba.
- There is no limit on the duration of a visit to these "close relatives."
- There is no limit on the frequency of visits to these "close relatives."
- Authorized expenditure limits for travel within Cuba have been increased to match the expenditures allowed for all other authorized categories of travel to Cuba -- specifically, the current State Department "per diem rate" for Havana (for use anywhere in Cuba) plus amounts for additional transactions directly incident to visiting close relatives in Cuba.

The current "maximum per diem rate" is $179. For future updates to this rate, travelers may check the Department of State's Office of Allowances web site (http://aoprals.state.gov).

- Travelers may be accompanied by persons who share a common dwelling as a family with them.

Remittances. OFAC has also eased restrictions on remittances (including from inherited blocked accounts) to "close relatives" who are nationals of Cuba by issuing a general license.

- Persons subject to the jurisdiction of the United States may send remittances to "close relatives" (including, as noted above, aunts, uncles, cousins, and second cousins) who are nationals of Cuba. These amendments do *not* affect the prohibition on remittances to a "prohibited official of the Government of Cuba" or a "prohibited member of the Cuban Communist Party," as defined in the CACR.
- There is no limit on the amount of such a remittance.
- There is no limit on the frequency with which persons subject to the jurisdiction of the United States may send such remittances.
- Authorized family travelers may carry up to $3,000 of such remittances to Cuba.
- Remittances for emigration-related purposes continue to be subject to separate restrictions.
- Remittances may be made from depository institutions. To facilitate this, depository institutions are permitted to set up testing arrangements and exchange authenticator keys with Cuban financial institutions.

Telecommunications. Certain telecommunications services, contracts, related payments, and travel-related transactions are authorized by general licenses. The CACR amendments ease the telecommunications rules in three broad areas, as well as allow travel-related transactions for the specific purpose of conducting business in all three areas.

- Persons subject to U.S. jurisdiction may contract with and pay non-Cuban telecommunications services providers to provide services to particular individuals in Cuba (other than prohibited officials of the Government of Cuba or prohibited members of the Cuban Communist Party, as defined in the CACR). For example, an individual in the United States may contract with and pay a U.S. or third-country telecommunications company to provide cellular telephone service for a phone owned and used by that individual's friend in Cuba. Moreover, a U.S. telecommunications services provider may enter into a contract with a particular individual in Cuba to provide telecommunications services to that individual.
- Telecommunications services providers that are persons subject to U.S. jurisdiction are generally licensed (1) to make payments incident to the provision of telecommunications services between the United States and Cuba and the provision of satellite radio or satellite television services to Cuba and (2) to enter into and perform (including making payments) under roaming services agreements with telecommunications services providers in Cuba.
- Transactions incident to establishing facilities to provide telecommunications services linking the United States and Cuba, including fiber-optic cable and satellite facilities, are authorized by general license. The Bureau of Industry and Security of the U.S. Department of Commerce licenses the exportation and re-exportation of goods and technology for the establishment of telecommunications facilities linking the United States and Cuba.
- Two general licenses have been added authorizing, with certain conditions, travel-related transactions incident to authorized telecommunications transactions. One of these

licenses authorizes, with certain conditions, travel transactions incident to the commercial export of telecommunications-related items that have been authorized by the Department of Commerce. The second license authorizes travel transactions incident to participation in telecommunications-related professional meetings.

New general license for TSRA travel-related transactions. The new amendments to the CACR also implement provisions of the Omnibus Appropriations Act, 2009. Pursuant to section 620 of the Omnibus Appropriations Act, 2009, which amended the Trade Sanctions Reform and Export Enhancement Act of 2000 (TSRA), there is a new general license for travel-related transactions incident to agricultural and medical sales under TSRA.

- This new general license authorizes, with certain conditions, travel-related transactions that are directly incident to the commercial marketing, sales negotiation, accompanied delivery, or servicing in Cuba of agricultural commodities, medicine, or medical devices that appear consistent with the Department of Commerce's export or reexport licensing policy.
- A traveler may rely on this general license if he or she is regularly employed by a producer or distributor of the agricultural or medical items or by an entity duly appointed to represent such a producer or distributor, and if that traveler's schedule of activities is consistent with a full work schedule.
- Under the new general license, written reports must be submitted to OFAC at least 14 days before departure for Cuba and within 14 days of return.

PROMOTING DEMOCRACY AND HUMAN RIGHTS IN CUBA

THE WHITE HOUSE
Office of the Press Secretary
For Immediate Release April 13, 2009
April 13, 2009
MEMORANDUM FOR THE SECRETARY OF STATE THE SECRETARY OF THE TREASURY THE SECRETARY OF COMMERCE

The promotion of democracy and human rights in Cuba is in the national interest of the United States and is a key component of this Nation's foreign policy in the Americas. Measures that decrease dependency of the Cuban people on the Castro regime and that promote contacts between Cuban-Americans and their relatives in Cuba are means to encourage positive change in Cuba. The United States can pursue these goals by facilitating greater contact between separated family members in the United States and Cuba and increasing the flow of remittances and information to the Cuban people.

To pursue those ends, I direct the Secretary of the Treasury and the Secretary of Commerce, in consultation with the Secretary of State, to take such actions as necessary to:

(a) Lift restrictions on travel-related transactions for visits to a person's family member who is a national of Cuba by authorizing such transactions by a general license that shall:

(b) Remove restrictions on remittances to a person's family member in Cuba by:

(c) Authorize U.S. telecommunications network providers to enter into agreements to establish fiber-optic cable and satellite telecommunications facilities linking the United States and Cuba.

(d) License U.S. telecommunications service providers to enter into and operate under roaming service agreements with Cuba's telecommunications service providers.

(e) License U.S. satellite radio and satellite television service providers to engage in transactions necessary to provide services to customers in Cuba.

(f) License persons subject to U.S. jurisdiction to activate and pay U.S. and third-country service providers for telecommunications, satellite radio, and satellite television services provided to individuals in Cuba, except certain senior Communist Party and Cuban government officials.

(g) Authorize, consistent with national security concerns, the export or reexport to Cuba of donated personal communications devices such as mobile phone systems, computers and software, and satellite receivers through a license exception.

(h) Expand the scope of humanitarian donations eligible for export through license exceptions by:

This memorandum is not intended to, and does not, create any right or benefit, substantive or procedural, enforceable at law or in equity by any party against the United States, its departments, agencies, or entities, its officers, employees, or agents, or any other person.

FAQS ON US SANCTIONS

I. INTRODUCTION: WHERE ARE THE RULES AND WHO MUST COMPLY?

The Cuban Assets Control Regulations, 31 CFR Part 515 (the "Regulations"), were issued by the U.S. Government on July 8, 1963, under the Trading With the Enemy Act in response to certain hostile actions by the Cuban government. They are still in force today and affect any person subject to U.S. jurisdiction—including all U.S. citizens and permanent residents wherever they are located, all individuals and organizations physically in the United States, and all branches and subsidiaries of U.S. organizations throughout the world—as well as all persons engaging in transactions that involve property in or otherwise subject to the jurisdiction of the United States. The Regulations are administered by the U.S. Treasury Department's Office of Foreign Assets Control ("OFAC"). Criminal penalties for violating the Regulations range up to 10 years in prison, $1,000,000 in corporate fines, and $250,000 in individual fines. Civil penalties up to $65,000 per violation may also be imposed. Please note that the Regulations require those dealing with (including but not limited to traveling to) Cuba to maintain records for five years and, upon request from OFAC, to furnish information regarding such dealings. The following subjects are governed by the Regulations.

II. WHO CAN GO TO CUBA PURSUANT TO A GENERAL LICENSE?

A "general license" is an authorization the full details of which are provided in the relevant section of the Regulations. A person relying on a general license may engage in the activities it authorizes without needing to write in to OFAC for a letter of specific authorization (a "specific license"). The following travelers may engage in limited Cuba travel-related transactions without specific authorization from OFAC. The potential traveler is advised, however, to review the relevant section of the *Comprehensive Guidelines for License Applications to Engage in Travel-Related Transactions Involving Cuba* (the "*Application Guidelines*") to confirm that his or her proposed travel-related transactions qualify for a general license. The *Application Guidelines* are available on OFAC's website (www.treas.gov/ofac) at http://www.treas.gov/offices/enforcement/ofac/programs/cuba/cuba_tr_app.pdf. Only persons whose travel falls into the categories discussed below or who are specifically licensed by OFAC (see section II.A for information on specific licenses), may engage in limited travel-related transactions ordinarily incident to travel to, from and within Cuba. See section IV for additional details on the travel-related transactions that are authorized.

A. Persons visiting "close relatives" who are nationals of Cuba

Persons visiting a "close relative" who is a national of Cuba, and persons traveling with them who share a common dwelling as a family with them, are authorized to engage in Cuba travel-related transactions pursuant to section 515.561(a)(1) of the Regulations. There is no limit on the duration or frequency of such travel to Cuba. Authorized expenditure limits for travel within Cuba are the same as for all other authorized categories of travel to Cuba (see section IV).

B. Persons visiting "close relatives" who are U.S. Government employees assigned to the U.S. Interests Section in Havana, Cuba

Persons visiting a "close relative" (see section II.A for a definition of "close relative") who is a U.S. Government employee assigned to the U.S. Interests Section in Havana, as well as persons traveling with them who share a common dwelling as a family with them, are authorized to engage in Cuba travel-related transactions pursuant to section 515.561(a)(2) of the Regulations. There is no limit on the duration or frequency of such travel to Cuba.

C. Journalists and support personnel

Journalists and supporting broadcast or technical personnel regularly employed in that capacity by a news reporting organization and traveling for journalistic activities are authorized to engage in Cuba travel-related transactions pursuant to section 515.563(a) of the Regulations. See section III.D below for information on specific licenses for free-lance journalists.

D. Official U.S. and foreign government travelers (traveling on official business)

U.S. and foreign government officials who are traveling on official business in their official capacities are authorized to engage in Cuba travel-related transactions pursuant to section 515.562 of the Regulations.

E. Officials of intergovernmental organizations of which the United States is a member (traveling on official business)

Officials of intergovernmental organizations, of which the United States is a member, who are traveling on official business in their official capacities, are authorized to engage in Cuba travel-related transactions pursuant to section 515.562 of the Regulations.

F. Full-time professionals engaging in travel related to:

1. Professional research

Full-time professionals are authorized to engage in Cuba travel-related transactions to conduct professional research in their professional areas pursuant to section 515.564(a)(1) of the Regulations, provided that their research (1) is of a noncommercial academic nature; (2) comprises a full work schedule in Cuba; and (3) has a substantial likelihood of public dissemination.

2. Professional meetings organized by an international professional organization

Full-time professionals are authorized to engage in Cuba travel-related transactions to attend professional meetings or conferences in Cuba pursuant to section 515.564(a)(2) of the Regulations, provided that (1) the meeting or conference is organized by an international professional organization, institution, or association that regularly sponsors meetings or conferences in other countries; (2) the organization, institution, or association sponsoring the meeting or conference is not headquartered in the United States unless it has been specifically licensed to sponsor the meeting; (3) the purpose of the meeting or conference is not the promotion of tourism in Cuba or other commercial activities involving Cuba that are inconsistent with the Regulations; and (4) the meeting or conference is not intended primarily to foster production of any biotechnological products.

G. Employees of a U.S. telecommunications services provider or an entity representing such a provider

Employees of a U.S. telecommunications services provider or an entity duly appointed to represent such a provider are authorized to engage in Cuba travel-related transactions under two separate general licenses. Each general license provides that the travelers' schedule of activities may not include free time, travel, or recreation in excess of that consistent with a full work schedule.

H. Employees of a producer or distributor of agricultural commodities, medicine, or medical devices or an entity representing such a firm

Individuals regularly employed by a producer or distributor of agricultural commodities, medicine, or medical devices or an entity duly appointed to represent such a producer or distributor are authorized to engage in Cuba travel-related transactions incident to the commercial marketing, sales negotiation, accompanied delivery, or servicing in Cuba of such items, provided that their schedule of activities does not include free time, travel, or recreation in excess of that consistent with a full work schedule and provided the activities appear consistent with the export or re-export licensing policy of the Department of Commerce. Please see section 515.533(e) of the Regulations for reporting and other requirements concerning these travel-related transactions.

III. WHO CAN GO TO CUBA PURSUANT TO A SPECIFIC LICENSE?

OFAC considers specific license requests on a case-by-case basis related to travel for the activities listed below. Please refer to the *Application Guidelines* for help with determining whether you may be eligible for a specific license. Individuals wishing to obtain a specific license must submit an application to OFAC, prepared either in letter format or using OFAC's automated application form, which is available on OFAC's website (www.treas.gov/ofac) at https://cubatravel.ofac.treas.gov/. Applicants must address the criteria set forth in the relevant section of the *Application Guidelines*. Applications should be mailed to the Licensing Division, Office of Foreign Assets Control, U.S. Department of the Treasury, 1500 Pennsylvania Avenue, NW, Washington, DC 20220.

A. Educational activities

OFAC may issue specific licenses for up to one year in duration to accredited U.S. undergraduate or graduate degree-granting academic institutions authorizing the institution, its students enrolled in an undergraduate or graduate degree program at the institution, and its full-time permanent employees to engage, under the auspices of the institution, in travel-related transactions incident to the activities listed below. Note that an individual relying on an academic institution's license must carry a letter from the licensed institution (the required content of the letter varies based on the type of activity). Please see the *Application Guidelines* and section 515.565 of the Regulations for more information on specific licenses for educational activities and related requirements. Note that for individuals whose academic institutions have not obtained a specific license, OFAC may issue a specific license to authorize the individual to engage in travel-related transactions incident to the activities described in section III.A.2 or section III.A.3, below.

1. Participation in a structured educational program

Participation in a structured educational program that includes at least 10 weeks in Cuba as part of a course offered at the licensed U.S. undergraduate or graduate institution.

2. Noncommercial, Cuba-related academic research

Noncommercial academic research in Cuba specifically related to Cuba and for the purpose of obtaining a graduate degree (i.e., the proposed research is independent research for writing a master's thesis, doctoral dissertation, or similar document).

3. Participation in a formal course of study at a Cuban academic institution

Participation in a formal course of study no shorter than 10 weeks at a Cuban academic institution provided the Cuban study will be accepted for credit toward the student's degree at the licensed U.S. institution.

4. Teaching at a Cuban academic institution

Teaching at a Cuban academic institution by an individual regularly employed in a teaching capacity at a licensed U.S. undergraduate or graduate institution, provided the teaching activities are related to an academic program at the Cuban institution and the teaching in Cuba is no shorter than 10 weeks.

5. Sponsorship of a Cuban scholar

Sponsorship, including payment of a stipend or salary, of a Cuban scholar teaching or engaging in other scholarly activities at a licensed institution in the United States.

6. Organization of and preparation for the educational activities described above

Organization of and preparation for the educational activities described above by full-time permanent employees of a licensed institution.

B. Religious activities

OFAC may issue specific licenses to religious organizations to authorize individuals affiliated with the organization to engage in travel transactions under the auspices of the religious organization. Applications by religious organizations for such licenses must include examples of the religious activities to be undertaken in Cuba. Travel-related transactions authorized by such a license must be for the purpose of engaging in a full-time program of religious activities in Cuba. All individuals traveling pursuant to a religious organization's license must carry with them a letter from the licensed organization citing the number of the license and confirming that they are affiliated with the organization and are traveling to Cuba to engage in religious activities under the auspices of the organization. Please see the *Application Guidelines* and section 515.566 of the Regulations for more information on specific licenses for religious activities.

Note that persons wishing to travel to Cuba to engage in religious activities that are not authorized pursuant to a religious organization's specific license may apply for a specific license to engage in these activities. Specific licenses may be issued authorizing transactions for multiple trips over an extended period of time to engage in a full-time schedule of religious activities in Cuba.

C. Humanitarian projects and support for the Cuban people

Specific licenses may be issued for (1) travel-related transactions intended to provide support for the Cuban people, such as activities of recognized human rights organizations; and (2) travel-related transactions directly incident to certain humanitarian projects in or related to Cuba that are designed to directly benefit the Cuban people. Licenses may be issued authorizing transactions for multiple trips over an extended period of time by applicants demonstrating a significant record of overseas humanitarian projects. Please see the *Application Guidelines* and sections 515.574 and 515.575 of the Regulations for more information on specific licenses for support for the Cuban people and humanitarian projects.

D. Free-lance journalism

Specific licenses may be issued for travel-related transactions incident to research in Cuba for a free-lance article, provided that certain conditions are met. Licenses may be issued for multiple trips over an extended period of time by applicants demonstrating a significant record of free-lance journalism. Please see the *Application Guidelines* and section 515.563(b) of the Regulations for more information on specific licenses for free-lance journalism.

E. Professional research and professional meetings

Specific licenses may be issued for travel-related transactions incident to professional research or to attend a professional meeting that does not meet the requirements of the relevant general license (described in section II.F.2) may apply for a specific license to engage in these activities. Licenses may be issued for multiple trips over an extended period of time by applicants demonstrating a significant record of research. Please see the *Application Guidelines* and section 515.564(b) of the Regulations for more information on specific licenses for professional research and meetings.

F. Public performances, athletic and other competitions, and exhibitions

Specific licenses may be issued for travel-related transactions incident to athletic competition by amateur or semi-professional athletes or teams traveling to Cuba to participate in an athletic competition held under the auspices of the relevant international sports federation. To qualify, the U.S. participants must have been selected for the competition by the relevant U.S. sports federation, and the competition must be one that is open for attendance and, in relevant situations, participation by the Cuban public.

Specific licenses may also be issued for travel-related and other transactions incident to participation in a public performance, athletic competition not covered by the above criteria, non-athletic competitions, or exhibition in Cuba. The event must be open for attendance and, in relevant situations, participation by the Cuban public, and all profits from the event after costs must be donated to an independent nongovernmental organization in Cuba or a U.S.-based charity, with the objective, to the extent possible, of benefiting the Cuban people. Please see the *Application Guidelines* and section 515.567(b) of the Regulations for more information regarding these specific licenses.

G. Activities of private foundations or research or educational institutions

Specific licenses may be issued for travel-related transactions incident to activities by private foundations or research or educational institutes that have an established interest in international relations to collect information related to Cuba for noncommercial purposes. Licenses may be issued for multiple trips over an extended period of time. Please see the *Application Guidelines* and section 515.576 of the Regulations for more information on specific licenses for the activities of private foundations or research or educational institutions.

H. Activities related to the exportation, importation, or transmission of information or informational materials

Specific licenses may be issued for travel-related transactions incident to the exportation, importation, or transmission of information or informational materials. Please see the *Application Guidelines* and section 515.545 of the Regulations for more information on these specific licenses.

I. Activities related to U.S. exportations to Cuba

Specific licenses may be issued authorizing travel-related transactions incident to the marketing, sales negotiation, accompanied delivery, or servicing in Cuba of exports that appear consistent with the export or re-export licensing policy of the Department of Commerce and are not authorized by the general licenses described above in sections II.G and II.H. (See section 515.533(g) of the Regulations.)

J. Persons visiting "close relatives" who are neither Cuban nationals nor U.S. government employees assigned to the U.S. Interests Section in Havana, Cuba

Specific licenses may be issued for travel-related and other transactions incident to travel to visit a "close relative" (see section II.A for a definition of "close relative") in Cuba who is neither a national of Cuba nor a U.S. Government employee assigned to the U.S. Interests Section in Havana (see section 515.561(b) of the Regulations).

IV. WHAT CUBA-RELATED TRAVEL TRANSACTIONS ARE AUTHORIZED BY OFAC LICENSES?

A. Generally

Unless authorized by a general or specific license, any person subject to U.S. jurisdiction who engages in any Cuba travel-related transaction violates the Regulations. Persons authorized to engage in Cuba travel-related transactions are allowed to engage in all transportation-related transactions ordinarily incident to travel *to and from* (not within) Cuba without any expenditure limitations. Authorized travelers also may engage in all transactions ordinarily incident to travel anywhere *within* Cuba, such as hotel accommodations, meals, local transportation, and goods personally used by the traveler in Cuba, provided that the total for such expenses does not exceed the State Department "per diem rate" Allowance for Havana, Cuba (http://aoprals.state.gov), in place during the period that the travel takes place (travelers can check the current per diem rate on the Internet at <<http://www.state.gov/www/perdiems/index.html>>) (see section 515.560(c) of the Regulations).

Pursuant to the separate travel sections referenced above, most authorized travelers may also spend additional money for transactions directly related to the authorized activities in Cuba. For example, journalists traveling in Cuba under the journalism general license (described above at section II.C) may spend money over and above the current per diem for extensive local transportation, the hiring of cable layers, and other costs that are directly related to covering a story in Cuba. Purchases of services unrelated to travel or a licensed activity, such as elective medical services, are prohibited. The purchase of publications, recorded music, and other informational materials is not restricted.

B. Vessels used for travel

All persons onboard vessels, including the owner and crew, must be authorized travelers, as listed above, to engage in travel-related transactions in Cuba. Unauthorized travelers may not purchase meals, pay for transportation, lodging, dockage or mooring fees, cruising fees, visas, or entry or exit fees. Vessel owners are prohibited from carrying passengers to Cuba , and vessels carrying goods or passengers to or from Cuba are prohibited from entering a U.S. port with such goods or passengers on board absent authorization from OFAC (see section 515.207(b) of the Regulations). Vessels traveling to Cuba are also subject to regulations implemented by the Department of Commerce (see 15 CFR Parts 730 *et. seq*) and the United States Coast Guard (see 33 CFR § 107.200 *et. seq*).

C. Travel Service Providers

Any person subject to U.S. jurisdiction who provides services akin to those of a travel agent (for example, arranging travel to, from, or within Cuba, selling tickets for direct charter flights between the United States and Cuba, reserving and selling accommodations for authorized travelers within Cuba, or other travel-related services involving property in which Cuba has an interest) must be specifically licensed as a Travel Service Provider prior to providing any of these services (see section 515.572(a)(1) of the Regulations). A traveler should not use any travel agent or tour operator in the United States that is not a Travel Service Provider. A list of authorized Travel Service Providers is available at http://www.treas.gov/offices/enforcement/ofac/programs/cuba/cuba_tsp.pdf. If you are interested in being licensed as a Travel Service Provider, please consult Circular 2006, which is available on the OFAC website (www.treas.gov/ofac) at http://www.treas.gov/offices/enforcement/ofac/programs/cuba/circ2006.pdf, for details on the Service Provider Program requirements.

D. Carrier Service Providers

Any person subject to U.S. jurisdiction who offers direct charter flights or vessel voyages between the United States and Cuba must be specifically licensed as a Carrier Service Provider prior to providing such services (see section 515.572(a)(2) of the Regulations). A list of authorized Carrier Service Providers is available at http://www.treas.gov/offices/enforcement/ofac/programs/cuba/cuba_tsp.pdf. If you are interested in being licensed as a Carrier Service Provider, please consult Circular 2006, which is available on the OFAC website (www.treas.gov/ofac) at http://www.treas.gov/offices/enforcement/ofac/programs/cuba/circ2006.pdf, for details on the Service Provider Program requirements.

V. WHAT CAN BE BROUGHT BACK FROM CUBA?

No goods of Cuban origin, other than information or informational materials, may be transported out of Cuba or brought into the United States (see section 515.560(c)(3) of the Regulations). There are no limits on the import or export of informational materials. Such materials—including books, films, posters, photographs, CDs—are statutorily exempt from regulation under the embargo and may be transported freely. However, blank tapes and blank CDs are not considered informational materials (see sections 515.206(a) and 515.332 of the Regulations).

VI. SENDING OR CARRYING MONEY TO CUBA: REMITTANCES

A. Family remittances

Pursuant to section 515.570(a) of the Regulations, persons subject to U.S. jurisdiction aged 18 or older is authorized (by general license) to send remittances to a "close relative" (see section II.A for a definition of "close relative") in Cuba or Cuban nationals in a third country, provided that the recipient is not a prohibited official of the Government of Cuba or a prohibited member of the Cuban Communist Party, as defined in sections 515.337 and 515.338 of the Regulations. There is no limit on the amount of such authorized remittances or the frequency with which they may be sent. The remittances must not be made from a blocked source and may not be for emigration-related purposes. An authorized traveler may carry up to $3,000 in authorized family remittances to Cuba (see section 515.560(c)(4) of the Regulations), and a national of Cuba departing the United States may carry back up to $3,000 received as remittances for him or herself (see section 515.560(d)(2) of the Regulations). Carrying remittances on behalf of others is prohibited.

B. Emigration-related remittances

Pursuant to section 515.570(b) of the Regulations, persons subject to U.S. jurisdiction are authorized (by general license) to send two one-time $1,000 remittances per payee to enable the payee to emigrate from Cuba to the United States. One remittance of no more than $1,000 may be sent before the payee has received a valid visa from the U.S. State Department or other approved U.S. immigration documents for the purpose of covering the payee's preliminary expenses associated with emigrating from Cuba to the United States.

Up to an additional $1,000 may be sent to a Cuban national for the purpose of enabling him or her to emigrate from Cuba to the United States, including for the purchase of an airline ticket and payment of exit or third-country visa fees or other travel-related fees, after the Cuban national has received a visa or other approved U.S. immigration document. A remitter must be able to provide the visa recipient's full name, date of birth, visa number, and visa date of issuance at the time this remittance is sent.

These emigration-related remittances may not be made from a blocked source except as discussed below in section VI.C. There is no limit to the amount of authorized per payee emigration-related remittances that an authorized traveler may carry to Cuba but none may be carried until a visa has been issued to each payee and the traveler can provide the visa recipient's full name, date of birth, visa number, and visa date.

C. Remittances from blocked accounts

Pursuant to a general license, all funds deposited in a blocked account in a banking institution in the United States held in the name of, or in which the beneficial interest is held by, a national of Cuba as a result of a valid testamentary disposition, intestate succession, or payment from a life insurance policy or annuity contract triggered by the death of the policy or contract holder may be remitted to that Cuban national provided that she or he is a "close relative" of the decedent. Such inherited blocked funds may also be remitted as emigration-related remittances in accordance with section VI.B. above to the Cuban national account-holder or beneficiary whether or not she or he is a "close relative" of the decedent. Up to $300 in any consecutive three-month period may also be sent from *any* blocked account in a banking institution in the United States to a Cuban national in a third country who is an individual in whose name, or for whose beneficial interest, the account is held. None of these remittances from blocked accounts may be remitted to a prohibited official of the Government of Cuba or a prohibited member of the Cuban Communist Party, as defined in sections 515.337 and 515.338 of the Regulations. Please see section 515.570(c) of the Regulations and section XII for more information on remittances from blocked accounts.

D. Specific licenses may be issued pursuant to section 515.570(d) to allow remittances to:

E. Remittance forwarders

Pursuant to section 515.572(c) of the Regulations, any person subject to U.S. jurisdiction (other than a depository institution, as discussed below) who seeks to provide services in connection with collecting, forwarding domestically, or transferring internationally authorized remittances must be specifically licensed as a Remittance Forwarder prior to providing any of these services. OFAC maintains a current list of Remittance Forwarders (other than depository institutions, which are authorized by general license), Travel Service Providers, and Carrier Service Providers on its website (www.treas.gov/ofac) at http://www.treas.gov/offices/enforcement/ofac/programs/cuba/cuba_tsp.pdf.

Depository institutions, as defined in section 515.333, are authorized by general license to forward remittances. To facilitate this, depository institutions are permitted to set up testing arrangements and exchange authenticator keys with Cuban financial institutions to forward authorized remittances, pursuant to section 515.572 of the Regulations. Depository institutions may not, however, open or use direct correspondent accounts with Cuban financial institutions.

Please consult Circular 2006, which is available on the OFAC website (www.treas.gov/ofac) at http://www.treas.gov/offices/enforcement/ofac/programs/cuba/circ2006.pdf, for details on the Service Provider Program requirements. Authorized Remittance Forwarders (including generally authorized depository institutions) must collect information from persons who use their services showing compliance with remittance provisions, must report to OFAC annually on their transactions, and retain the information for five years. Those seeking to become a Remittance Forwarders also should consult Circular 2006.

VII. GENERAL PROHIBITIONS ON EXPORTS, IMPORTS, AND CERTAIN OTHER TRANSACTIONS

A. Exporting to Cuba

Except for publications, other informational materials (such as CDs and certain artwork), certain donated food, certain licensed legal and telecommunications services, and certain goods licensed for export or re-export by the U.S. Department of Commerce (such as medicine and medical devices, food, agricultural commodities, and gift parcels), no products, technology, or services may be exported from the United States to Cuba, either directly or through third countries, such as Canada or Mexico, absent a specific license from OFAC. This prohibition includes dealing in or assisting with the sale of goods or commodities to or from Cuba, even if done entirely offshore.

Such brokering is considered to be dealing in property in which Cuba has an interest and is therefore prohibited. Provision of consulting services is also prohibited. Thus, no U.S. citizen or permanent resident alien, wherever located, and no foreign subsidiary or branch of a U.S. organization, may export products, technology, or services to Cuba or to any Cuban national, wherever they may be located, or broker the sale of goods or commodities to or from Cuba or any Cuban national.

Pursuant to section 515.533 of the Regulations, transactions ordinarily incident to the exportation of items from the United States to Cuba or the reexportation of 100% U.S.-origin items from a third country to Cuba are authorized by general license provided the export is licensed or otherwise authorized by the Department of Commerce. Pursuant to provisions of the Cuban Democracy Act of 1992 (the "CDA") and the Trade Sanctions Reform and Export Enhancement Act of 2000, the Commerce Department maintains a favorable license policy with respect to the sale and export or re-export of medicine and medical devices, food, and agricultural commodities to Cuba. Those interested in engaging in such exports or re-exports must first obtain authorization from the Commerce Department's Bureau of Industry and Security. All licensed sales must be financed by cash-in-advance or by third-country banks that are not persons subject to U.S. jurisdiction or owned or controlled by Cuba or Cuban nationals. Foreign subsidiaries of U.S. banks, however, are authorized to directly finance licensed sales of agricultural products. All U.S. banks may advise or confirm any of the transactions authorized above. Section 1705(b) of the CDA provides for donations of food to independent non-governmental organizations or individuals in Cuba. Shipments of food may be donated to non-governmental organizations from the U.S. or from third countries without a license from the U.S. government.

In the mid-1970s, section 515.559 was added to the Regulations to publicize OFAC's policy of licensing foreign subsidiaries of U.S. firms to conduct trade in commodities with Cuba so long as several specific criteria were met. Section 1706(a) of the CDA, however, prohibits the issuance of licenses that would have been issued pursuant to section 515.559, except where a contract was entered into prior to enactment of the CDA or where the exports at issue are medicines or medical supplies or certain telecommunications equipment. Accordingly, OFAC does not license foreign subsidiaries of U.S. firms to conduct trade in commodities with Cuba except in limited circumstances.

Pursuant to the CDA and section 515.207 of the Regulations, no vessel carrying goods or passengers to or from Cuba or carrying goods in which Cuba or a Cuban national has any interest may enter a U.S. port absent authorization from OFAC. The prohibition applies to vessels even if they enter only to take on fuel and supplies (bunker), whether from U.S. fuel providers within the port limits or at offshore points, as well as vessels discharging or loading merchandise offshore, by lighter or otherwise. In addition, vessels that enter a port or place in Cuba to engage in the trade of goods or services are prohibited from entering a U.S. port for the purpose of loading or unloading any freight for 180 days. Pursuant to section 515.550 of the Regulations, a general license authorizes entry into U.S. ports notwithstanding these two vessel prohibitions provided the vessel is engaging solely in trade with Cuba that is authorized by license or exempt from the Regulations (e.g., vessels carrying authorized exports of agricultural products or donations of food to nongovernmental organizations or individuals).

B. Importing Cuban-origin goods or services

No goods or services of Cuban origin (including most souvenirs) may be imported into the United States either directly or through third countries such as Canada or Mexico. The only exceptions are information or informational materials such as publications or certain artwork, defined in section 515.332 of the Regulations.

C. Transactions involving property in which Cuba or a Cuban national has an interest

In addition to the prohibitions on exports to and imports from Cuba, the Regulations prohibit any person subject to U.S. jurisdiction from dealing in any property in which Cuba or a Cuban national has or has had any interest. Under the Regulations, "property" includes but is not limited to contracts and services. For example, unless authorized, persons subject to U.S. jurisdiction (including U.S. overseas subsidiaries) may not purchase Cuban cigars in Mexico; may not sign a contract with a U.K. firm if the contract terms include Cuba-related provisions (even if those provisions are contingent upon the lifting of the embargo); and may not provide accounting, marketing, sales, or insurance services to a Cuban company or to a foreign company with respect to the foreign company's Cuba-related business.

D. Nationals of Cuba; specially designated nationals

The Regulations prohibit buying from or selling to Cuban nationals whether they are physically located on the island of Cuba or doing business elsewhere. Most transactions with nationals of Cuba who are lawfully present in the United States in a non-visitor status, however, are generally authorized by section 515.505 of the Regulations. Specific licenses may be granted on a case-by-case basis to unblock Cuban nationals permanently resident in third-countries.

Individuals or organizations who act on behalf of Cuba anywhere in the world are considered by OFAC to be nationals of Cuba. A non-exhaustive list of these names is published in the Federal Register, an official publication of the U.S. Government. This list may be obtained by calling OFAC at 800/540-6322 or on OFAC's website (www.treas.gov/ofac). The listing, however, is a partial one and any individual or organization subject to U.S. jurisdiction engaging in transactions with foreign nationals must make certain that such foreign nationals are not Cuban nationals.

E. Accounts and assets

There is a total freeze on Cuban assets, both governmental and private, and on financial dealings with Cuba; all property of Cuba and Cuban nationals in the possession or control of persons subject to U.S. jurisdiction is blocked. Any property in which Cuba or a Cuban national has an interest that comes into the United States or into the possession or control of persons subject to U.S. jurisdiction is automatically blocked by operation of law. Banks receiving unlicensed wire transfer instructions in which there is a Cuban interest, or any instrument in which there is a Cuban interest, must freeze the funds on their own books or block the instrument, regardless of origin or destination. "Suspense accounts" are not permitted. Blocking imposes a complete prohibition against transfers or transactions, aside from those authorized by the Regulations. Other payments, transfers, withdrawals, or other dealings may not take place with regard to blocked property unless authorized by the Treasury Department. Banks are permitted to take normal service charges. Blocked deposits of funds must be interest-bearing. "Set-offs" are not allowed.

Persons subject to U.S. jurisdiction should exercise extreme caution in order not to involve themselves in unlicensed transactions in which Cuba or a Cuban national has an interest. Except as authorized, no bank in the United States or overseas branch or subsidiary of a U.S. bank may advise a letter of credit involving Cuba or a Cuban national nor may it process documents referencing Cuba. All such property must be blocked as soon as it comes within the bank's possession or control. All persons in possession of blocked property are required to register with OFAC. Persons subject to U.S. jurisdiction who engage in any transaction involving Cuba or a Cuban national, either directly or indirectly, risk substantial monetary penalties and criminal prosecution.

VIII. HUMANITARIAN DONATIONS

There is joint OFAC and Department of Commerce administration over export of gift parcels and humanitarian goods to Cuba to meet basic human needs. OFAC generally licenses certain financial and other transactions related to exports that are licensed by the Commerce Department. See part 740 and 746 of the Department of Commerce's Export Administration Regulations (15 CFR Chapter 7), which are available online at www.access.gpo.gov/bis/ear/ear_data.html, for the relevant Department of Commerce regulations. Please note that travel-related transactions incident to humanitarian donations must be separately licensed by OFAC.

IX. SENDING GIFT PARCELS

The sending of gift parcels is covered by the Department of Commerce's regulations at 15 CFR Parts 740 and 746. Gift parcels may be sent or carried by an authorized traveler to an individual or to a religious, charitable, or educational organization in Cuba, subject to limitations set forth in the Department of Commerce's regulations.

Organizations that consolidate and send multiple gift parcels in single shipments must obtain a validated license from the U.S. Department of Commerce. Each gift parcel in the single shipment must meet commodity, dollar-value, and frequency limitations. If a parcel being shipped or carried to Cuba fails to meet these standards, it is subject to seizure by the U.S. Government. Please contact the Department of Commerce for specific restrictions and details.

X. MAIL AND TELECOMMUNICATIONS SERVICES IN CUBA

A. Mail

All transactions of common carriers incident to the receipt or transmission of mail between the United States and Cuba are authorized.

B. Telecommunications services

Certain telecommunications services, contracts, related payments, and travel-related transactions are authorized by general licenses, pursuant to sections 515.533, 515.542, and 515.564 of the Regulations.

XI. FAIR BUSINESS PRACTICES

Anyone authorized by the U.S. Department of the Treasury to provide Cuba travel-or remittance-related services is prohibited from participating in discriminatory practices of the Cuban government against individuals or particular classes of travelers. The assessment of consular fees by the Cuban government, which are applicable worldwide, is not considered to be a discriminatory practice. However, requiring the purchase of services not desired by the traveler is not permitted. Persons wishing to provide information on such activities should call OFAC's Miami office at 786/845-2829. All information regarding arbitrary fees, payments for unauthorized purposes, or other possible violations furnished to the U.S. Treasury Department will be handled confidentially.

XII. ESTATES

An estate becomes blocked whenever a Cuban national is an heir or is the deceased; money from a life insurance policy is blocked whenever the deceased or beneficiary is a Cuban resident. Please see section 515.570 of the Regulations (discussed above in section VI.) for more information about the ability to make certain remittances from inherited funds.

XIII. SAFE DEPOSIT BOXES

A safe-deposit box is blocked whenever a Cuban has an interest in the property contained in the box or an interest in the box itself. Access to a blocked safe deposit box is authorized under certain conditions. Please see section 515.517 of the Regulations for more information.

XIV. PAYMENTS FOR OVERFLIGHTS

A specific license is required to make payments for charges in connection with overflights of Cuba or emergency landings in Cuba. Banks should request to review the originals of such licenses before executing transfers and should keep a copy for their files. Please see section 515.548 of the Regulations for more information.

XV. EMERGENCIES

In case of emergencies while in Cuba, a traveler should contact the U.S. Interests Section in Havana at 537/833-3551. In case of emergencies requiring financial transactions such as emergency repair of vessels or medical treatment, travelers are urged to contact OFAC at 202/622-2480, to discuss necessary authorizations.

If you have information regarding possible violations of the Cuban Assets Control Regulations, please call OFAC at 786/845-2829. Your call will be handled confidentially.

This document is explanatory only and does not have the force of law. The statutes, Executive Orders, and implementing regulations relating to Cuba contain the legally binding provisions governing the sanctions, and this document does not supplement or modify those statutes, Executive Orders, or regulations.

The Treasury Department's Office of Foreign Assets Control also administers other sanctions programs involving, for example, certain countries and regimes, designated terrorists and international narcotics traffickers, Foreign Terrorist Organizations, and designated foreign persons who have engaged in activities relating to the proliferation of weapons of mass destruction. For additional information about these programs or about the Cuban sanctions program, please contact the:

OFFICE OF FOREIGN ASSETS CONTROL
U.S. Department of the Treasury
Washington, D.C. 800/540-6322
Miami, Florida 786/845-2829
www.treas.gov/ofac

STRATEGIC INFORMATION FOR CONDUCTING BUSINESS

The Republic of Cuba is an archipelago formed by the island of Cuba, with an extension of 106,007 km2, the Isle of Youth, with 2 200 km2 of surface, and around 4 200 keys and small islands. It's total surface covers 110 922 km2, lying at the entrance of the Gulf of Mexico, in the Caribbean Sea. It limits to the north with the peninsula of Florida (United States of America), at a distance of 180 km; to the south with Jamaica, at 140 km; to the east with Haiti, at 77 km, and to the west with the Yucatan peninsula (Mexico), which lies 210 km away.

Flat lands which cover 70% of its territory make Cuba an essentially plain territory, with three big mountain chains: Sierra de loss Organos, in the western region; Sierra del Escambray, in the center of the island, and Sierra Maestra in the eastern part, the latter including the main height in the country, Pico Real del Turquino, with 1 974 meters (5 933 feet) above sea level.

Cuba's climate is considered subtropical moderate, with predominance of tropical maritime conditions. The average annual temperature is 25,2 degrees Celsius (77 degrees F) in summer and 22 degrees C (71,6 degrees F) in winter, with two very well defined seasons: the dry season, from November through April, and the rainy season, from May through October.

Average rain fall totals 1 059 mm during the rainy season and 316 mm in the dry season, for an annual average of 1 375 mm.

The Cuban coasts have a length of 5 746 km, the north coast being the largest with 3 209 km. The coastal zones have numerous excellent beaches as well as bays, ports and cities.

According to estimated figures, Cuba's population reaches 11,2 M inhabitants, with an annual growth rate of 0,6 per 100. Since the decade of the 90s, a gradual aging of the population has become evident, the number of persons over 60 years of age now reaching 12,9% of the total.

Spanish is Cuba's official language, while English is used extensively in commercial and cultural circles as well as in international contacts.

Politically and administratively, Cuba is divided into 14 provinces, 158 municipalities and one special municipality.

From west to east, the provinces are Pinar del R¡o, La Habana, Ciudad de La Habana, Matanzas, Villa Clara, Cienfuegos, Sancti Spiritus, Ciego de Avila, Camagüey, Las Tunas, Holguín, Granma, Santiago de Cuba, Guantánamo y Las Villas. The special municipality of Isla de la Juventud (Isle of Youth) consists of that island, located south of the province of La Habana.

Ciudad de La Habana is Cuba's capital. Also important because of their economic development and population are the cities of Santiago de Cuba, Holguín, Camagüey, Cienfuegos, Matanzas, Pinar del Río, Ciego de Avila, Bayamo and Guantánamo.

Cuba is a socialist State of workers, independent and sovereign, organized as a unitary and democratic republic.

The National Assembly of People's Power is the supreme organ of power of the State, having constituent and legislative power in the Republic of Cuba as parliamentary regime.

The Council of Ministers is the highest executive and administrative organ and constitutes the government of the Republic of Cuba.

The country has only one political party: the Communist Party of Cuba.

The State is ruled by the Constitution of the Republic of Cuba, approved on February 24, 1976, with reforms introduced in July, 1992.

Education is free of cost at all levels, as well as the teaching materials. There are no illiterates in the country, which has 300 000 teachers more, 47 higher education centers and 300 OOO students.

There are universities or university faculties in all the provinces, as well as medium level, specialized, polytechnical and other educational centers.

Cuba's health care system, covering the whole country, is considered unique in Latin America. Medical services are free of cost for all Cuban citizens.

Cuba possesses the lowest infant mortality rate in Latin America and one of the lowest in the world. 7.2 out of 1000 born alive. Life expectancy reaches 75.2 years.

According to the Ministry of Public Health, in 1997 Cuba had 62624 doctors (56.8 / 10000 inhabitants) being 28855 family doctors (26.2 / 10000 inhabitants), 9816 dentists (26.2/ 10000inhabitants) 81333 nurses and assistants; 283 hospitals, 12 investigation institutes 440 policlinics, 166 dentist clinics, 26 blood banks, 164 medical offices, 220 mother's homes, 196 aged clinics and 27 homes for the physical disabled.

THE DOMESTIC POLITICAL SITUATION IN THE 1990S

During the mid-1990s the overriding domestic policy concern for Cuban leaders was to arrest the economic free-fall caused by the breakup of the Council of Mutual Economic Assistance (CMEA) and the Soviet Union and to establish a basis for future growth without significantly altering the current political regime. The economic crisis of the early 1990s, in which Cuba's Gross Domestic Product (GDP) declined by almost half, and already low living standards plummeted, was the greatest challenge to ever face Fidel Castro and the communist leadership. Faced with a sharp worsening of economic conditions on the island and the reemergence of small, isolated pockets of domestic opposition, the government resorted in the early 1990s to a dual policy of liberalization of the external economic sectors and heightened repression in an effort to head off an impending political crisis.

The political component of the regime's survival strategy began to take shape in 1991, when Fidel Castro dismissed any significant moves toward political liberalization at the PCC's Fourth Party Congress. At that Congress, Castro prepared the country for the so-called "zero-option," a strategy of economic autarchy designed to address the worst case scenario of a total cutoff of oil imports from Russia, to whom Cuba owed US$28 billion. The contingencies foreseen in the zero option were extreme. According to the plan, most motorized vehicles would be replaced by human and animal-powered transport, and Cuban farmers would resort to organic agriculture to compensate for an absence of fertilizer. Hundreds of thousands of urban dwellers would be compelled to move to the countryside to procure their own food. Under the logic of the zero-option plan, the prospects for legalization of an organized opposition became more remote than ever, given the purported need for absolute unity in a time of dire crisis. As part of a crackdown on dissidents and government opponents, the government established Rapid Reaction Brigades--civilian mobs organized by the Directorate of State Security (*Seguridad del Estado*) to intimidate and physically assault dissidents in so-called "acts of repudiation."

As economic conditions on the island continued to worsen and hopes for a democratic transition faded, the most desperate individuals--mainly young men in their twenties and thirties--began to take to the sea on homemade rafts bound for the United States. The number of rafters (*balseros*) rescued at sea by the United States Coast Guard rose nearly tenfold in three years, from 466 in 1990 to 4,169 in 1993.

In late 1993 and early 1994, there were growing signs of unrest and indications that the regime was losing its ability to maintain law and order. Nightly blackouts encouraged a rash of urban crime, and for the first time since the early 1960s the neighborhoods of Havana reverberated with the clanging of pots and pans in noisy antigovernment protests. In July 1993, a civil disturbance broke out in the fishing town of Cojímar, when residents attacked police who had fired on Cubans trying to escape the island. In October 1993, a second civil disturbance broke out in the Havana suburb of Regla, during the funeral of a man who had been shot and killed by police in another escape attempt.

Dramatic refugee departures continued to mount in early 1994, sparking an intensification of police presence in coastal areas and increased coastal patrols. In the first half of the year, thirteen boats were hijacked and diverted to the United States. Several aircraft, including an airliner and a military transport helicopter, were also hijacked and diverted to southern Florida. Some of the escape attempts produced violent clashes between police and the escapees. Alarmed over the thefts of state property and concerned that word of the dramatic refugee escapes would destabilize the regime, the government embarked on a crackdown against refugees caught attempting to flee the country.

On July 13, 1994, Cuban government fire boats rammed and sank a tugboat with 72 refugees aboard. Forty-one refugees, including 12 children, drowned as a result of the ramming which broke the tugboat in half. According to survivors, before the ramming, high pressure water hoses had been used against persons found above deck. After the boat sank, the pursuing government boats refused for more than 30 minutes to lend assistance to the survivors in the water. Only after a passing foreign vessel was seen observing the drama did Cuban Coast Guard boats attempt to rescue the survivors. In the aftermath, the Cuban government portrayed the incident as an accident, but the regime's actions were condemned as deliberate by Amnesty International and the Inter-American Commission on Human Rights. Shortly after the incident, Pope John Paul II sent a private message of condolence and solidarity to the families of the victims.

Social tension reached a peak on August 5, 1994, when several hundred (by some estimates more than a thousand) people rioted in a seafront Havana district. Videotape footage of the event showed rioters looting shops, battling police, and shouting anti-government slogans. This was the first major civil disturbance to take place in Havana since the consolidation of the regime in the early 1960s. Although the police regained control of the situation in a matter of hours, Cuban officials later admitted that they were badly shaken by the disturbance. Appearing on state-run Cuban television, Fidel Castro declared that Cuba would no longer prevent "illegal" departures from the island. During the next several weeks, tens of thousands of people congregated on the northwestern coast of Cuba seeking opportunities to emigrate from the island by sea. During August and early September, the United States Coast Guard intercepted more than 30,000 people in the Florida Straits attempting to flee Cuba on homemade rafts. A large number of empty rafts were also found at sea, suggesting that several hundred (by some estimates several thousand) people may have drowned while traveling on vessels.

Responding to the uncontrolled mass exodus and seeking to curb unsafe departures by raft, on August 19 the Clinton administration announced that Cubans intercepted at sea would no longer be granted automatic political asylum in the United States, but would instead be given safe haven at the United States Naval Base at Guantánamo Bay, Cuba. The flow of refugees continued unabated until September 9, 1994, when the Cuban and United States governments reached a migratory agreement to stem the exodus. In the September 9 agreement, Cuba agreed to use mainly "persuasive" means to prevent unsafe departures in exchange for United States approval of 20,000 visas annually to legal Cuban "migrants" (despite Cuba's commitment to employ nonviolent means to avoid departures, "attempted illegal departure" remains a felony carrying a 2-year prison sentence). The United States in turn would adopt a "wet feet vs. dry feet" policy toward Cuban refugees. Hereafter, Cuban refugees who make it to U.S. shores would be released to family and relatives in the United States, whereas those intercepted at sea by the U.S. Coast Guard would be immediately returned to Cuba unless a very strong claim for political asylum could be made.

In the aftermath of the August 1994 riot and the *balsero* crisis, the Cuban government took additional steps to alleviate shortages and stabilize the political situation. The most significant changes were the reestablishment of the farmers markets that had been shut down in 1986 and the authorization of individual self-employment in about 100 trades. In the meantime, the Cuban government continued to maintain a strict clampdown on independent civic organizations and opposition political activity.

GOVERNMENT STRUCTURE

COUNCIL OF MINISTERS

The Council of Ministers is a large cabinet-like body that comprises the leadership of all of the national-level ministries, state committees, and national institutes. The Council incorporates both the executive and the high-level administrative leadership of the national government. Article 98 of the 1976 constitution stipulates the broad powers of the Council of Ministers. These include the issuance of administrative regulations, the submission of a draft national budget to the National Assembly of Popular Power (Asemblea Nacional de Poder Popular--ANPP), and the handling of foreign policy. In addition, the Council of Ministers is responsible for "organizing and conducting the political, economic, cultural, scientific, social, and defense activities of the state as outlined by the National Assembly."

The Council of Ministers consists of a president, who is considered the head of government, a first vice president, and the heads of major ministries and central government agencies. Ministers are appointed by the ANPP at the initiative of the Council of State, headed by Fidel Castro. Within the Council of Ministers, there exists an Executive Committee comprising the president, the first vice president, the executive secretary, and five vice presidents. This group forms the inner cabinet within the Council of Ministers and is the highest administrative and executive authority of the Cuban state. Prior to a major cabinet reorganization in 1994, each Executive Committee member had oversight authority over a group of functionally related ministries. All Executive Committee members are also members of the PCC Politburo. By virtue of his dual presidency of the Council of Ministers and the Council of State, and his status as PCC first secretary and commander in chief of the armed forces, Fidel Castro is the most powerful figure in the Executive Committee and has a disproportionate influence over all executive decision making.

In April 1994, the central state apparatus was thoroughly reorganized in an effort to streamline the cumbersome bureaucracy and consolidate the activities of functionally related agencies. The reorganization of the bureaucratic framework established during the 1970s was most pronounced among the agencies dealing with economics, foreign trade, science and technology, and tourism--areas where supply-and-demand considerations were being introduced. These changes were a prelude to a systematic government downsizing that was begun in the summer of 1995.

The bureaucratic reorganization, carried out under the terms of Decree Law 147 of April 22, 1994, abolished several state committees and national institutes formerly belonging to the Council of Ministers and subsumed their operations under existing or new ministries. Significantly, the state committee structures that were abolished or absorbed were part of the central planning apparatus of the Cuban state. In addition, the reorganization law consolidated the National Academy of Sciences and the Executive Secretariat of Nuclear Affairs under a newly created Ministry of Science, Technology, and the Environment. The decree law also upgraded the National Tourism Institute to ministerial status.

A total of seven new ministries were created, while the organizational category of state committee was abolished and the number of national institutes was reduced. The newly established ministries are Economy and Planning; Finances and Prices; Foreign Investment and Economic Cooperation; Labor and Social Security; Metallurgy and Electronics Industry; Science, Technology, and the Environment; and Tourism.

The Executive Committee of the Council of Ministers was also reorganized. Two of seven vice presidencies were abolished and the oversight authority of vice presidents over clusters of ministries was revoked. Instead, vice presidents would chair interagency task forces and committees, but would not necessarily exercise executive authority beyond their respective ministries. This latter provision, which is apparently intended to reduce potential turf battles among ministers, also reduces the chances that any single individual might develop an inter-bureaucratic power base from which to challenge Castro's authority.

In January 1995, the Cuban government announced a second major cabinet reshuffle, this time affecting only the economics and trade-related ministries. Eight cabinet-level officials, including two vice presidents of the Council of Ministers, were removed in an effort to place reform-minded technocrats in high-level economic posts. The appointments were widely believed to have been taken at the initiative of Carlos Lage, the recently appointed secretary of the Council of Ministers and a key figure in Cuba's economic reform process. In an interview published by the official daily, Granma, in January, Lage described the cabinet changes as "favoring the reorganization of the state apparatus with the participation of other valuable cadres" with the objective of making the state "more rational, more energetic, more efficient, less costly and adjusted to the conditions we face today."

COUNCIL OF STATE

The Council of State serves as the permanent committee of the ANPP when the Assembly is not in session. The Council of State, which is comparable to the Presidium of the Supreme Soviet of the former Soviet Union, can issue decree laws, propose legislation and constitutional reforms, and appoint and dismiss ministers. All of these activities are closely coordinated with the PCC. The Council of State has thirty-one members, elected from among ANPP deputies who are also top PCC leaders. Thus, Fidel and Raúl Castro, as well as most of the PCC Politburo, are periodically elected to the Council of State in orchestrated Assembly votes.

The Council of State includes a president, a first vice president, five vice presidents, a secretary, and twenty-three regular members. According to the constitution, the Council of State president is officially the head of state. This position, along with the presidency of the Council of Ministers, has always been held by Fidel Castro. By virtue of his dual status as head of state and government, and his authority as PCC first secretary, Castro is able to control and coordinate executive and legislative decision making. Castro's presidency of the Council of State also gives him legal authority to appoint and remove government ministers. Castro's presidential authority thus complements his control over personnel and policy decisions as PCC first secretary. As president, Castro may also assume personal command of any government ministry during a crisis. A 1992 amendment to the constitution made explicit the president's authority to assume direct command over the armed forces under conditions of national emergency, thereby reaffirming Castro's status as commander in chief.

There is a pronounced overlap of membership in the Council of State and the PCC Politburo, with sixteen out of thirty-one Council of State members being Politburo members as well. The majority presence of Politburo members within the Council of State guarantees that all internal decisions, decided by majority vote, coincide with PCC directives. The Council of State thus serves, along with the Council of Ministers, as a fail-safe legal channel for PCC control of the state.

The Council of State also usurps the legislative authority of the National Assembly. The Council of State's decree law authority renders the ANPP little more than a rubber stamp parliament, convened during brief biannual sessions in order to ratify directives from the PCC leadership. As a permanent committee of an elected National Assembly, the Council of State provides a thin democratic façade to authoritarian rule by Fidel Castro and the top leadership of the PCC.

NATIONAL ASSEMBLY

The National Assembly of People's Power (Asamblea Nacional del Poder Popular--ANPP) was established by the 1976 constitution as the unicameral national legislature.

The Assembly, which currently has 589 members representing territorial districts nationwide, is directly elected every five years. Elections to the ANPP are noncompetitive, with the nominating and voting process under the control of the local PCC organizations, such as the Committees for the Defense of the Revolution (CDRs) and other mass organizations. Campaigning is prohibited, and the main criterion for electibility is commitment to the Revolution under the direction of the PCC and the leadership of Fidel Castro. Candidates are usually nominated on the basis of their personal popularity and their "active integration" into the political system. The latter quality is essential to being placed on the candidate list because dissidents, regime opponents, and even mild critics of the regime are systematically shut out of the nominating process. Seventy percent of the current Assembly membership are either PCC members or members of PCC-affiliated organizations, and all appear to be loyal to the status quo.

Although it is legally empowered by the constitution to debate and pass legislation, in practice the ANPP general chamber abdicates all substantive decision-making authority to the Council of

State, whose thirty-one members are elected from among the Assembly's ranks. The debility of the Assembly is assured by the infrequency and short duration of its biannual plenary sessions, which last no more than two weeks. Although the Assembly has eight standing committees, they do not exercise any effective authority to publicly debate or modify bills. During its biannual plenums, the Assembly plays a passive role as audience for various government speakers. Once the Council of State's legislative proposals have been presented, they are summarily ratified by unanimous or near unanimous vote of the general chamber.

ANPP deputies, who are predominantly young and politically inexperienced PCC members with minimal background in parliamentary procedure, are little inclined to challenge the party leadership in public debate. Moreover, deputies are amply aware that--proclamations of collegiality notwithstanding--any attempt to challenge the leadership on substantive issues is paramount to political and professional suicide. Like membership in the PCC Party Congress, an ANPP deputyship is generally considered an honorific position, usually granted as a reward for loyalty and valuable service to the Revolution. Moreover, the remarkably high rate of turnover within the ANPP--83 percent in the last election--prevents deputies from forging an independent power base. Perhaps the most telling indicator of parliamentary weakness is the ANPP's lack of a permanent meeting place. During its brief sessions, the ANPP convenes in the Havana Convention Center, while the historic national Capitol building, towering formidably over the city center, houses a government ministry.

The Council of State is not representative of the Assembly membership, but consists instead of high PCC officials, including members of the Politburo, who also hold ANPP seats. Thus, Fidel Castro, who holds a deputyship from Santiago de Cuba and has been president of the Council of State since the office was created, is periodically reelected by unanimous vote of the general chamber. Under the supervision of the ANPP president, a position currently held by Politburo member Ricardo Alarcón, Castro's nominees for the remaining thirty seats in the Council of State are ratified by unanimous or near-unanimous vote. Among the top Politburo members elected to the Council of State, Raúl Castro customarily occupies the first vice presidency.

JUDICIARY

Article 120 of the 1976 constitution establishes the People's Supreme Court as the nation's high court and authorizes the creation of lower courts. The Supreme Court is organized into five chambers: criminal, civil and administrative, labor, state security, and military. The lower court system comprises fourteen people's provincial courts and 169 people's basic courts at the municipal level.

Under Cuba's Marxist-Leninist legal system, the judiciary is not recognized as an independent branch of government but is instead subordinate to the Council of State and the ANPP. In practice, the courts are nearly powerless to defend individuals against acts of the state, especially when dealing with politically relevant cases. There is no known instance of a revolutionary Cuban court ruling against the government in a political trial. Moreover, the Court is not authorized to decide on constitutional matters, a prerogative legally held by the ANPP. The Court is thus limited to ruling on individual civil and criminal cases.

Justices of the People's Supreme Court--about half of whom are PCC members--are nominated by the Council of State and are elected by the ANPP. Lower court judges are nominated by the Ministry of Justice and are elected by their respective provincial and municipal assemblies. In addition to its 700 professional judges, the Cuban judiciary employs 14,000 "lay judges," who share the bench with the professionals. The ostensible purpose of the lay judges is to inject popular attitudes and values into the administration of justice. In practice, lay judges are used to pack the courts with PCC loyalists. In this manner, the regime undermines the judiciary's institutional autonomy and ensures that all judicial rulings are sympathetic to the government and the PCC.

CUBAN COMMUNIST PARTY

Since the mid-1960s, Cuba's sole legally recognized political party, the PCC, has been the paramount institution of the regime. In the early 1990s, the PCC claimed almost 1.5 million members, or approximately 10 percent of the population. The party is rooted in an uneasy alliance among the core leaderships of fidelista veterans of the "26 of July" movement and members of the former Popular Socialist Party (Partido Socialista Popular--PSP), Cuba's pro-Soviet communist party. Although Fidel Castro declared his allegiance to Marxism-Leninism in the early 1960s, it was not until the ratification of the constitution of 1976 that the PCC's hegemony over society and the political system came to resemble that of Soviet and East European communist regimes. Article 5 of the constitution of 1976 recognizes the PCC--whose organization and activities intrude on practically all aspects of Cuban life--as the "organized vanguard of the Cuban nation" and "the supreme guiding force of society and the state."

The PCC performs many roles within Cuban society. Among them, the most important is that of ideological "rudder" of the regime. As the sole institution with exclusive authority to decide fundamental political, economic, and social issues, the PCC determines the parameters within which all other institutions--most notably the state--may operate. Working in concert with a network of mass organizations under its control, the PCC is also a vital intermediary between the regime and society, bearing principal responsibility for propaganda, socialization, and elite recruitment. The PCC's capacity to act as the exclusive intermediary between regime and society derives from its singular influence over the state (the country's only legal employer), the mass media, and the education system.

Through its Committees for the Defense of the Revolution (Comités por la Defensa de la Revolución--CDRs), the PCC also serves as the regime's most important instrument of control over society. The CDRs, which consist of approximately 80,000 neighborhood block committees, are one of the key totalitarian components of the political system. They keep civil society atomized and weak by usurping its functions and preventing its resurgence through surveillance, intimidation, and constant interference in the private sphere. The mass organizations also hinder the development of civil society by monopolizing the public sphere and claiming exclusive representation of officially recognized social and occupational groups.

PARTY CONGRESS

Following the practice of the former Soviet Union and East European communist parties, the PCC convenes party congresses every five years to review and adjust its policies and institutions and to map out national strategy for the next five-year period. Party congresses, typically lasting one to two weeks, are large gatherings of hundreds of delegates from all sectors of the PCC, as well as the top party leadership. The PCC held party congresses in 1975, 1980, 1986, 1991 and, most recently, in February 1997.

Like other large representative gatherings in Cuba, party congresses serve mainly as a forum for the introduction of new initiatives by the top PCC leadership, rather than as an arena for debate of fundamental issues. The general chamber does not formulate policy, but merely ratifies decisions made in advance by the PCC leadership. In preparation for the congress, working groups may be assembled to elaborate the new party program, but these tend not to contravene the policy preferences of the top leadership. Whereas the working groups may discuss in closed session issues beyond the scope of the leadership's agenda, only proposals approved in advance by the Politburo are brought to the floor of the general chamber. In the final reckoning, a party congress only goes as far to initiate reform as it is allowed to go by Fidel Castro and the top Politburo membership.

Despite their theatrical character, the congresses draw the attention of domestic and international observers because they portend significant change in PCC institutions and policies. The First Congress, held in 1976, ratified the current constitution and marked the beginning of the "institutionalization" of the regime along Soviet lines; the Second Congress in 1980 emphasized improving economic efficiency and accepted minor concessions to economic rationality by authorizing the formation of the farmers' markets. The Third Congress in 1986 initiated the process of "rectification," wherein the Party was exhorted to return to its socialist ideological roots and the farmers' markets experiment was discontinued.

The Fourth Party Congress was especially significant because it coincided with the crisis and collapse of Soviet and East European communism and the disbanding of the Council of Mutual Economic Assistance (CMEA) trade and aid system. These extraordinary events presented a formidable challenge to Cuba's political and economic institutions. In the wake of the collapse of its key trading partners and the international repudiation of its totalitarian political model, the regime faced its most severe test of survival since the early 1960s.

Prior to the Fourth Congress, a number of observers had speculated that Fidel Castro might accept incremental political and economic reforms as a tactical move to relegitimize the regime and avoid a violent Romania-style rupture. Instead, Castro--who had opposed Mikhail Gorbachev's policy of restructuring (perestroika) in the Soviet Union--reaffirmed single-party rule and rejected the possibility of legalizing alternative political organizations. In the economic arena, however, the Congress approved a constitutional amendment that allowed the return of foreign direct investment (after a thirty-year hiatus) and authorized self-employment in a limited number of service sector occupations. In addition, the PCC announced an end to discrimination against Roman Catholics and other religious groups by allowing religious believers to join the party. Finally, Castro conceded to changing external circumstances and disavowed any further attempts to spread revolution to the Third World. Thus, Jorge Domínguez observes that the Fourth Party Congress:

> in short, was not responsive to the wishes of those who wanted to liberalize and democratize Cuba substantially, but it was responsive to some of the wishes of its core constituency, the middle-level cadres who staffed the regime and on whose personal prestige, the polls showed, the allegiance of ordinary citizens rested.

The Fourth Party Congress also produced significant institutional change within the PCC. Pursuing a policy of political retrenchment, Castro engineered a far-reaching purge of reform-minded leaders within the party and strengthened his own position as the central figure in the regime. The Fourth Congress also approved a high turnover of Politburo and Central Committee members in a process whereby young and inexperienced cadres replaced more established leaders who could potentially challenge Castro's authority. Upon Castro's initiative, the Congress abolished the PCC Secretariat and eliminated candidate membership in the Politburo. By absorbing some of its former candidate members and adding several new members, the Politburo was expanded to twenty-five posts.

CENTRAL COMMITTEE

The principal institution of the PCC between party congresses is the Central Committee. The Committee, which consists of 150 high-ranking party members (including the PCC Politburo), oversees party activities at all levels of the state and society and is responsible for carrying forward the programs initiated at the congresses. In addition to the top PCC political leadership at the national and provincial levels, the current Central Committee also includes members of the armed forces, municipal party secretaries, leaders of mass organizations, the heads of large state enterprises, and a variety of PCC activists from the fields of economics, education, medicine, the sciences, and sports.

Central Committee members are selected from among delegates to the party congresses. Although the general chamber of the Central Committee delegates day-to-day governing authority to the Politburo, membership in the larger body confers high prestige and is a stepping stone toward appointment to the highest organizations of the party and the state.

In October 1990, the Central Committee's bureaucracy was cut back as part of a broader effort to reduce waste and excessive interference by the PCC in administrative affairs. The Committee's nineteen departments were consolidated into nine, and its work force was cut by half. However, the Committee was given special powers to circumvent local, provincial, and national state and party organs in the event of a national emergency requiring rapid popular mobilization. The Central Committee was also authorized, through the Politburo, to override the decisions of government ministries in situations of national emergency.

POLITBURO

The Politburo, which is appointed from the ranks of the Central Committee, is the highest authority of the Cuban political system. It not only sets party policy, but also "recommends" legislative and executive action to be taken by the state. The coordination of party and state policies is facilitated by the overlapping partisan, legislative, and executive responsibilities of key leaders in the Cuban political system, most notably Fidel Castro.

Castro's indefinite tenure as "Maximum Leader" is recognized in the preamble to the constitution, which mentions him by name as the founder and head of the Cuban revolutionary process being carried forward by the PCC. His legal authority over the "party-state" stems from his dual occupancy of the highest party and government posts, as reflected in his formal titles of president of the Council of State and of the Council of Ministers, first secretary of the PCC Politburo, and commander in chief of the Revolutionary Armed Forces. Castro is thus the unchallenged head of state, head of government, and chairman of the PCC. This arrangement is consistent with the organic concept of the state promoted by the constitution, which accepts the tutelary role of the PCC in the affairs of state.

In addition to Fidel and Raúl Castro, the Politburo includes influential government ministers, provincial PCC party secretaries, the leaders of some of the mass organizations, and high-ranking military officers. The Fourth Party Congress approved substantial structural and personnel changes to the Politburo. Veteran revolutionary leaders such as Minister of Culture Armando Hart Dávalos and Women's Federation president Vilma Espín were replaced by younger Castro loyalists, such as former Union of Young Communists General Secretary Roberto Robaina González, President of the Writers' and Artists' Union Abel Prieto Jiménez, and presidential staff member Carlos Lage Dávila. In all, eleven of the Politburo's twenty-five members have been appointed since 1991. Of the eleven new members, none was older than forty-nine at the time of his or her appointment.

Castro's courting of young fidelistas at the expense of senior party leaders appeared to fulfill a dual purpose. First, it strengthened Castro's relative authority by reducing the amount of collegiality within the inner policymaking elite. Instead of having to deal with fellow "historic figures" (históricos)--who, as Castro's contemporaries, hold significant independent authority--Castro would preside over a cabinet containing far more junior subordinates. Lacking the standing of their predecessors and owing their political rise to Castro, these new Politburo members are considered less likely to challenge the "Comandante's" initiatives or to question his judgment in internal policy debates.

A second reason for Castro's overtures to young cadres stems from his desire to reverse widespread alienation among Cuban youth from the political culture of the Revolution. By promoting popular young leaders such as Roberto Robaina, the regime appeared to revitalize itself, despite the fact that, as Castro's foreign minister, Robaina exercised little independence in formulating policy. The appointment of a young foreign minister was also designed to elicit a favorable reaction in the foreign media. However, despite their youth, there is little indication that the new crop of revolutionary leaders is any more inclined to introduce fundamental political reform than their predecessors--at least not while Castro remains in office.

In contrast to the stagnation he has imposed on political affairs, Castro has yielded to economic necessity by allowing his chief economic advisor, Carlos Lage, to pursue limited economic reforms. The dire shortage of foreign exchange since the collapse of the CMEA has forced Castro grudgingly to accept the introduction of joint ventures with foreign corporations, primarily in the tourism industry. Since the approval of a constitutional amendment allowing foreign direct investment and the legalization of dollar transactions and limited self- employment in 1993, Lage's economic team has cautiously proceeded with reforms intended to steer foreign hard currency into state coffers and bring the large black market economy under profitable regulation by the state (see Economy). However, reforms of the domestic economy have lagged far behind those of the external sectors, providing only minimal relief to the Cuban population.

DECISION MAKING

Within Cuba's totalitarian political system, state-society relations follow Fidel Castro's well-known maxim: "Within the Revolution everything; outside the Revolution nothing." Thus, the regime is somewhat receptive to currents of opinion within its own ranks and within the broader "revolutionary family" (the PCC and the mass organizations under its control). However, regime leaders do not recognize the rights of expression of individuals who are not "integrated" or those whose dissenting views surpass established limits.

Within the hierarchical structure of the PCC, the main organizing principle is that of "democratic centralism," wherein the lower levels of the party are accountable to the higher levels, which presumably rule by popular mandate. The PCC proclaims the sovereignty of the people and goes to extraordinary lengths to generate the appearance of mass participation. Consequently, it generates great fanfare over its theatrical electoral processes, and it employs sophisticated polling techniques to discern the popularity of its policies. "Participation" in the Cuban context generally does not entail open, adversarial debate on substantive issues.

Instead, consultation between the party hierarchy and the rank-and-file more often than not involves orchestrated ratification of the leadership's agenda. Instances of public disagreement on fundamental political issues are rare, and these usually result in the purging of the offending subordinate if he or she happens to be on the "wrong" side of an issue of importance to the top leadership (such was the suspected fate of former Foreign Minister Roberto Robaina, who was replaced in 1998 and subsequently disappeared from public view). As a result, deviation from the official line on matters submitted for discussion does not take the form of a rejection of the leadership's objectives or a questioning of its motives, but is framed in the form of "suggestions" relating to peripheral issues. Thus, even within the PCC rank and file, communication is constrained by self-censorship and the prevailing attitude among the lower levels is one of complacency.

Public opinion is not considered by government leaders in deciding matters pertaining to the fundamentals of the political system or in addressing issues of vital interest to the top leadership. Thus, for example, when Fidel Castro decided in 1986 that the highly popular farmers' markets introduced earlier in the decade were undermining socialism and the regime's economic control capabilities, he decreed their closure without the benefit of public debate. The regime is not completely unresponsive to currents of public opinion, however. It is willing to accommodate, in certain instances, some of the demands of the PCC-affiliated mass organizations. In the past, mass organization leaders have expressed reservations over policies of the central administration that adversely affect their constituents. Nevertheless, most such disagreements are voiced discreetly in private and are always carefully worded to avoid any implied criticism of Fidel or Raúl Castro.

REPRESSION OF DISSENT

Whereas the regime demonstrates some flexibility in accommodating the demands of its partisans, its response to public dissidence and opposition has consistently been uncompromising and repressive. During the first two decades of the Revolution, thousands of regime opponents, including many individuals who today would be classified as prisoners of conscience, were executed by firing squad or "disappeared" in prison. During the 1960s, the Castro regime's campaign to destroy the autonomous institutions of civil society produced a raft of excesses, including mass deportations and imprisonments, and--during the mid-1960s--the internment of opponents and suspicious individuals in agricultural labor camps. During the 1970s, it is estimated that Cuba's prison system held more than 40,000 long-term political prisoners, giving Cuba one of the world's highest per capita rates of political incarceration.

During the late 1970s and early 1980s, approximately 20,000 political prisoners were freed on condition that they immediately leave the country. In its 2000 Annual Report, Amnesty International classifies approximately 300 imprisoned Cubans as political prisoners, but acknowledges that its estimates are conservative. Amnesty International and Human Rights Watch/Americas have consistently reported ill treatment of detainees in prisons and police stations, and frequent short-term detention and harassment of human rights and political activists.

In 1992 Freedom House documented dozens of cases of political detainees being subjected to unnecessary psychiatric treatments, including multiple doses of electroshock therapy, in efforts to alter their personalities and as a method of torture. Political prisoners are regularly subjected to physical and psychological torture, including beatings, neglect, and isolation in cramped, unventilated cells. Political prisoners are also frequently housed alongside common criminals, including violent felons. Prison conditions are known to be extremely poor through testimonial evidence and through evidence gathered by the United Nations Commission on Human Rights (UNCHR).

From 1991 until 1997, the UNCHR designated a Special Representative (upgraded in 1992 to Special Rapporteur) to investigate the human rights situation in Cuba. The Cuban government consistently denied the Special Rapporteur permission to enter the country and refused to respond to the Rapporteur's written inquiries on human rights matters. Based on reports from Cuba's independent human right groups, every year but one since 1991, the UNCHR has adopted resolutions condemning Cuba's human rights record. For example, in 1995, the Commission approved a resolution that regretted profoundly Cuba's violations of basic human rights and fundamental freedoms and expressed "particular concern at prevailing intolerance for freedom of speech and assembly in Cuba."

Government encroachment on the rights of Cuban citizens is systematic. Rights violations are carried out within the parameters of the legal system and at the behest of the highest political authorities. The Cuban constitution of 1976 recognizes only "social rights," and prioritizes these over the civil liberties of individuals. The Cuban Penal Code does not meet international standards of due process and protection of individual rights. Among the felonies listed in the code are thought crimes such as "dangerousness," "illegal association," and "dissemination of enemy propaganda." These charges, which carry sentences ranging from one to fifteen years, are often lodged against nonviolent political dissidents and human rights monitors. More vocal opponents who call for fundamental political change may be charged with "rebellion," which carries sentences exceeding fifteen years and, in some cases, may warrant capital punishment. Individuals who are convicted of insulting the commander in chief face prison sentences of up to three years, and Cubans caught attempting to emigrate illegally may be imprisoned for up to two years. Trial procedures are skewed against defendants, who do not enjoy the right of habeas corpus and are usually not assigned a public defender until the actual date of their trial.

The regime not only violates basic civil liberties, but also uses political criteria to discriminate in the provision of employment, education, and social services. Thus, for example, individuals who display "antisocial" tendencies may be denied promotions or may be dismissed altogether from their jobs, or their children may be expelled from universities. Human rights monitors and independent journalists who attempt to report on Cuban human rights conditions have had their telephone service and other utilities disconnected and their communications equipment confiscated. These and other sanctions provide the government with a broad range of lesser coercive mechanisms to dissuade the discontented from joining opposition groups.

During crisis situations, the regime has used emigration as a "safety valve" to rid itself of dissatisfied elements of society. The result has been a diaspora of more than 1.5 million people during the past four decades. Most refugees have fled to the United States, Canada, Spain, and several countries of Latin America. The majority of Cuban refugees have settled in the United States, mostly in southern Florida, home to the largest Cuban exile community.

OFFICIAL CORRUPTION

Despite official rhetoric extolling egalitarianism and the regime's purported commitment to "the new socialist man," corruption and clientelism are endemic to Cuban institutions, almost all of which are controlled by the state. Like a well-oiled urban political machine, the regime relies on the allocation of goods and services based on demonstrated political loyalty to maintain the support of the military and the Communist Party rank and file. In the circumstances of scarcity that pervade life in Cuba, and with the discrediting of Communism as the legitimizing ideology of the regime, government largesse has become a highly effective method of maintaining the support of traditional regime loyalists within the Communist Party (PCC).

High PCC functionaries and military officers constitute a privileged class (mayimbes) within Cuban society. They enjoy a variety of perks, including luxury housing, priority access to scarce transportation resources, freedom to travel overseas and to import foreign luxury items duty free, and access to segregated medical and recreational facilities. Moreover, the children of high party functionaries enjoy superior educational opportunities and are exempted from the military draft and from agricultural labor.

In 1997 Forbes magazine placed Fidel Castro among the world's richest individuals, with a personal fortune estimated at US$1.5 billion. Many observers have suggested that this is a conservative estimate. It is rumored that Castro maintains more than a dozen residences across Cuba, as well as large tracts of land for personal recreational use.

In addition to traditional forms of corruption, strong evidence emerged during the 1980s of Cuban involvement in international organized crime. Evidence from that period suggests that high-ranking officials, most notably Armed Forces head, Raul Castro, knowingly allowed Cuban territory and military facilities to be used for the transshipment of narcotics into the United States

The 1989 drug scandal that led to the trial and execution of Division General Arnaldo Ochoa Sánchez and several other high-ranking military officers provided a wealth of information on the lifestyles of Cuban officials and on alleged government- sponsored participation in drug trafficking. Testimonies from the trial corroborated allegations by Cuban government defectors that Cuban officials, under the direction of Minister of Interior José Abrantes and with the tacit consent of Raúl Castro had cooperated with the Colombian Medellín Cartel in transshipping cocaine bound for the United States.

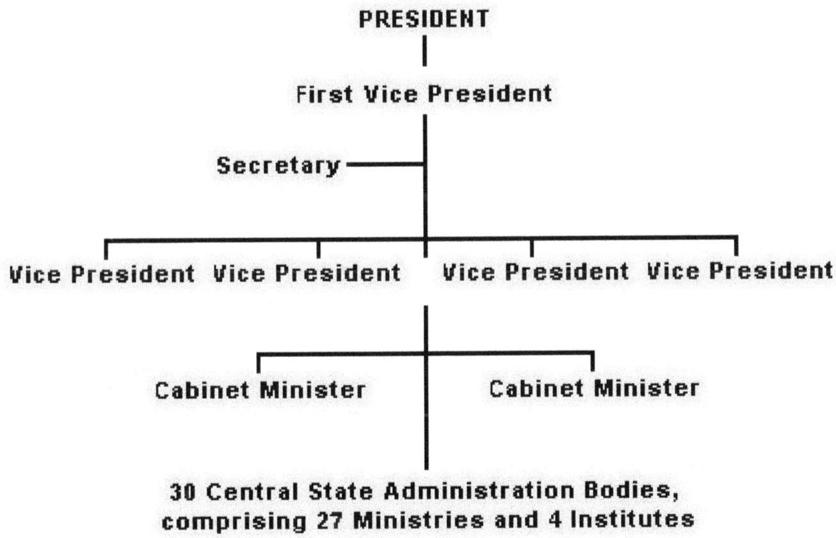

COUNCIL OF STATE

Members of the Council of State elected by the Cuban Parliament - February 24, 1998

PB indicates a member of the Politburo of the Communist Party.		
President:		
	Fidel Castro Ruz (PB)	First Secretary of the Central Committee of the Cuban Communist Party, President of the Council of Ministers
First Vice-President:		

	Raul Castro (PB)	Second Secretary of the Cuban Communist Party, First Vice-President of the Council of Ministers, Minister of the Armed Forces
Vice Presidents:		
	Juan Almeida Bosque (PB)	Commander of the Revolution
	Corps Gen. Abelardo Colome Ibarra (PB)	Minister of the Interior
	Carlos Lage Davila (PB)	Vice President of the Council of Ministers, Secretary of the Executive Committee of the Council of Ministers
	Jose Ramon Machado Ventura (PB)	Chief of the Organization Department of the Central Committee of the Communist Party
	Esteban Lazo Hernandez (PB)	First Secretary of the Communist Party in Havana
Secretary:		
-	Jose Miguel Miyar Barrueco	-
Members: (Holdovers)		

	Pedro Miret Prieto (PB)	Vice President of the Council of Ministers
	Jose Ramon Balaguer Cabrera (PB)	Head of the Department of Intl. Relations and Ideology of the Communist Party
-	Vilma Espin Guillos	President of the Cuban Women's Federation
-	Armando Hart Davalos	Director of the Jose Marti Programs Office
-	Orlando Lugo Fonte	President of the National Assn. of Small Farmers
	Felipe Ramon Perez Roque	Foreign Minister Personal Assistant to Fidel Castro
	Marcos Portal Leon (PB)	Minister of Basic Industry
	Pedro Ross Leal (PB)	Secretary-General of the Cuban Worker's Union
	Rosa Elena Simeon Negrin	Minister of Science and Technology
New Members:		
	Sergio Corrieri Hernandez	President of the Cuban Friendship Institute

	Roberto Diaz Sotolongo	Minister of Justice
	Jose Luis Rodriguez Garcia	Minster of Economy and Planning
-	Caridad del Rosario Diego Bello	Head of Office of Religious Affairs of the Communist Party
-	Salvador Antonio Valdes Mesa	Minister of Labor and Social Security
-	Roberto Fernandez Retamar	President of Casa de las Americas
-	Regla Martinez Herrera	President of the Consejo Popular de los Sitios of Havana
-	Maria Caridad Abreus Ruiz	President of the Municipal Assembly in La Palmira, Cienfuegos Province
-	Conrado Martinez Corona	President of the Municipal Assembly, Havana
	Div. Gen. Julio Casas Regueiro (PB)	First Substitute of the Revolutionary Armed Forces Minister
-	Otto Rivero Torres	First Secretary of the Union of Young Communists
-	Juan Cotino Aslan	National Coordinator of the Committees for the Defense of the Revolution (CDRs)
-	Marcos Raul Aguilera Gueton	Director of the Central Oil Company
-	Carlos Manuel Valenciaga Diaz	President of the University Students Federation

Source: CUBANews (March 1998); Domingo Amuchastegui. 1998. "Government: Inside Look at the Council of State." CUBANews. March, p.4.

COUNCIL OF MINISTERS:

The Council of Ministers is the highest executive and administrative body and constitutes the Government of the Republic.

The number, designation and functions of the ministries and central bodies which form part of the Council of Ministers are established by law.

The Council of Ministers comprises the Head of State and Government, who is its President, the First Vice President, the Vice Presidents, the Ministers, the Secretary and the other members, as determined by law.

The President, the First Vice President, the Vice Presidents and the other members of the Council of Ministers selected by the President, make up its Executive Committee.

The Executive Committee may make decisions regarding matters pertaining to the Council of Ministers in the period of time between meetings of the Council.

FUNCTIONS OF THE COUNCIL OF MINISTERS:

- To organize and direct the implementation of political, economic, cultural, scientific, social and defense activities agreed upon by the National Assembly of People's Power
- To draft proposals related to general plans for economic and social development, and, once approved by the National Assembly of People's Power, to organize, direct and monitor their implementation
- To direct the foreign policy of the Republic and its relations with other governments
- To approve international treaties and submit them to the Council of State for ratification
- To direct and monitor foreign trade
- To draft the state budget, and, once it has been approved by the National Assembly of People's Power, take responsibility for its implementation
- To adopt the necessary measures to strengthen the country's monetary and credit systems
- To draft new legislation and submit it for consideration by either the National Assembly of People's Power or the Council of State, as appropriate
- To attend to national defense, the maintenance of internal order and security, the protection of citizens' rights, and the safeguarding of human lives and property in the event of natural disasters
- To manage the administration of the state and to unify, coordinate and monitor the activities of the central state administration bodies and of local authorities
- To implement laws and agreements made by the National Assembly of People's Power, as well as decree-laws and provisions introduced by the Council of State, and when necessary, to pronounce corresponding regulations
- To pronounce decrees and provisions based on and in fulfillment of current laws, and monitor their implementation.
- To revoke decisions made by authorities subordinate to the Provincial or Municipal Assemblies of People's Power, adopted as a result of powers delegated by central state administration bodies, when these decisions contravene superior regulations, which are

binding decisions.

- To propose to the Provincial and Municipal Assemblies of People's Power that provisions adopted by subordinate provincial and municipal authorities as part of their specific function be revoked when they contravene regulations approved by central state administration bodies in the exercise of their powers
- To revoke provisions made by the heads of central state administration bodies when these contravene the superior regulations, which are binding decisions
- To propose to the National Assembly of People's Power or to the Council of State the suspension of agreements made by Local Assemblies of People's Power, when these contravene current laws and provisions, or when they affect the interests of other communities or of the country in general
- To set up the committees deemed necessary to fulfill the tasks which it has been assigned
- To designate and remove officials in accordance with the powers granted to it by law
- To undertake any other function which is entrusted to it by the National Assembly of People's Power or the Council of State

The Council of Ministers is responsible for all its activities and periodically reports to the National Assembly.

FUNCTIONS OF THE MEMBERS OF THE COUNCIL OF MINISTERS

- To direct the affairs and tasks of the Ministry or body for which they are responsible, pronouncing any provisions and resolutions necessary for this purpose
- To pronounce, when it is not the express function of any other state body, the regulations required for the implementation and application of the laws and decree-laws which correspond to them
- To attend sessions of the Council of Ministers, as voting members, and to present to the council draft laws, decree-laws, decrees, resolutions, agreements, or any other type of proposal which they consider appropriate
- To designate, in accordance with the law, the officials for whom they are responsible
- Any other function ascribed to them by the Constitution or the law

MINISTRY OF SUGAR

The Ministry of Sugar is the body responsible for directing, implementing – within its jurisdiction – and monitoring state and government policy related to sugar cane cultivation and the processing of sugar cane and its derivatives, with the aim of achieving sustainable development of production, in order to meet domestic and export demands.

MINISTRY OF AGRICULTURE

The Ministry of Agriculture is the body responsible for directing, implementing – within its jurisdiction – and monitoring state and government policy related to:

- The use, conservation and improvement of land used for cultivation and the ownership and possession of agriculture and forestry land
- Plant Health
- Veterinary medicine
- The conservation, management, rational use and sustainable development of forest resources and the country's wild flora and fauna
- The protection and growth of the country's cattle stocks
- The mechanization and irrigation of production programs within its jurisdiction
- The production of agricultural crops other than sugar cane, livestock and forestry
- The cultivation and production of rice, tobacco, citrus fruits, apicultural products, poultry, feed, forestry products, and others for which it is given responsibility by the Executive Committee of the Council of Ministers
- The harvesting and use of agricultural and forestry products

THE MINISTRY OF SCIENCE, TECHNOLOGY AND THE ENVIRONMENT

The Ministry of Science, Technology and the Environment is the body responsible for directing, implementing and monitoring state and government policy related to science and technology, environmental policy and the non-violent use of nuclear energy, promoting its systematic integration in the country's development, as well as regulating biological security and monitoring chemical substances controlled by the convention on chemical weapons.

THE MINISTRY OF FOREIGN TRADE

The Ministry of Foreign Trade is the body responsible for directing, implementing and monitoring the application of state and government policy related to foreign trade operations.

THE MINISTRY OF DOMESTIC TRADE

The Ministry of Domestic Trade is the body responsible for directing, implementing and monitoring the application of state and government policy related to domestic wholesale and retail commerce in foods, other goods and services for personal and commercial consumption.

THE MINISTRY OF COMPUTER SCIENCE AND COMMUNICATIONS

The Ministry of Informatics and Communications is the body responsible for regulating, directing, supervising and monitoring state and government policy on activities related to information technology, telecommunications, information and communication networks, value-added services in communications, broadcasting, the radio spectrum, automation, postal services and the electronics industry.

THE MINISTRY OF CONSTRUCTION

The Ministry of Construction is the body responsible for directing, implementing – within its jurisdiction – and monitoring state and government policy related to:

- Geological engineering explorations for construction purposes
- The drafting of designs for construction and installation projects
- Civil construction and industrial installation
- Maintenance and repair of housing and urban developments
- Building maintenance
- The development of civil, industrial, road, waterway and dredging projects, which are of benefit to the state
- The manufacturing of concrete and asphalt and prefabricated concrete products
- The implementation of measures for monitoring the application of the General Housing Act and the housing supply, including the pronouncement or proposal of necessary regulations

THE MINISTRY OF CULTURE

The Ministry of Culture is responsible for directing, guiding, monitoring and implementing, within its jurisdiction, the application of state and government cultural policy. It is also responsible for guaranteeing the protection, preservation and enhancement of Cuba's cultural heritage.

THE MINISTRY OF THE ECONOMY AND PLANNING

The Ministry of the Economy and Planning is the body responsible for directing, implementing and monitoring the application of state and government policy related to the economy, planning, statistics, standardization, measurement and quality control, community services, physical planning and industrial design.

THE MINISTRY OF EDUCATION

The Ministry of Education is the body responsible for directing, implementing and monitoring the application of state and government policy related to education, with the exclusion of higher education.

THE MINISTRY OF HIGHER EDUCATION

The Ministry of Higher Education is the body responsible for directing, implementing – within its jurisdiction – and monitoring state and government policy related to higher education.

THE MINISTRY OF FINANCE AND PRICES

The Ministry of Finance and Prices is the body responsible for directing, implementing and monitoring the application of state and government policy related to finance, taxes, prices, auditing and insurance. It is responsible for giving advice concerning these policies and directing and monitoring the organization of state finances and the utilization of financial resources.

THE MINISTRY OF THE REVOLUTIONARY ARMED FORCES

The Ministry of the Revolutionary Armed Forces is the body responsible for directing and implementing state and government policy to defend the country's sovereignty and independence and the principles of the Socialist Revolution.

THE MINISTRY OF THE FOOD INDUSTRY

The Ministry of the Food Industry is the body responsible for directing, implementing and monitoring state and government policy related to the production of:

The dairy industry

The meat industry

Vegetable preserves

Flour and its derivatives

Oils and fats

Snack foods

Alcoholic and non-alcoholic beverages

THE MINISTRY OF BASIC INDUSTRY

The Ministry of Basic Industry is the body responsible for directing, implementing and monitoring state and government policy related to the following activities:

- The generation, transmission, distribution and marketing of electrical energy
- The production and distribution of fuel and lubricants
- The prospecting, exploration and extraction of oil and gas
- The prospecting, exploration, extraction and exploitation of solid minerals
- The production of fertilizers, chemical fibers, industrial gases, plastic articles, pesticides, paints, colorants, varnishes and other chemical products
- The production of tires, inner tubes and rubber products

- The production and conversion of paper, cardboard and wood pulp
- The production of glass and glass products

THE MINISTRY OF LIGHT INDUSTRY

The Ministry of Light Industry is the body responsible for directing, implementing and monitoring state and government policy related to the following activities:

- The production of textiles, clothing and leather goods
- The production of soaps and perfumes; wood furniture; wood, paper, cardboard and bristol board packaging; clay, earthenware and porcelain goods; and metal products
- The production of plastic articles, objects of art, and other cultural products that are primarily for personal and domestic use.

THE MINISTRY OF THE FISHING INDUSTRY

The Ministry of the Fishing Industry is the body responsible for directing, implementing and monitoring state and government policy related to the exploration, conservation, extraction, cultivation, processing and marketing of fishing resources and the merchant fleet.

THE MINISTRY OF THE IRON, STEEL, MACHINE AND ELECTRONICS INDUSTRY

The Ministry of the Iron, Steel, Machine and Electronics Industry is the body responsible for directing, implementing and monitoring state and government policy related to the following activities:

- The iron, steel, machine and electronics industry
- The application of information technology and industrial automation

THE MINISTRY OF THE INTERIOR

The Ministry of the Interior is the body responsible for directing, implementing and monitoring the application of state and government policy related to the organization, maintenance and defense of the country's security and internal order.

THE MINISTRY OF JUSTICE

The Ministry of Justice is the body responsible for assisting the government with the preparation and implementation of legal policies; it advises on legislative processes and employs the powers granted to it by the law with respect to Provincial and Municipal Courts. It is responsible for the management and technical, regulatory and methodological control of the activities for which it is responsible, and for promoting the development of legal activities.

THE MINISTRY OF FOREIGN AFFAIRS

The Ministry of Foreign Affairs is the body responsible for researching, contributing to the drafting of and implementing the foreign policy approved by the state and government.

THE MINISTRY OF PUBLIC HEALTH

The Ministry of Public Health is the body responsible for directing, implementing and monitoring state and government policy related to public health, the development of medical sciences and the medical-pharmaceutical industry.

THE MINISTRY OF LABOR AND SOCIAL SECURITY

The Ministry of Labor and Social Security is the body responsible for directing and monitoring state and government policy related to employment, salaries, social assistance, and safety and prevention.

THE MINISTRY OF TRANSPORTATION

The Ministry of Transportation is the body responsible for directing, implementing and monitoring state and government policy related to land, sea and river transportation, auxiliary or connected services, and civil maritime navigation.

THE MINISTRY OF TOURISM

The Ministry of Tourism is the body responsible for directing, evaluating, monitoring and implementing, within its jurisdiction, state and government policy related to tourism.

THE MINISTRY OF FOREIGN INVESTMENT AND ECONOMIC COOPERATION

The Ministry of Foreign Investment and Economic Cooperation is the body responsible for promoting foreign investment in Cuba, on the basis of the development strategies and policies established by the state and government. In coordination with the authorized bodies, it directs the corresponding negotiation processes and coordinates and advises on the implementation and fulfillment of state and governmental policy concerning economic cooperation.

THE CUBAN CIVIL AVIATION INSTITUTE

The Cuban Civil Aviation Institute is the body responsible for directing, implementing and monitoring state and government policy related to air transportation, civilian air navigation and its auxiliary and connected services.

ECONOMY AND ECONOMIC DEVELOPMENT

MAIN OBJECTIVES

- Growth of 5 % rate of the Gross Domestic Product.
- An advance in the most important indicators of economic efficiency, as the main support to economic and social development.

  Work Productivity : 4,3 %
  Energy intensity: -2,6 %
- Rate of growth of investments by approximately 14 %.
- Developing tourism, to reach 2 millions of visitors, and 15% in terms of total gross income.
- A growth of industrial production of 7,4 %.
- Sugar industry will have a 3,7 million tons sugar harvest.
- Equivalent production of petroleum and gas is planned to reach 4 millions tons. Generation of electricity on the base of domestic fuel will rise to 90 %.
- Constructions will grow 18 % and non sugar cane agriculture around 10 %.
- In industry, important growths are planned in nickel production, to reach 75 thousand tons (increase 5%), steel production 15%, and stainless steel will also be duplicated.
- Increase exports more than 20 % specially bent tobacco and rum. Imports will growth more than 4 %. These projections will support a reduction of the balance of trade deficit.
- Internal financial balance will be maintained, decreasing the liquidity as a proportion of the GDP.
- A fiscal deficit of 779 million pesos, which in terms of the proportion of the Gross Domestic Product represents 2,7 % .

ECONOMIC REPORT MINISTRY OF ECONOMY AND PLANNING

ECONOMIC PERFORMANCE

In spite of the deepening of the US actions against the country through the strengthening of the blockade with the application of the Helms-Burton Law, the adverse climatic behavior including an extensive dry season and the increasingly financial difficulties that the country had to cope with, the Gross Domestic Product grew by 1,2%, reaffirming the continuity of the process of recovery of the economy, which dates from 1994 on.

The growth of the industrial sector was of a 3,1 % and of construction of 5,2%. Agricultural production decreased by 6,7%, due to a decline of the sugar cane production. However, the gross aggregated value of the non sugar cane agriculture grew by 2%, and the corresponding to cattle raising production kept itself similar to the previous year, despite the aforementioned climatic difficulties.

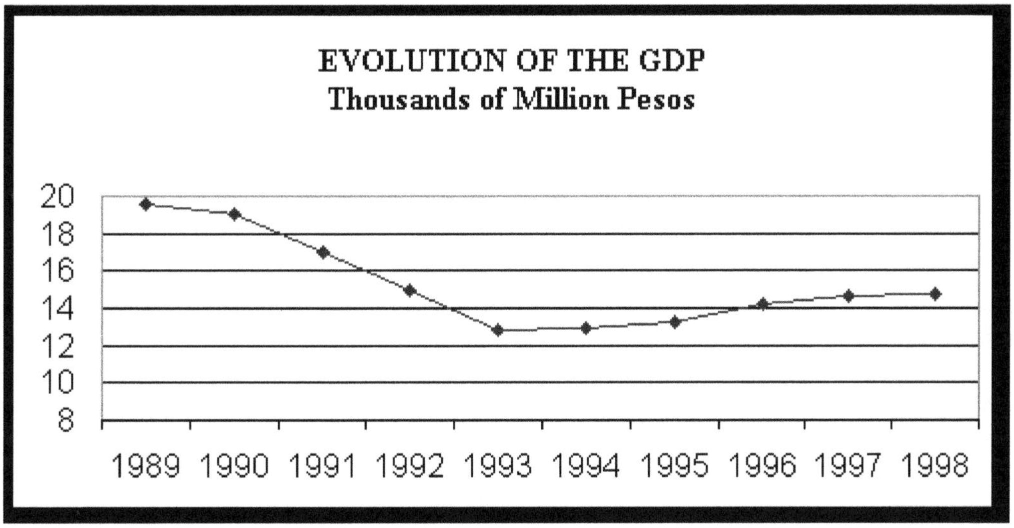

Economic policy has focused on the growth of efficiency in the use of all resources. This is materialized in an increase of the efficiency within the investment process of around 33%; and an increase in the efficiency in the use of energy, where for the first time in this decade the GDP grows, while at the same time it is registered a drop of 1,2% in the physical consumption of energy.

A trend toward recovery is prevalent within the non sugar sectors of the economy, with an increase of 7,1% in gross investments; of 4% in non sugar industrial production ; of 2% in non sugar cane agricultural production; and of 18% in the gross income of tourism.

In addition, the internal market shows a favourable trend towards financial equilibrium, with an important growth of the segment which operates with freely convertible currency, and a stable exchange rate between the Cuban peso and the USD.

These elements demostrate that during 1998, the factors, which have determined the trend towards a gradual recovery of the national economy, are maintained in spite of the difficulties confronted.

Selected economic indexes	MU	1997	1998
Average population (June)	MM habitants	11,0	11,1
Gross Domestic Product (GDP)	MMP	14572,4	14754,1
Dynamics: (Previous year = 100%)			
Gross Domestic Product (GDP)	%	102,5	101,2
Work Productivity	%	100,9	100,2
Investments	%	99,5	107,1
Exports	%	97,5	79,4
Imports	%	111,7	104,8

Foreign Debt (in freely convertible currency)	MMUSD	10145,6	11208,9
Exchange Rate (Unofficial market)	Ps : $US	22,82	21,81
Unemployment rate	%	7,0	6,6

INVESTMENTS

Gross investments grew by 7,1% attaining a value above 2300 MMP. By 1998, foreign capital investment already reached 345 agreements of association with Cuban enterprises, to which 243 operators of free trade zones are added.

Somewhat more than 50% of joint investments and economic associations with foreign capital are concentrated in the industrial sector, mainly in the generation of electricity and oil activities, 27% in communications and 16% in tourism and real state activity.

By the end of 1998, 34 Agreements of Promotion and Reciprocal Protection of Investments were already signed with 35 countries.

Investments within the tourism program reaches a total performance of over 560MMP and 3553 rooms were finished to start with their exploitation in international tourism.

GROWTHS OF THE GDP ACCORDING TO ITS SECTOR OF ORIGIN

(Percentage)

	1997	1998
Agriculture, hunting, fishing and forestry	99,8	94,8
Manufacturing industry	108,3	103,3
Construction	103,2	105,7

SELECTED PRODUCTIONS

	MU	1998	1998/97
Sugar (96%)	MT	3229,4	0,76
Nickel	MT	67,7	1,13
Cigars	MMU	263,5	1,23
Rice for consumption	MT	90,3	0,62
Viands	MT	1383,7	1,02
Vegetables	MT	846,5	1,41
Fishing (gross capture)	MT	133,8	0,98
Fertilizers	MT	156,7	0,85
Fabrics	MMm^2	54,0	1,00
Steel	MT	278,0	0,83

Oil production	MT	1678,2	1,15
Generation of electricity	GWh	14145,1	1,00

External sector

Cuban total exports decreased by 20,6% while imports increased by 4,8% with a trade deficit of 569 MMP, more than in 1997.

EXPORTS

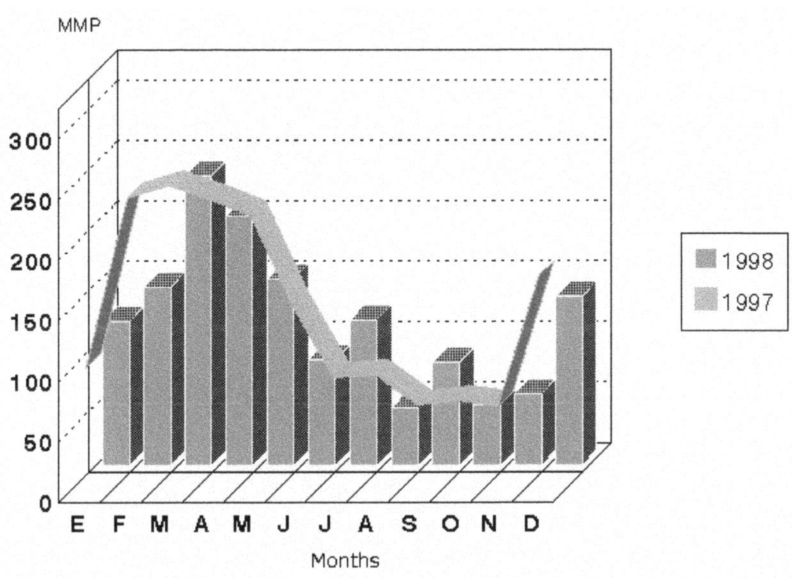

A comparison of a group of products with actual results in 1997, shows that the deterioration of the export price index is influenced to a great extent by: fresh and frozen shrimp (35%), nickel sulfide (34%), sinter-nickel oxide (31%), crude coffee (19%) and sugar (2%).

To the adverse external financial conditions, a climatically disastrous year was added due to the effects of "El Niño" with excessive rains and also droughts, and the effects of hurricane George, a phenomenon which cost around 520 million pesos to the economy.

Though income from tourism increased by 18% in relation to the previous year, the aforementioned situation led to a plan with less financial resources than in 1997.

FINANCE AND THE DOMESTIC MARKET

Internal financial equilibrium has been achieved since 1996, with a positive performance, evidenced by the appreciation of the national currency whose quotation has gone from 150 pesos per dollar in 1994, to a level between the 19 and 22 pesos in the last three years. In 1998 the average quotation was of 21,81 pesos per dollar.

It is estimated an end-year fiscal deficit of around 560 MMP, thus continueing a trend towards stability, which in relative terms to the Gross Domestic Product represents approximately 2,5%.

This result shows that the performance of the State Budget has not constituted cause for imbalance in public finances, in the last three years.

Consumer Price Index

The consumer price index (CPI) increased around 3%. The agricultural market shows an increasing trend in 1998 in the value of sales (7,3%) as well as in quantity of products (11,5%), while the price index for this market was reduced by 1,1%. The sales in the industrial and artisan markets rose in volume, and their value also rose to 8,9%.

Personal income rose by 11,7% and household consumption increased by 3,2%.

Employment

The unemployment rate continues to decline and in 1998 was 6,6%. Working conditions were improved and pay-incentives schemes were broaden, comprising more than 1020 workers, with an increase of 9,7 % in relation to 1997.

Women's participation in total employment is around 37%.

STANDARD OF LIVING

Education, health and social assistance services continue to show a gradual improvement.

During the academic course of 1998-1999 more than 2,2 million students were enrolled, with 15 thousand more students in pre-school, primary and middle education. The most important increase took place in secondary education where 34% of the students are boarding-pupils. Enrollment in higher education is still above 100,000 students. More than 12,000 schools and 145 institutes are functioning. The fundamental resources for study and living conditions were guaranteed for this year.

In regard to health services, surgical activity is a priority within the strategies to strengthen hospital activities and it has behaved satisfactorily by the end of 1998. More than 884 716 interventions were made representing an increase of 13 932 more interventions than those registered in 1997.

Optical services have been improved in relation to the previous year. This is shown by the number of cases resolved, representing an increase of 18% in relation to the previous year. In regard to dentistry, services have been provided to 20 consultations representing an increase of 15% in relation to the previous year for the same period.

The coverage for special services for the attention to elders was increased. Care centers for grandfathers and grandmothers increased by 2690, gerontologic equipments by 74, special care rooms by 5, and around 14 thousand more elders receive domiciliary attention.

The death rate for elders have kept at the 1997 levels, while the rates for tuberculosis and severe diarrheal diseases have been reduced.

Infantile mortality reached a rate of 7,1 for one thousand borne alive, which compares favorably to 7,2 in 1997. The rates in the provinces where they are the lowest, represent a little more than

5%, where as in the province with the highest rate, it is of 8,6 deaths of minors under one year of age for one thousand borne alive.

Main objectives for the 1999 Plan

The main objectives for the 1999 Plan can be summarized in the following aspects:

- Growth of 2,5% rate of the Gross Domestic Product.
- An advance in the most important indicators of economic efficiency, as the main support to economic and social development.
- A growth in work productivity by 1,6%
- To decrease in energy intensity by almost 4%
- To increase investment yield by 4,5%
- To increase investments by approximately 11,5%
- To continue developing tourism, where growth is expected to be of 18%.
- To attain a growth of industrial production of 2%
- To start recuperating the sugar production so as to reach 3,6 million tons, for a growth of 11,5% in relation to the previous year.
- To grow by 3,1% in the agricultural sector, and 3,75% in construction works.
- To increase exports by 7,2% diversifying them and restricting imports to a growth of 5,4%.
- To maintain liquidity in hands of the population at levels similar to those by the end of 1998. To continue strengthening the purchasing power of the national currency.
- Not to surpass the fiscal deficit by 3% in relation to the GDP.

PERFORMANCE OF THE ECONOMY IN THE FIRST SEMESTER OF 1999.

In the first semester of 1999 the economy recorded a growth of the Gross Domestic Product of 6,1%, measured at constant prices. The growth foreseen for the year was of 2,5%, placing the economy in conditions to surpass the initially considered rate.

It is significant that the total consumption of energy products derived from oil, including the national crude and natural gas, increased by only 0,8%, which evidences that the growth attained was obtained with greater efficiency. The generation of electricity grew by 2,8%, and national energy sources for that production represented 43%. On the other hand, savings programs and load accommodation allowed a reduction of peak demand of electricity by 5%. Likewise, oil extraction increased by 23%, and the usage of natural gas five fold. The sugar industry, which in 1997-1998 experienced one of its lowest levels in recent years, and which constituted an obstacle to the economy's recovery achieved an increase of somewhat more than half a million tons in the just concluded harvest of 3,78 million tons in 1998-1999. Practically all the productive branches present growths which confirm the trend toward recovery evidenced since 1995.

GROWTH IN THE FIRST SEMESTER OF 1999,

In relation to the same period for last year

Industry	**6,4**

Sugar industry	23,4
Non sugar industry	5,9
Agriculture	**10,7**
Sugar cane agriculture	12,5
Non sugar cane agriculture	17,8
Construction	**8,2**
Comunications	**7,9**
Conmerce	**5,5**

Tourism shows a favorable performance above the considered projections for the first semester, with a growth of 23% in the number of visitors. Moreover, the efficiency indicators are improving, the capacity utilization rate has increased by 3%; and the daily income per tourist has increased by 1%. On the other hand, despite salary raises for the public health, education sectors and others, domestic finance have kept stable. Besides, about 12 thousand people had access to new jobs in this period. Nevertheless the aforementioned, difficulties still remain present in the economy within the consumption sphere, which does not reach the existing levels before the crisis at the beginning of the 90's, and also tensions are manifested with respect to external financing.

ECONOMIC RESULTS YEAR 2000

During the last seven years the Gross Domestic Product of Cuban economy has increased, reaffirming the continuity of the process of recovery. In the year 2000 this increment of the GDP reached 5,6 % measured at constant prices.

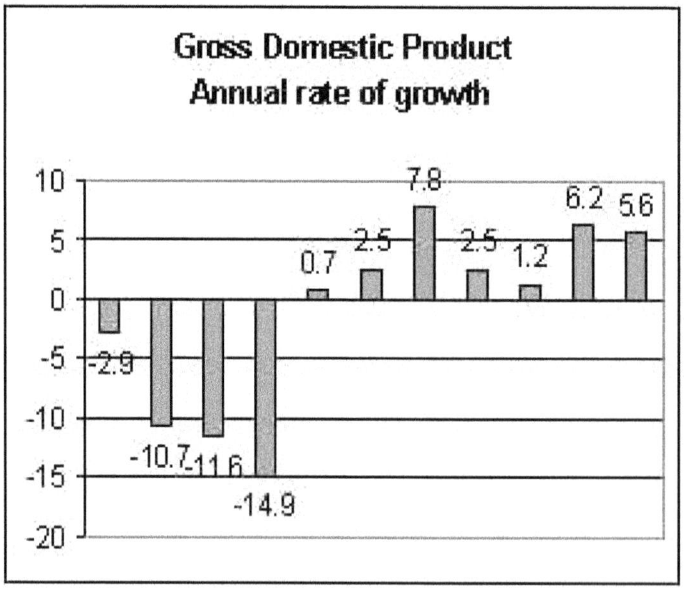

This growth in the Gross Domestic Product was accompanied by the improvement of economic efficiency in different spheres. The coefficient of the energy intensity decreased 2,9%, labor productivity grew in 3,5%; and investment efficiency increased 7,1 %.

In this last year advances were observed in the recovery of the sugar industry, which reached a production of 4059 thousand metric tons, a equivalent to a 7,3% growth.

The internal market showed a sustained trend toward financial equilibrium, with an significant growth of the segment which operates in convertible currency; and a stable exchange rate between the Cuban peso and the USD, as well as a fiscal deficit not larger than 2,7% of the Gross Domestic Product.

These results were obtained in spite of the significant increment of the prices of the petroleum and a descent of the prices of important export products, such as sugar. It algo must be mentioned the complex external financial situation that the economy had to face, as well as the negative effects originated by the economic blockade of United States.

Selected economic indicators	
Half population (June) (Millions of inhabitants)	11,2
Gross Domestic Product (Millions of pesos, at constant prices of 1981)	16556,4
Rate of growth 2000/1999 (%) **(Preliminary figures)**	
SECTORS	
Agriculture	14,5
Industry	5,0
Construction	9,3
Transport and communications	9,1
Trade and tourism	5,4
Communal, social and personal services	3,4
Rate of change (Informal market) (pesos/US dolar)	21,7
Unemployment rate	5,5

The growth of some of the main productions is shown below.

Selected productions	U M	2000	00/99
Sugar (96°) (harvest)	Mt	4059,1	1,07
Nickel	Mt	71,4	1,07
Tobacco	Mt	38,0	1,01
Citric	Mt	892,6	1,18
Edible roots	Mt	967,9	1,12
Vegetables	Mt	1558,0	1,41
Fishing (gross capture)	Mt	155,3	1,07
Petroleum Extraction	Mt	2695,3	1,26
Natural gas	Mt	522,4	1,25
Steel	Mt	336,3	1,11
Electricity	GWh	15028,8	1,04

INVESTMENTS

In the year 2000, investment reached more than 3100 million pesos. This represents more than double the level attained in 1995, and a growth of 16 % compared with 1999.

Investments in the tourist program reached over 522 millions of pesos. There were 3273 rooms completed, ready for exploitation in international tourism, for a total number of rooms of 35 000.

FOREIGN TRADE

This year the proportion of services en total export revenues reached 62%.

In the case of export goods, foreign trade showed a favorable behavior, with an increment of 16,2 % in exports, and a remarkable growth in non traditional products. Imports grew 11 % at current prices.

In tourism the number of visitors was of 1,7 million people, with total revenues of nearly 2000 million dollars.

EXTERNAL OPENING

By the end of 2000, foreign capital investment reached 394 association agreements with Cuban enterprises, with a committed capital of 5 thousand million dollars. The year 2000 ended with 31 new business, including mixed companies and association agreements.

Mixed exterprises and other associations with foreign capital showed significant economic advances. The year ended with a higher level of sales of 1200 millions dollars. Up to now 51 Agreements of Promotion and Protection of Investments have been signed and more than ten are being negotiated.

FINANCES AND INTERNAL MARKET

The population income in national currency increased 8,3 % and the expenses rose 6,1 %. Income from salaries experienced an increment of 7,7 %, due principally to the improvement of wages for teachers, health care personal and other groups. Retail sales increased 4,9 %.

Although monetary liquidity grew 5,9 % in the year 2000, the internal financial balance presents a positive behavior, as attested by the diminishin tendency of the consumer price index (CPI) and the revaluation of the national currency, tendency that has been manifest from 1996 to date.

The rate of exchange in the informal market has gone from 150 pesos per dollar in 1994, to a range between 19 and 22 pesos in the last four years. In 2000 the average rate was of 21,7 pesos per dollar and the price index decreased by 2,3%.

In the State Budget spending grew 8,6 %; education increased 16,1 %, and public health 11,1 %. Revenues show an increment of 8 %, and the estimated fiscal deficit should be around 730 millions of pesos, thus continuing a trend towards stability, which in relative terms to the Gross Domestic Product should be of the order of 2,7 %.

This results shows that the performance of the State Budget has not constituted cause for imbalance in public finances in the last 5 years.

EMPLOYMENT

The unemployment rate continues to decline and in 2000 was 5,5 % Working conditions were improved, and pay-incentive schemes were broaden, comprising more than 1158 thousand workers.

Women¢ s participation in total employment is around 43,3% in the state sector.

STANDARD OF LIVING

The daily levels of kilocalories is considered in 2585 Kcal, and 68 grams of protein per inhabitant. In 2000 the building of housing by the State must reach 42,5 thousand units.

Education, health, security and social assistance services continue to show a gradual improvement.

During the academic course of 2000-2001, 2,253 thousand of students were enrolled in the general education. Although substantial variation doesn't exist in the global indicator, it should be pointed out that in the structure the tendency continues to the decrease of the primary education (36 thousand) and the concentration of the students in middle education, which presents an increase of 39 thousand students. In turn the total of internal students is increased reaching the figure of 351,5 thousand students.

Enrollment in higher education is about 128,4 thousand. This represents an increase of 8,5 % regarding the course 1999-2000. The new enrollment to higher education increases in more proportion reaching 13 %.

In regard to health services, surgical activity is a priority within the strategies to strengthen hospital activities. In the 2000 were made about 950 thousand interventions.

Attention to serious ill patients has continued improving its indicators, with a strengthen coordination among the integrated system of medical urgency, and the attention of urgency that offers the system of primary attention of health. Thanks to that has been achieved the goals outlined for the main chronic illnesses not transferable.

Infantile maternal program of attention has maintained a high priority for the system of health and for all the sectors of the society. Infantile mortality rate reached 7,2 for one thousand born alive. This locates Cuba among the first 20 countries of the world.

Related to the program for the attention to eldest population, the Circles of Grandparents, which mantained an active social activity with this group of the population, arrived to almost 14 thousand, with more than 542 thousand participants. Also were increased the Houses of Grandparents, where special attention is given for orientation and recreation for elder people receiving domiciliary attention.

FINANCIAL SITUATION

BUDGET PROJECT OF THE STATE FOR THE YEAR 2000 PRESENTED BEFORE THE NATIONAL ASSEMBLY OF PEOPLE'S POWER (CUBAN PARLIAMENT).

Commander in Chief Fidel Castro, President of the Council of State and of the Council of Ministers.

Comrade Ricardo Alarcón de Quesada, President of the National Assembly of People's Power.

Comrade Deputies.

Honorable Guests.

Just eleven days have to go by to finish the fiscal year corresponding to the budget that was endorsed for this year at the end of 1998.

Consequently, it is compulsory to give you a report on the results expected from the budget of 1999, preceding the presentation of the budget for the year 2000 before this assembly on behalf of the Council of Ministers.

The Act passed pondered a maximum fiscal deficit of 720 million pesos. Considering the growth that had been planned for the national economy, the deficit approved meant a 2.9 % of the GDP.

A set of measures were passed along the year and they caused an increase in budgetary expenditures by 700 million pesos of which, 620 were used for salary raises and the payment of contributions for social security and mostly for education and public health.

Considering the experience of previous years, 150 million pesos were also allotted to the creation of a fund to keep up with production in the cases of loses which can not be charged on business management, including loses due to adverse climatic conditions. The agricultural sector has top priority in this case.

It is stimulating to report that in spite of this increase in expenditures, we expect to liquidate this year's budget with a deficit lower than endorsed, around 100 million pesos less than foreseen.

This favorable result has been possible by the fulfillment over scheduled plans of the plan of incomes originally stipulated by the law.

As it is plainly put in the report, economic recovery registered along the year raising the GDP by more than 6% above GDP in 1998 has been a decisive factor for this overly fulfillment of the plan of incomes. The figure is more than the double of predictions for last year.

The result is also favored by the measures taken to increase the offer of products so as to balance the rise in demand caused by the raise in salaries mentioned, the increased efficiency in productive sectors and a dynamic fund raising policy of the National Tax Office. These measures haven been duly supported by the procedures and control of the Communist Party and the local governments in the provinces and the municipalities.

The advantageous results obtained in the year about to end let us cut down deficit relation with the GDP to 2.4% under current prices. Such results are the foundations to commit us with higher goals in the socioeconomic development of the country. These goals are contained in the budget for the year 2000 we are presenting before the Assembly for approval.

Comrades:

This project of State Budget covers the threats meant by external financial restrictions caused by the outrageous American blockade against our country for more than four decades and the limited access to international credits for development.

But the project also covers the strength that springs from a people united, brave and decided to face hardships and work with continued perseverance to defend its social achievements, the equity of our system and continue with the sustained economic development of our country.

The project fully meets the General Guidelines issued by the Secretary Office of the Executive Committee in the middle of the year. Its main objectives are the continue increasing efficiency in state business, the consolidation of the fiscal policy and the role of budget to achieve macroeconomic stability without affecting the social policy. The General Guidelines are in line with the contents approved in the Economic Resolution of the 5th Congress of the Communist Party.

I should stress on the outstanding increase proposed for the amounts allotted to cover current expenditures of budgeted activities. As a whole, 9.166 million pesos have been projected and more than 70% of this figure is appointed for top priorities: education, public health, social security and social assistance, housing maintenance and repairs and communal services. This figure is 17,5% higher than the figure allotted in the budget of 1999.

In the case of education, expenditures of 2.050 million pesos have been envisaged. This means an additional 185 million as compared to expenditures for 1999. Out of this budget, approximately 94 million will be used for salaries and contributions to social security. Salary raises were approved and paid for 12 months after last March and also, 4 500 fresh teachers joined education at the end of 1999 and a similar amount will be joining at the beginning of the academic course 2000 - 2001.

The budget guarantees finances for a full coverage of school age population with an enrolment of more than 2 million 250 thousand students in pre-school, primary and medium level education and 115 thousand students in different areas of university education.

The program for the repairs and maintenance of schools will continue. An additional 20 million pesos as compared to the current year have been allotted to this end.

An amount of 23 million has been financed to re-establish the allowance recently approved for higher education students.

The budget for public health will rely on more than 1.732 million pesos and it will also cover for 2 376 new doctors, 162 dentists, 1 919 bachelors of nursing as well as 3 230 mid level technicians of which 1 700 are nurses.

When these graduates join the services of public health there would be one doctor per every 168 inhabitants and a dentist per 1 123 inhabitants. They would be distributed all over the country in the wide range of health facilities currently available for service: 283 hospitals, 440 policlinics and 14 622 community doctor's offices.

An increase in other expenditures larger by 19.5% as compared to the budget of this year is included. The objective is to increase the repairs and maintenance of hospitals and continue with vaccination programs, antivector campaigns and other indispensable requirements for priority programs of health and prevention.

It has been estimated that 78 000 workers will retire next year so the figure of pensioners will amount to more than 1 400 000. Every month they receive their pension without failure or delays.

An amount of 1.800 million pesos are allotted from the budget to pay for pensions, including 26 million for partially disabled persons and loans to working women to care for their children up to the age of six months.

On the other hand, funds allotted to social assistance programs were increased by more than 15%.

From the figure of 699 million pesos envisaged for housing and services to the community, 143 million are devoted to conservation of the housing stock. Though it still insufficient because of the limitations with construction materials it represents an increase by 13% as compared to this year's budget. Two hundred and ninety five million have been allotted to the program of road repair and maintenance, whether urban or rural.

An amount of 217 million pesos are appointed to improve communal services, mainly in the City of Havana. Out of this figure, eleven million pesos would be used to raise salaries of workers in this sector.

The increases shown in the budget for defense and for interior order are almost entirely referred to the raise in the salaries of police officers.

On the point of culture, not only the 1 658 cultural centers have been kept in operation in all the municipalities and the development of cultural activities in everyone of its forms has been intensified. But also, funds have been appointed for the reanimation of cultural activities at community level and to subsidize projects regardless of the incomes they might return.

Allocations to support the creation of four local TV stations and three local radio stations were increased. This was also aimed to increase the time of radio and TV broadcastings, besides a plan to improve the quality of broadcastings based on new equipment joined and raises in salaries.

The Budget of the State covers approximately 53% of the total expenditures of technical and scientific programs giving priority to the sugar industry, food production, energy, agricultural biotechnology and biopharmaceutical products among others. The remainder 47% is covered with the resources of enterprises, high above what has been achieved this year. This shows a closer link between technical-scientific researches and the interests of production.

Six million pesos will be allocated for the development of the Forum of Science and Technique and the Exhibitions of Developers of the Future.

It is worth underlining that more than 150 million pesos are allocated to the protection of the environment and to this, one has to add the resources used by business to observe legislation in force on the issue of environmental protection

Deputies:

Only seven years ago, in 1993, the Budget of the State subsidized loses of state business by 5 434 million pesos.

Measures endorsed by the National Assembly (parliament) in 1994 to improve the situation of finances and cut down the excess of circulation contributed to a outstanding reduction of such subsidies. These measures were endorsed after a wide process of consultation with the workers all over the country, a magnificent example of socialist democracy together with other important economic measures. It is expected that subsidies will not surpass 1.040 million pesos by 1999 and for the year 2000 we have planned 608 million. i.e., only 11% of the figure financed by the state in 1993.

Though there are other factors that benefit the results of business, it is obvious that an outstanding improvement in the efficiency of state business have been accomplished during these years and it will be sped even more by joining the program of business management improvement already being introduced.

Out of 318 business that have planned loses for the coming year, 279 belong to the Ministry of Sugar and the Ministry of Agriculture. These two agencies hold 84% of the total of business loses. But one has to recognize that the figure of 510 million envisaged for subsidies in the year 2000 for business in these two entities is lower by 45% if compared to plans for this year

From the figure of business considered with loses in the budget presented, 6 are subordinated to the Ministry of Basic Industry, 5 belong to the Ministry of Light Industry and three shipping business remain in this situation. The remainder 25 is non-profitable business that belongs to the bodies of the People's Power.

As it is explained in this report, the economic assistance to cooperatives in agriculture is only granted to Basic Cooperatives Production Units (UBPC) not growing sugar cane. In the case of sugar cane cooperatives, farmers rely on more efficient forms of financing, only to compensate state decisions that cause expenditures that can not be charged on the farmers.

The 51 million pesos of assistance to the non-sugar cane cooperatives represent a reduction of 139 million pesos as compared to the budget for the year 1999. These cooperatives have been benefited by an increase in the prices paid by the state collection centers of agricultural products and the planned increase of efficiency.

It is also important to stress on the increase of 100 million pesos against the figure allocated in 1999 to subsidize the prices of certain products needed by the people: a group of foodstuff, domestic fuel and some industrial products. Five hundred and sixty million pesos are allocated for this end.

And finally, 1.700 million are financed for investments and other capital expenditures. The budget for the year 2000 will assume 60% (approximately) of the plan of investments endorsed by the Ministry of Economy and Planning and it will be mostly used for housing construction, road and water supply and sewerage programs and works of the infrastructure. For the case of business investment, the participation of the budget would be limited to projects related to agriculture, the sugar industry and the development of tourism.

Summing up, expenditures by 14.270 million pesos have been planned. This figure is larger by 8.2% as compared to the original budget for this year and it is almost 2% above estimates after considering the decision to raise salaries and others, endorsed as budgetary adjustments.

In order to face expenditures and keep budgetary deficit within the range desired, no less than 13.575 million pesos would have to be collected for next year. This figure is larger by 8.5% than the current budget and 1% above estimates for this year.

The tendency to increase the incomes from taxes is maintained as a consecuence of a policy to join all business to the Taxation System as well as the increase (within those income taxes) of the share of direct tax incomes related to the results of business.

The payment of tax on profits and use of the labor force and yield of the state investment by business to the Budget have been calculated in 3.548 million pesos. This figure exceeds by 1.510 million pesos the amount of money they receive from the Budget for subsidies and other allocations. This figure improves the amount envisaged for 1999 in 608 million pesos, thus continuing with the sustained improvement of state business management observed during the last few years. Of course, there are many efficiency reserves that would have to be increased and there, business management improvement should play a vital role, as I said before.

Summing up, we propose that the Act of Budget endorsed should consider 745 million pesos as maximum for deficit and this would mean a ratio of 2.8% over the GDP envisaged, with an economic growth of 4% for next year.

Some final remarks on the budgets of provincial and municipal councils of administration.

In recent years I made reference to the discipline of local administrations on the point of budget management and the actions they have been implementing for the gradual reduction of budget deficit under difficult economic conditions. In this point, more knowledge of presidents of local governmentss and councils has been observed on the issue of budget and more powers have been vested on them to improve the management of financial resources allocated.

However, the increase in expenditures for the raise in salaries and road and housing maintenance endorsed for this year take a large share of local budgets, thus increasing their deficits remarkably. It is necessary to take measures to increase the interest of local governments to continue promoting actions to reduce local deficits. These actions should turn into concrete tasks to increase efficiency, the search of new products and services and the best use of land. Indeed, these actions should provide more jobs, better living standards and more income for the people.

It is for this reason that in the draft of the Act of Budget for the year 2000 it has been envisaged to empower the Ministry of Finances and Prices to evaluate and apply a more equitable distribution of incomes currently collected by the Central Budget. This would be done on technical and properly documented basis. By nature, these incomes can and should be allocated as incomes of the provinces and municipalities. I think it is fair to implement that work that will provide for a better distribution of resources between the Central Budget and that of the provinces and municipalities without changing the total deficit endorsed by the Budget of the State.

Comrade deputies:

When the European socialist community collapsed at the beginning of the 90's, Cuba lost 3/4^{ths}of its trade exchange over night and the fair trade conditions enjoyed during years were also lost. Important investments where large amounts of finances and resources had been invested stayed unfinished and those that had been completed on the basis of integration with those European countries ran out of markets and sources of raw materials. Only a few abroad believed that a small country under such difficult conditions would be able to subsist and keep with the technical and social advances and the equality and solidarity of the citizens that had been achieved in a short term.

We are about to finish the last year of the 90's and it is right to make a good retelling of what has been done during these hard years to properly judge what has been done and where we stand.

Let's see:

After the year 1990, 301 599 professionals have graduated from the universities. Out of this figure, 60 508 belong to medical sciences, 121 178 have graduated as teachers and 59 098 have graduated from technical and agricultural careers.

Slowness in general education has been reduced by 2.3%. More than 1.400 000 students have finished the sixth grade of education during this decade. More than 1 180 000 have finished secondary education and approximately 393 000 have finished high school and about 692 000 have graduated from polytechnic education.

Right in 1999 we have 74 975 doctors and dentists, 29 300 more than in the year 1990; and already at the end of 1998 we had 82 600 nurses. Out of this figure 17 568 were bachelors in nursing. The community doctor service covers almost all the population. This high availability of health professionals and their state-of-the-art skills and their extraordinary human values guarantees service all over the country in all the fields of medicine. Not only this, but also we are able to help other countries as part of our solidary support to other countries.

The infant population has been kept protected against 12 communicable diseases and the infant mortality rate has been reduced from 10.7 per thousand births alive in 1990 to 6.5, according to estimates for this year.

In the last ten years, the amount of 16.200 million pesos has been allocated to Social Security and Assistance. Today, more than 1 500 000 citizens enjoy these benefits and the figure represents 261 000 more than ten years ago.

We have been able to keep a wide range of cultural facilities under operation. Among them 277 art community centers, 352 public libraries, 247 museums and 123 art galleries can be pointed out. As to art courses we may say that 5 305 have graduated from mid level art schools and 980 from art schools of university level.

Our writers and artists have been acknowledged internationally and are renowned in the international arena. Many of them and their works have been awarded in international events.

The success in sports is outstanding. We keep number one position in the Central American and Caribbean Games and in 1991 we were successful with the celebration of the 11th Panamerican Games where we ranked in the first place. In the Panamerican Games celebrated in 1995 and 1999 we took second place among all the countries of the continent and we were only surpassed taking into account the amount of medals, by the most powerful and with the largest resources of the world, with a population 25 times larger than our population.

In the Olympic Games celebrated in Barcelona we took 5th place and in Atlanta we ranked 8th.

During this period 105 Cuban athletes have become world champions in 15 sports and right now we have classified in 21 sports and 229 athletes for Sydney 2000.

The tremendous momentum in the development of our science is outstanding in these years. The international reputation of our centers of research and production with the latest state-of-the-art are the pride of Cubans.

Let it be enough talking of the success in the development of vaccines. The most important are the antimeningococcic vaccine, the recombinant vaccine against B hepatitis and against leptospirosis and the management of state-of- the-art technology to obtain humanized recombinant monoclonal antibodies.

The development and production of medical equipment with the latest state-of-the-art with important contributions in the Ultramicroanalytic System (SUMA), technologies for fast diagnosis and the introduction of more than 450 finished drugs in the process of production increase the quality of medical assistance in the country.

The human capital educated by the revolution during all these years linked to the scientific development of the country has been decisive for the accomplishment of these results.

The defense of our fatherland and the achievements of the Revolution have been kept firm and increasingly strengthened. Most Cubans are trained fighters ready to defend the country.

These are facts undeniable facts that do not astonish those who can assess the capacities of a people convinced of its ideals, of its aspirations and of the final victory. This is happy and responsible people with an indisputable leader heading all the economic, political and military battles.

The Budget we present and which endorsement I request guarantees the national finance to go ahead with these programs.

Thank you.

PUBLIC FINANCES IN CUBA

PUBLIC FINANCES

The Ministry of Finances and Prices is the State's Central Administration Institution in charge of the management, implementation and control of the application of the fiscal, financial, taxes, prices, auditing and insurance policy of the State and the Government. It also provides advice on these policies to these Institutions of the administration of the country and manages and controls the organization of public finances and the use of financial resources.

As part of the arrangement of public finances, Law Decree 192 **"On Financial Administration of the State"**, was endorsed in April 1999 as one of the most outstanding steps in the arrangement of public finances. Its objective is to impart more clearness, arrangement and organicity to the process of planning, implementation and control of public finances so as to meet the goals and policies set by the state.

Law-Decree 192 substitutes Act 29 "Organic Act of the State Budget" in force since 1980, but now obsolete because it could not meet overall current conditions of the economy in general neither those of finances particularly approached.

The law-decree defines and covers a group of principles, standards, systems, institutions and management procedures which make it possible to gather public resources and use them to meet state goals, endeavoring to meet the needs of society. It is made up by the following systems:

a. Taxes
b. Budget
c. Treasury
d. Public credit
e. Government accountancy

The System of Taxes is ruled by special legislations, mostly Act 73 **"On the System of Taxes"** passed by the Cuban Parliament in 1994 and by other provisions. These legislations are gradually applied with the elementary principles of social justice to protect low-income sectors and stimulate work and production and control cash liquidity.

The act mentioned above acknowledges eleven (11) taxes, three rates (3) and one (1) contribution which are applied based on the principles of generality and equity of taxes, in line with the economic capacity of people that should pay for them.

Taxes:

- Tax on gross profits
- Tax on personal incomes

- Tax on sales
- Tax on special products
- Tax on public services
- Tax on the property or possession of certain goods
- Tax on land transport
- Tax on the transfer of goods and heritage
- Tax on documents
- Tax on the use of labor force
- Tax on the use and exploitation of natural resources and for the protection of the environment

Contributions:

- Contribution to social security

Rates:

- Rate for tolls

Rate for airport and travelers service

- Rate for the settlement of adds and commercial propaganda

Taxes put in force has been introduced gradually in line with conditions set for that end.

The system has achieved consolidation and institutionalization and in a short term it has been able to reestablish a tax paying oriented mind, the timely collection of taxes and the collection of non-tax incomes payable to the state by legal and natural persons.

The **budget systems** keeps up with the accomplishments in this issue derived from the previous act and introduces new principles according to the most common international practice in the issue of budgeting and register. Stress is made on the principles of non-compensation of expenditures and incomes and the register of expenditure by earning.

Classifiers of financial resources and uniform expenditures were established for all the system. They provide the necessary information for control and efficiency in the management of public resources at the different levels of the budget.

Although Cuba is a unitary republic by definition of its Constitution, the system of government was structured after 1976 by a central government, 14 provincial governments and 169 municipal governments in line with the political and administrative division of the country. Consequently, for each level of the government there is a budget that is the financial basis for the fulfillment of its role of top authority of the state within the limits of the corresponding territory. This gives rise to the Budget System made up by 200 budgets:

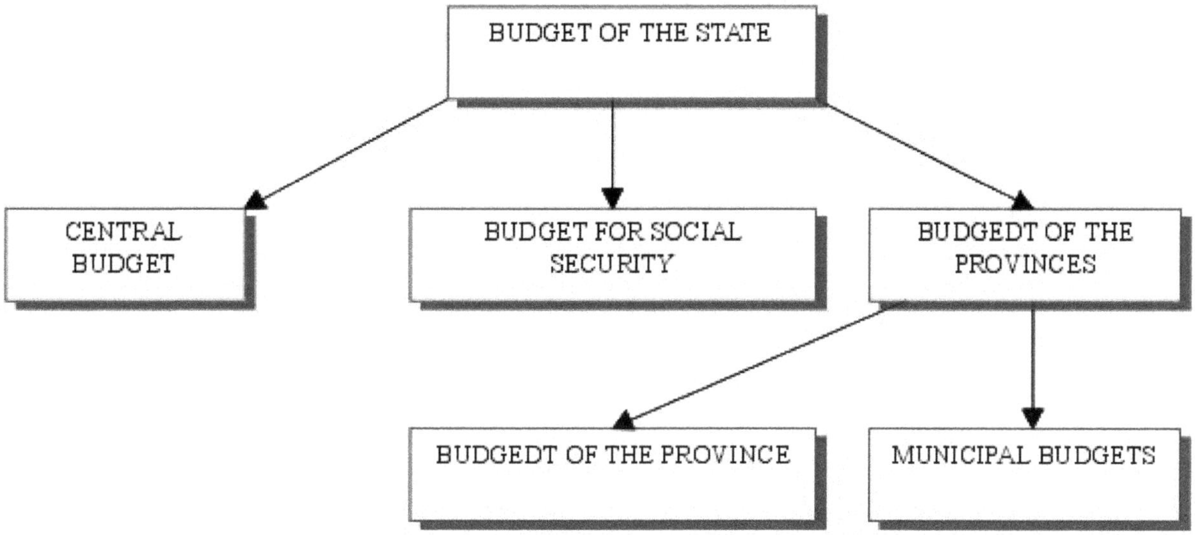

The combination of a central management principle, which recognizes and gives powers to the local bodies of the, People´s Power is present in the Cuban budget system so that they can extensively participate in working out, implementing and liquidation of budgets.

Legislative and normative functions of all the system are concentrated in the central bodies as well as the necessary proceedings to achieve macroeconomic stability and guarantee timely financial support of crucial tasks of the economic development. And the distribution of financial resources that might provide for equity and implementation of programs, regardless of economic development in the territories is also accomplished through the concentration of the functions above mentioned

Local bodies of the government concentrate a large share of financial resources that guarantee the implementation of the economic policy together with the corresponding autonomy for planning and use of resources. The end is to join the interest of every territory and those of society as a whole. The relation between the central budget with the provincial budgets is further explained.

The budget of the state is discussed and endorsed by the Cuban Parliament every year during its sessions at the end of the year and this budget rules from January 1st to December 31st every year.

Working out starts during May-June once the Council of Ministers issue its guidelines and top priorities. Then, the Ministry of Finances and Prices works out specific guidelines considering the characteristics of every sector, branch, activity or territory based on the considerations of the Council of Ministers. These specific guidelines are the basis on which bodies linked to the Central Budget and to Provincial and Municipal Budgets work out preliminary plans and present them before the Ministry of Finances and Prices in October. A process of analysis, evaluation and negotiation of figures for further submittal before the Council of Ministers starts after this date

After the analysis, the Council of Ministers submits the project before the National Assembly of People's Power (Cuban Parliament) that approves it by the following items:

a. The Budget of the State, by the total amount of financial resources and expenditures and within them, by its main sources and ends and in its opening, by current budgets and capital budgets.
b. The Central Budget divided into current budget and capital budget and consigning the main sources of financial resources, the total sum of expenditures and the detachment of its destination.
c. The Budget for Social Security, by the total amount of its financial resources and expenditures.
d. The percentages of participation of provincial budgets in the incomes of the Central Budgets
e. Direct transfers to grant to provincial budgets, bearing on the Central Budget

After the endorsement of the Budget of the State, the Ministry of Finances and Prices gives notice with the corresponding figures to the agencies related to it and periodically allots budgetary credits.

During implementation, there can be changes and adjustments made by the different organizations and institutions if they do not affect limits set forth in the notices.

The Ministry of Finances and Prices has the power to implement changes as long as they do not affect the balance of incomes and expenditures, i.e., they can not change the Fiscal Deficit endorsed by Parliament.

Periodically, the different organizations and institutions are compelled to report on the implementation of the budget. This provides for the evaluation of fulfillment and at the end of the fiscal year they should present the liquidation that serves as the basis for the rendering of accounts of the Ministry of Finances and Prices before the Government and the Parliament

Concerning the System of the Treasury, its implementation has been propelled by requirements needed not only by an efficient financial management including the flow of funds but also, by the reform sped up in the banking system of the country.

Though it is not valid to speak of a system of the treasury, certain basic principles are being applied. The most outstanding are: working out a budget for payments; monthly financial programs of budget distribution; shortening the terms to hand budgetary credits.

All the territories have created mechanisms to operate under the principles of treasury set by the Law - Decree and to manage the accounts of the Central Budget in the different territories.

And parallel to this, work has been done on the System of Government Accounting. The establishment of income and uniform expenditure classifiers has been crucial for this end.

Accountancy of management entities was worked out and introduced, establishing heritage and budget control. These are the basis to know efficiency and economy of public expenditure management and the proper use of funds allotted by the State budget

Though the Law - Decree authenticates the legal frame for the introduction of the System of Public Credit it will not come into force in a short term because it is conditioned by other factors.

RELATIONS OF BUDGET WITH PUBLIC BUSINESS

The changes that have occurred as a result of the crisis and the restatement needed in the organization and management of public administration and the endorsement of Act 73 on the Tax System conditioned a change in the relations between public business and the Budget of the State. This change provides for a clearer concept of the state in its double role of Treasury and owner.

Under this concept, all public business is compelled to pay taxes, rates and contributions to the Treasury, in line with Act 73. Commitments with the Treasury are compulsory and failure to comply under the terms and amounts set leads to penalties established by law.

Profits after honoring the Treasury can be used for different ends previously defined by the representatives of the State. The most important are the contribution to the budget by the yield of the state investment, the capitalization and finance of investments and stimulation to workers teams.

The system conceives a closest link of the business with the result of its economic management when it grants autonomy on the issue of financial management. It favors the capacity and initiative of business managers and strengthens their responsibility for the work they carry out.

In this sense, the system allows for the creation of reserves and provisions from the gross income to cover eventual losses and risks as well as provisions for voluntary expenditures aimed for general repairs.

Besides profits, the use of other sources for financing such as decentralized resources from the accumulated depreciation, the sale of active assets and bank credits are recognized to start a process of investments. In this way, agencies and institutions are progressively separated from the Budget on the issue of finance for investments, increase of working capital, stimulation to workers and other plans for development.

Due to state needs there is public business producing under conditions that can not cover expenditures with profits. They are unprofitable. In this case, the State Budget subsidizes their production based on a plan endorsed under the guidelines of the Annual Law of Budget

RELATIONS OF THE CENTRAL BUDGET WITH THE PROVINCIAL BUDGETS

The Central Budget allots budgets to the provinces based on certain criteria of distribution and in line with the policy of decentralization of resources explained in the Budgetary System for organizations and institutions of the local bodies of the government so that they can efficiently manage their budgets. The criteria for budget allotment are the following:

Incomes transferred or owned: These incomes come from institutions managed by local bodies of the government or linked to collections from a past or future expenditure that should be paid by the community e.g. the reproduction and education of labor force causes expenditures in education, public health, recreation and cultural and social ones. It is for this reason that the Tax on the Use of Labor Force is fully transferred to the provinces and municipalities regardless of subordination of the institution that pays.

Participative incomes: These incomes are derived from taxes at the central level collected in the provinces / municipalities, with rates ranging from 10 to 20% on the Tax of Circulation and the Tax on Profits of business of national subordination

The Central Budget allots Direct Transfers as subsidies to balance fiscal capacities between provinces and municipalities and are not aimed to finance any particular expenditure. Likewise, Direct Transfers are made to finance investments in programs of the infrastructure, housing and road construction and social and cultural works.

Consequently, local governments and the institutions subordinated to them are responsible for the management and use of financial resources allotted. This makes it possible to increase efficiency and efficacy in the service of these institutions.

Decentralization in the management of public expenditures to the provinces / municipalities guarantees an effective application of the social policy established. It also provides for a more active performance since the institutions of local governments have the power to define and approve the objectives of expenditures, considering the needs and characteristics of every territory according to the established limits of their budgets.

During the fiscal year and according to the implementation, they can transfer financial resources from one thing to another by way of budgetary changes without permission from higher budgetary organizations. This provides more flexibility in the decentralized management of budget and a more efficient allotment and use of resources and the timely attention to financial needs.

MAIN CHARACTERISTICS OF BUDGET FOR THE YEAR 2000

State Budget for the year 2000 has regarded that in spite of a favorable forecast for next year's economy, external financial restrictions, the blockade and the limited access to international credits under favorable terms are still in force.

Consequently, a deficit amounting to 745,0 million pesos has been projected following the fiscal policy laid for the last four years. This figure represents 2.8% of the GDP calculated at current prices and it meets the principles of stability and sustainability that have made possible the stability of finances during this stage.

An amount of 9.166 million pesos have been allotted to budgeted business. This figure is higher than estimates by 607 million pesos out of which 176, 0 million pesos were used for rises in salaries in different sectors in 1999; 275,0 million pesos are used for maintenance and renovation in housing and road and social/cultural facilities. More than 90,0 million come from the rise in prices and almost 54,0 million to back the natural growth of the amount of professionals joining the fields of health and education. The entire expenditures represent 34.8% of the GDP.

An amount of 2.601 million pesos are disposed for transfers to the business sector and from this figure, 608.0 are allotted to subsidies for losses in state business. It should be stressed that all the institutions reduce the amount of loses scheduled as compared to 1999.

Resources appointed for subsidies due to the difference of prices are growing (subsidies to consumer families). The reason is the rise in prices of state collection centers of agricultural products without changing retail prices, considering that these are products of the basket of good sold to the population on the ration card. An amount of 560,0 million pesos are allotted for this end.

As a whole, transfers to the state business sector are lower by 9.8% as compared to the budget for 1999 and this means 292, 0 million pesos less than in that year.

Economic assistance to basic units for cooperative production (not involved in sugar cane plantations) is reduced due to the positive effects provoked by the rise in the prices of milk and meat and due to the increased management efficiency.

A Central Reserve of 190.0 million pesos has been considered for this year and it exceeds the figure budgeted for 1999 by 90.0 million pesos. The objective of this is to face new decisions including the continuation of a wage reform in the sectors that were not benefited in 1999.

An amount of 1.700 million pesos is appointed to finance investments and other capital expenditures (6.5 % of the GDP). This figure is below the budget of 1999 by 50,0 million pesos but it is in line with the forecasts for the end of the year according to the results of calculations showing that 100.0 million pesos would not be expended. So, when you compare with estimates it is foreseen that a growth of 3.0% would be attained.

So as to meet these needs of resources it has been envisaged to obtain incomes by an amount of more than 13.525 million pesos that exceed the plan for 1999 by 8.5%.

It should be stressed that the amount planned exceeds the estimates for 1999 only by 0.8% because non-repetitive incomes have been purged from the year 2000 mostly by reductions of tax rates that reduce the collection of such taxes.

Notwithstanding, these reductions are balanced by the prediction of higher collection of direct taxes linked to the profit of businesses and the Contributions by Yield according to the growth projected by the economy, the increase in business efficiency and the fiscal discipline of tax payers.

From the total amount of resources to collect via budget, 78% is made up by taxes and 22% comes from non-tax incomes.

THE POLICY OF PRICES

The price determination is fitted to the current conditions of the Cuban economy and generally, there is advance in establishing them centrally. Wholesale prices are based on our foreign trade prices or the domestic prices in hard currency.

Mechanisms are being introduced to make prices formation flexible and provide business with the possibility to negotiate them; this without renouncing to the central establishment of the policy of prices. So, wholesale trade in the local hard currency market develops under prices generally determined by business depending on the market.

It is under these conditions that a new complementary system of financial relations has been born. It sets the actions of the Cuban state as an owner, defining the procedures for the contribution by the yield of state investment in state businesses as part of the distribution of profits obtained once fiscal obligations are met.

This system conceives a closer link of business with the results of its economic management because it grants autonomy on the issue of financial management and stimulates the capacity and initiative of managers and strengthens their role to account for the efficiency of their actions.

In this sense, the system allows the creation of reserves and provisions from gross earnings so as to cover future loses and other eventualities as well as provisions for voluntary expenditures aimed at general repairs.

On the other hand, it allows for the partial allotment of retained profit to finance investments, regardless of the existence of other sources of finance such as decentralized resources from accumulated depreciation and the sale of idle capital assets or the bank credits. In this way, business progressively separate from the Budget on the issue of finance for investments, increase of working capital, stimulation of workers and other plans for development.

INSURANCE SUPERINTENDENCE

The Superintendency of Insurance of Cuba was created under Law-Decree No. 177, "On the arrangement of insurance and its agencies", dated on September 2nd, 1997. It is assigned to the Ministry of Finances and Prices and its role is to control and superintend institutions dealing with insurance and reinsurance procedures, support services for insurance and brokerage and insurance agencies. The protection of the insured is its mission.

Its scope is not limited to agencies operating in the national territory. It also deals with Cuban agencies or with Cuban interests based abroad that work in the field of insurance.

Currently, there are three national companies of direct insurance operating in Cuba: International Insurance of Cuba S.A., (ESICUBA), National Insurance Co. (ESEN) and Tourism Insurer, La Isla S.A. There are other institutions related to insurance such as Intermar S.A., a tallying and inspection agency and others; Asistur, providing assistance to tourism; Rado and Associates, consultant and lawyers; Conavana S.A., consultants of valuation.

There are branches of foreign life insurance companies liquidating contracts signed up to 1962 represented in Cuba and the Offices of the Lloyd's Register of Shipping and the Veritas Bureau. There is also a Center of Accounting, Financial and Insurance Studies.

INDUSTRY

The management, implementation and control of how State and Governmental policy is applied, in relation to industrial development there are seven specialised industrial ministries which are responsible:

- **Ministry of Basic Industry.**
- **Ministry of Iron and Steel Mechanics Industry**
- **Ministry of the Fishing Industry**
- **Ministry of the Food Industry (Only available in spanish).**
- **Ministry of Light Industry.**
- **Ministry of Sugar.**

The Ministry of Steel – Mechanical Industry (SIME) is the Cuban entity committed in the leading, execution and control of the State and Government policy regarding the activities of the Steel and Mechanical Industry and Recycling.

It was founded in 1974 as a result of the strengthening of investor process in the industrial sphere, a visionary conception of Major Ernesto Che Guevara in the dawn of the Revolution, when he was heading the Ministry of Industries.

Mechanical industry is undoubtedly a creation of Cuban revolution, one of its products. Before the Revolution this industry did not exist in Cuba, everything was imported, we depended entirely on American industry. In this primary stage, the creation of SIME meant the consolidation of a whole series of productions prioritized by the country, which were essentially necessary for the economic development of our nation.

Since its creation, SIME has had a vertical development line thanks to a properly structured and well thought investment plan aimed to the production of automotive and railroad equipment, agricultural machinery, iron & steel industry, construction equipment, machine tools, medical equipment and clinical furniture, supplies for hotel industry, etc.

This investor process started as early as years 1963-64, when such industries still belonged to the Ministry of Industries, which was created by Major Guevara and it was carried out in cooperation with the socialist countries, commissioning productive complexes in the central and eastern regions of the country.

Its creation was an important step that allowed the agglutination of human resources that were being significantly oriented from the beginning of the Revolution toward sectors of vital importance for our socialist development.

So can we see in statistics that soon after its creation, in 1976 it produces 246 millions of dollars, in 1977, 278 millions; in 1978, 304 millions; in 1979, 360 millions, till reaching in 1985 the quantity of 760 millions. This situation starts a sudden downward trend in 1989, because of the diminishing trade with the USSR and former socialist countries, and gets to its climax in 1992.

From 1993 on, the organism enters a recovery process, re-ordering its capacities toward new products lines, related to *the needs of the emerging sector of the economy* in this stage of special period, and *exports*. Other activities were incorporated in 1994, such as electronics, information science, recycling and the import – export possibilities in its competent activities, as a consequence of a re-ordain in the state apparatus whose objective was to transfer, on a mid term, the management of economy to enterprises in an important proportion and diminish the leading role of the central organism in an important quantity of decisions that should actually be taken by enterprises themselves.

These years have served to SIME for consolidating and make grow excellent workers' groups, who know their profession, are skilled and able to make our factories work in hard conditions, and will also be capable of making them evolve and develop.

These years have seen incorporating to SIME a large quantity of technicians and professionals, massive entering of university graduates who have enriched the possibilities and potential of its enterprises.

At the moment, the Ministry relies on:

12 Industrial Groups;
178 Enterprises;
6 Research and Development Centers;
4 Associations;
9 Commercial Firms
1 Formation Centers
6 Joint Ventures
4 Economic Associations in Cuba

Total quantity of SIME workers is 62642, 15% of which are professionals.

- **ACINOX Industrial Group**
- **ALCUBA Industrial Group**
- **CICLEX Industrial Group**
- **DIVEP Industrial Group**
- **GIMAC Industrial Group**
- **Caribbean Ironworks**
- **Raw Material Recovery**
- **Refrigeration and Boilers**
- **BK-CETI Industrial Group**
- **General Machinery**
- **FERROTAINO Industrial Group**
- **UNECAMOTO Industrial Group**

MAJOR GOVERNMENT AGENCIES

- Ministry of Sugar (MINAZ)
- Ministry of Agriculture (MINAGRI)
- Ministry of Science, Technology and Environment (CITMA)
- Ministry of Foreign Trade (MINCEX)
- Ministry of Domestic Trade (MINCIN)
- Ministry of Communications (MINCOM)
- Ministry of Construction (MICONS)
- Ministry of Culture (MINCULT)
- Ministry of Economics and Planning (MEP)
- Ministry of Justice (MINJUS)
- Ministry of Labor and Social Security (MTSS)
- Ministry of Education (MINED)
- Ministry of Higher Education (MES)
- Ministry of Finances and Prices (MFP)
- Ministry of the Food Industry (MINAL)
- Ministry of the Basic Industry (MINBAS)
- Ministry of the Light Industry (MINIL)
- Ministry of the Industry of Construction Materials (MIMC)
- Ministry of the Fishing Industry (MIP)
- Ministry of the Iron, Steel, Mechanical and Electronical Industry (SIME)
- Ministry of Foreign Affairs (MINREX)
- Ministry of Public Health (MINSAP)
- Ministry of Transportation (MITRANS)
- Ministry of Tourism (MINTUR)
- Ministry for Foreign Investment and Economic Cooperation (MINVEC)
- Institute of Civil Aeronautics of Cuba (IACC)

- National Institute of Hydraulic Resources (INRH)
- National Institute of State Reserves (INRE)
- National Institute of Sports, Physical Education and Recreation (INDER)
- Cuban Institute of Radio and Television (ICRT)
- Central Bank of Cuba (BCC)

GOVERNMENT AGENCIES SUPERVISING FOREIGN TRADE ACTIVITY

The Cuban State rules and controls foreign trade through the Ministry of Foreign Trade, guiding, controlling and supervising the country's foreign trade activities and those of entities empowered to perform them.

To such ends and with the authorization of the competent organ, it disposes the creation, merger, modification and extinction of foreign trade enterprises, with an independent juridical character and patrimony of its own, granting them faculties to perform export and import operations.

The following institutions participate directly or indirectly in Cuban foreign trade::

- Ministry of Foreign Trade, leading organ of foreign trade activity.
- Central Bank of Cuba, leading institution of the national banking system, which acts as central State bank.
- Ministry for Foreign Investment and Economic Cooperation, in charge of directing and controlling those negotiations related with the investment process.
- Ministry of Finances and Prices, in charge of leading and controlling the State and Government's financial policy.
- General Customhouse of the Republic, entity empowered to enforce the country's customs policy.
- Ministry of Economy and Planning, organ in charge of directing the State and Government's economic policy.
- Ministry of Foreign Affairs, organ in charge of international political relations.
- Chamber of Commerce of the Republic of Cuba, independent agency promoting and cooperating in the development of Cuban external relations.

There are other banking and financial institutions linked to the commercial activity and wich are detailed in the chapter of Banking System.

REGULATIONS

In accordance with the new changes happening in the Cuban economy, in its international economic relations, the experience gathered and the international practice, the Cuban legislation offers by means of the decree No.206 from April 1996 and the resolutions No. 24,25 and 26 from 1997 as a complement to that decree and that were stated by the Minister of Foreign Trade and by means of which possibilities are established that permit a better development of its foreign trade.

To such purposes, the branch offices of foreign mercantile societies and individual entrepreneurs interested in performing trade activities in the Cuban territory may establish themselves in it or be represented by previously authorized national entities, which will act as intermediaries.

Branch offices and agents authorized to act in the national territory must previously obtain the license issued by the National Registry of Branch Offices and Agents at the Chamber of Commerce of the Republic of Cuba, and be entered in the Registry of that organization.

Cuba's great concern for human health and the prevention of animal and plant disease has become evident by the enactment of a number of laws, decrees and regulations for the issuance of the corresponding export or import permit.

Public health regulations for the registration of foodstuffs, cosmetics, as well as personal and household articles The Ministry of Public Health through Instituto Nacional de Nutrición e Higiene de los Alimentos establishes the regulations for the registration of foodstuffs, cosmetics and articles for personal and household use consistent with the Cuban standards NC 38-03-06'87 for the import and export of foodstuffs and NC 95-37'87 for perfumes and cosmetics.

The Registry is designed to protect consumers' and users' health and is independent from the Veterinary

Registry for Goods of Animal Origin and the Phitosanitary Registry for Goods of Plant Origin established by the Ministry of Agriculture.

ANIMAL-HEALTH REGULATIONS

Decree-Law No. 137 of April 16, 1993 rules the veterinary activity and establishes the requirements for the export and import of animals and their products. Decree No. 181 of April 17 of the same year provides for transgressions of the law and corrective measures. The National Veterinarian Medicine Institute, under the Ministry of Agriculture, enforces such a legislation.

Animal species, either alive or preserved in any manner; animal-based products for consumption, industrial,decoration, experimental or research purposes; germ or parasitic agents; serum, vaccines, hormones or fermentations of animal origin; culture and diagnostic means using animal-based ingredients, and any item, product or packaging material of any origin that may carry animal diseases are all subject to veterinary control.

Animals and animal-based goods and raw materials destined for export must comply with the registrations established by the veterinary regulations in force as well as those demanded by the competent authorities from the importing country or the international treaties of which Cuba is a party.

In order to guarantee the veterinary conditions of the animals and animal-based goods and raw materials destined for export, the Ministry of Agriculture, through the National Veterinarian Medicine Institute, will issue the corresponding Veterinary Export Certificate.

PLANT HEALTH REGULATIONS

The National Plant Health Center, under the Ministry of Agriculture, is responsible for plant health control. The import and export of plants and related components are regulated by Resolution No. 366 of May 29, 1990, as amended by Resolution No. 45 of October 28, 1994.

Live plant species and related parts, crop and wild-plant seeds, food products of plant origin, both in their natural or semiprocessed form; feed and fodder; forest products; packages and containers that may carry pests; earth, soil or organic fertilizers; raw materials of plant origin; tobacco;

organisms or microorganisms hazardous to agriculture and any agent that may act as a disease or pest carrier are all subject to plant-health controls.

Cuba does not apply any import or export license regime, regulations, quotas, etc. which may be obstacles to foreign trade.

All Cuban entities or international associations created under law 77 which have given authority to export or to import by Resolution of the Ministry of Foreign Trade could do operations of foreign trade, for the nomenclature of products listed in said Resolution.

Other regulations in force are those related to the preservation of the national patrimony and drug prohibitions, as well as health regulations and others relative to the preservation of the environment, protection of endangered species and movement of refuse and other dangerous materials beyond the frontier.

INTERNATIONAL ORGANIZATIONS

Cuba is a member state of the World Trade Organization, which became valid on January 1st 1995, as a successor body on the General Agreement on Custom's taxes and Trade.

Among the most important compromises to be fulfilled by Cuba we have the anti-dumping measures, the safeguard to commerce technical obstacles and the implementation of tax reductions.

Cuba's participation in the WHO has generated new obligations, but at the same time permits the defense of the country's commercial interests, and the denunciation of illegal measurements and opposite to the principles and objectives of free trading.

Cuban is also a member of many international agencies among them:

- United Nations Organization (UNO)
- United Nations Conference on Trade and Development (UNCTAD)
- Economic Commission for Latin America
- International Sugar Organization (ISO)
- International Coffee Organization (ICO)
- Wheat International Council (WTC)
- Permanent Court of Arbitration
- Group of Latin American and Caribbean Sugar Exporting Countries
- Universal Postal Union (UPU)
- Non-Aligned Countries Movement
- International Civil Aviation Organization
- World Organization of Industrial Property
- International Standardization Organization (ISO)
- Association of Caribbean States (ACS)
- UNICEF (UN Children´s Fund)
- International Labor Organization (ILO)
- United Nations Economic and Social Council (ECOSOC)
- Latin American Economic System
- International Air Transportation Association (IATA)
- United Nations Food and Agriculture Organization (FAO)

- United Nations Industrial Development Organization (UNIDO)
- United Nations Development Program (UNDP)
- Latin American Energy Organization
- World Health Organization (WHO)
- Pan American Health Organization (PAHO)
- United Nations Educational, Scientific and Cultural Organization (UNESCO)
- International Olympic Committee (IOC)
- International Court of Justice

ECONOMY

After the dissolution of the external economic relations with the socialist block, especially the Soviet Union, as a result of the political changes in those countries, and the tightening of the U.S. embargo on the island, the Cuban economy has gone through a process of transformation in the 90's which has enabled its reentrance in the international economy.

This transformation of the Cuban economy covers all spheres prone to changes.

Great transformations have happened in the spheres of foreign capital, the state no longer runs the monopoly of foreign trade. There are different organizations and types of property; there is now a possibility for the creation of joint ventures with foreign currency and more possibilities for entrepreneurial and territorial management.

The institutional changes carried out include the improvement of organization, direction and planning of the economy, where financial bases prevail.

As a result of these measures in 1994 the Cuban economy stopped its deterioration, and in 1995 the recovery process started, reaffirmed in 1996.

Last year a growth of a 2,5% in the Gross National Product was observed. These figures show comparable results with many Latin American and Caribbean countries.

The projection of The Gross National Product for that year was of a 4%, it was not achieved because of certain factors, such as the low production of the sugar economy, the deterioration of exchange relations as a result of a decrease in the production of that product and a decrease in the international prices for nickel, which are major exports of the economy. On top of that there was a fracture in the external financing due to the Helms Burton Act, damaging the economy. The negative effects of Lili Hurricane were felt, affecting the agriculture, and there appeared a number of plagues in different crops.

Incomes generated by tourism in 1997 increased over a 12% when the number of 1.18 millions of tourists was reached.
For 1998 a GNP increase of 2.5-3.5 is expected, taking into account the foreseen financial unbalance.

Foreign Trade and the economy were seriously affected in the decade of the 90's. One of these factors was the disappearance of commercial relations with the Soviet Union and CAME, what provoked the loss of preferential markets and investment projects, import and export preferential prices, elimination of collaboration agreements, and interruption of essential supplies for the development of the national economy.

On top of this we had the strengthening of the embargo on our island and the approval of the Torricelly and Helms-Burton Acts. As a result of them the access of financial credits to Cuba was limited, as well as commercial operations and foreign investment was being threatened.

The high banking interest rates in an international scale, fluctuations in the currency markets' quotations and the unfavorable alterations of exchange terms internationally were also factors that exerted a negative influence over the economy and its foreign trade.

This group of factors provoked a decrease in our commercial exchange, so the application of measures aimed at the reinsertion of Cuba in the international economy and the reorganization of its external markets was necessary.

The State's monopoly over foreign trade was eliminated with the aim of speeding external commercial activity and foreign investment was promoted because of its capital, technology and market's meaning.

This decentralization process of the Cuban foreign trade allowed for the appearance of state, private and joint enterprises, authorized to perform operations in this sphere, and other foreign enterprises and entrepreneurs were given opportunities to open a branch or to be represented in the country by an agent as well as the establishment of warehouses in free zones and industrial parks in custom's deposits.

An special emphasis has been placed in the strengthening of relations with Latin America and the Caribbean, thus reaching partial agreements with member states of the Latin American Integration Association (ALADI). Other talks have begun with MERCOSUR and is member of the Caribbean State's Association and CARIFORUM. Cuba is working on an agreement with the European Union which enables the development of commercial ties with that organization.

The trend towards recovery in commercial exchange has kept steady since 1995 and in 1997 despite the harsh national financial situation this orientation remained firm.

(Valor en pesos cubanos)

Años	Exportaciones	Importaciones	Intercambio Total	Saldo Comercial
1988	5518.3	7579.8	13098.1	-2071.5
1989	5399.2	8139.7	13538.9	-2740.5
1990	5415.0	7416.6	12831.6	-2001.6
1991	2961.5	4149.0	7110.5	-1187.5
1992	1784.0	2315.0	4099.0	- 537.0
1993	1156.7	2008.2	3164.9	- 851.5
1994	1330.8	2016.8	3347.6	- 538.3
1995	1491.6	2882.5	4374.1	-1390.9
1996(1)	1848.9	3480.6	5329.5	-1631.7
1997(2)	1860.0	4173.2	6033.2	-2313.2
1998(3)	2094.4	4584.3	6678.7	-2489.9

The Cuban economic policy has substantially evolved towards a process of adjustment according to the new circumstances under which its relations develop, the bank system playing a new and important role.

Bearing in mind this reality, the Cuban banking system has entered into an unavoidable process of reforms and decentralization, with the separation of the functions of central and commercial bank which Banco Nacional de Cuba had been conducting and the creation of Banco Central de Cuba as central bank.

In an autonomous form and with independent organization and juridical character, Banco Central de Cuba exerts the ruling, regulating and supervising authority of the financial institutions and of the representative offices established in the country, including the extra-territorial banking center, duty-free zones and industrial parks.

It performs other functions related to those of other countries' central banks.

In the process of reorganization of the national banking system have been conceded new licenses authorizing to different banks to do functions of national banking.

The new banking system is formed by:

- **Banco Central de Cuba (BCC)**, whose functions have already been explained.
- **Cuban National Bank BNC**. It gets and gives credits in national and hard currencies, accepts discounts negotiates and validates in any form exchange letters, checks and other negotiable documents. It keeps the record, control service and attention of the foreign debt contracted with foreign creditors, up to the date of validation of the decree No. 172 from 1997 from the Central Bank of Cuba.
- **International Financing Bank BFI.** It receives and gives deposits in cash at sight or by terms, loans or other forms of financing credits and funds transfer to and from abroad.
- **Commerce and Credit Bank BANDEC.** It performs typical functions of the commercial bank and thus all kinds of operations and businesses of financial mediation.
- **Popular Savings Bank BPA.** It attracts, keeps and receives cash in deposits at sight or by terms in the convenient modalities. It also lends money, credit and financing lines of all types, short medium and long-term, as well as invoices, financial leasing and other financing modalities.
- **Commerce International Bank S.A. (BICSA).** Exchange of hard currency; transfers, common accounts and deposits, deposits by terms and all kinds of document operations.

Within the reorganization process of the Cuban bank, it has also been created the New Bank Group which is made up of the following entities:

- National Financing (FINSA). It performs operations for export financing, imports and investment, leasing factoring and collecting management; forfaiting, financial engineering service and business management.
- Investment Bank S.A. (BI). It performs all kinds of banking businesses, especially those of investment financing and administration; it gets funds and gives credits on its own, or as a trustee agent.
- Exchange Offices (CADECA). It offers services of hard currency or Cuban convertible peso buying or sailing.
- Metropolitan Bank S.A. (BM). It offers normal account services in national currency and in hard currency. Accounts in deposits at a fixed term in hard currency; tax collections, payments sales of traveler's checks and credit cards.

- Trusteeship Companies (TC). Accepts and performs requests of all types given to the company by any person, corporation or judiciary authority, could also be a fiscal agent, testament executor, Judicial Administrator Trustee and other fiduciary activities recognized internationally; inter-enterprises money collections.

Other financial non-banking institutions and not belonging to the Nueva Banca group are:

- Rafin S.A. It finances export operations, imports and investments. Leasing, factoring and forfeiting.
- Finalse S.A. It finances export operations, imports and investment; it performs operations of leasing and invoices, it participates in operations of refinancing debts and it also brings engineering services and business management.
- Fimel S.A. It finances export and import operations, it gives services of financial engineering, business management, it promotes export projects, it serves as a consultant firm in economic financing and statistic matters.
- Panamerican Finance Society S.A.PANAFIN SA. It finances fuel import operations, food and chemicals with incomes coming from export pre-financing. Deals with the contracts necessary to clearly establish its rights and obligations and to guarantee the support of its records. According to the generally accepted principles.

Under the existing legislation there are 12 representative offices of foreign banks in the country, which constitute a relevant promotion and coordination link in the relations with their respective head offices. These banks are:

- The Netherlands Caribbean Bank
- The ING Bank (International Nederlanden Group)
- Havana International Bank Ltd.
- Banco Exterior de España
- National Bank of Canada
- Banco Sabadell
- Fransabank Sal
- Banco Bilbao Vizcaya
- Banco Nacional de Comercio Exterior de Mexico
- INKOMBANK
- Stolichny Bank of Savings

The national currency is the Cuban peso. Since 1993, the US dollar is also in circulation.

The official exchange rate fixed by BCC is 1 Cuban peso = 1 USD.

QUALITY CONTROL

To guarantee the quality of the products that enter or leave the country and the fulfillment of their standards, foreign trade enterprises include in their contracts, supervision of their goods in origin and destination in function of the technical parameters and others requirements to check.

CUBACONTROL's services are offered to more than 144 countries, with permanent offices in Russia and Mexico and itinerant inspectors in other countries, at the request of clients. In 1961, CUBACONTROL signed an agreement with the Societe Generale de Surveillance (SGS) from Switzerland, the leading multinational company in the world for merchandise certification.

Services that offer this enterprise are of inspection, customhouse and transitaries and posses a laboratory duly equipped with trail methods recognized for the executions of analysis to chemical products, fresh and canned goods, alcohol and beverages. Other enterprises offer similar services are ADESA S.A and AISA.

FOREING TRADE.

The Cuban economy and foreign trade were severely affected by a number of events that took place in the nineties. As a result, Cuba lost access to preferential markets and investment projects, to preferential prices for import and export, collaboration agreements were cancelled and supply of essential products for the development of our economy was discontinued.

All that was compounded by the strengthening of the United States embargo against Cuba and the adoption of Torricelli and Helms-Burton acts, which limit Cuba's access to financial credits in international institutions, hinder business transactions and put pressure on potential foreign investors.

Other factors also had serious damaging effects on Cuba's economy and its foreign trade during the nineties, namely, high bank interest rates at the international level, fluctuations in money market quotations as well as an unfavorable change in worldwide exchange terms.

All those factors as a whole caused a decrease in our business exchange. Therefore, it was necessary to take a number of measures intended to reinvigorate our economy with a view to inserting it into the global economy and reorganize our external markets.

For the purpose of facilitating our external trade activity, foreign trade stopped being a State-only function and foreign investment began to be given great support due to its significant contribution to bringing capital, technology and market into the country.

The role played by the Ministry of Foreign Trade of Cuba was reinforced as a leading, executing and monitoring institution for implementing State and Government foreign trade policies. In that respect, the Ministry is intended to guide, control and supervise the country's foreign trade activities and those carried out by authorized entities.

Such a decentralizing process in foreign trade operational management allowed for the establishment of State enterprises and joint ventures, as well as international economic associations having direct access to the overseas market. Foreign companies and businessmen were allowed to open branch offices or have representative agents in Cuba. Furthermore, consignment stocks and bonded warehouses were established and free zones and industrial parks were opened.

Special emphasis has been placed on the strengthening of Cuba's relations with Latin America and the Caribbean. In that respect, Cuba has signed Partial Scope Agreements with most member States of the Latin-American Association of Integration (ALADI), except for Paraguay: Argentina, Bolivia, Brazil, Colombia, Chile, Ecuador, Mexico, Peru, Uruguay and Venezuela.

Once Cuba enters into that Association, our country will have to renegotiate or adapt those agreements to the rules governing for those instruments established among member States, which would imply that concessions would only be granted to signatory countries. Thus, a "4+1" agreement would then be negotiated with MERCOSUR participants.

Cuba has an observer status in the Group of countries associated to the Lomé Convention, an association made up by African, Caribbean and Pacific countries and the European Union, with which we are working in order to sign an agreement that will allow for the development of closer commercial links.

Preliminary figures of our foreign trade activity in 1998 show a decrease in exports estimated at 11%, along with a 6% increase in imports. Those results were given by a number of internal and external factors, namely:

- Growing external financial tension influenced by: a more acute crisis caused by worldwide credit contraction and a price fall in the main Cuban exports;
- Problems relating to the economic embargo and aggression affecting the country;
- Serious damages to agricultural and sugar production due to excess rain, followed by a severe drought. All that was compounded by the damage caused by Hurricane George, which struck the country in September 1998.

Nevertheless, progress has been made in the commercial exchange with other countries. The geographical distribution of trade has radically changed with an increase in the proportional participation of countries. Europe has a 47% share in total commercial exchange, where Spain, Russia, France, Italy and Germany score most highly, followed by America with 37%, where Canada, Venezuela, Mexico and the Netherlands Antilles stand out as our most active business partners in the Hemisphere. Asia follows next with a 14% share.

Export goods have been improved and diversified mainly due to a decrease in sugar production and international prices, but also to an increase in other export items.

The best performing export items in 1998 over 1997 were raw sugar, rolled tobacco, rum, coffee, bottled genuine honey, citrus juice, electric wires and cables, scrap, houses, frozen fish, textiles, some biotechnology pharmaceuticals, medical equipment, cocoa products and bagasse boards.

Non traditional export items have a significant potential, taking into account existing and potential productive capacities. Some progress has been achieved in this area and the country is still working to this end.

Imports in 1998 showed an increase of 6%, as a result of a rise in the price of food, fuels and other raw materials, as well as in those inputs necessary to maintain an economic recovery. That increase in import expenses widened the country's commercial gap, having a negative effect on our foreign debt, along with additional prices that Cuba has to pay to its suppliers and the necessary expenses to reinvigorate our economy.

The decentralization process in foreign trade has continued with a rise in the number of entities separately involved in related activities. Consequently, production has been increasingly linked to international market conditions and new ways of business management have been established.

These changes have brought about a higher share of responsibility of enterprises in the stewardship of resources and closer links to the overseas market.

IMPORT AND EXPORT REGIME.

Cuba does not apply any import or export license regime, regulations or quotas that may hinder foreign trade.

All Cuban entities or international associations established under Act 77 as well as those granted an import and/or export permit under resolution by the Ministry of Foreign Trade for nomenclature of goods listed in said resolution will be able to do foreign trade transactions.

Other regulations in force are those relating to preservation of our national heritage, restraints on drugs, environmental preservation, protection of endangered species, across-the-border movements of waste and other dangerous materials and sanitary regulations.

REGULATIONS FOR THE ESTABLISHMENT OF BRANCH OFFICES AND AGENTS.

The Cuban legislation authorizes, under Decree 206 of April 1996, the establishment of offices by foreign business corporations or individual investors interested in having a branch office in the country for direct management of their business relations with Cuban enterprises and agencies. The above is based on the changes undergone by the Cuban economy in its international economic relations and the experience acquired in international practice.

Those foreign entities or individual businessmen who prefer to have a representative in the country rather than setting an office will need to apply for an agency contract, in order to be represented by a Cuban national entity legally entitled to act as an agent in our country.

Enrollment in the National Registry of Foreign Branch Offices and Business Corporation Agents is indispensable for the establishment of an office in the Republic of Cuba. The document accrediting such enrollment is the license issued by said Registry.

Note: The figures about increase and decrease of exports and its causes were taken from the Statement by José Luis Rodríguez during the second National Assembly Session, Granma newspaper, 23 December 1998.

DUTY FREE ZONES

The development of duty-free zones and industrial parks through foreign investment is an attractive option given Cuba's international communications facilities both by sea and air, geographical location, political and social stability and availability of skilled labor, among other advantages.

According to Decree-Law No. 165 of 1996, any individual or body corporate based abroad or any local body corporate may apply for a concession in respect to a duty-free zone, being committed to start up, operate, develop, maintain, manage and administer this concession.

The National Office of Free Zones of the Ministry for Foreign Investment and Economic Cooperation (MINVEC) is in charge of regulating and controlling the activities of the Duty-Free Zones. Facilities in the duty-free zones will be managed by the operators; i.e. individuals or body corporate based abroad or local individuals or body corporate duly authorized by MINVEC at the proposal of the concessionary. Any individual or body corporate that holds a may also act as an operator.

The duty-free zone operator may obtain approval for the following activities: production, manufacture, finished or semifinished product processing; trading, operations, banking, financial and insurance services; general and technological services, scientific research services, agricultural activities or others to be determined.

The operator may reserve up to 25 percent of productive, manufacturing, processing, trade and agricultural activities to the domestic market. Any higher proportion will require MINVEC approval.

The applicable preferential conditions on customs and taxes are similar to those existing in Latin America and the Caribbean.

Duty-free zones have the advantage that productions from those territories compete with imported ones since they are exempt from taxes, both for the purchase of raw materials and for their exports.

Duty-free zones have the advantage that domestic clients pay no customs tariffs if the product has a national aggregated component exceeding 50percent of its value, where by the cost of salaries, water and energy supply and other services may be calculated within that sum.

Presently there are in operations three industrial parks of the four authorized, one in the Wajay zone and other in Berroa Valley, both in the capital of the island and the third in the Mariel Port of Havana province.

The industrial park of Ciudad de La Habana is managed by Havana in Bond S.A., belonging to CIMEX Corporation, and is located in Berroa Valley, east of Ciudad de La Habana, with an easy access to Havana's port and airport.

TRADEMARKS

The protection of rights on inventions, scientifical discoveries, industrial models, trademarks and trade names, advertising of establishments, commercial slogans as well as the indication of origin and source is regulated by Decree Law No. 68 of May 14, 1983, as amended by Decree Law No. 160 on the application for patents of chemical and pharmaceutical products for agriculture.

Cuba is a member state of the World Organization for Intellectual Property (1975) and it is part of the treaties and agreements which protects these rights which are: The Paris Convention for the Protection of Industrial Property (1904), the Madrid Agreement Concerning the Repression of False Origin Indications in the Products (1905) The Madrid Agreement Concerning the International Register for Trademarks (1989) and the Protocol Concerning The Madrid Agreement on the Trademark International Agreement (1995), the Cooperation Treaty on Patents (1996), and the Lisbon Agreement concerning the protection of original denominations and their International Register (1958), and the Treaty on Trademarks Rights (1997).

PACKAGING

As a member of the World Trade Organization, Cuba is represented in its Committee of Trade Technical Obstacles by the National Standardization Office as competent national entity. This Office also acts as Information Point of the National Information Service on standards, technical regulations and procedures for the evaluation of acceptance (certification, inspection, trials, verification, quality control, among others).

The National Standardization Office represents Cuba in the International Standardization Office, the International Organization of Legal Metrology, the Codex Alimentarius Commission, the Pan American Commission of Technical Standards, the Inter-American Metrology System and the Inter-American Crediting Cooperation.

The implementation of the ISO 9000 standards started in Cuba in 1991. Many of the country's goods and service enterprises are involved in this process.

The ONC is the national certification organ, acknowledged by the Ministry of Economy and Planning.

The National Metrology Service, whose organization and control are conducted by the Office, is based on internationally acknowledged principles and particularly follows the recommendations of the International Organization of Legal Metrology(OIML).

The technical services of standardization, metrology and quality rendered by the Office are commercialized through the Cuban enterprise MACNOR S.A.

LABELING AND PACKAGING

The Cuban standards comply with the international praxis and basic principles on labeling, packing and marking with regard to the required information related to production and expiration dates, composition, marking, etc., with due regard to the ISO standards. The National Packing and Packaging Center is the Cuban entity overseeing this matter within the country on a central basis.

INVESTMENT REGULATIONS

Law No. 77 of September 5, 1995, rules foreign investment in Cuba and therefore has the purpose of promoting and incentivating foreign investment in the national territory, to perform profitable activities contributing to the strengthening of its economic capacity and sustainable development of the country, on the basis of respect to the national sovereignty and independence, and of the protection and rational utilization of natural resources.

Ministry for the Foreign Investment and Economic Collaboration (MINVEC) is charge of controlling negotiations to make the different types of economic associations with foreign participation.

It is possible to invest in all sectors except those of health and education services to the population, and in the armed forces except its entrepreneurial system.

Investments may take the form of mixed enterprises by nominative shares, contract of international association which does not imply the creation of a juridical person other than that of both contracting parties, and enterprises with a totally foreign capital.

Regarding payment of taxes and customs duties, a special regime has been created establishing payment of taxes by mixed enterprises, foreign investors and nationals who are part of international economic association contracts, on income and the use of labor force, as well as the contribution to social security, customs duties and remaining collectable rights in customs, land transportation and documents.

The law authorizes to export the production and import directly everything required for its purposes.

Concerning guarantees, these may include from compensation in case of expropriation to the assurance to the foreign investor of the free transfer of his income abroad.

Likewise, the - having received governmental authorization - may sell or transfer his total or partial participation to the State or to a third party, receiving the corresponding price in convertible currency.

The Cuban State also guarantees the foreign investor the free transfer in convertible currency, without payment of taxes or any other contribution related with that transfer; in the cases of:

- net profits, dividends or payments for expropriation
- his share of the liquidation, upon expiration of the authorization granted for his operations, in any of the investment forms he may be engaged in
- the sale or transfer to a third party of his total or partial participation in the investment.

Cuba has signed 19 promotional bilateral agreements and agreements of reciprocal investment's protection with Italy, Spain, Russia, Colombia, England, China, Ukraine, Bolivia, Viet Nam, Argentina, Lebanon, South Africa, Chile, Rumania, Barbados, Brazil, Federal Rep. of Germany, Greece, Switzerland, Venezuela, Eslovaquia, France, Lao, Ecuador, Cape Green, Jamaica, Namibia, Indonesia, Malaysia, Turkey and Belize.

Also approved and working are 317 associations with foreign capital mainly from Spain, Canada, Italy, France, Mexico, the Netherlands, Venezuela, Argentina, England and Chile in many sectors.

Cuba is a party to multilateral treaties that provide for significant trade rules on certain categories of sensitive products. These treaties include the following:

- Ozone Layer Protection Agreement, its protocol and amendments
- International Agreement on Trade of Endangered Species from the Flora and the Fauna (CITES)
- Basel Convention on Across-the-Border Movement and Disposal of Hazardous Wastes
- United Nations Convention on Illicit Traffic of Narcotics and Psychotropic Substances

AIR SERVICES

42 foreign lines from 3 continents and 26 countries participate in the Cuban market.

Europe: Spain Germany, Switzerland, Italy, Austria, The Netherlands, France, England, Russia, Ukraine, Sweden, Belgium, Denmark, Portugal and Finland.

North America: Canada.

Center and South America: Colombia, Panama, Costa Rica, Guatemala, Ecuador, Mexico, Brazil, Jamaica, West Indies

Africa: Angola

CUBANA AIRLINES. With almost 70 years of operations, it covers a range of 40 international destinies from Europe, America and the Caribbean, together with 15 local points.

AEROCARIBBEAN. This Cuban Regional Airline has over 15 years of experience in the Caribbean, Central America and the North of South America, with charter flights. It transports all kinds of loads with a fleet of Antonov-26 of up to 55 tons and IL-18 of up to 135 tons.

AEROGAVIOTA. Operates routes from Central America and the Caribbean, it takes loads to any destination, in executive-type planes, with a capacity of 40 metric tons in AN-26 and IL-76, 30.

AEROCARIBE. Airline Caribe S.A. C.V., it is the Mexican regional airline, their services are in DC-9. The destination to Cuba reaches a frequency of 4 weekly flights.

IBERIA. 6 weekly frequencies to Havana in Boeig-747, this enterprise offers connections from Madrid to all European capitals and countries from Asia and Africa. It does 312 flights a month non-stop from Spain to America.

AOM. This French airline partenaire de Swissair does 4 weekly flights to Cuba in planes DC-10-30.

Cubana de Aviacion and its cargo division, Cubana Cargo, provide their services all around the world and have established flight connection arrangements with other airlines.

Cubana Cargo has regular flights to Spain, Portugal, France, Italy, Germany, the United Kingdom, Russia, Canada, Mexico, Jamaica, the Dominican Republic, Martinique, Guadeloupe, St. Martin, Panama, Costa Rica, Venezuela, Ecuador, Colombia, Perú, Argentina, Brazil and Chile.

Other air transportation enterprises operating in Cuba appear among the service enterprises in this Directory.

SEA TRANSPORT

In Cuba there is a wide number of entities that are devoted to the international maritime service, which covers all necessary aspects to carry out import and export commercial operations, including insurance.

These companies transport dry and liquid cargoes, refrigerated, loose loads and by containers. They operate with services of regular lines, direct or combined, as well as TRAMP services.

Such firms are:

- Coral Container Lines SA
- Poseidon
- Mar America
- Friomar
- Nexus Reefer
- Melbridge Container Lines
- Nirint Shipping BV
- Acinox Shipping
- Petrocost
- Expedimar SA
- Melfi Marine Corporation SA

- Norstrand Maritime and Trading CO. LTD
- Transcargo International
- Cuflet Chartering
- Naviera Cubalse
- Navegacion Caribe
- Naviera Caribena

There are also entities which act as cargo agents, ship chartering, custom agent, supervisors inspections etc.

- International Supervision Services (Cubacontrol)
- Expedimar SA
- Transcargo Internacional
- Cuflet Chatering
- Transitorios Coral
- Intermar
- Adesa S.A.
- Arandia
- Perez SA
- Marinter SA
- Schenker International
- Servitally

The entities that work as ship consignors and as protector agents are:

- Consignataria Mambisa

- Servimar
- Destino
- Perez SA
- Marinter SA
- Maritima Caribeña

The principals ports of the country are:

- Havana
- Mariel
- Matanzas
- Cienfuegos
- Isabela
- Nuevitas
- Santiago de Cuba
- Antilla
- Felton
- Manzanillo
- Nueva Gerona

In Havana, Cienfuegos, Santiago de Cuba and Antillas there are facilities specialized for the unloading of cereals. There are also facilities specialized for sugar shipping in the ports of Mariel, Matanzas, Cienfuegos, Palo Alto, Guayabal, Carupano, Ceiba Hueca and Boqueron.

Details on the services offered by a group of enterprises:

- **EXPEDIMAR SA.** It gives services of cargo international expedition, ship chartering and cargo agencies to any country. Conventional cargo as wells, in containers or refrigerated. It has a transportation service regular to the Caribbean.
  Teleph. 242440/241881 Fax 240080/ 249472
- **TRANSCARGO.** It performs operations of cargo international maritime transportation according to destination out of regular lines, with trips to the north of Europe and the Mediterranean and it also has a line of containers.
  Teleph. 622425/ 622450 Fax. 338626
- **NEXUS REEFER.** It operates a service of refrigerated cargo with a frequency of two weekly trips to Progreso (Mexico) and another weekly from Santiago de Cuba to Dominican Republic (Boca Chica or Rio Haina). It also offers maritime transportation service between Cuba the Caribbean and Canada.
  Telephone: 629000/ 338448 Fax. 338446/ 338708
- **CORAL CONTAINER LINES SA.** It offers regular lines for Canada, Central America Barcelona, Genoa, where it uses containers with a 600TEUS capacity of 20 and 40 feet. It also offers transferring service by means of subcontracting.
  Telephone: 621071/ 622120 Fax.621867
- **MELFI MARINE CORP SA.** It has regular lines to Panama every 15 days, to Tampico and Veracruz (Mexico) every 10 days, to Progreso right in Mexico every 7 days and to The Dominican Republic every 15 days.
  Telephone: 334263/64 Fax 334265
- **COMPAÑIA TADAY MARINE SA.** Has its own container terminals for dry cargo and refrigerated In Havana and Santiago de Cuba provinces, offering their services to the Mediterranean and American geographical zone.
- **MARAMERICA.** It possesses a regular line Mariel (Cuban western part)-Tampico (Mexico) and it has general cargo ships for chartering operations. It has cement transporters of among 2500 and 5512 t of TDW.
  Telephone: 292076/298077 Fax. 248889
- **NAVEGACION CARIBE.** It offers cargo service to the Caribbean basin, on the basis of time chartering. It has to towed 800t rafts, with a 29-containers capacity (20-40 feet or 1300m3) and two Roll On-Roll Off cement containers.
  Telephone 615611 Fax. 338564
- **PETROCOST.** It operates tankers for liquid cargoes.
  Telephone 616528// 669498
- **NAVIERA POSEIDON.** It operates general cargo ships and performs chartering contracts.
  Telephone: 248887 Fax. 248627
- **NIRINT SHIPPING BV.** It operates ship in the European zone.
  Telephone: 243643/ 802784 Fax. 243332/ 240153
- **FRIOMAR.** It operates refrigerated ships.
  Telephone: 639580 Fax. 335185
- **ACINOX.** It performs trips to Colombia on a monthly basis, Nicaragua, Honduras, Dominica, Haiti and Trinidad and Tobago to Ecuador from time to time, Peru and Chile. It has 5 ships for the services.
  Telephone: 331643-47 Fax. 331648

ENTERPRISE FOR MARITIME WORKS

It possesses 5 ships that operate under the chartering system, three of general cargo and two of 499t asphalt-carrying tanker, dead weight each, though not given to transport for foreign trade, it could be contacted in the case of suing, and negotiable possibilities for the service.

Foreign Shipping enterprises represented in Cuba:

- **MELBRIDGE.** It trasnports merchandise for the north of Europe, being able to widen its service by means of transferring. It has a regular service every 14 days. Telephone. 244728 Fax. 244729
- **PEREZ NV.** Maritime transportation service to several destinations. Tel. 338224 Fax. 338225
- **MARINTER.** Maritime transportation service to several destinations. Tel. 338342 Fax. 338343

PORT SERVICES AND CUSTOMS HANDLING

Port services are offered by the state enterprise Consignataria Mambisa, which in turn subcontracts them from independent suppliers and operators. The service include harbor pilot, loading and unloading, hoisting means, water and fuel supply, health control inspectors, inmigration and others.

Importers are not allowed to conduct customs formalities directly, being obliged to employ a specialized agency or a representative of the importing enterprise, duly trained and registered with the Cuban Customs. There is a minimum tariff for these services.

The list of authorized agencies operating in the country appears in the service enterprises section.(Custom Services)

CUSTOMS

The Customs Tariff of the Republic of Cuba, promulgated by Decree-Law No. 124 of October 15, 1990, has undergone changes which have allowed a substantial reduction of its tariffs and their adequation to the changes occurred in the country's economic policy and reordering of its foreign trade, which include the gradual transfer of that activity to the productive entities.

The Customs Tariff has two columns:

a) the General Tariff (the highest), which is applied to non-member countries of the World Trade Organization, or countries which have not signed bilateral trade agreements with Cuba

b) the Most Favored Nation tariff, which is applied to member countries of the World Trade Organization which have signed bilateral trade agreements with Cuba.

This has brought about changes in the customs tariff structure, contained in the Joint Resolution of the Ministries of Finances and Prices and Foreign Trade, No. 5 of May 17, 1996, which became in force on January 1, 1997.

The changes in the simple tariff averages of the Customs Tariff show the following behavior:

General Column
51.5%
34.0%
23.8%
16.9%
Most Favored Nation

17.0%
14.0%
11.9%
10.7%

In addition, the Cuban customs regime has the following preferential systems:

> *a group of goods from countries making up the Global System of Trade Preferences (SGPC) among developing countries are granted lower customs tariffs than those corresponding to most-favored nation*
>
> *likewise, lower customs tariffs than those corresponding to most-favored nation are granted to products negotiated in the framework of the Agreements of Partial Reach with the member countries of the Latin American Integration Association (ALADI).*

Cuba has signed these agreements with Argentina, Brazil, Colombia, Mexico, Uruguay, Bolivia, Venezuela, Peru and Ecuador. As well as with Chile, waiting to be ratified by that country.

Besides, Cuba is part of the agreements on seeds and cultural goods signed by ALADI member countries, which derogate customs tariffs for these products.

The highest customs tariff in the General Column is 40 percent, and 30 percent in the Most Favored Nation column, which places Cuba at the same level of the Latin American country averages.

With regard to antidumping and compensatory duties and the adoption of safeguarding measures, Cuba abides by the provisions of the World Trade Organization on the subject.

GENERALIZED SYSTEM OF PREFERENCES

Cuba benefits from the Generalized System of Preferences (GSP) in the following countries:

- European Union
- Switzerland
- Hungary
- Norway
- Poland
- Czech Republic
- Bulgary
- Canada
- Japan
- New Zealand
- Australia

From CEI countries preferences are given to Russia, Belarus, Georgia, Ukraine and Kazajastan.

GSP gives Cuban exporters the opportunity to enjoy a preferential customs treatment for the goods covered by this scheme exported to the above markets. The Chamber of Commerce of the Republic of Cuba issues the corresponding certificates of origin (Form A) upon request of Cuban exporters.

From the 15 preferential schemes favoring goods, the most widely used by Cuba is that of the European Union, since this market is a recipient of most of the Cuban exports under this regime.

EXPORT-PODUCTS

Other food products

HARMONIZED SYSTEM CODE	DESCRIPTION
0208.90.	Cocodrile meat
0301.99.	Peces vivos para la alimentaci6n
0302.66.	Anguiles, chilled
0302.69.	Tilapias,and carps, fresh or chilled
0303.76.	Anguiles, frozen
0303.79.	Tilapias and carps, frozen
0304.10/20	Tilapia and carp fillets and other meat, fresh, chilled or frozen.
0306.21.	Lobster, alive, fresh or chilled
0306.23.	Shrimps, fresh or chilled (including culture shrimps)
0409.00.	Natural honey
0504.00.	Guts and other edible offal
0901.21.	Coffee, toasted and grounded
1701.91.	Flavoring blends for beverages (instant soft-drinks)
1806.10.	Chocolate powder
1806...	Chocolate bars and tablets
2007.99.	Fruit pulp
2009...	Juice and concentrate of natural fruits
2201.10.	Bottled mineral water
	Purified and carbonated water
210390	Mayonnaise sauce
2202.10.	Soft-drinks
2203.00.	Beer
220421/29	Wines
	Ham, bacon

LIVE ANIMALS

HARMONIZED	DESCRIPTION

SYSTEM CODE	
0101.11/19	Horses - purebred breeding animals
0102.10.	Bovines - purebred breeding animals (for milk, meat, etc)
0105.91.	Fighting roosters
0106.90.	Fantasy birds (guacamayoes, cockatoos, flamingoes, buzzards)
0106.30.	Laboratory animals
0301.10.	Ornamental fishes

AGRICULTURE AND CATTLE INDUSTRIES

HARMONIZED SYSTEM CODE	DESCRIPTION
0511.10.	Bovine semen
0511.99.	Bovine embryo
0602.20.	Plantain, malanga and other "in vitro" plants
0602.00	Citrus fruit cuttings for graphting
1209.91.	Horticultural seeds (tomatoes, pimentos and others)
1209.99.	Papaya seeds
1209.99.	Citrus fruit seeds
1209.99.	Tropical forest tree seeds
3105.90.	Biofertilizers and organic fertilizers
3402.90.	Detergent citrus fruits washing
3404.00.	Wax for citrus fruits coating
3808.10.	Biological insecticide for mosquitoes
3808.20.	Insecticide against citrus fruit ants
3808.90.	Biological rodenticide and anti-parasites
130190	Natural pine resin
4201.00.	Leather saddles
0505.10	Goose and duck feathers
	Crop protectors and hothouses

	Orange and citron capsular cells

MEDICAL INSTRUMENTS AND EQUIPMENT

HARMONIZED SYSTEM CODE	DESCRIPTION
9018.11	Electrocardiograph (computerized)
9018.19	Ultrasonic system with Elisa techniques
9018.19	Dynamic system for ultrarapid antibiogram
9018.19	Digital electroencephalograph system
9018.19	Digital multimodal avoked potential system
9018.19	Register and processing system for biomedical signals
9018.19	Other laser and ultrasonic medical equipment .
9018.19	External bone fixer (plastic)
9018.90.	Diagnostic equipment and instruments (pipettes, washing pit, etc)

ART AND COLLECTION ARTICLES

HARMONIZED SYSTEM CODE	DESCRIPTION
3706.00.	Cinematographic films
4202.00.	Stamping on fine leather
4303.10.	Leather clothing
4901.10.	Text and children books
4904.00.	Written music
4905.00.	Maps and nautical charts
7118.00.	Collection coins of no legal tender
8524.32.	Compact discs, records and cassettes recorded by cuban artists and musical groups of all genre
8524.32.	Recorded radio programmes
9701/2/3	Works of modern Cuban art and decorative art
9704	Postage stamps for philatelic use, new or canceled from Cuba or abroad
9601	Handicraft of worked bones, tortoise shells and other materials(including miniatures)

FRUITS AND VEGETABLES

HARMONIZED SYSTEM CODE	DESCRIPTION

0701.90.	Potatoes
0709.60.	Pimento
0702 - 09	Other fresh or refrigerated vegetables
0801.11.	Dry coconut
0804.40.	Avocado
0804.50.	Mangoes
0805...	Citrus fruits
0807.20.	Papaya
091010	Ginger

MACHINES AND EQUIPMENT

HARMONIZED SYSTEM CODE	DESCRIPTION
8201...	Agricultural hand tools
8421.22/3	Vacuum rotary filter
8432...	Agricultural machinery- founded and Forged iron And steel products
8438.30	Machinery and equipment for the sugar industry-rolls, spindels cushions, bearings, couplings, transports, condensers etc. Rough machined roller shells Grooved roller shells without shaft and complete with shaft Machine finished roller shafts Rough and machine finished cast iron scrapers Rough and machine finished cast iron trash plate Machine finished mill brass bearings Cast iron mill couplings Pumps for various industrial uses Cane carrier chain Bagasse carrier chain Steam boilers and parts for the same Vacuum pans Evaporators Juice clarifiers Grain crystallisers Seed pans Large vessels Cane carriers, bagasse carriers, sugar belt and grasshopper conveyors Hoppers for sugar, filter cake, etc Sugar cane cutter KTP-3S
8479.10.	Machinery and equipment for the sugar industry-Winches, evaporators, elevators, machinery for the production of dovetail blocks, compacting machine, ceramic and wood saw, etc

ELECTRIC AND ELECTRONIC PRODUCTS

HARMONIZED SYSTEM CODE	DESCRIPTION
8504.10.	Ballast for fluorescent lamps
8544.20.	Electrical and telephone cables and wires
9028.30.	Electricity single-phase meter

INTERMEDIATE PRODUCTS

HARMONIZED SYSTEM CODE	DESCRIPTION
7408.11.	Copper wire 8 mm.
	Aluminum framework (doors, windows, etc)

OTHER INDUSTRIAL PRODUCTS

HARMONIZED SYSTEM CODE	DESCRIPTION
3304.00	Medicinal mud and water beauty products for care of the skin
3401.11/19	Toilet and washing soap
340220	Detergents
3922/23/24	Plastic products (multipurpose containers, buckets, brooms and brushes, absorbents, PVC and polyethylene pipes, etc)
3925/26	Plastic water tanks and boothes, with all the components, like electricity and water installations etc.
3925/26	Velum leather for musical instruments
4520..	Humidity control cases for cigar storing
4819.50.	Egg trays
6403.59.	All leather shoes
6406.99.	Leather soles
6908.10.	Bricks and paving tiles of acid resistant ceramic
6909.19/90	Ceramic products for technical use (rasching, leasing rings, etc)
6912.00.	Ceramic plates and other table service pieces
6913.90.	Ornamental ceramic
7017.00.	Laboratory glass ware
7615.00.	Kitchen and other household or hotel articles of aluminum (including pressure cooker), teflon pans.
8303.00.	Safe and strong-boxes, individual and wall fitting.
8480.00.	Molds and headers or shapers
9017.20.	Drawing and designing instruments
9306.00.	Cartridges caliber 5.6 and 12/16 for hunting
9403.20.	Stainless steel equipment for gastronomy, tourism and hospitals
9403.50/60	Wooden style furniture
94.03.30/40/50	Wooden furniture for all uses
94.03.70.	Plastic furniture reinforced with fiberglass

9403.80.	Rattan Furniture
9405.10/20	Decorative lamps
9502.10.	Dolls
9503...	Didactic toys
9506.99.	Sport articles for boxing, softball and baseball

MEDICAL PRODUCTS

HARMONIZED SYSTEM CODE	DESCRIPTION
3001.90	Natural pulmonary surfactant
3002.10	Blood products:Human Albumin Inmunoglobulin, etc.
3002.20	Human vaccines: Diphteria-Tetanus Leptospirosis Becterian polivalent
	Anti-hepatitis B recombinant
3002.20	Antimeningococcicus
3002.20	Other common monovalent and polivalent vaccines
3002.30	Veterinary vaccines, Anti PVC (anti parvovirus canine)
3002.30	Viral encephalomiocarditis (for pigs)
3002.30	Anti coccidiosis (for poultry)
3002.30	Other veterinary vaccines: (tetanus toxoid, Inactivated Aujeszky, Brucela, Symptomatic carbunco, pig cholera, contagious ectyme, equine encephalomielitis, canine hepatitis, leptospirosis, etc.
3002.90	Hiperimmune Gamma anti PVC (Parvovirus Canino)
3004.90	Streptokinase (recombinant)
3004.90	Epidermal growth factor
3004.90	Human trasfer factor
3004.90	Interferons
3004.90	Therapeutical Monoclonal antibodies (specially for kidney transplant)
3004.90	Citostatics, cephalosporines, antiarthritics, antiulcersand others
3004.90	Other therapeutic medicaments and dietetical supplements
3004.90	Hipocholesterolemic (PPG)
3004.90	Antivitilige
3004.90	Natural antiseptic healing for veterinary use
3004.90	Anti-mastitis (veterinary use)

3004.90	Natural antidiaharrea bulbs (for new born pigs)
3005.90	Plaster of Paris
3006.60	Oral contraceptives
3821.00	Culture means
3822.00	Monoclonals antibodies for diagnosis, purification, cell identification and lab investigation.
3822.00	Diagnostic kit for vaginal Candisiass, Trichomoniasis y Gerdnerella vaginales
3822.00	Diagnostic for VIH 1 y 2
3822.00	Other kits of diagnosis means
3822.00	Diagnostic kits for veterinary and agricultural desease detection

CONSTRUCTION INDUSTRY PRODUCTS

HARMONIZED SYSTEM CODE	DESCRIPTION
2522.00.	Calcium carbonate
5984.81/82	Sanitary hardware and fittings
6810.19.	Tiles, flagstone, bricks and similar cement or concrete articles
6810.91.	Rail concrete ties
6810.91.	Prefabricated structural components made from wood for houses
6905.10.00	Roofing tiles
6908.10.00	Glazed ceramic tiles or mosaics
6910.10.00	Sanitary furniture and accessories
7207.19/20	Corrugated steel bars and others
7214.20.	Corrugated steel bars and others
7218.99	Carbon stainless billet
9406.90.	Prefabricated structural components of concrete for houses
9406.90.	Low-cost building-material made from ecomaterial

TEXTILE PRODUCTS

HARMONIZED SYSTEM CODE	DESCRIPTION
5208/09	Unbleached woven fabrics of 100% cotton (including those for tablecloth, curtains, sheets, etc)
6114.20/90	Pullovers and other products with serigraphy images
6301.40.00	Linen clothes, docker trousers, pyjamas, socks

OTHER SERVICES

HARMONIZED SYSTEM CODE	DESCRIPTION
	Minting any kind of coins
	Postage stamp printing
	Medical services in specialized clinics and hospitals Ophthalmic Surgery Centre for Pigmentary Retinosis Neurological Restoration Centre Placental Histotherapy Centre Orthopedic, Pediatric and Gynecobstetric Specialized Centres
	Spare parts recuperation service for rail and shipping transport
	Recuperation and automatization service for machinery tool
	Aircraft reparation and maintenance service
	Naval reparation and maintenance service
	Designs for vessels' construction, reconstruction and repair
	Design development for construction and repairing of shipyards
	Marines construction
	Construction of fishing centres
	Designs and development of equipment and systems for the fish-processing industry
	Port dredging service
	Yacht building according to orders
	Designs of coast works
	Reproduction of publicity images in posters, serigraphy and other types of promotional articles.
	Serigraphy service
	Tampography service
	Musical shows (soloists and groups of all genre)
	Sport training service
	Low-cost appartment construction made from ecomaterial
	Freighter frozen cargo service to all the world
	Fishing agreements
	Frozen cargo storing capacity for handling and distribution
	Designs in health and sport branches: Hospitals, rehabilitation centres, sports and physical culture centres.

TRANSPORT

HARMONIZED	DESCRIPTION

SYSTEM CODE	
8409/8708	Cars and spare parts
8609.00.	Containers 20' y de 40' new and recuperated
8711.00.	Motorcycles
8712.00.	Bicycles
8902.00.	Fishing boats of small and medium sized
8903.00.	Sport boats

AGRICULTURAL TECHNOLOGIES

HARMONIZED SYSTEM CODE	DESCRIPTION
	Feasibility studies of soil, agroindustry diagnosis, equipment assembly and installing, post sale services, automation and reparation in all that concerns sugar industry
	Micropropagation of plants "in vitro"
	Technology to avoid deterioration of sugar cane
	Technology to obtain biofertilizer and fodder from sugar industry wastes
	Production and conservation of animal feeding products
	Machanization of green sugar cane harvest
	Forest consulting programmes
	Technology for poultry and birds viral sickness diagnosis
	Technology for the use of germoplasma of different species
	Application of biotechnology to vegetables and fruits improvement
	Non conventional pork feeding
	System for the genetic improvement of porks
	System for pork residue treatment
	Earthworm breeding for animal feeding
	Projects for citrus fruit plantation founding
	Citric packing industry project
	Technical assistance in the administration and exploitation of citrus fruit plantation and agricultural plantations in general.
	Training programmes in citrus fruits techniques
	Disease diagnosis and phytosanitary measures handling
	Whole plants and equipment installation services in citrus industry

INDUSTRIAL TECHNOLOGIES

HARMONIZED SYSTEM CODE	DESCRIPTION
	Social interest construction technologies
	Production technologies for glucose-fructose, tensoactives, inverted syrups enzimatique means, anticorrosives, printing paper and pulp.
	Other sugar industries technologies- bagasse drying, rum's rapid aging, residues treatment.

OTHER NATURAL PRODUCTS

HARMONIZED SYSTEM CODE	DESCRIPTION
0510.00.	Propoleo tincture
0510.00.	Apicultural diet supplements
0510.00.	Shark cartilage for diet supplement in form of dry powder or pills
0510.00	Bee poison
1211.90	Spirulina extracted from algae as a diet supplement
	Diet supplement (Estimulante PV-2)
	Diet supplement (Bioestimulín)
	Diet supplement (Ferrical)

OTHER PRODUCTS NOT CLASSIFIED

HARMONIZED SYSTEM CODE	DESCRIPTION
	Lactoperoxidasa system activator for the conservation of milk
	Braille module and other means for teaching blinds
	Diverse softwares and multimedia products
	Veterinarian biotechnological modules (bioterium, vivarium, etc)
	Educational programmes for technical and professional specialization in different branches of the agriculture and animal raising techniques
	Post-graduate and specialization programmes for medical science
	Post-graduate and summer school programmes on all university specialties, scientific, consultancy, projects and services, international events, guided scientific tours, etc.

CUBA EXPORT PRODUCTS

HARMONIZED SYSTEM CODE	DESCRIPTION

0208.90.	Cocodrile meat
0301.99.	Peces vivos para la alimentación
0302.66.	Anguiles, chilled
0302.69.	Tilapias,and carps, fresh or chilled
0303.76.	Anguiles, frozen
0303.79.	Tilapias and carps, frozen
0304.10/20	Tilapia and carp fillets and other meat, fresh, chilled or frozen.
0306.21.	Lobster, alive, fresh or chilled
0306.23.	Shrimps, fresh or chilled (including culture shrimps)
0409.00.	Natural honey
0504.00.	Guts and other edible offal
0901.21.	Coffee, toasted and grounded
1701.91.	Flavoring blends for beverages (instant soft-drinks)
1806.10.	Chocolate powder
1806...	Chocolate bars and tablets
2007.99.	Fruit pulp
2009...	Juice and concentrate of natural fruits
2201.10.	Bottled mineral water
	Purified and carbonated water
210390	Mayonnaise sauce
2202.10.	Soft-drinks
2203.00.	Beer
220421/29	Wines
	Ham, bacon

CENTER FOR EXPORT PROMOTION OF CUBA (CEPEC)

CEPEC offers specialized services to exporters of goods and services, particularly to small and medium enterprises, in order to create a space for them in the international market which contributes to the promotion, development and diversification of the Cuban export offer.

With that purpose, it carries out activities such as the spreading of information on the export offer, market research, consultant services to Cuban enterprises for the development of new items, creation of promotion programs, organization of trade missions and search of trade information.

CEPEC also participates in both domestic and international fairs, offering trade information services and professional assistance in market and promotion techniques to the Cuban enterprises, as well as promoting trade contacts with foreign firms.

Special emphasis has been placed on the Caribbean Fairs, which should be the most important trading partner for Cuba, participating there not just as a promoter of Cuban trade but also representing small enterprises, helping to identify potential clients and presenting their promotional materials. The results of these contacts are transmitted to the interested enterprises in order to give answers to the offer and information requests.

CEPEC has developed direct relations with the enterprises, allowing a wide spreading of their offers, according to their commercialization policy and target markets, based on their relations with trade promotion organs in developing or underdeveloped countries, by inserting the offer in specialized publications and using importer data bases.

The Center has been fostering international relations with similar entities and with imports promotional centers from European countries, Canada and Japan. These ties favor the acquisition of valuable information, on exportable offer among the foreign importing firms as well as the necessary information for trade development.

The canalization of trade opportunities detected in the provinces of the country allow to expand the possibilities of Cuban trade, specially of the new export products whose insertion to the exportable offer constitutes an essential element in the economic development of the country.

CEPEC' direct work with the export goods manufacturers allows the detection of their export potential and production obstacles, advising ways and forms to solve them in order to make their products comply with the requirements of the international markets.

Though recently created (1995), CEPEC carries out market research and is in charge of trade information since 1976, when was create. A considerable number of product and country market studies contain recommendations which have proven very useful when placing Cuban products in the market, since they have enabled the identification of trade opportunities as well as the regulations to be complied with and the intrinsical and apparent characteristics required of products to win a space in those markets.

Although the Center does not work with imports, it may render services to foreign enterprises wishing to sell their products in the Cuban market or invest in the country, since it has importer databases. Any Cuban exporting or importing enterprise may address CEPEC to identify trade opportunities.

SELECTED EXPORTERS

ALCONA S.A.

Direc: Calle 42 No. 514, Miramar, Ciudad de La Habana, Cuba
Tel: (537) 24-9227/ 22-2526/27
Fax: (537) 24-9227
Contacto: Loreta García, Gerente General

CARIBEX S.A.
Direc: Aparthotel Las Brisas, Edificio 3C Apto.42, Villa Panamericana, Habana del Este, Ciudad de La Habana, Cuba
Tel: (537) 95-1140/ 95-1141
Fax: (537) 95-1142

E-mail: CARIBEX@fishnavy.inf.cu

Contacto: Lazaro Fundora Alvarez, Director

Sitio Web: http://www.ceniai.inf.cu/CUBAMAR/caribex/caribex.htm

CUBAEXPORT
Direc: Calle 23 No. 55, 8vo piso, Vedado, Ciudad de La Habana, Cuba
Tel: (537) 55-0595/ 543130
Fax: (537) 33-3587

E-mail: cexport@infocex.cu
Contacto: Milda Picos Rivers, Directora

STELLA S.A.
Direc: Calle 3ra A No. 9007 e/ 90 y 92, Miramar, Ciudad de La Habana, Cuba
Tel: (537) 24-0828
Fax: (537) 24-0829
Contacto: Leila Aguilar, Gerente

EMPRESA PRODUCTORA-EXPORTADORA "VICTORIA"
Direc: Calle Real No. 466, Rpto. Sta. Fé, Guanabacoa, Ciudad de La Habana
Tel: (537) 97-0006 24-6137
Fax: (537) 80-1947 33-6899
Contacto: Jorge Delgado, Director

CUBA EXPORT-IMPORT & CUSTOMS REGULATIONS

IMPORT AND EXPORT

Articles 37 - 41, Customs Decree-Law No. 162/96.

Import and export operations fulfilled by natural or legal persons shall be controlled by Customs in order to corroborate whether goods correspond to declaration, that the established requirements have been made met and that the payment of duties and taxes due has been satisfied.

Import or export of live animals, plants, vegetable or animal goods or products - in addition to the fulfillment of strictly Customs procedures shall be subject to compliance with measure of sanitary or veterinary character, environmental licensing and other permits prescribed by national legislation.

IMPORT

It shall be deemed to be import goods those which having come from abroad enter national territory for a temporary or definite period, whether or not free from the payment of duties and taxes or enjoying from suspension, exemption or relief of payment.

It shall be understood that an import operation has begun from the moment the means of conveyance of the goods destined to national territory enters the territorial boundaries of the Republic of Cuba, and therefor are subject to Customs control from that moment on.

EXPORT

It shall be deemed to be export goods those proceeding from national territory and destined to foreign countries. It shall be understood that an export operation has begun from the moment when the first solid or liquid lot, or the first package or group of packages forming a lot has been loaded aboard the means of conveyance, and that export has ended on the moment when the means of conveyance abandons the boundaries of the Republic of Cuba.

CUSTOMS PROCEDURES

Imported or exported goods enter or leave the country under a specified Customs procedure.

MEANS OF TRANSPORT

Means of transport arriving or departing from the country or circulating in Customs premises shall be submitted to Customs control, except for Vessels and Aircrafts of States and International Organizations devoted to non-commercial purposes and not included as exceptions in any of the Conventions, Treaties and Agreements of which Cuba is a Party.

VESSEL CONTROL

Vessels arriving in Cuban ports shall be represented by a Consignor who shall inform Customs in writing about the vessel's entry or departure, the pier or place of anchorage, the beginning of goods loading and unloading operations, the beginning of food provisioning operations, water and fuel provisioning, ewnrooling and un-enroling of crew members, or any other operation that Customs determines.

In order to proceed to the clearance of the vessel its Captain or representative shall be in the obligation of showing or handling over to Customs authorities - as the case should be - the established documents. These documents shall conform to those established in Treaties, Conventions and Agreements on facilitation of International Maritime Traffic of which Cuba should be a Party.

A vessel's manifest shall contain the relevant details required in international practice. In every national port of destination it shall be necessary to produce the manifest for the goods to be unloaded. Original manifests shall be presented in Spanish or English languages. Translated manifests shall be presented in Spanish language.

For the purpose of providing more agility to clearance operations the consignor of the vessel shall present an advanced manifest to Customs authorities. In cases where there are errors in the documents produced during the Customs clearance of a vessel, such errors could be repaired within the term provided for each given case and begining by the certification of the Captain of the vessel or his representative, as the case might be.

When presumen that inside a vessel located in national territorial waters there are hidden goods or objects which could be ilegally introduced into the country - notrwithstanding the fact that the said vessel should not be transporting goods destined for the national territory or should it be only in its dead weight - Customs authorities could submit the vessel to Customs control. In the same manner Customs could submit to revision any vessel and the travellers it transports when ther are reasonable grounds to presume that a violation of the established Customs Standards is to be attempted.

AIRCRATS CONTROL

Aircrafts arriving in Cuban airports from abroad shall be submitted to Customs control and shall produce to Customs authorities the following documents:

- General Declaration
- Cargo Manifest
- Air Guides of transported goods

All aircrafts departing from national territory shall have to be cleared by Customs authorities. During clearance operation Customs shal verify that all established requirements for aircraft operations have been met and that duties, taxes and other amounts due have been paid. The representative of the aircraft shall be held responsible for the failure to meet these requirements.

CUSTOMS LAW

Article 127: Clearance for home good is the Customs procedure enabling imported goods to definitely remain within Customs territory and implies the payment of Customs rights, tariffs and other payable duties imposed on imports, as well as compliance with all the established formalities.

Article 128: In order to apply for the procedure of "Clearance for Home Use" the seaport or airport operating agency shall lodge in Customs the Goods Declaration. The lodgement shall be made in a term not exceeding thirty (30) calendar days starting from the date when the document advising on the results of the classification and counting of the unloaded goods was produced to Customs authorities.

Article 129: Notwithstanding the provisions of the previous article, import goods could be declared for clearance for home-use their arrival into the national territory.

Article 130: The goods shall be extracted from the docks, warehouses or designated areas during a term not exceeding thirty (30) calendar days from the date of acceptance of the Declaration of Goods.

Article 131.- The term "Customs transit of Goods" means the Customs procedure by which goods are transported under Customs control from one Customs House to another located in the national territory.

It shall be considered to be under Customs transit:
goods circulating from an entry Customs House to a departure Customs House;
goods circulating from an entry Customs House to an internal Customs House;
goods circulating from an internal Customs House to a departure Customs House; and

goods circulating from an internal Customs House to another internal Customs House.

Article 132.- Goods arriving from abroad and transported under the Customs Transit procedure with destination to another country, shall be declared to Customs in the Transit Cargo Manifest which shall contain the particulars required for in international practice according to Treaties, Conventions and Agreements of which the Republic of Cuba is signatory.

Article 133.- For goods destined to a Cuban port or airport which are unloaded in another port or airport different from the one originally stated and which are intended to be transported to their destination without being cleared, it shall be required from the consignee of the goods or his agent or the transporting agency to apply for a Customs transit procedure authorization.

Article 134.- Goods in transit, as well as the warehouses where they are kept can be inspected whenever Customs deem it convenient during the stay of the transporting vessel or aircraft at a port or airport.

Article 135.- Should it be necessary to unload goods in transit destined to foreign ports or airports because of any cause preventing from continuing their route on board the vessel or aircraft originally transporting them, the unloading operation shall be performed only under authorization granted by Customs on request of the captain of the vessel or its consignee, the commander of the aircraft or his representative or of the port or airport operator. Customs authorization shall also be required for loading the goods on board the vessel or aircraft transporting them to their final destination.

Authorization for Customs transit can be requested by any person having the right to act as declarant for the goods (consignee, transporter, etc.) and shall be responsible to Customs for the compliance of transportation conditions and for the presentation of goods at the destination Customs house, as well as for the remaining obligations that he could have been undertaken.

Article 136.- Transhipment is the Customs procedure enabling goods to be transfered - under Customs control - from one means of transport to another, or to transfer the goods to the same means of transport in a different journey, for the purpose of taking them to their final destination.

Transhipment may be either direct - when not involving the placing of the goods in a temporary warehouse - or indirect if warehousing should be involved.

Article 137.- The vessel consignee shall previously notify the commencement of such operations with due observation of the established form, content and terms.
Notification for a transhipment operation of goods between aircrafts shall be made through presentation of the Transit Cargo Manifest.

Article 138.- In cases when goods intended for transhipment are to be placed under temporary storage, Customs shall be informed on the place of storage, the estimated time of stay in the said warehouse and other aspects which might be deemed useful. The Captain of the vessel or aircraft, or his consignee or agent - according to the given particular case - are in the obligation to provide such information.

Article 139: Temporary admission of goods intended for re-exportation in the same state means the Customs procedure enabling to receive in the Customs territory - with relief from customs duties - goods imported for a specific purpose and destined to be re-exported within a given period of time, without undergoing any other transformation apart from the normal depreciation as a consequence of its use.

Article 140: Temporary import for re-exportation in the same state shall be allowed for:

- technical material - including spare parts and accessories - for certain professions or crafts with the purpose of performing in Cuba a specific work or function;
- goods intended to be exhibited or used in fairs, exhibitions and other technical or cultural events, including the necessary elements for the decoration of shelves and the advertising material destined to promote the goods and according to Treaties, Conventions and Agreements of which Cuba should be a Party;
- samples without commercial value;
- animals and plants destined to participate in exhibitions or in sports and recreational events;
- construction equipment and of other designation for constructive activities;
- production machinery and equipment or their parts provisionally and freely placed at the disposal of the importer in order to replace similar ones while being repaired abroad as a result of damage;
- musical instruments, technical material, scenery parts and equipment for artists, orchestras, theater groups, circuses and similar groups;
- land automotive vehicle, airplanes, boats and other vehicles and vessels;
- equipment for mining prospecting and research; and
- others items of interest to the country.

Article 141: Temporary admission of goods for inward processing is the Customs procedure allowing to receive - with relief from import duties and taxes - certain goods intended for re-export within a given period of time, after having undergone total or partial process of transformation, elaboration or repair leading to an increase in their value due to the value thus added within the national territory.

Article 142: Goods referred to in this Section - wether used alone or combined with other national or nationalized goods or also with goods imported under the same temporary admission procedure for inward processing and having undergone the afore mentioned transformation - shall solely have re-exportation as their inmediate destination.

Article 143: All goods - packagings included in this concept - may be object of temporary admission for inward processing provided their compliance with legal provisions and their being considered as profitable for national economy.

Article 144: Granting temporary admission for inward processing procedure shall - in each case - depend upon a Resolution issued by the Cuban Ministry of Finances and Prices, as a result of a previous report from the General Customs of the Republic and with the participation - when so required - of other organizations and institutions.

Article 145: Requests for granting this procedure shall be addressed in writing to the Minister, Finances and Prices vía the General Customs of the Republic.

Article 146: The Minister of Finances and Prices - taking into consideration the opinion of the General Customs of the Republic - shall dictate the proceedings for implementing the procedure described under this Section.

Article 152: It will be considered replacement through franchise the customs regime allowing duty-free import of equivalent merchandise, identical in its kind, quality and technical caracteristics to the one transformed while in free circulation to obtain products exported from customs territory.
Article 153: Duty-free import operations shall be authorized by the Minister of Finances and Prices for exporting manufacturers certifying that the goods to be imported are equivalent in kind, quality, quantity and technical characteristics to the goods incorporated to export products with a right to replacement.

Article 154: Under this procedure and in the fulfillment of a security provided by the producer or supplier it shall be possible to import - with relief from Customs duties - goods repaired abroad or goods replacing other damaged, defective or inadequate for the purpose they were imported.

Article 155: The relief referred to in the previous Article shall be granted to importers crediting to Customs:

- that the exported goods are identical or equivalent to the one imported;
- the existence of the security provided by the manufacturer or supplier; and

the transportation document.

Article 156: Customs warehousing is the procedure under which imported goods are stored under Customs control in a place designated for that purpose, without payment of Customs duties until their placement under a nother Customs procedure.
Article 157: To enforce an effective Customs control of the goods placed under this procedure, the storage facilities shall be previously inspected and approved by the Customs authorities. Customs shall maintain control on the compliance of the warehousing facilities with the required security conditions.

Article 158: Clearance for home use of goods placed under this procedure shall conform to the requirements for the Goods Declaration as if the goods entered the Customs territory directly from abroad after satisfying the payment of Customs duties, tariffs and other payable rights.

CLASSES OF WAREHOUSES

Customs Warehouses means the facilities where imported goods are to be stored under Customs warehousing procedure. Warehouses could be either public or private.

Public Warehouses means duly authorized facilities in which several depositors entitled to use the Customs warehousing procedure store goods, depositors being legal persons different from the depositaries.

Private Warehouses means those warehouses reserved for the exclusive use of the person authorized to enjoy the benefits of the procedure for storing the goods. The owners of private warehouses shall simultaneously hold the condition of depositaries and depositors.

AUTHORIZATION OF A WAREHOUSE

Applications for establishing a public Customs warehouse shall be made in writing and addressed to the Head, General Customs of the Republic.
In the case of private warehouses, applications for authorizing it shall be made as part of the application for the granting of the procedure.

AUTHORIZATION OF THE CUSTOMS WAREHOUSING PROCEDURE

The Customs warehousing procedure can be granted to natural and legal persons, whether Cuban or foreigners, living in the national territory and devoted to trade and production.

In the case of legal Cuban persons they should be authorized to perform foreign-trade operations, meaning import and export. Foreign persons should be credited in the country and registered in the existing registries according to the kind of activity they develop.

In both cases those interested in applying for an authorization shall comply with the conditions and prescriptions established for such purpose in the regulations in force.

REMOVAL OF GOODS FROM THE WAREHOUSES

The depositor shall have - at all times - the right to dispose of the goods placed in the warehouse and shall be entitled to re-export, to transfer ownership, abandon or sell all or part of them.

Clearance for home use of goods placed under Customs warehousing procedure shall only be allowed for legal persons authorized to perform foreign trade operations, and the declared goods must be in correspondence with those included in their authorized nomenclature.

In order to declare for home use the goods placed under Customs warehousing procedure importers shall fulfill the prescriptions and shall produce the relevant documents requested for this new procedure as if goods had been arriving from abroad.

The Declaration of Goods imported for home-use shall be supported with the Sales Invoice issued by the depositor. When deemed necessary the control Customs office could request presentation of documents other than those normally established in the Standards for Customs Clearance of Goods.
On the other hand, provided that Customs control is not affected and that the volume of operations should so require, Customs could grant interested persons larger facilities - upon request and in compliance with the relevant conditions - in order to remove goods from the warehouse before lodging the Goods Declaration.

Article 161: Temporary exportation of goods subject to re-importation in the same state is the Customs procedure enabling to re-import - into the Customs territory with relief of Customs rights - goods previously exported from that same territory in order to be used abroad and provided this use has not implied any modifications of the goods except for the normal depreciation due to the use made of them.

Article 162: In the declaration for temporary export the goods shall be identified by their permanent characteristics with the purpose of their identification during re-importation.

PARCEL POST, COURIERS AND PACKAGE CONSIGNMENTS

Articles 42 - 46 of the Decree-law No. 162/96
Ruling No. 26-94 of the Head, General Customs of the Republic, Standards for Postal Traffic.
Ruling No. 25-96 of the Head, General Customs of the Republic, Standards for Courier Consignments.

Article 42: It shall be considered to be a consignment all items - whether sent towards or received from foreign countries by sea, air or post - in the form of packages, mail, parcels or courier deliveries, and they will be classified as follows:

- Post consignments: any of the forms of the International Postal Service recognized by the Universal Postal Union which are grouped into mail consignments and parcel post consignments;
- Package consignments: any consignment received or sent by air or sea using the services offered by enterprises and agencies functioning under express authorization of the Cuban State, and duly registered in the Central Customs Registry; and
- Courier consignments: any consignment received or sent using the services offered by enterprises and agencies functioning under license granted by the Ministry of Communications and duly registered in the Central Customs Registry.

Article 43: Import and export of parcel post, courier and package consignments shall abide the common applicable standards approved by the Universal Postal Union for international postal service.

Article 44: Goods imported or exported through parcel postal, courier and package consignments shall be declared and legalized with Customs authorities, in compliance with the existing requirements and through presentation of the special authorizations required in the cases subject to restrictions.

Article 45: The Post Administration shall be responsible for the conveyance, storage, protection and presenting of postal consignments to Customs authorities, and for their subsequent delivery to the consignees.

Article 46: The inspection of parcel post, courier post and package consignments shall correspond to the Customs authorities which - for the said purpose - shall apply selectivity criteria determined by the Head, General Customs of the Republic.

TRAVELLERS AND TRAVELLERS LUGGAGE

Article 51: Upon arrival and departure from national territory, travellers shall declare to Customs any items they carry and which are not part of their personal belongings. The declaration may be oral or written.
Article 52: Concerning the declaration - provided there was no evil intention - any oblivion or omission could be amended through oral statement to the Customs authority at the beginning or during luggage control.
Article 53: When deemed necessary Customs authorities could proceed to confront declared items against the real contents of the luggage.
Article 54: Personal belongings of travellers shall be subject to Customs control. Such control could be extended to body search procedures in cases where there are reasonable suspicion of objects being hidden with an intention of either illegal introduction or extraction .
Article 55: In the case of items subject to payment of Customs duties they shall not be removed from seaport or airport areas until such payment has been satisfied
Article 56: When deemed necessary in the case of products subject to import or export special regulations, Customs shall require compliance with the established requirements, including presentation of the authorization issued by a competent organization.
Article 57: Precious metals and stones and jewels elaborated with them, cultural patrimonial goods, protected endangered flora and fauna species and other goods and valuables included in special regulations will only be taken out of the country by travellers in condition to prove - to

Customs satisfaction - having previously imported them or upon presentation of an authorization issued by a competent organization.
GENERAL
Travellers means persons arriving or departing from the country on board an international means of transport whether they are passengers or crew members.
Customs, on the grounds of previous requierement and for reasons deemed valid, could authorize that formalities regarding clearance of travellers and their luggage be performed outside Customs premises . All expenses of such procedure shall be bore by the interest requiring party.
Transporting organizations shall notify to Customs the appearance of unclaimed luggage in order to proceed to their proper control.
TARIFF POLICY
Items imported by travellers shall be subject to the payment of Custioms duties according to rates established by national legislation, except for the cases of items relieved from payment of duties.
Travellers not permanently residing in Cuba - and also travellers permanently residing in Cuba having travelled abroad due to personal reasons - shall proceed to pay Customs duties in Cuban Convertible Pesos. The rest of the travellers shall perform their payments in Cuban Pesos.
As a general rule in order to determine Customs value of imported items it will be accepted the value declared by the traveller at the moment of clearance. However, Customs authorities could require presentation of documents supporting the declared value or - if such declared value should not be acceptable - proceed to their valoration.
In the case of non-resident travellers Customs could establish a security in order to ensure that certain items are actually re-exported. The said security shall be reimbursed to the traveller in its full amount while leaving the country through any of the departure Customs offices.

CENTRAL CUSTOMS REGISTRY

The functions of the Central Customs Registry include the maintenance of a register of natural and legal persons which - as a result of the activities they develop - have to establish links with Customs during the clearance procedure of goods, travellers and means of transport.
At present all Registry and invoicing operations have been fully automated, this being a condition enabling not only to have a more effective control, but also to provide - without delay and in reduced terms - statistical reports and other information deemed of interest.

It is compulsory for the following to be registered in the Central Customs Registry:

- Trade importers and exporters.
- Customs Agencies;
- Customs agencies brokers and registered brokers of enterprises.
- Depositants and Depositors.
- Travel agencies.
- Persons authorized to enjoy relief from payment of Customs duties and taxes.
- Vessels consignors.
- Courier and Post consignment Agencies.

Applications for inscription in the Central Customs Registry shall be made through fulfillment of requirements established for each given case.
At the moment of the inscription applicants shall pay the tariff established by regulations in force. Payment shall be made in fiscal stamps with a value of seventy (70.00) pesos in the case of new inscriptions and forty (40.00) pesos in the case of any modification to previous inscriptions.

In the case of state enterprises the required fiscal stamps shall correspond to Cuban pesos while for the rest of the cases the fiscal stamps shall correspond to freely convertible currency.

Inscription in the Central Customs Registry entails assignment of a coded number to identify given persons on their clearance related proceedings. In every case the Central Customs Registry shall provide legal persons with a Certificate of Inscriptions and natural persons with an Identification Carnet.

Organizations using registered brokers and Customs agents agencies shall be liable to pay the established monthly service tariffs equivalent to fifty (50.00) pesos per each broker or agent. The payment shall correspond to the elapsed month and shall be satisfied before the tenth day of each month.
For Cuban entities the service fees shall be calculated in Cuban Pesos while for the rest will be calculated in freely convertible currency. Entities so willing could proceed to make advance payments for periods of three (3), six (6) and twelve (12) months. In cases where the terms of payment should not be met the brokers and agents accreditation will be suspended until updating arrears due.

For any further information or consultation addressed to the Central Registry of Customs please address to:

- Central Customs Registry. Calle 6 esquina a 39. Plaza. Ciudad Habana. Cuba. CP 10600.
- Telephone: (53-7) 81-0605 or through switch board numbers (53-7) 55-5466, Extension 217.
- Fax: (53-7) 815-631; (53-7) 335-222.
- E-mail; registro@agr.aduana.cu

The person in charge of the Registry is Mr. Oscar Morales Gago.

REQUIREMENTS FOR INSCRIPTION

Customary importers and exporters

- Duly completed application form for inscription in the Central Customs Registry.
- Photocopy of the Certificate of Inscription in the National Importers and Exporter Registry of the Chamber of Commerce of the Republic of Cuba.
- In the case of Trading Societies or Joint Enterprises - certificate of inscription in the relevant Registry.
- Copy of the Resolution from the Ministry of Foreign Trade authorizing import and/or export and attach to it the authorized nomenclature of items.
- Application from the Customs brokers - according to the case.
- Fiscal stamps for an amount of seventy (70.00) pesos. In the case of joint or private enterprises fiscal stamps shall be purchased in freely convertible currency.

BRANCHES OF FOREIGN TRADING SOCIETIES

- Duly completed application form for inscription in the Central Customs Registry.
- Photocopy of the License issued by the National Registry of the Chamber of Commerce of the Republic of Cuba for Branches and Agents of Foreign Trading Societies.
- Photocopy of the Tax - Payer Identification Card or photocopy of model RC-01 issued by the National Tax Administration Office (ONAT)
- Fiscal stamps for an amount of seventy (70.00) dollars.

Travel Agencies

- Duly completed application form for inscription in the Central Customs Registry.
- Photocopy of the License issued by the Travel Agencies National Registry of the Chamber of Commerce of the Republic of Cuba. The original shall be produced in order to confront it with the photocopy.
- Photocopy of the Tax - Payer Identification Card or photocopy of model RC-01 issued by the National Tax Administration Office (ONAT)
- Fiscal stamps for an amount of seventy (70.00) dollars.

CUSTOMS BROKERS AGENCIES

- Duly completed application form for inscription in the Central Customs Registry.
- Photocopy of the Tax - Payer Identification Card or photocopy of model RC-01 issued by the National Tax Administration Office (ONAT).
- Application of the Agents to be employed
- Fiscal stamps for an amount of seventy (70.00) dollars.

COURIER AND POST PACKAGE CONSIGNMENT AGENCIES AND SHIP CONSIGNORS

- Duly completed application form for inscription in the Central Customs Registry.
- Copy of the document issued by the organization invested with faculties to authorize exercising the relevant activity.
- Photocopy of the Tax - Payer Identification Card or photocopy of model RC-01 issued by the National Tax Administration Office (ONAT).
- Fiscal stamps for an amount of seventy (70.00) dollars.

CUSTOMS AGENCIES BROKERS AND REGISTERED BROKERS OF ENTERPRISES.

Applications to accredit Customs agencies brokers and registered brokers of enterprises shall be made by the Director or Manager of the employing Customs Brokers Agency or of the Import - Export Organization.
Persons interested in working as Customs agencies brokers and registered brokers of enterprises shall meet the following requirements:

- To be a Cuban citizen.
- To be in full exercise of legal faculties.
- To approve tests of the National School for Customs Officials (Escuela Nacional de Formación Aduanera) qualifying for the position of Customs agencies broker or registered broker of enterprises.
- Not having been active member of the Customs system within the last 12 months nor having been discharged due to indiscipline.

In order to apply for accrediting Customs agencies brokers and registered brokers of enterprises the Agencies or Enterprises shall lodge in the Registry:

- A letter of application signed by the Director.
- List of the persons to be credited as Customs agencies brokers and registered brokers of enterprises. The list shall include full name and surnames, home address and serial number of the Identification Carnet.
- Two 1x1 inch photographs. Both photographs shall be identical and updated.

- Photocopy of the Certificate issued by the National School for Customs Officials (Escuela Nacional de Formación Aduanera) for each one of the persons listed. The original certificate shall be produce for confrontation with the copies.

LEADING INDUSTRIAL AGENCIES

BUFETE INTERNACIONAL

Casa Matriz
5ta. avenida No. 16 202, esquina 162, Miramar, Playa, Ciudad de La Habana.
Teléfonos: (537) 24 6749
Fax: (537) 24 6750
Sucursal Ciudad de La Habana
Calle 47 No. 815, entre Santa Ana y Conill, Nuevo Vedado, Plaza, Ciudad de La Habana.
Teléfonos: (537) 33 5459, 33 5469
Fax: (537) 33 5448
Rebeca Babeth García Monroy

CLAIM

Consultores de Marcas y Patentes.
Lamparilla # 2. Lonja del Comercio. Oficina 6. Habana Vieja. Ciudad de La Habana. CP 10100.Cuba.
Teléfonos: (537) 330743 y 330755
Fax: (537) 330746
Rogelio Rafael Valdés Pila
María Lourdes Ruiz Sotolongo
Reynold Sampedro Vázquez
Raúl Sancho Valladares
Annia Susana Rodríguez Sarraff

CONAS

Consultores Asociados.
5ta. avenida No. 2 201, esquina 22, Miramar, Playa, Ciudad de La Habana.
Teléfonos: (537) 24 0207 y 24 2988
Fax: (537) 24 4320
María Antonia Carrillo de Albornoz y Martínez

CONSULTORÍA JURÍDICA INTERNACIONAL

Calle 16 No. 314, entr 3ra y 5ta. avenida, Miramar, Playa, Ciudad de La Habana.
Teléfonos: (537) 24 4090
Fax: (537) 24 2303
Dania Teresita Gálvez Fernández
Roberto Vizcaíno Martínez

LEX, S.A.

Servicios Jurídicos de Marcas y Patentes.
Calle 1ra No. 1001, esquina 10, Miramar, Playa, Ciudad de La Habana.
Teléfonos: (537) 24 9093
Fax: (537) 24 9533

Ada Acosta Martínez
Olga Lidia Moreno Samper
Dánice Vázquez De Alvaré
Sara Marta Díaz Rodríguez
Zahily Ramírez Cabrera

PROVINCIAL CHAMNERS OF COMMERCE

Sección Provincial de Matanzas.
Fué creada el 20 de julio de 1999.
Nombre: Lourdes M. Rodríguez Rodríguez y Oreste Bello García.
Dirección: Calle Jovellanos No. 5, entre Medio y Río, Matanzas, Cuba.
Teléfonos: (052) 24 2483
E-mail: propind@atenas.inf.cu
Sección Provincial de Villa Clara.
Fué creada el 21 de julio de 1999.
Nombre: Osmel Aroche Pérez (Abogado), Aleyda Hernández y Carmen Elisa Roché.
Dirección: Cuba No. 364, entre Carretera Central y Serafín Sánchez, Santa Clara, Villa Clara, Cuba. C. Postal 50100
Teléfonos: (422) 7 3567
E-mail: ocpivc@civc.inf.cu

Sección Provincial de Camagüey.
Fué creada el 16 de noviembre de 1999.
Nombre: Boris Rodríguez Porrata y Aldo Alonso Muñoz (Abogado).
Dirección: General Gómez No. 325, entre San Miguel y Perro, Apartado 384,Camagüey, Cuba.
Teléfonos: (322) 9 7901
E-mail: boris@caonao.cmw.inf.cu

Sección Provincial de Holguín.
Fué creada el 17 de noviembre de 1999.
Nombre: Martha Morejón Borjas.
Dirección: Calle 18, entre 1ra y Maceo, Reparto "El Llano", Holguín, Cuba.
Teléfonos: (24) 42 2203, 46 8306
E-mail: mar@holguin.inf.cu, ciget@holguin.inf.cu

Sección Provincial de Santiago de Cuba.
Fué creada el 18 de noviembre de 1999.
Nombre: Yordanka Masó Dominicico (Abogada), Ma. Angeles Alpizar Terrero, Isabel Rodríguez Moreno, Blancet García Querol.
Dirección: Calle Carnicería No. 459, entre Enramada y San Gerónimo, Santiago de Cuba, Cuba. C. Postal 90100
Teléfonos: (226) 2 7402, 2 8291, 2 6909
E-mail: yordanka@megacen.ciges.inf.cu, mangeles@megacen.ciges.inf.cu

PRACTICAL INFORMATION FOR BUSINESS AND INVESTMENT ACTIVIRY

INVESTING IN CUBA: POLICY AND LEGAL FRAMEWORK

In 1988 a new stage opened when the first joint venture was created between a Cuban enterprise and a Spanish company with the purpose of building a hotel in the tourist resort of Varadero on the basis of Decree-Law No. 50 of 1982.

From 1991 to 1994, foreign investment was accelerated as one of the important steps taken by the Cuban authorities to recover from the serious impact to the Cuban economy caused by the disappearance of the Soviet Union and the economic links with other Socialist countries in the framework of the Council of Mutual Economic Aid (COMECON). This impact resulted in the loss of 35% of Cuba's GDP in the first three years of the nineties with strong economic and social effects. From 1997 on, foreign investment further expanded and more complex deals were agreed with important partners in newly opened sectors.

At the present time, this activity is promoted by Law 77, the Foreign Investment Act, approved by the National Assembly on September 5, 1995. It stipulates that foreign investment should contribute to strengthening the country's economic capacity and sustained development, on the basis of respect for national sovereignty and independence, and the protection and rational use of natural resources.

This new legislation offers more guarantees, greater security and new benefits for the investor, as well as providing a more significant opening in various economic sectors, where associations with foreign capital can be constituted.

The opening is oriented toward meeting specific needs within the Cuban economy, among them: export diversification, in terms of quality and quantity; the acquisition of raw materials; the need for new capital; insertion into new markets; the acquisition of advanced technologies; and the introduction of more modern economic management practices.

Foreign investment, which rose from less than $100 million USD in 1990 to more than $2.1 billion in 1995, now plays an important role in the search for the markets, technology and financing that disappeared simultaneously with the collapse of the socialist bloc.

In addition to the benefits previously mentioned, the process of opening up to foreign investment in Cuba has played a complementary role to national efforts to maintain capitalization in those economic branches that offer the largest rate of return. Even in sectors such as tourism, where foreign capital has been present since its current stage of development began, it is calculated that only 20 % of the investments in new capacities has been financed by foreign partners.

Neither can it be said that in Cuba the foreign investment opening is part of an ongoing privatization process. Certainly economic association with foreign capital supposes that certain assets are no longer state property, at least for as long as the agreement is in effect, which is generally long-term. But, as Minister of the Economy and Planning José Luis Rodríguez recently stated, national policy is aimed at defending the prevalence of state property in all forms of joint ventures and only accepting a majority investment or 100 % foreign control in justified cases.

Foreign capital represents barely 3 % of the gross domestic product, and the work force employed in this sector is approximately 5 % of the country's total.

Cuba has signed bilateral investment promotion and reciprocal protection agreements with 18 countries: Italy (1993); Argentina (1995); Russia (1993); Lebanon (1995); Spain (1994); South Africa (1995); Colombia (1994); Romania (1995); United Kingdom (1995); Chile (1996); China (1995); Barbados (1996); Ukraine (1995); Greece (1996); Bolivia (1995); Germany (1996); Viet Nam (1995); Switzerland (1996).

The evolution of economic associations with the foreign capital has had several phases. The first one went from the emergence of the first association up until September 1991, when there were still very few associations and they consisted of small and medium-sized companies, aimed at braking the drop of global indicators.

Between that date and 1993 there were no significant variations, although more than 60 entities of that kind were constituted. Starting in September 1994, a new wave of joint ventures emerged, mainly in services, housing construction, real estate and telecommunications, and at that point associations were allowed in all the productive branches of the country. At that time, companies with great prestige and international ranking, mainly European, began to do business on the island.

In this process, ever increasing interest has been expressed by entrepreneurs from United States. Consultancies such as the U.S.-Cuba Trade and Economic Council, Inc., with headquarters in New York, have experienced significant growth in their membership since that Cuban legislation went into effect.

In recent years several Cuba-United States business encounters have taken place, with the participation of executives and representatives of major international companies such as Mobil Oil Corporation, Texaco Inc., Bristol Myers Squibb Co., Pharmacia and Upjohn Co., Continental Grain Co., Wyeth Ayerst International Inc., Caterpillar Inc. and Lincoln Property Co.

Economic associations with foreign capital have grown steadily, going from 20 in 1990 to 260 in 1996 and 317 in 1997. At the present time, there are a total of 332. Since the beginning, only 63 have been dissolved, for various reasons. In 1998, 74 % of the associations with foreign capital were concentrated in six sectors: basic industry, tourism, light industry, the food industry, construction and agriculture.

The most far-reaching agreements are those established in telecommunications, the nickel industry, tourism and petroleum exploration and extraction. Prospects in tourism are very positive and Cuban authorities plan to continue creating new capacities and remodeling existing facilities. The most recent additions to the regulations promoting foreign investment were the Duty-Free Zones and Industrial Parks Act and the new tariff system, which went into effect on July 1, 1996.

Furthermore, there are three duty-free zones functioning in the country: Berroa and Wajay, in City of Havana, and Mariel, in La Habana province. By late 1997, a total of 190 operators had been authorized to do business in the duty-free zones, 140 of them commercial

Today, investors from 46 countries operate in almost 400 ventures in 32 sectors of the Cuban economy; 52 % of those investors are from European Union countries: 24% from Spain, almost 15% from Italy, 4% from France, 3.5% from the United Kingdom. Tourism, Oil and Gas, Mining,Energy and Telecoms are the main sectors of investment. Thus, foreign direct investment, focused on the search for new external markets, competitive technologies and financing (mainly long term) has played an important role in the country's economic recovery.

Cuba is located in a region whose share in world investment flows is rapidly growing. This, together with the country's potential and prospects for attachment to the Latin American integration process, makes hundreds of business people contact the Economic Office of the Cuban Embassy in London in search for information about investment opportunities.

Foreign investment is not associated to a privatisation process in Cuba; it is rather focused on specific objectives that complement national development efforts. Hence it is important to note what those objectives are and and the space they offer for foreign capital involvement.

In 1992, the National Assembly of the People's Power (Cuba's Parliament) approved a number of ammendments to the Constitution of the Republic with a view to recognising forms of ownership other than the State ownership.Joint ventures were legalised and FDI-associated aspects defined. The latter include: the recognition by the Cuban State of the assets of legally constituted joint ventures and economic partnerships, and their use, enjoyment and disposal shall be governed by the provisions of the law and treaties, as well as by their own by-laws and rules.

A new Foreign Investment Legislation (Law No.77) was passed in 1995. This legislation is in line with international practice. Some of the regulations thereof are:

Ø Foreign investment in Cuba may adopt the form of: a Joint Company, an Economic Association Contract or a Wholly-owned Foreign Company -where the investor is acknowledged full conduction of the company and enjoyment of all rights, as well as the responsibility for all the obligations stipulated in the authorisation

Ø The authorisation of investments in Cuba is a faculty of the State. There are two organs empowered to grant authorisations: the Executive Committee of the Council of Ministers and a Government Commission appointed by that Council, according to the case.

The procedure to obtain the authorization results from a previous negotiation between the national investor and the foreign investor, in the case of a joint venture of a contract of international economic association, or between the foreign investor and the ministry in charge of the corresponding branch, sub-branch or economic activity in which the investment is to be carried out, which is the case of a company totally of foreign capital. Both parties, the national and the foreign investor, will submit the corresponding application to the Ministry for Foreign Investment and Economic Cooperation (MINVEC) to examine and channel the proposal for final approval. Once the required economic and legal documentation on the proposed business has been prepared and submitted to MINVEC, the decision denying or approving such foreign investment is handed down within a period of 90 calendar days.

Ø Some of the guarantees granted to investors, as provided for in the Law include:full protection and security; their asset cannot be expropriated, save cases of extreme social interest, in which case prior compensation to be paid; tax-free freely transfer of their dividends; right to sell or transfer, subject to prior authorisation by the Government, their shares.

Ø Foreign investors can directly export and import whatever is necessary for their purposes.

Ø A special taxation regime provides for:

. the application of a 30% net profit tax and,

. the application of a 11% payroll tax and 14% as a employer's contribution to social security which apply to the total wages and other income that may be received by workers of the entity except those granted as economic stimulation.

Ø Authorisation for the establishment of duty free zones and industrial parks in properly delimited regions within the Cuban territory.

Ø Foreign investment in Cuba has increased.Today almost 400 joint ventures are operating in the country , with a strong presence in sectors such as mining, oil prospecting and extraction, tourism, industries and telecommunication. Lately other ventures and negotiations have expanded in new sectors, such as power generation by natural gas, expansion of the cities domestic gas supplies, etc.

Ø Investors from more than 40 countries have placed their capital in Cuba. Outstanding among them are: Spain, Canada, Italy, France and the United Kingdom.

The Economic Office of the Cuban Embassy in London can help with the general and specific information that may be necessary to participate in the Cuban foreign investment procedure: including the organisation of contacts, meetings or other arrangements with Cuban officials or possible counterparts which could facilitate British investment.

CUBA'S COMPARATIVE ADVANTAGES FOR FOREIGN INVESTMENT
Cuba's comparative advantages for foreign investment include the following:

Ø A highly skilled labor capable of assimilating, in a short period of time, any new technology;

Adequate infrastructure; 95% of the national territory is electrified; additionally, the country's basic infrastructure in terms of power generation and distribution, oil extraction, prospection and refining, and communications, has remained and even developed supported by foreign investment.

Ø Social stability and safety climate for foreign investors;

Ø Bilateral agreements on promotion and reciprocal protection of investments entered into with more than 50 countries, and 5 agreements for the avoidance of double taxation, while others are being negotiated.

FREE ZONES AND INDUSTRIAL PARKS
After approval of Law No.77 of Foreign Investment, Decree Law No. 165 on Free Zones and Industrial Parks was issued on June 22, 1996. This legislation defines Free Zones as areas within the national territory, duly limited, without a resident population , of free import and export of goods, not linked to the customs boundaries. Industrial, trade, agriculture, technological and services activities will be allowed in this area under application of a special regime.

This special regime is concerned with regulations relative to the customs, banking, tax, labour, migratory and public order systems, less burdensome and strict than the ordinary regulations, as shown below:

Customs regime:

- It rules the total exception of custom duties and other duties to be collected by customs for the introduction of goods destined to the development of the authorized activities;

Tax regime:

- For concessionaires and operators of productive activities there is total exemption of income taxes and taxes for the use of labor force, for a period of 12 years, and a bonus of 50% for another 5 years.

- In the case of operators of trade and service activities, the total exemption of the above mentioned taxes will be for 5 years, and the 50% bonus for another 3 years.

- More favorable exemptions may be granted after particular analysis of each case, and the terms may be extended.

Concessionary:

Promotes and develops with his own resources the necessary infrastructure for the operation of the duty free zone and assumes or delegates its management.

Operator:

Is authorized to establish himself in the duty free zone in order to carry out production, trade or service activity.

Banking and financial regime:

- The possibility exists of establishing banking and financial services if the license is previously obtained from Banco Central de Cuba;

- The capital obtained from operations may be freely transferred abroad; and

Labor regime:

- The Ministry of Labor and Social Security will determine the minimum salaries.

- The concessionary of mixed capital may act as employing entity to engage his workers and those required by the operator. The concessionary of wholly foreign capital will engage the workers through an entity proposed by the Ministry for Foreign Investment and approved by the Ministry of Labor and Social Security.

Other incentives of the Cuban legislation are the following:

- It creates a system that allows the investor to perform any application or handling before state entities or institutions through a sole point or Central Office at the Free Zone.

- It allows the operator to allocate up to 25% of the goods resulting from his activities in the domestic market.

- For reasons of availability of labor force, transportation or handling of raw materials, the operator may be authorized to perform specific activities outside the duty free zone area.

- Both concessionaires and operators may purchase goods and services offered by the country's enterprises outside the area where they are established. In this regard, a program of cooperation between the industries located in the duty free zone and the national industry is being drawn up.

These regulations are applicable to concessionaries and operators of free zones as incentives for investment.

There are 3 zones operating: Berroa and Wajay, both in the City of Havana, and Mariel in the Province of Havana, with 365 authorised operators.

THE MINISTRY FOR FOREIGN INVESTMENT AND ECONOMIC COOPERATION

The Ministry for Foreign Investment and Economic Cooperation (MINVEC) is the Central Administration Agency of the Cuban Estate responsible for governing and controlling the foreign investment process and the development of Free Zones and Industrial Parks. It is also in charge of preparing the relevant legislation in this field.

Its main functions include:

Ø Promotion of inward and outward foreign investment;

Ø Guiding the negotiation process for the establishment of economic associations or any other forms of foreign investment;

Ø Assestment of compliance with the bases and principles set forth for economic associations between Cuban and foreign entities;

Ø Implementation of the economic cooperation policy; governing and controlling the development of the technical assistence provided to and by the country;

Ø Preparation, negotiation and signing of agreements and conventions entered into with official foreign institutions dealing with foreign investment.

THE INVESTMENT PROMOTION CENTRE

The Ministry for Foreign Investment has, since 1994, its own Investment Promotion Centre (CPI) which is responsible for promoting the existing business opportunities for foreign capital involvement in Cuba, as well as overseas investment by Cuban companies.

Main services provided by CPI include:

Ø Provision of up-to-date information on the country, foreign investment regulations, and opportunities for foreign investment involvement in the domestic economy;

Ø To arrange meetings with would-be Cuban partners for foreign investors interested in investing in Cuba;

Ø To prepare for business delegations the required program of meetings with Cuban agencies and entities, as well as to organise tours to places of business interest;

Ø Provision of information on investment-aid programmes that may favor investment flows into Cuba;

Ø Organising investment seminars, lectures, meetings, events and fora, both in Cuba and abroad;

Ø Making consultations within Cuba or from abroad in connection with the feasibility of any investment project in particular;

Ø Provision of up-to-date information to the business press and international institutions that contribute to promote investment;

Ø Overseas promotion of investment by Cuban companies with comparative advantages.

To render such services, CPI relies on a highly qualified staff composed of updated experts with broad knowledge and skills on business promotion techniques used at international level and for the carrying out of opportunity-prefeasibility studies. This group of experts works jointly with national organisations and entities in defining projects for foreign capital involvement.

CPI is a member of the Geneva-based World Association of Investment Promotion Agencies (WAIPA), under the auspices of UN

EXPORTS AND REEXPORTS TO CUBA, IRAN, LIBYA, AND SUDAN UNDER THE TRADE SANCTIONS REFORM AND EXPORT ENHANCEMENT ACT

Summary: On July 12, 2001, the Bureau of Export Administration (BXA) and the Department of the Treasury's Office of Foreign Assets Control (OFAC) published regulations implementing certain provisions of the Trade Sanctions Reform and Export Enhancements Act of 2000 (TSRA) (Title IX of Public Law 106-387). The regulations went into effect on July 26, 2001 and both agencies have instituted procedures that will allow U.S. exporters and reexporters in other countries to engage in certain transactions that are subject to TSRA. BXA implemented the requirements of TSRA for exports and reexports of agricultural commodities to Cuba. BXA created License Exception Agricultural Commodities (AGR) to permit such exports and reexports to Cuba. Exports and reexports of medicines and medical devices to Cuba are not eligible for AGR, but are eligible for existing BXA license application procedures. OFAC regulates exports of agricultural commodities, medicines, and medical devices to Iran, Libya, and Sudan.

Explanation of

License Exception Agricultural Commodities (AGR)

TSRA Eligible Agricultural Commodities

TSRA Eligible Medicines and Medical Devices

BXA's Prior Notification Procedures under License Exception AGR

Commodity Classification Requirements

Summary of BXA Requirements for Treasury Department authorized Exports to Iran, Libya, and Sudan

Frequently asked Questions

LICENSE EXCEPTION AGRICULTURAL COMMODITIES (AGR):

The Bureau has created a new License Exception Agricultural Commodities (AGR) in section 740.18 of the Export Administration Regulations (EAR) .

License Exception AGR authorizes exports and certain reexports of eligible agricultural commodities that are classified as EAR99 (i.e., not listed on the Commerce Control List) to Cuba, subject to certain criteria and restrictions.

License Exception AGR does not authorize exports or reexports of medicines or medical devices to Cuba.

Exporters must notify BXA and obtain confirmation from BXA that no agency of the U.S. Government that reviews these notifications objects to use of License Exception AGR prior to any export or reexport under authority of License Exception AGR. The proposed export must meet all of the criteria and restrictions listed below.

Exports and reexports must be made pursuant to a written contract and must take place within 12 months of the signing of the contract, unless the shipment is a commercial sample or a donation, in which case the contract requirement does not apply.

No exports may be made to a terrorist entity, including a Specially Designated Terrorist (SDT) or Foreign Terrorist Organization (FTO), a person denied export privileges by the Department of Commerce if the export would violate the terms of the denial order, or for use in weapons of mass destruction (WMD) programs (i.e., biological, chemical, nuclear warfare or missile proliferations activities). The Treasury Department's Office of Foreign Assets Control lists of SDTs and FTOs as part of the list of Specially Designated Nationals and Blocked Persons

No U.S. owned or controlled foreign firm may export or reexport from a third country to Cuba a foreign produced agricultural commodity.

TSRA ELIGIBLE AGRICULTURAL COMMODITIES

Agricultural commodities are defined in Section 102 of the Agricultural Trade Act of 1978 (7 U.S.C. 02).

For purposes of License Exception AGR, agricultural commodities include, but are not limited to, food, feed, fish, shellfish and fish products; beer, wine and spirits; soft drinks; livestock; fiber, including cotton, wool and other fibers; tobacco and tobacco products; wood and wood products, including lumber and utility poles; seeds; and reproductive materials such as fertilized eggs, embryos, and semen.

A list of eligible agricultural commodities is available for review at the U.S. Department of Agriculture Web site[2]. If you have questions regarding whether an item is eligible, you should consult Ms. Emiko Purdy at the Department of Agriculture, Foreign Agricultural Service, phone: 202-720-0762, fax: 202-720-0069.

Vitamins, minerals, food additives and dietary supplements, and bottled water are also considered to be agricultural commodities for the purposes of License Exception AGR.

Some organic and inorganic fertilizers are eligible and some are not. The distinction is as follows:

Dry fertilizers containing 15% or less ammonium nitrate are eligible for License Exception AGR.

Dry fertilizers containing more than 15% ammonium nitrate are classified as Export Commodity Classification Number (ECCN) 1C997 and are not eligible for License Exception AGR.

Liquid fertilizers are eligible for License Exception AGR regardless of the concentration of ammonium nitrate they contain.

Some agricultural commodities are not eligible, such as:

items on the Commerce Control List (CCL), including western red cedar and live horses;

items on the U.S. Munitions List;

items for use in weapons of mass destruction (WMD).

Agricultural commodities do not include furniture even if made from wood; clothing; agricultural equipment (whether hand tools or motorized equipment); pesticides, insecticides, or herbicides; or cosmetics (unless derived entirely from plant materials).

TSRA ELIGIBLE MEDICINES AND MEDICAL DEVICES

Medicines are drugs as defined in Section 201 of the Federal Food, Drug and Cosmetic Act (21 U.S.C. 321).

Medicines include prescription medicines and over the counter medicines for humans and animals.

Medical devices include medical supplies, instruments, equipment, equipped ambulances, institutional washing machines capable of sterilizing hospital clothing and bedding, and vehicles with installed medical testing equipment.

If you have questions regarding whether an item meets the definition of medicine or medical device under the Food, Drug and Cosmetic Act, you should consult the Food and Drug Administration (FDA). For medicines, contact the FDA's Office of Drug Information at 301-827-4570 (telephone); 301-827-4577 (fax); For medical devices, contact the FDA's Division of Small Manufacturers' Assistance at 800-638-2041 (telephone); 301-443-8818 (fax);

Medicines on the Commerce Control List are not eligible.

[2] See Supplements

Ineligible Medicines:

The following vaccines, immunotoxins, medical products, diagnostic and food testing kits are controlled on the Commerce Control List in Export Control Classification Number (ECCN) 1C991 and are not eligible for export under the expedited procedures authorized by the Trade Sanctions Reform and Export Enhancement Act of 2000.

- Controlled vaccines are those which contain items listed in Category 1 on the Commerce Control List in ECCNs 1C351, 1C352, 1C353 and 1C354. To view a description of these items, go to the Export Administration Regulations on the Access GPO web site, scroll down to "Category 1" and select the format in which you wish to view the document.

- Controlled immunotoxins are antibody-toxin conjugates intended to destroy specific target cells (e.g., tumor cells) that bear antigens homologous to the antibody, where the toxin portion is listed in 1C351.d.

- Controlled medical products are pharmaceutical formulations designed for human administration in the treatment of medical conditions, prepackaged for distribution as medical products and approved by the Food and Drug Administration to be marketed as medical products, which contain toxins listed in 1C351.d.

- Controlled diagnostic and food testing kits are specifically developed, packaged and marketed for diagnostic or public health purposes, which contain toxins listed in 1C351.d.

Medical devices do not include general purpose furniture such as desks, tables, or lamps used in hospital offices and waiting rooms.

For Cuba, medicines and medical items are not eligible for License Exception AGR. These may be authorized for export to Cuba according to the provisions of the Cuban Democracy Act under an export license issued by BXA. A BXA export license is valid for two years.

BXA'S PRIOR NOTIFICATION PROCEDURES UNDER LICENSE EXCEPTION AGR:

Before making any shipment under License Exception AGR, exporters must submit a notification to BXA and obtain confirmation that no agency has raised an objection to the use of License Exception AGR for the transaction described in the notification. BXA informs exporters within 12 business days from the date the notice is registered in BXA's electronic database whether such objections have been raised. BXA's confirmation that no objections have been raised does not relieve parties to the transaction from the obligation to assure that they meet all of the requirements of License Exception AGR, other requirements of the Export Administration Regulations (EAR), and any other applicable law. The procedures for using this license exception are:

-Exporters must notify BXA prior to any export or reexport.

-Exporters provide this prior notification by submitting a completed BXA Multi-purpose Application Form (BXA-748P) or electronically through BXA's Simplified Network Application Process (SNAP).

Within two business days of the notification's registration in BXA's electronic database system, BXA will refer the notification electronically to the Departments of State, Defense, and other agencies, as appropriate, for review.

Any reviewing agency that objects to the use of License Exception AGR must provide notice of such objection to BXA within nine business days of the referral.

-An agency may object for one or more of the following reasons:

the commodity is not an agricultural commodity;

the items are not EAR99;

the export would violate the terms of a denial order;

the recipient may promote international terrorism; or

the transaction raises nonproliferation concerns.

If any agency objects, BXA will convert the notification into a license application and process it under standard export license application procedures.

An exporter may ship the goods after 12 days if no agency has raised an objection. Applicants may check the status of their notification or application via BXA's System for Tracking Export License Applications (STELA) at 202-482-2752 using the "Z" number on the 748-P form or provided by SNAP. Applicants may not make the export without confirming via STELA that no agency has raised an objection.

BXA also will notify the applicant in writing of the outcome of the interagency review.

COMMODITY CLASSIFICATION REQUIREMENTS:

Exporters must be sure that they are not attempting to use AGR as authority to export any item that is on the Commerce Control List (CCL). Only items classified as EAR99 are eligible for BXA's License Exception AGR or OFAC's expedited review procedures. EAR99 items are items that are subject to the Export Administration Regulations, but they are not specifically listed on the CCL.

Exporters may need to include, with their notification or application, an official BXA commodity classification to confirm the classification of an item as EAR99, as specified in greater detail below.

BXA is responsible for providing commodity classifications. Exporters may obtain a commodity classification by submitting a completed BXA's Multipurpose Application Form (BXA-748P) or electronically through BXA's Simplified Network Application Process (SNAP) indicating that they wish a commodity classification. See Section 748.3 of the Export Administration Regulations for more information.

BXA has already determined that most items that meet the definition of agricultural commodity are classified as EAR99. This includes most of the items on the Department of Agriculture's Eligible Commodities List (pdf) available from its Economic and Trade Sanctions Web page. This means that items on this list do not require a commodity classification with three exceptions: live horses; western red cedar; and fertilizers.

For these three types of agricultural commodities, BXA and OFAC require a BXA commodity classification for fertilizers, live horses or western red cedar prior to submission of a notification to BXA or a license application to OFAC, as these agricultural commodities may be on the Commerce Control List.

Medicines do not require a BXA commodity classification prior to OFAC review, unless you are unsure whether your item is a medicine (e.g., vaccines and immunotoxins) that BXA has identified on the Commerce Control List and thus on BXA's list of ineligible medicines.

Medical supplies (e.g., syringes, bandages and gauze) and devices require a BXA commodity classification prior to OFAC review, unless BXA has listed the item on the list of EAR99 medical supplies found on BXA's Web site.

EXPORTS AND REEXPORTS TO IRAN, LIBYA, AND SUDAN:

OFAC is responsible for authorizing exports of agricultural commodities, medicines, and medical devices to Iran, Libya, and Sudan. It is also responsible for authorizing reexport of these items by U.S. persons to Iran, Libya and Sudan.

BXA has licensing responsibility for reexports to Libya by U.S. or foreign persons of items requiring a license to Libya under the EAR, e.g., foreign produced medical equipment containing U.S. controlled content, reexports of U.S. origin medical equipment (see section 746.4 of the EAR).

If OFAC authorization is needed, exporters must submit an application in writing to OFAC identifying the item they would like to export and the purchaser, any intermediaries, and the end-user involved in the proposed transaction.

OFAC also has expedited procedures for reviewing such applications.

Exporters should check OFAC's Web site for additional information on OFAC's requirements.

Exporters can check the status of their OFAC applications by calling the OFAC Licensing Division at (202) 622-2480 between 9:00 AM and 5:30 PM Eastern time.

As described in the Commodity Classification Requirements summary above, to comply with OFAC regulations, exporters may need a BXA commodity classification.

FAQ ON CONDUCTING BUSINESS AND VISITING CUBA

U.S.-Cuba Trade and Economic Council, Inc.
30 Rockefeller Plaza New York, New York 10112-0002
Telephone (212) 246-1444 Facsimile (212) 246-2345
Internet: http://www.cubatrade.org

Can I export to Cuba?

The legislation liberalizes U.S. sanctions on exports to Cuba of agricultural commodities. However, strict laws remain in place on using U.S. dollars in Cuba, financing transactions, traveling to Cuba, and limiting U.S. Government assistance. Some Federal regulations and instructions will need to be developed regarding these issues. The principal agencies involved and where to turn for more information about regulations are USDA, U.S. Department of State, U.S. Department of the Treasury's Office of Foreign Assets Control, and the U.S. Department of Commerce's Bureau of Export Administration.

Until all these new regulations are in place, what can I do in Cuba?

Representatives of U.S. industry associations, state governments, and private companies may travel to Cuba provided they apply for and receive a specific license from the Treasury Departments Office of Foreign Assets Control. Under current regulations, travel transactions related to marketing, sales negotiation, and accompanied delivery of agricultural products are possible. Exporters are required to apply to the Treasury Department's Office of Foreign Assets Control for a license to engage in such transactions and to spend funds in Cuba. For information you may visit OFAC's website www.treas.gov/ofac or call (202)622-2520. Exporters should also check with the State Department for the most recent regulations for travel of U.S. citizens. Monitor the ***Federal Register*** to see proposed regulations on Cuba as they emerge and offer comments on how those regulations should be structured.

How do I find potential buyers?

U.S. exporters must vie for Cuba's trade with other, more established competitors such as Canada, France, and Mexico that already export agricultural commodities to Cuba. U.S. proximity to Cuba, the high quality of U.S. agricultural products, and the marketing expertise of the U.S. industry will slowly grow the Cuban marketplace for U.S. products, but only after considerable energy and effort has been made. For general information on Cuba, the U.S. Government operates a U.S. Interests Section in Havana located at Calzada between L & M Streets, Vedado, Havana, tel: (53-7) 33-3551 thru 3559, fax: (53-7) 33-3700. Also, the U.S. Department of Agriculture has a trade office in Miami , tel: (305) 536-5300 or fax: (305) 536-7577 that can help U.S. exporters search for markets throughout the Caribbean Basin, including Cuba. To do business in Cuba and find importers, an exporter should do in-depth market research and develop payment strategies that will conform to U.S. law.

Can representatives of U.S. agricultural cooperatives, trade associations, or state governments visit Cuba and perform market development activities?

Yes, but they must obtain a license and follow Federal law and regulations. The use of Federal funds to support export promotions is specifically prohibited by Congress. Private companies, cooperatives, trade associations, or state governments may use their own funds for market development purposes, but the use of funds in Cuba is tightly controlled. U.S. agricultural industry trade associations, such as FAS Foreign Market Development Cooperators or Market Access Program participants, are allowed to undertake market development activities in Cuba provided they obtain a license, but not with Federal funds. U.S. industry can use its own resources to explore the Cuban market, but prior to using any funds in Cuba, U.S. industry and associations must apply to the Office of Foreign Assets Control for a license.

How will I get paid?

The new law prohibits any U.S. person or company from providing payment or financing credit terms to anyone in Cuba. The law specifically rules out open account transactions, requiring cash in advance arrangements. Foreign banks may, however, finance transactions and U.S. banks may confirm or advise such foreign bank letters of credit or similar arrangements. Exporters should be alert to these provisions in law and how payment strategies will be affected by U.S. regulations. The U.S. Treasury Department's Office of Foreign Assets Control is the regulatory authority on currencies and payments with sanctioned countries and consulted regarding payment issues. For information you may visit OFAC's website www.treas.gov/ofac or call (202)622-2520.

What is the current level of Cuba's agricultural trade? What products?

Cuba imports about $600 million worth annually, primarily grain, pulses, meat, soybeans, vegetable oil, and dairy products. This amount has trended downward in recent years due to Cuba's current economic hardship. Cuba's 11 million inhabitants have an estimated per capita income of $1,500, equal to Guatemala. Adjusted to account for purchasing power parity this per capita income estimate rises to $3,500. This figure adjusts income for the relatively low cost of many items in the Cuban economy including subsidized rents and indicates that Cubans have greater purchasing power than indicated by that low nominal GDP figure. Growth in tourism and some reform of Cuba's centralized economy have the potential to turn around this picture and raise demand for imported foods. Tourism earns Cuba substantial foreign currency and is its No. 1 economic sector for growth. The United States might find new markets in Cuba for consumer-ready foods for the hotel and restaurant industry as tourism grows and as the United States begins to compete with other suppliers for bulk and intermediate commodity sales. Other agricultural products that hold promise for future U.S. sales are wood products and cotton.

VISITING THE REPUBLIC OF CUBA AND TRANSACTIONS WITH THE REPUBLIC OF CUBA

The following information is provided as a general overview of the regulations administered by the United States Department of the Treasury and the United States Department of Commerce. For specific information, including legal opinion, requests should be made directly to the appropriate representative of the United States government. Relevant information is contained within the Code of Federal Regulations (CFR)- 31 CFR Part 515.

Who is an Individual Subject To United States Law?

An individual subject to United States law includes: 1) Any individual, wherever located, who is a citizen or resident of the United States 2) Any person who is within the United States [a non-United States citizen in transit at an airport, for example] 3) Any corporation organized under the laws of the United States or of any State, territory possession, or district of the United States 4) Any corporation, partnership, or association, wherever organized or doing business, that is owned or controlled by persons specified in 1 and 3. Non-United States citizens who have visas are considered to be subject to United States law.

The Office of Foreign Assets Control (OFAC) of the United States Department of the Treasury in Washington, D.C., administers the regulations governing ***travel and financial transactions*** with respect to the Republic of Cuba by individuals subject to United States law.

Mr. R. Richard Newcomb
Director
Office of Foreign Assets Control
United States Department of the Treasury
Washington, D.C. 20220
Telephone: (202) 622-2480
Facsimile: (202) 622-1657
Internet: http://www.treas.gov/ofac

The Bureau of Export Administration (BXA) of the United States Department of Commerce in Washington, D.C., administers regulations governing the ***export of products*** (including donations and general aviation aircraft temporary sojourn licenses) to the Republic of Cuba by individuals subject to United States law and by businesses subject to United States law. However, Non-United States-based subsidiaries of United States-based companies must apply to the OFAC for licenses to export products to the Republic of Cuba. Applicants seeking to export products (including temporary sojourn licenses) to the Republic of Cuba (other than informational materials, which are exempt from licensing requirements) are required to use the Multipurpose Application Form BXA-748P which can be obtained by contacting the Office of Exporter Services at telephone (202) 482-4811 press 0.

Mr. John Bolsteins
Office of Strategic Trade and Foreign Policy Controls
Bureau of Export Administration
United States Department of Commerce
Washington, D.C. 20230
Telephone: (202) 482-3283
Facsimile: (202) 482-6088
Internet: http://www.bxa.doc.gov/

The Office of Cuban Affairs (OCA) United States Department of State in Washington, D.C., ***establishes the policies*** by which the OFAC and the BXA ***interpret the regulations by which laws are enforced***.

Mr. Charles Shapiro
Coordinator
Office of Cuban Affairs
United States Department of State
Washington, D.C. 20520
Telephone: (202) 647-9273
Facsimile: (202) 736-4476
Internet: http://www.state.gov/

Individuals subject to United States law can travel to the Republic of Cuba if they do so under the auspices of either an OFAC General License or an OFAC Specific License.

Individuals subject to United States law traveling to the Republic of Cuba (with the exception of individuals subject to United States law traveling to the Republic of Cuba on a "fully hosted" basis) under the auspice of an OFAC General License or OFAC Specific License are authorized to spend up to US$195.00 per day for hotels, meals, ground transportation, etc. Not included in the US$195.00 per day spending limit are expenses for telephone calls. Individuals who are full-time journalists traveling to the Republic of Cuba under a general license from the OFAC may also spend above the US$195.00 for expenses "incidental to journalist activities."

Exemptions to the US$195.00 per day authorization can be requested from the OFAC. "Fully hosted" travelers are not subject to spending limits while within the Republic of Cuba.

In August 1999, the OFAC increased the Per Diem allowance for employees of the United States government visiting the Republic of Cuba to US$195.00 (US$113.00 for lodging and US$82.00 for meals) from US$183.00 (US$102.00 for lodging and US$81.00 for meals), representing an increase of US$12.00 per day, or 6.16% from the Per Diem rate in effect from 1 December 1996. An increase in the Per Diem reflects an evaluation by the United States Department of State that prices within the Republic of Cuba have increased. Per Diem rates within the Republic of Cuba are based upon the Per Diem Rate For Foreign Areas issued by the Office of Allowances (202-663-1121) within the Office of Operations of the Bureau of Administration of the Under Secretary of Management of the United States Department of State in Washington, D.C. Per Diem values for travel to the city of Havana from 1995 through August 1999:

Effective Date	Lodging	Meals & Incidentals	Total Per Diem	% Increase From Previous Year
1 June 1999 to Present	US$113.00	US$82.00	US$195.00	6.16%
1 June 1999 to 1 December 1996	US$102.00	US$81.00	US$183.00	15.85%
1 December 1996 to 1 November 1995	US$90.00	US$64.00	US$154.00	-0-

Individuals (non-employees of the United States government) subject to United States law traveling to the Republic of Cuba under a general license from the OFAC or a specific license from the OFAC were permitted to spend US$100.00 per day (no distinction with respect to lodging and meals) from 1985 through May 1999. Since May 1999, individuals subject to United States law traveling to the Republic of Cuba under a general license from the OFAC or a specific license from the OFAC have been permitted to spend at parity with representatives of the United States government traveling to the Republic of Cuba on official business.

Individuals subject to United States law traveling to the Republic of Cuba under the auspices of either an OFAC General License (excluding "fully hosted" travelers subject to United States law) or an OFAC Specific License may return from the Republic of Cuba to the United States with up to US$100.00 worth of Republic of Cuba-origin products (such as cigars, rum, tee-shirts, crafts, etc.) for their personal use. For cigars, the United States Customs Service permits up to 100 cigars, but the total value must not exceed US$100.00. For example, if a traveler returns with 100 cigars which cost US$1.00 each, the traveler would not be permitted to bring any other

Republic of Cuba-origin products (such as rum) because the total value of imported Republic of Cuba-origin products would then exceed US$100.00. If a traveler purchased 100 cigars for US$50.00, then the traveler would have an additional US$50.00 to spend on other Republic of Cuba origin products such as rum, tee-shirts, crafts, etc. Travelers subject to United States law should retain a receipt showing the amount paid for all Republic of Cuba-origin products.

OFAC General License:

An individual subject to United States law traveling to the Republic of Cuba under the auspice of an OFAC General License is neither required to inform the OFAC in advance of their visit to the Republic of Cuba nor obtain a written license from the OFAC.

1) Representatives of the United States government on official business, representatives of non-United States governments on official business, representatives of international organizations of which the United States government is a member on official business.

2) Individuals subject to United States law who are regularly (full-time) employed by a news gathering organization (television network, television station, television production company, radio station, newspaper, newsletter, magazine, video production company, etc.). Travelers are advised to have company identification (with photograph), business card, and/or a letter from the company confirming full-time employment of the traveler. United States Customs Service inspectors may request this information at the point of entry into the United States.

3) Individuals subject to United States law traveling once in a twelve (12) month period to visit close relatives in circumstances of self-defined humanitarian need.

4) Individuals subject to United States law who are professional researchers. This includes individuals who are acting on behalf of an organization with an established interest in international relations.

5) Individuals subject to United States law who are graduate students, under graduate students, or secondary school students under the auspice of a specific license issued to a school, college, university, etc.

6) Individuals subject to United States law traveling on a "fully hosted" basis. "Fully hosted" travel requires that the individual subject to United States law who is traveling to the Republic of Cuba does not spend any funds of their own while within the Republic of Cuba. Funds used to make payments for hotels, meals, ground transportation, sundries, etc., must originate from a) an entity within the Republic of Cuba b) an entity within another country or c) an individual within another country. The use of indirect transfers is not permitted. For example, the individual subject to United States law sends funds to another country within which a relative, friend, or business associate resides. The relative, friend, or business associate then makes payments within the Republic of Cuba on behalf of the individual subject to United States law. "Fully hosted" individuals subject to United States law traveling to the Republic of Cuba and departing from the Republic of Cuba are not permitted to use their own funds for the purchase of an airline ticket or a cruise ship ticket for such travel if the airline or cruise ship is controlled by an entity within the Republic of Cuba. For example, a "fully hosted" traveler subject to United States law is not permitted to use their own funds to purchase an airline ticket on Cubana Airlines to travel to the Republic of Cuba, but the traveler could use their own funds to purchase an airline ticket on Mexicana, Air Jamaica, Lacsa, Iberia, etc. A "Fully hosted" traveler subject to United States law may return from the Republic of Cuba to the United States with an unlimited value of artwork and informational materials (books, magazines, music tapes, CD ROM's, photographs, films, posters,

phonograph records, microfilm, microfiche, compact disks, and newswire feed, etc.) A "Fully hosted" traveler subject to United States law may not return from the Republic of Cuba to the United States with Republic of Cuba-
origin products such as those authorized for individuals subject to United States law who travel to the Republic of Cuba under an OFAC General License or an OFAC Specific License such as cigars, rum, tee-shirts, crafts, etc. A "Fully hosted" traveler subject to United States law may return from the Republic of Cuba to the United States with any gift received from a Republic of Cuba national. However, the gift must remain with the United States Customs Service at the point of entry into the United States. The "fully hosted" traveler subject to United States law may then request a license from the OFAC to take possession of the gift.

"FULLY HOSTED" TRAVELERS WARNING

Officials at the United States Department of State, officials at the Office of Foreign Assets Control (OFAC) of the United States Department of the Treasury, officers of the United States Customs Service, and officers of the Immigration and Naturalization Service, have re-confirmed that any individual subject to United States law returning to the United States after visiting the Republic of Cuba on a "fully hosted basis" will be subjected to increased scrutiny. This is especially true for high profile groups. Extreme caution should be taken as there is no longer a presumption of innocence, there is now a presumption of guilt and fines will be assessed. The term "fully hosted" means that all expenses within the Republic of Cuba (including travel to and from the Republic of Cuba if using a Republic of Cuba government-operated air carrier, such as Cubana Airlines, or other means of transportation) on behalf of the individual subject to United States law are paid for by an individual or entity not subject to United States law. No direct or indirect payments are permitted. A "fully hosted" traveler may return to the United States with an unlimited amount of informational materials (books, magazines, newspapers, music tapes, etc.) and an unlimited amount of artwork. A "fully hosted" traveler may not return to the United States with any other Republic of Cuba-produced products (such as cigars, rum, coffee, tee-shirts, etc.). The OFAC and the United States Customs Service confirm that "fully hosted" travelers should now expect the following: ***A)*** *A letter from an individual or entity not subject to United States law (or a letter from a United States-based law firm) confirming that the individual subject to United States law was "fully hosted" will not be accepted as "proof" that a visit was "fully hosted."* ***B)*** *The individual subject to United States law will be required to produce receipts for all daily expenses within the Republic of Cuba which demonstrate that all of the expenses were paid by an individual or entity not subject to United States law.* ***C)*** *At the entry point to the United States, the United States Customs Service may make a photocopy of the passport of the individual subject to United States law. The passport number may be entered in a permanent data base.* ***D)*** *The individual subject to United States law will be required to submit a signed letter confirming, under penalty of perjury, that all daily expenses incurred within the Republic of Cuba on behalf of the individual subject to United States law were paid for by an individual or entity not subject to United States law.* ***E)*** *The OFAC may send a letter to the individual subject to United States law requiring additional proof that the visit to the Republic of Cuba was "fully hosted."*

OFAC Specific License:

An individual subject to United States law traveling to the Republic of Cuba under the auspice of an OFAC Specific License is required to obtain a written license from the OFAC. An individual(s) subject to United States law who wishes to travel to the Republic of Cuba under the auspice of an OFAC Specific License should write a letter to the OFAC and include the following information: a) the date of the planned visit and the length of stay b) the specific purpose(s) of the visit c) name(s), title(s) of individual(s), and background(s) of the traveler.

1) Individuals subject to United States law who wish to identify commercial opportunities in the fields of agricultural products, air charter services, artwork, communications, entertainment, farm supplies, food sales, informational materials, medical equipment, medical instruments, medical supplies, medicated products, medicines, money transfer services, package delivery services, pharmaceuticals, telecommunications; travel services; register trademarks and patents; and organize and participate in trade shows;

2) Individuals subject to United States law more than once in a twelve (12) month period to visit close relatives in circumstances of self-defined humanitarian need.

3) Individuals subject to United States law who are employed as freelance journalists.

4) Individuals subject to United States law accompanying licensed (from the BXA) humanitarian donations.

5) Individuals subject to United States law traveling in conjunction with activities of recognized human rights organizations investigating human rights violations.

6) Individuals subject to United States law who are professional researchers. This includes individuals who are acting on behalf of an organization with an established interest in international relations.

7) Individuals subject to United States law who are graduate students or secondary school students.

8) Individuals subject to United States law who are athletes competing in an event(s).

9) Individuals subject to United States law who are members of a religious organization.

10) Individuals subject to United States law who wish to lecture at educational institutions.

11) Individuals subject to United States law who wish to engage in a public exhibition, such as a concert, trade show, etc.

Travel Visas From The Republic Of Cuba:

Individuals subject to United States law can travel to the Republic of Cuba using either an a) official visa or b) a tourist visa. Official visas are obtained from the Cuban Interests Section in Washington, D.C. A tourist visa can be obtained from: **1)** a travel agent licensed by the Office of Foreign Assets Control (OFAC) of the United States Department of the Treasury **2)** a non-United States-based travel agent **3)** at the ticket counter of the non-United States-based airline providing travel to the Republic of Cuba from a country other than from the United States or **4)** in some cases, upon arrival at an airport within the Republic of Cuba, although this is unadvisable.

The official visa is used for individuals subject to United States law who are traveling to the Republic of Cuba for any purpose other than tourism. Generally, if an individual subject to United States law travels to the Republic of Cuba using a tourist visa and then, while within the country, wishes to change his or her visa status, the change can be completed by contacting the United States Department of the Ministry of Foreign Affairs of the Republic of Cuba.

His Excellency

Dr. Fernando Remirez
Cuban Interests Section
2630 16th Street, Northwest
Washington, D.C. 20009
Telephone: (202) 797-8518 or (202) 797-8522
Facsimile: (202) 797-8521
Mr. Jose Barrios
Director- United States Department
Ministry of Foreign Affairs
Calle Calzada No. 360 e/ G y H, Vedado
Havana, Republic of Cuba
Telephone: 011 53 7 32 9190 or 011 53 7 30 50 31
Facsimile: 011 53 7 31 23 14 or 011 53 7 33 3085

Travel Arrangements To/From/Within The Republic Of Cuba:

Individuals subject to United States law traveling to the Republic of Cuba should only use travel agents which have been licensed by the Office of Foreign Assets Control (OFAC) of the United States Department of the Treasury:

Tico Travel
161 East Commercial Boulevard
Fort Lauderdale, Florida 33334
Telephone: (954) 493-5335 or (800) 493-8426
Facsimile: (954) 493-8466
E-mail: tico@gate.net
Internet: http://www.destinationcuba.com/
Mr. Joel Sanz
United States and Puerto Rico Division
Havanatur
Corporation Cimex S.A.
Edificio Sierra Maestra, Calle 1ra y O, Mirara, Playa
Havana, Republic of Cuba
Telephone: 011 53 7 23 97 16
011 53 7 23 97 90
011 53 7 23 97 91
011 53 7 24 24 24 (emergencies)
Facsimile: 011 53 7 24 2912 or 011 53 7 24 29 12
E-mail: joels@cimex.com.cu or georgina@cimex.com.cu

IS IT LEGAL TO GO TO CUBA? US LAW AND TRAVEL TO CUBA

"Fully hosted" Travelers

Individuals subject to US law traveling on a "fully hosted" basis can travel without a specific license so long as they do not spend any funds of their own while in Cuba. This includes travel on a prepaid, all-inclusive tour package with companies such as Last Frontier Expeditions (see Organized Tours in the Transportation chapter). Funds used to make payments for hotels, meals, ground transportation, sundries, etc., must originate from a) an entity within Cuba b) an entity within another country (Last Frontier Expeditions is an Aruba and Mexican based company) or c) an individual within another country. The use of indirect transfers is not permitted. A "fully hosted" traveler may pay for transportation only if aboard a non-Cuban carrier such as Mexicana, Air Jamaica, Lacsa, Iberia, etc. Travelers whose expenses are covered by a person not subject to US jurisdiction may not bring back any Cuban origin goods, except for informational materials (books, magazines, posters, etc.) and an unlimited amount of artwork. Gifts from Cuba nationals may be brought into the USA, but the gift must remain with the US Customs Service at the point of entry; the traveler subject must then request a license.

Qualified Travel Service Providers Referring to travel agencies and tour operators, "It is possible to provide travel services to US persons legally able to travel to Cuba for family visits, professional research, or news gathering," says Michael Krinsky, a partner in the law firm of Rabinowitz, Boudin, Standard, Krinsky and Lieberman, which represents the Cuban government in the United States. US travel agencies can also provide services to third countries, from where a traveler makes his or her own arrangements for travel to and within Cuba. They may also be able to provide services, such as travel arrangements to Jamaica, where a component includes an excursion to Cuba. Treasury Department regulations do not "show a clear penalty against travel agents who book travel this way."

Contrary to popular belief, US law does not prohibit US citizens from visiting Cuba. However, to visit Cuba legally you must either spend no money there, or qualify for a license issued by the US Treasury Dept. in order to buy goods (a meal at a hotel, for example) or services (an airline ticket, tour package, or hotel room). In order to apply, you need a good reason. Except as specifically licensed by the Office of Foreign Assets Control, payments in connection with any other travel to Cuba are prohibited, whether travelers go directly or via a third country such as Mexico, Canada, or another Caribbean Island. US citizens and any person in the USA is subject to these restrictions, regardless of citizenship. Under these restrictions, spending money relating to Cuban travel is prohibited unless the traveler is licensed. The regulations change frequently and are open to interpretation by the understaffed office (interpretation often shifts with the political breeze). For example, in May 1999 the Clinton administration announced new regulations that will expand travel opportunities. US universities and non-governmental organizations may now apply for two-year travel permits to Cuba that will permit any of its members to travel to Cuba without requiring individual certification. And the amount that U.S. citizens can spend in Cuba was raised from US$100 to US$185 per day.

- To determine if you or your organization qualify for a general license (which does not require prior government authorization) or a specific license (which does require prior government authorization), contact:

  Licensing Division, Office of Foreign Asset Control (OFAC)
  US Department of the Treasury
  1500 Pennsylvania Ave.
  NW, Washington, D.C. 20200
  tel. 202-622-2520 or 202-622-2480
  fax 202-622-1657
  - Request the ***Cuban Assets Control Regulations***.

- **The Office of Cuban Affairs (OCA)**
  Department of State
  Washington, D.C. 20520
  tel. 202- 647-9273
  fax 202-736-4476
  web site: **www.state.gov**
  -establishes the policies by which the OFAC interpret the regulations by which laws are enforced. The following regulations applied at press time:

Who is an "Individual Subject To United States Law"

An individual subject to US law includes: any individual, wherever located, who is a citizen or resident of the USA; any person who is within the US (a non-US citizen in transit at an airport, for example); any corporation organized under the laws of the USA or of any State, territory possession, or district of the USA; any corporation, partnership, or association, wherever organized or doing business, that is owned or controlled by persons an individual or individuals subject to US law. (Non-US citizens who have H-1 visas are generally considered to be subject to US law.)

GENERAL LICENSES?

The following categories of travelers are permitted to spend money for Cuban travel without the need to obtain special permission from OFAC, nor are they required to inform OFAC in advance of their visit to Cuba:

Official Government Travelers: US and foreign government officials, including representatives of international organizations of which the United States is a member, who are traveling on official business.

Journalists: Individuals who are regularly (full-time) employed by a news gathering organization (television network, television station, television production company, radio station, newspaper, newsletter, magazine, video production company, etc.). Travelers are advised to have company identification (with photograph), business card, and/or a letter from the company confirming full-time employment.

Persons who are visiting close relatives: People with close relatives in Cuba may visit them in circumstances of humanitarian need. This authorization is valid only once every 12 months.

SPECIAL LICENSES?

A specific license requires written government approval. Applicants should write a letter to the OFAC stating the date of the planned visit and the length of stay; the specific purpose(s) of the visit; plus the name(s), title(s), and background(s) of the traveler. OFAC has been understaffed and is notoriously slow: allow two or three months. Special licenses are issued by OFAC on a case by case basis authorizing travel transactions by persons in connection with the following travel categories:

Humanitarian Travel: Persons traveling to Cuba to visit close relatives in cases involving hardship more than once in a 12 month period; persons traveling to Cuba to accompany licensed humanitarian donations (other than gift parcels); or persons traveling in connection with activities of recognized human rights organizations investigating human rights violations.

Educational Research: Travel in connection with professional research or similar activities, for clearly defined educational or religious activities, including academics intending to lecture at educational institutions or attend a meeting or conference, and activities related to study for an undergraduate or graduate degree sponsored by a college or university located in the United States.

Commercial "Opportunists": Individuals wishing to identify commercial opportunities in the fields of artwork, communications, entertainment, informational materials, medical equipment, medical instruments, medical supplies, medicated products, medicines, pharmaceuticals, and telecommunications; register trademarks and patents; organize and participate in trade shows; authorize consumer credit cards to be valid for use; and provide travel services and provide air transportation services.

Others: Freelance journalists; athletes competing in an event; and individuals wishing to engage in a public exhibition, such as a concert, trade show, etc. Many travelers have successfully been approved as "freelancers." If you want to go it alone and try the "journalist" or "researcher" angle, write to the OFAC, which requires a written statement of why your proposed trip falls within the rules for permissible travel.

WHAT YOU MAY SPEND?

Licensed travelers are authorized to spend up to US$185 per day. Exemptions to the US$185 per day authorization can be requested from the OFAC. "Fully hosted" travelers are not subject to spending limits while within the Republic of Cuba.

Money may be spent only for purchases of items directly related to travel such as hotel accommodations, meals, and goods personally used by the traveler in Cuba, or for the purchase of $100 worth of Cuban merchandise to be brought into the United States as accompanied baggage. Purchases of services related to travel, such as nonemergency medical services, are prohibited. The purchase of publications and other informational material is not restricted in any way. Licensed travelers may return from Cuba with up to US$100 worth of Cuban products (such as cigars, rum, tee-shirts, crafts, etc.) for their personal use. For cigars, the US Customs Service permits up to 100 cigars, but the total value must not exceed US$100. For example, if a traveler returns with 100 cigars which cost US$1 each, the traveler would not be permitted to bring any other Cuban products (such as rum). Travelers should retain a receipt showing the amount paid for all Republic of Cuba-origin products.

VISAS FOR LICENSED TRAVELERS?

All licensed travelers to Cuba must have a visa from the Cuban government prior to reserving your flight. Tico Travel and Marazul (see above) can assist you in acquiring your visa. (Tico Travel charges US$120 for the visa and preparing the documents.) There are two different forms: one for those born in Cuba and one for those born outside Cuba. Allow thirty days for processing.

* See the Immigration and Customs section in the Information chapter for information on tourist visas.

Cubans and Cuban-Americans: Anyone who permanently left Cuba after December 31, 1970 must have a valid Cuban passport (people born in Cuba who left Cuba permanently before that date don't need a Cuban passport). If you don't have a Cuban passport and you left Cuba after December 31, 1970 you must contact the Cuban Interests Section in Washington D.C., tel. 202-797-8609, 797-8610. to get the required paperwork. Cubans who left Cuba permanently prior to 1959 can acquire a slightly less expensive 359 Visa, acquired directly with the Cuban Interests Section.

ILLEGAL TRAVEL?

About 103,000 US citizens visited Cuba in 1998. The majority did so legally (most went with organized groups), while the rest slipped in through third countries and spent freely without a license. The US government has recently sought to tighten control of unsanctioned travel. Since May 1998, persons subject to US jurisdiction who travel to Cuba without a license bear a "presumption of guilt" and may be required to show documentation that all expenses incurred were paid by a third party not subject to US law.

IS IT SAFE IN CUBA?

The oftentimes negative statements from our government and the media about Cuba has left many of us with the false impression that Cuba is unsafe. Few places in the world are as safe for visitors as Cuba. Most visitors are far less likely to run into problems in Cuba than they are in their own cities and towns. Cubans are very honest and friendly towards foreign guests and each other.

CAN US CITIZENS USE CREDIT CARDS OR TRAVELERS CHECKS IN CUBA?

Cash is King in Cuba! US citizens can only use US dollars in Cuba as is the policy with all other foreign countries. Only credit cards issued from a foreign bank may be used by US citizens.

Please do not confuse the new "convertible pesos" that you may receive in change with the real Cuban peso. The convertible peso is only for tourist and is in reality just a much more colorful US dollar. And, there is really no need to have any Cuban pesos since they are not accepted in any of the government run tourist establishments.

American Express and Thomas Cook travelers checks can be redeemed at Cuban banks and many of the larger hotels. But, please be advised not to say that you are taking them to Cuba when you are ordering them from your bank or travel agency. Recently the agency for Thomas Cook checks has refused to issue them to US citizens traveling to Cuba.

DO WE NEED A US PASSPORT TO GO TO CUBA?

Yes: Unlike Mexico, a birth certificate will not gain you entry into the Republic of Cuba.

HOW DO YOU GET TO CUBA?

The most popular points of demarcation for US citizens going to Cuba are Cancun, Mexico; Nassau, Bahamas and Toronto, Canada. Beware that in both Nassau and Toronto US Customs pre-clears incoming passengers who are returning to the USA.

Last Frontier Expeditions has been utilizing Cancun, Mexico for entry into Cuba for many reason.

1. It is accessible from the USA via many air charter companies.
2. We maintain an office and staff in Cancun and personally make sure you get your visa, airline tickets and get on the plane. In fact, our representatives personally meet you upon arrival in Cancun, Mexico.
3. Cancun offers flights to Cuba on Aerocaribe Airlines (Mexicana) so we do not have to take the additional risk of violating US law by using the Cuban government airlines (Cubana).
4. With departures from Cancun we are able to offer our clients airport VIP service in Havana. This needs to be requested ($20 fee) in advance. The good part? While the

others are waiting in Customs lines you are in the VIP lounge with a cool drink and/or a cigar!

5. Whether on an organized tour, traveling in small groups or alone, you will always be personally be met in Havana by one of our representatives.

MEDICAL INSURANCE

For a $5.00 USD per day you will be covered for a maximum of $25,000.00 USD in medical benefits at Havana's International Hospital. Arrangements to be made in advance

TRADE WITH CUBA

In October 2000, the U.S. Congress passed legislation, later signed by the President into law on October 28, 2000, which changed the U.S.-Cuba trade relationship by enacting certain exceptions from U.S. sanctions legislation for agricultural and medical exports. The Trade Sanctions Reform and Export Enhancement Act of 2000 was not comprehensive and some prohibitions remain. The ban on U.S. imports from Cuba was not changed by this legislation.

FOOD AND AGRICULTURAL EXPORTS TO CUBA

NEW INITIATIVE ALLOWS LICENSED EXPORTS OF FOOD AND AGRICULTURAL ITEMS FOR SALE TO INDEPENDENT ENTITIES IN CUBA

To implement the President's January 5, 1999 initiative to expand the export of food and agricultural commodities to Cuba, the Department of Commerce, Bureau of Export Administration (BXA), has amended its regulations to allow the sale of food and certain agricultural commodities to non-government entities in Cuba. Applicants may apply to BXA for such exports using the standard Commerce Department Multipurpose Application Form BXA-748P. You may also request copies of Form 748-P by calling the Export Counseling Division at (202) 482-4811 or the Western Regional Office at (949) 660-0144.

The United States will approve on a case-by-case basis exports of food (i.e. both solids and liquids normally consumed by humans or animals) and certain agricultural commodities if destined to independent non-government entities, individuals or organizations in Cuba. Such entities may not be controlled, owned or operated by the Cuban government.

Applicants must demonstrate on the application form in block 24, Additional Information, that the prospective end-user is independent from the Cuban government. Independent non-government entities in Cuba include, but are not limited to, religious groups, private farmers and private sector enterprises such as restaurants.

SUPPLEMENTS

STRATEGIC GOVERNMENT AND BUSINESS CONTACTS

"Jose Martí" International Airport
Rancho Boyeros, Cuba
Telf. : 45-3133, 33-5666,33-5777, 33-5753
Telex : 51-1304
Fax : 33-5169

General Customhouse of the Republic of Cuba
Calle 39 esq. 6, Nuevo Vedado Ciudad de La Habana, Cuba
Telf. : 55-5466 AL 71
Fax : 33-5222

Havana Subcontracting Exchange
Calle 17 No. 55 Apto. 1-B Edif. FOCSA, Vedado, Plaza Ciudad de La Habana, Cuba
Telf. : 30-9556
Telex : 51-1555
Fax : 30-9556

Chamber of Commerce of the Republic of Cuba
Calle 21 No. 661, esq. A, Vedado, Ciudad de La Habana, Cuba
Telf. : 30-3356 al 58
Telex : 51-1754 CAMAR CU
Fax : 33-3042

National Packing and Packaging Center (CNEE)
Ave. Del Bosque No. 121, Nuevo Vedado, Ciudad de La Habana, Cuba
Telf. : 81-0197 / 81-2100 / 81-3422
Fax : 33-3150

National Plant Health Center
Ayuntamiento No.231 e/ San Pedro y Lombillo, Siboney, Ciudad de La Habana, Cuba
Telf. : 79-1339 / 78-4976 al 79
Fax : 70-3277 / 79-6654

Center for Export Promotion of Cuba (CEPEC)
Infanta No. 16 esq. 23, Vedado, Ciudad de La Habana, Cuba
Telf. : 55-0428 / 54-2185 / 54-2194 /55-0405 / 55-0425
Telex : 51-1174 / 1175 y 1176 MCEX CU
Fax : 66-2220 / 55-0376
E-Mail: cepecdir@infocex.cu
cepecsic@infocex.cu
cepecmer@infocex.cu

Cuban Radio and Television Institute
Calle 23 No. 258, Vedado, Ciudad de La Habana, Cuba
Telf. : 32-1568 / 32-4775 / 33-4256
Fax : 33-3107

Cuban Civil Aviation Institute
Calle 23 No. 64 esq. Infanta, Vedado, Ciudad de La Habana, Cuba
Telf. : 33-4412
Fax : 30-4618

Hydraulic Resources National Institute
Virtudes No.680 esq. a Belascoaín, Centro Habana
Telf. : 70-5571

Institute of Veterinary Medicine
Calle 12 No. 355 e/15 y 17, Vedado, Ciudad de La Habana, Cuba
Telf. : 3-7330 / 3-7077 / 30-6615
Fax : 30-3537

National Institute of Sports, Physical Education and Recreation
Ave. Independencia y Vía Blanca, Ciudad de La Habana, Cuba
Telf. : 40-3390 / 81-5176 / 41-1415
Fax : 33-5310

Ministry of Science, Technology and the Environment
Industria y Barcelona, Capitolio Nacional, Ciudad de La Habana, Cuba
Telf. : 62-0420 / 60-3411
Telex : 51-1290
Fax : 33-8654

Ministry of Labor and Social Security
23 y P, Vedado, Ciudad de La Habana, Cuba
Telf. : 70-4571 / 70-9311

Ministry of Culture
Calle 2 No. 258 e/ 11 y 13, Vedado, Ciudad de La Habana, Cuba
Telf. : 55-2236 / 55-2239-40 / 55-2256
Fax : 33-3013 / 66-2284

Ministry of Economy and Planning
20 de Mayo y Ayestarán, Plaza, Ciudad de La Habana, Cuba
Telf. : 51-5371 / 81-3798
Telex : 51-1421 / 51-1806

Ministry of Education
Obispo No. 160, Habana Vieja, Ciudad de La Habana, Cuba
Telf. : 61-4534 / 62-8011
Fax : 62-2547

Ministry of Finances and Prices
Calle Obispo No.211 esq. a Cuba, Habana Vieja, Ciudad de La Habana
Telf. : 57-3000
Fax : 33-8050

Ministry of Construction
Ave. Carlos Manuel de Céspedes y Calle 35, Plaza, Ciudad de La Habana, Cuba
Telf. : 82-0244 / 81-6978

Telex : 51-1275
Fax : 81-5376

Ministry of the Construction Materials Industry
Calle 17 esq. O, Plaza, Ciudad de La Habana, Cuba
Telf. : 32-2541 al 49 / 32-9494
Telex : 51-1517 / 51-1329 / 51-1205
Fax : 33-3004

Ministry of Agriculture
Ave. Independencia e/Conill y Santa Ana, Ciudad de La Habana
Telf. : 81-2875 / 84-5770
Telex : 51-1966 / 51-1968
Fax : 33-5086

Ministry of the Food Industry
Calle 41 No. 4455 esq. 50, Playa, Ciudad de La Habana
Telf. : 23-6801 al 09 / 23-4671
Telex : 51-1123
Fax : 29-6089 / 24-0517

Ministry of the Sugar Industry
Calle 23 No. 171 e/ N y O, Vedado, Ciudad de La Habana, Cuba
Telf. : 55-3194
Telex : 51-1292
Fax : 33-3193

Ministry of the Basic Industry
Salvador Allende No. 666 e/ Oquendo y Soledad, Ciudad de La Habana, Cuba
Telf. : 57-5031 al 37
Telex : 51-1325
Fax : 33-5345

Ministry of Foreign Trade
Infanta No. 16 esq. 23, Vedado, Ciudad de La Habana, Cuba
Telf. : 54-3237 / 54-2265
Telex : 51-1174, 1175 MCEX CU
Fax : 550356

Ministry of Domestic Trade
Obispo No.302, Habana Vieja, Ciudad de La Habana, Cuba
Tlf. : 60-3311

Ministry of Communications
Ave. Independencia y 19 de Mayo, Plaza, Ciudad de La Habana, Cuba
Telf. : 82-0088
Telex : 51-1713, 51-1915
Fax : 33-5253

Ministry of the Light Industry
Empedrado No. 302 esq. Aguiar, Ciudad de La Habana, Cuba

Telf. : 57-0387
Fax : 62-5575

Ministry of Justice
Calle O No. 216 e/23 y Humboldt, Vedado, Ciudad de La Habana, Cuba
Telf. : 55-3451 al 59
Fax : 33-3038

Ministry of Foreign Affairs
Calzada No. 360 esq. G, Vedado, Ciudad de La Habana, Cuba
Telf. : 31-2206 / 30-5031 / 55-3260
Telex : 51-1122
Fax : 33-3460 / 32-5178

Ministry of Public Health
Calle 23 No. 201 esq. N, Vedado, Ciudad de La Habana, Cuba
Telf. : 55-3332 al 41 / 55-3345 al 48
Telex : 51-1149
Fax : 66-2537

Ministry of Tourism
Calle 19 e/ A y Paseo, Vedado, Ciudad de La Habana, Cuba
Telf. : 33-4319 / 33-4323
Fax : 33-4325

Ministry for Foreign Investment and Economic Cooperation
Calle Primera 18 y 20, Miramar, Ciudad de la Habana, Cuba
Telf. : 29-2828 / 22-5196
Telex : 51-1445 / 51-1341
Fax : 24-6951 / 24-3183

Ministry of the Fishing Industry
5ta. Ave. y Calle 248, Barlovento, Santa Fé, Ciudad de La Habana, Cuba
Telf. : 24-1189 / 29-7930 / 29-7942
Telex : 51-1206
Fax : 24-9167/68

Ministry of Transportation
Ave. Independencia y Tulipán, Plaza, Ciudad de La Habana, Cuba
Telf. : 81-1782 / 55-5031 al 39
Telex : 51-1181
Fax : 33-5118

Ministry of the Iron, Steel, Mechanical and Electronic Industry
Ave. Rancho Boyeros y Calle 100, Altahabana, Ciudad de La Habana
Telf. : 45-3911 / 45-3978
Telex : 51-1179 / 51-1473
Fax : 27-1163

Ministry of Justice (Special Notary's Office)
Calle O entre 23 y 25, Vedado, Ciudad de La Habana, Cuba

Telf. : 55-3451 al 59
Fax : 33-3038

Cuban Office of Industrial Property
Picota No.15 e/ Luz y Acosta, Habana Vieja, Ciudad de La Habana, Cuba
Telf. : 61-0185 / 61-3602
Fax : 33-5610

National Standardization Office
Calle 13 esq. E, Vedado, Ciudad de La Habana, Cuba
Telf. : 30-0022

National Office of Free Zones
Calle 22 No.318 e/ 3ra y 5ta, Mirarnar, Ciudad de La Habana, Cuba
Telf. : 29-0686 / 24-7636 / 29-0685 al 89
Fax : 24-7637

Food Nutrition and Health National Institute
Calzada de Infanta No.1158 e/ Llinaz y Clavel, Centro Habana, Ciudad de La Habana Cuba
Telf. : 70-3104 / 78-5919 / 78-1429

City Havana Free Zone
Carretera de Berroa Km 1, Habana del Este, Ciudad de La Habana, Cuba
Telf. : 33-8137 al 39 / 33-8923
Fax : 33-8140 / 66-9898
E-Mail: victor p.@cimex.com.cu

Mariel Free Zone
Carretera de Quiebra Hacha Km 8 ½, Vista del Mar.
Península de Angosta, Mariel, Ciudad de La Habana
Telf. : 33-5924
Fax : 33-5925

Wajay Free Zone
Carretera Aerocaribbean, Km 1 ½, Wajay, Ciudad de La Habana, Cuba
Telf. : 33-5884
Fax : 33-5885

MINCEX Territorial Delegation
Santiago de Cuba-Granma-Guantánamo
Santo Tomás No.565, 3er piso e/ Aguilera y Enramada, Santiago de Cuba
Telf. : (0-226)2-9144 / 2-6725
Fax : (0-226)8-6290

MINCEX Territorial Delegation
Holguín-Las Tunas
Calle 10 de Octubre No.3 e/ Luz y Mario Pozo, Rpto.Luz, Holguín
Telf. : (0-244) 6-2379 / 6-2865
Fax : (0-244) 6-2379

MINCEX Territorial Delegation
Camaguey-Ciego de Avila

Calle 6ta. E/ 1ra y B, Rpto. Julio A. Mella, Camaguey
Fax : 7-1725

MINCEX Territorial Delegation
Cienfuegos
Ave.37 (Prado)No.4406 e/ 44 y 46, Cienfuegos
Telf. : (0-432) 3321 y 8591
Fax : (0-432) 8951

National Code(537)

TRADE SHOWS AND EXIBITIONS

Cuba hosts several specialized trade fairs and general trade fairs:

February:
International Agriculture and Cattle Fair (PABEXPO)
International Book Fair (Biennial, PABEXPO)
International Fair on Informatics, Industrial Automation and Communications (Biennial, PABEXPO)
International Fair on Sport, Recreation and leisure time(PABEXPO)

March:
International Fair on Food, Packaging, Graphics Arts (ALIMEXPO)(PABEXPO)
International Handicraft Fair (FIART) (PABEXPO)

April:
Health for All (Biennial) (PABEXPO)
International Fair on Construction. (FECONS)(PABEXPO)

May:
International Fair of the Music, Images and the Sound (CUBADISCO) (PABEXPO)
International Fair of the Furniture, Decoration and Lighthing (PABEXPO)
International Salon of Technology and Goods for the Tourist
Industry (TECNOTUR)(PABEXPO)
Turist Convention (PABEXPO)

June:
Caribbean International Fair (EXPOCARIBE)(HEREDIA CONVENTION CENTER)
Cubagua (PABEXPO)
July:
International Fashion Salon (MODA)(PABEXPO)
International Metallurgical, Electronical and Industrial Subcontracting Fair (METANICA) (PABEXPO)

September:

International Fair on Sugar Agroindustry (EXPOAZUCAR)(PABEXPO)
International Fair of Transport (FIT)(PABEXPO)

November:

Havana International Fair (FIHAV)(EXPOCUBA). The principal fair of Cuba

CUBA ECONOMIC SITUATION

SOCIO-ECONOMIC CONDITIONS IN PRE-CASTRO AND PRESENT DAY CUBA

An enduring myth is that 1950's Cuba was a socially and economically backward country whose development was jump-started by the Castro government. In fact, according to readily-available historical data, Cuba was a relatively advanced country in 1958, certainly by Latin American standards and, in some areas, by world standards. The data appear to show that Cuba has at best maintained what were already high levels of development in health and education, but at an extraordinary cost to the overall welfare of the Cuban people. These include access to "basics" such as adequate levels of food and electricity, but also access to consumer goods, the availability of which have increased significantly in other Latin American countries in recent decades.

It is true that Cuba's infant mortality rate is the best in Latin America today, but it also was the best in Latin America -- and the 13th lowest in the world -- in pre-Castro Cuba. Cuba also has improved the literacy of its people, but Cuba had an excellent educational system and impressive literacy rates in the 1950's.

On the other hand, many economic and social indicators have declined since the 1959 revolution. Pre-Castro Cuba ranked third in Latin America in per capita food consumption; today, it ranks last. Per capita consumption of cereals, tubers, and meat are today all below 1950's levels. The number of automobiles in Cuba has fallen since the 1950's -- the only country in Latin America for which this is the case. The number of telephone lines in Cuba also has been virtually frozen at 1950's levels. Cuba once ranked first in Latin America and fifth in the world in television sets per capita. Today, it barely ranks fourth in Latin America and is well back in the ranks globally.

Cuba's rate of development of electrical power since the 1950's ranks behind every other country in Latin America except Haiti. Cuba is the only country in the hemisphere for which rice production today is lower than it was four decades ago. By virtually any measure of macroeconomic stability, Cuba was in far better shape in 1958 than it is today. Finally, the Castro government shut down what was a remarkably vibrant media sector in the 1950's, when the relatively small country had 58 daily newspapers of differing political hues and ranked eighth in the world in number of radio stations.

METHODOLOGY

This paper assesses Cuba's level of development in a variety of economic and social indicators during the revolutionary period (1959-present), especially relative to that of other countries during the same period. It relies most extensively on UN data, particularly from the statistical yearbook and demographic yearbook, which are considered among the most prestigious data compendiums in the development field. Trade data is derived from the IMF's Direction of Trade Statistics, which provides a consistent data series dating back to the 1950's. For the various international comparisons and rankings listed below, only those countries acquiring independence prior to 1958 and having relatively consistent data available for the period 1955-present have been included. (The former stipulation excludes many highly-developed Caribbean countries from consideration.)

HEALTH

The health care system is often touted by many analysts as one of the Castro government's greatest achievements. What this analysis ignores is that the revolutionary government inherited an already-advanced health sector when it took power in 1959.

Cuba's infant mortality rate of 32 per 1,000 live births in 1957 was the lowest in Latin America and the 13th lowest in the world, according to UN data. Cuba ranked ahead of France, Belgium, west Germany, Israel, Japan, Austria, Italy, Spain, and Portugal, all of which would eventually pass Cuba in this indicator during the following decades.

Today, Cuba remains the most advanced country in the region in this measure, but its world ranking has fallen from 13th to 24th during the Castro era, according to UN Data. Also missing from the conventional analysis of Cuba's infant mortality rates is its staggering abortion rate -- 0.71 abortions per live birth in 1991, according to the latest UN data -- which, because of selective termination of "high-risk" pregnancies, yields lower numbers for infant mortality. Cuba's abortion rate is at least twice the rate for the other countries in the table below for which data are available.

In terms of physicians and dentists per capita, Cuba in 1957 ranked third in Latin America, behind only Uruguay and Argentina -- both of which were more advanced than the United States in this measure. Cuba's 128 physicians and dentists per 100,000 people in 1957 was the same as the Netherlands, and ahead of the United Kingdom (122 per 100,000 people) and Finland (96).

Unfortunately, the UN statistical yearbook no longer publishes these statistics, so more recent comparisons are not possible, but it is completely erroneous to characterize pre-Revolutionary Cuba as backward in terms of healthcare.

WORLD: INFANT MORTALITY		
(DEATHS PER 1,000 LIVE BIRTHS)		
	1957	1990-95
JAPAN	40	4
ICELAND	16	5
SWEDEN	18	5
FINLAND	28	5
SWITZERLAND	23	6
BELGIUM	36	6
GERMANY (A)	36	6
NETHERLANDS	18	7
AUSTRALIA	21	7

DENMARK	23	7
UNITED KINGDOM	24	7
CANADA	31	7
IRELAND	33	7
FRANCE	34	7
LUXEMBOURG	39	7
AUSTRIA	44	7
SPAIN	53	7
NORWAY	21	8
ITALY	50	8
UNITED STATES	26	9
ISRAEL	39	9
GREECE	44	10
PORTUGAL	88	10
CUBA	32	12
MALAYSIA	76	13
(A) - FOR 1957, INCLUDES ONLY FRG.		
SOURCE: UNITED NATIONS.		

EDUCATION

Cuba has been among the most literate countries in Latin America since well before the Castro revolution, when it ranked fourth. Since then, Cuba has increased its literacy rate from 76 to 96 percent, which today places it second only to Argentina in Latin America. This improvement is impressive, but not unique, among Latin American countries. Panama -- which ranked just behind Cuba in this indicator during the 1950's -- has matched Cuba's improvement when measured in percentage terms.

LATIN AMERICA: LITERACY RATES (A)					
(PERCENT)					
	LATEST				

	AVAILABLE				
	1950-53		1995		
ARGENTINA	87	(B)	96		
CUBA	76		96		
CHILE	81		95		
COSTA RICA	79		95		
PARAGUAY	68		92		
COLOMBIA	62		91		
PANAMA	72		91		
ECUADOR	56		90		
BRAZIL	49		83		
DOMINICAN REPUBLIC	43		82		
EL SALVADOR	42		72		
GUATEMALA	30		56		
HAITI	11		45		
(A) - DATA FOR 1950-53 ARE AGE 10 AND OVER.					
DATA FOR 1995 ARE AGE 15 AND OVER, REFLECTING					
A CHANGE IN COMMON USAGE OVER THIS PERIOD.					
(B) - 1947 DATA, THE LATEST AVAILABLE, ARE					
FOR AGE 14 AND OVER.					
SOURCE: UNITED NATIONS.					

CONSUMPTION

Rationing has been a staple of Cuban life since the early 1960's. During the early 1990's, Cuba's food consumption deteriorated sharply, when massive amounts of Soviet aid were withdrawn. On its own without Soviet largesse and abundant food imports, Cuban agriculture was paralyzed by a scarcity of inputs and poor production incentives resulting from collectivism and the lack of appropriate price signals. In pre-Castro Cuba, by contrast, food supplies were abundant. The 1960 UN Statistical yearbook ranked pre-Revolutionary Cuba third out of 11 Latin American countries in per capita daily caloric consumption.

This was in spite of the fact that the latest available food consumption data for Cuba at the time was from 1948-49, almost a decade before the other Latin American countries' data being used in the comparison. Looking at the same group of 11 countries today, Cuba ranks last in per capita daily caloric consumption, according to the most recent data available from the UN FAO Indeed, the data show Cuba with a poorer food supply situation than even Honduras.

LATIN AMERICA:				
PER CAPITA FOOD CONSUMPTION				
(CALORIES PER DAY)				
	LATEST			
	DATA			
	1954-57		1995	
MEXICO	2420		3135	
ARGENTINA	3100		3110	
BRAZIL	2540		2834	
URUGUAY	2960		2826	
CHILE	2330		2769	
COLOMBIA	2050		2758	
PARAGUAY	2690		2560	
VENEZUELA	1960		2442	
ECUADOR	2130		2436	
HONDURAS	2260		2359	
CUBA	2730	(A)	2291	
(A) - FOR 1948-49.				
SOURCE: UN FAO FOOD BALANCE SHEETS				

A closer look at some basic food groups reveals that Cubans now have less access to cereals, tubers, and meats than they had in the late 1940's. According to 1995 UN FAO data, Cuba's per capita supply of cereals has fallen from 106 kg per year in the late 1940's to 100 kg today, half a century later. Per capita supply of tubers and roots shows an even steeper decline, from 91 kg per year to 56 kg. Meat supplies have fallen from 33 kg per year to 23 kg per year, measured on a per capita basis.

Although some would blame Cuba's food problems on the U.S. embargo, the facts suggest that the food shortages are a function of an inefficient collectivized agricultural system -- and a scarcity of foreign exchange resulting from Castro's unwillingness to liberalize Cuba's economy, diversify its export base, and pay off debts owed to its Japanese, European, and Latin American trading partners during the years of abundant soviet aid. This foreign exchange shortage has severely limited Cuba's ability to purchase readily-available food supplies from Canada, Latin America, and Europe. The U.S. Embargo has added, at most, relatively small increases in transportation costs by forcing Cuba to import food from non - U.S. sources elsewhere in the hemisphere.

The statistics on the consumption of nonfood items tell a similar story. The number of automobiles in Cuba per capita has actually fallen since the 1950's, the only country in the hemisphere for which this is the case. (Unfortunately, the latest available data for Cuba are from 1988.) UN data show that the number of automobiles per capita in Cuba declined slightly between 1958 and 1988, whereas virtually every other country in the region -- with the possible exception of Nicaragua -- experienced very significant increases in this indicator. Within Latin America, Cuba ranked second only to Venezuela in 1958, but by 1988, had dropped to ninth.

The 1988 data on automobiles also reveal that countries in Asia and Europe that once ranked far behind Cuba in this measure have since surpassed Cuba by a wide margin. Japan, with four cars per 1,000 inhabitants in 1958, was far behind Cuba (24) that year, but by 1988, Japan's number had grown to 251, whereas the figure for Cuba remained frozen at its 1958 level. Similar comments could be made for Portugal (increased from 15 in 1958 to 216 in 1988), Spain (increased from six to 278), and Greece (increased from four to 150). Indeed, Italy's 29 cars per capita was not far ahead of Cuba's 24 in 1958, but by 1988, Italy boasted 440 cars per capita, whereas the figure for Cuba was unchanged from the 1950's.

LATIN AMERICA: PASSENGER CARS PER CAPITA (A)					
(CARS PER 1,000 INHABITANTS)					
	1958		1988		Average Annual Growth (PERCENT)
ARGENTINA	19		129		6.6
URUGUAY	22	(F)	114		5.3
VENEZUELA	27		94		4.3
BRAZIL	7		73		8.1

MEXICO	11	(C)	70		6.4
PANAMA	16	(B)	56		4.3
CHILE	7		52		6.9
COSTA RICA	13		47	(C)	4.4
CUBA	24		23		-0.1
DOMINICAN REPUBLIC	3	(B)	23	(G)	7.3
COLOMBIA	6		21	(D)	4.3
PARAGUAY	3	(C)	20		6.5
PERU	7	(E)	18		3.1
ECUADOR	2		15		7.0
BOLIVIA	3	(C)	12		4.7
GUATEMALA	6		11		2.0
EL SALVADOR	7		10		1.2
NICARAGUA	7	(B)	8		0.5
HONDURAS	3		6		2.3
(A) - FOR MOST COUNTRIES, EXCLUDES POLICE AND					
MILITARY CARS.					
(B) - EXCLUDES ALL GOVERNMENT CARS.					
(C) - INCLUDES POLICE CARS.					
(D) - INCLUDES CARS NO LONGER IN USE.					
(E) - 1957.					
(F) - 1956.					
(G) - 1987.					
SOURCE: UNITED NATIONS.					

Telephones are another case in point. While every other country in the region has seen its teledensity increase at least two fold -- and most have seen even greater improvements -- Cuba's has remained frozen at 1958 levels. Today, Cuba has only 3 telephone lines per 100 people, placing it 14th out of 20 Latin American countries surveyed in 1994 and far behind countries that were less advanced than Cuba in this measure in 1958, such as Argentina (today 14 lines per 100 inhabitants), Costa Rica (13), Panama (11), Chile (11), Venezuela (11), and several others.

Cuba also has not kept pace with the rest of Latin America in terms of radios per capita. During the late 1950's, Cuba ranked second only to Uruguay in Latin America, with 169 radios per 1,000 people. (Worldwide, this put Cuba just ahead of Japan.) At that time, Argentina and Cuba were very similar in terms of this measure. Since then, the number of radios per capita in Argentina has grown three times as fast as in Cuba. Cuba also has been surpassed by Bolivia, Venezuela, El Salvador, Honduras, and Brazil in this indicator. Today, Cuba ranks just above average for Latin American countries.

In terms of television sets per capita, 1950's Cuba was far ahead of the rest of Latin America and was among the world's leaders. Cuba had 45 television sets per 1,000 inhabitants in 1957, by far the most in Latin America and fifth in the world, behind only Monaco, the United States, Canada, and the United Kingdom. In fact, its closest competitor in Latin America was Venezuela, which had only 16 television sets per 1,000 people. Today, Cuba has 170 televisions per thousand, behind Uruguay (232 per capita), Argentina (220), and brazil (209). Of these three countries, Uruguay in 1957 had fewer than one television per 1,000 people, and Argentina and Brazil each had five per 1,000 people -- far behind Cuba's 45 per capita.

PRODUCTION

Post 1959 Cuba falls short in areas of industrial production once prioritized by Soviet client states, such as electricity production. Although Cuba has never been a regional leader in public electricity production per capita, its relative ranking among 20 Latin American countries has fallen from eighth to 11th during the Castro era. In fact, in terms of the rate of growth for this measure, Cuba ranks 19th of 20 countries in the region, with only Haiti showing less accelerated development.

Cuba is the only country in Latin America whose production of rice has fallen since 1958, when it ranked fourth in the region in production of this staple. Two of the countries ranking ahead of Cuba in rice production in 1958 -- Colombia and Peru -- have since seen their rice production grow by more than three fold. Cuba's Caribbean neighbor, the Dominican republic, has increased its rice production by four fold since 1958. Perhaps even more telling are Cuba's yields per hectare in rice production. Whereas the Dominican Republic has increased rice yields from 2100 kg per hectare in 1958 to 5400 kg per hectare in 1996, Cuba's yields today are only 2500 kg per hectare, a negligible increase from the 2400 kg per hectare registered in 1958, according to UN FAO data.

LATIN AMERICA: RICE PRODUCTION				
(1,000 MT)				
				Average
				Annual
				Growth
	1958		1996	(PERCENT)
BRAZIL	3829		10035	2.6
COLOMBIA	378		1787	4.2

ECUADOR	176		1346	5.5
PERU	285		1203	3.9
ARGENTINA	217		974	4.0
URUGUAY	58		868	7.4
VENEZUELA	22		733	9.7
DOMINICAN REPUBLIC	99		555	4.6
MEXICO	240		455	1.7
BOLIVIA	11		296	9.1
PANAMA	86		230	2.6
CUBA	261		223	-0.4
NICARAGUA	33		219	5.1
COSTA RICA	34		186	4.6
CHILE	102		154	1.1
PARAGUAY	20		119	4.8
HAITI	42	(A)	96	2.3
EL SALVADOR	27		51	1.7
HONDURAS	21		41	1.8
GUATEMALA	11		33	2.9
(A) - 1959.				
SOURCE: FAO YEARBOOK (UN)				

FOREING TRADE AND BALANCE OF PAYMENTS

Cuba's exports have not kept pace with other countries of the region. Of the 20 countries in the region for which comparable IMF data are available, Cuba ranks last in terms of export growth -- below even Haiti. Mexico and Cuba had virtually identical export levels in 1958 -- while Mexico's population was five times Cuba's. Since then, Cuba's exports have merely doubled while Mexico's have increased by almost 130-fold, according to IMF statistics. Cuba's exports in 1958 far exceeded those of Chile and Colombia, countries which have since left Cuba behind. The lack of diversification of Cuba's exports over the past 35 years also is remarkable, when compared with other countries in the region.

Cuba's enviable productive base during the 1950's was strengthened by sizable inflows of foreign direct investment. As of 1958, the value of U.S. foreign direct investment in Cuba was $861 million, according to United States government figures published in 1959. Adjusting for inflation that foreign investment number amounts to more than USD 4.3 billion in today's dollars.

Contrary to popular perception, U.S. investors were not focusing on the sugar industry in the 1950's. U.S. firms began to gradually sell their Cuban sugar holdings to Cuban firms beginning in 1935. By 1958, U.S. firms owned fewer than 40 of Cuba's 161 mills. While U.S. firms were moving away from sugar, they were rapidly investing in a range of other ventures, especially in infrastructure development. According to U.S. government statistics, 41 percent of U.S. direct investments in Cuba were in utilities as of 1958.

LATIN AMERICA: TOTAL EXPORTS			
(MILLION USD)			
			Average
			Annual
			Growth
	1958	1996	(PERCENT)
MEXICO	736	95991	14
PANAMA	23	2722	13
ECUADOR	95	5243	11
COSTA RICA	92	3826	10
CHILE	389	15396	10
BRAZIL	1243	47747	10
PARAGUAY	34	1282	10
HONDURAS	70	2469	10
ARGENTINA	994	23794	9
COLOMBIA	461	10437	9
GUATEMALA	103	2330	9
PERU	291	5854	8
BOLIVIA	65	1216	8
URUGUAY	139	2397	8
VENEZUELA	2319	23149	6
EL SALVADOR	116	1020	6
NICARAGUA	71	621	6

DOMINICAN REPUBLIC	136	886	5
HAITI	48	181	4
CUBA	732	1831	2
SOURCE: IMF DIRECTION OF TRADE STATISTICS.			

As the numbers above imply, Cuba had a very favorable overall balance of payments situation during the 1950's, contrasted with the tenuous situation today. In 1958, Cuba had gold and foreign exchange reserves -- a key measure of a healthy balance of payments--totaling $387 million in 1958 dollars, according to IMF statistics. (That level of reserves would be worth more than 1.9 billion USD in today's dollars.) Cuba's reserves were third in Latin America, behind only Venezuela and Brazil, which was impressive for a small economy with a population of fewer than 7 million people. Unfortunately, Cuba no longer publishes information on its foreign exchange and gold reserves.

MASS MEDIA

It is no exaggeration to state that during the 1950's, the Cuban people were among the most informed in the world, living in an uncharacteristically large media market for such a small country. Cubans had a choice of 58 daily newspapers during the late 1950's, according to the UN statistical yearbook. Despite its small size, this placed Cuba behind only Brazil, Argentina, and Mexico in the region. By 1992, government controls had reduced the number of dailies to only 17.

There has also been a reduction in the number of radio and television broadcasting stations, although the UN no longer reports these statistics. However, it should be noted that in 1957, Cuba had more television stations (23) than any other country in Latin America, easily outdistancing larger countries such as Mexico (12 television stations) and Venezuela (10). It also led Latin America and ranked eighth in the world in number of radio stations (160), ahead of such countries as Austria (83 radio stations), United Kingdom (62), and France (50), according to the UN statistical yearbook.

STRATEGIC STATISTICS

GENERAL INDICATORS

General Indicators	
Area (km^{2}):	110 860
Cuba	104 945
Isle of Youth	2 200
Adjacent Keys	3 715
Highest Elevation:	
Pico Real	1 974

Longest River:	
Cauto(Km)	370
Social and Demographic Indicators for 2000:	
Resident population on December 31 (thousands)	11 217,1
Working age resident population (thousands)	6 645,0
Life expectancy at birth (94-95) (years)	74,8
Infant Mortality Rate (per 1000 live births)	7,2
Doctors per inhabitants	
Access to fresh water (%)	93,8
Illiteracy (10 years of age or over) (Housing and Population Census, 1981)	3,8
Employed (thousands)	...
Average monthly salary - state entities (pesos)	...
Figures for 1998 are preliminary	

TOURISM

TOURISM		MU	1998	1999	2000
Visitors by region		M	1 416	1 603	1 774
	Africa		6	6	7
	Americas		594	597	783
	Europe		793	874	949
	East Asia/Pacific		16	20	27
	Middle East		2	2	3
	South Asia		5	4	5
Turists		M	1 390	1 561	1 741
Excursionists		M	26	42	33
Income per tourists		MMUSD	1 759,3	1 901,0	1 939,9
Tourist-days		MM	10,1	11,0	11,8
Camping					
	No. of camping bases	U	82	82	82
	Capacity-beds	MU	20,8	20,6	20,6
	Users	M	797,8	851,4	849,9

INDUSTRIAL PRODUCTIONS

INDUSTRIAL PRODUCTIONS	MU	1998	1999	2000
Electrical power generation	Gw.h	14 145,1	14 487,5	15 028,8
Oil extraction a/	Mt	1 678,2	2 136,3	2 695,3
Natural Gas	MMm^3	124,2	460,0	574,5
Ordinary steel	Mt	278,0	302,7	327,3
Nickel + Cobalt (metal content)	tc	67,7	66,5	71,4
Automobile Batteries	MU	197,8	209,4	133,2
New tires	MU	164,7	156,6	160,5
Oxygen	M	21,0	19,3	30,5
Detergent for household use	Mt	12,2	12,9	13,1
Whole fertilizers	Mt	156,7	138,3	118,2
Gray cement	Mt	1 713,4	1784,6	1632,7
Crushed rock	Mm3	2 860,0	2 950,3	3 301,3

Corrugated asbestos-cement tiles	Mm2	2 830,0	3 099,2	2 679,8
Concrete blocks	MMU	42,8	42,3	41,4
Cotton threads	Mt	4,5	3,2	2,2
Whole fabrics	MMm2	54,0	51,0	47,5
Gas stoves	MU	72,7	138,8	153,8
Physical raw sugar a/	MMt	3,1	3,7	3,9
Rice consumption	Mt	90,3	107,8	66,1
National wheat flour	Mt	291,1	299,9	285,9
Fluid milk	Mt	272,0	285,9	295,6

ECONOMIC INDICATORS

Economic Indicators	MU	1998	1999	2000
Gross Domestic Product	MMP			
At current prices		23 900,8	25 503,6	27 634,7
At constant prices		14 754,1	15 674,4	16 556,4
External Sector	MMP			
Current account		-392,4	-456,1	...
Export of goods and services		1 540,2	1 465,5	...
Import of goods and services		4 229,0	4 343,5	...
External debt (in freely convertible currency)		11 208,9	11 078,0	...
Tourism				
Tourism income accrued	MM USD	1 759,3	1 901,1	1 939,9
Visitors	M	1 416	1 603	1 774
State Budget	MMP			
Income		12 502,0	13 419,2	14 505,0
Expenditures		13 061,7	14 030,9	15 243,0
Deficit		-559,7	-611,7	-738,0
Monetary Circulation	MMP			
Liquidity accrued		9 710,0	9 902,2	10 489,8
Cash in circulation		4 282,7	4 568,0	5 054,8
Ordinary savings		5 427,3	5 334,2	5 435,0

CONSTRUCTION

CONSTRUCTION	MU	1998	1999	2000
Selected Finished Works	U			
Culture, sports and recreation		...	35	70
Industrial			44	37
Hospitals		11	8	10
medical clinics		...	28	7
Hotels, motels and tourist villages		20	10	15
Dams			1	2
Total No. of housings completed:	U	44 963	41 997	42 940
By the population a/	U	14 201	16 313	16 074
C.S.C	U	...	2 166	2 559
Existing capacity of dams and reservoirs b/	MMm^3	9 061,5	9 035,5	9 003,2
a/ Certified to be occupied				
b/ Includes dams with a capacity over 3 MMm3				

RESIDENT POPULATION

			Thousands
RESIDENT POPULATION (on December 31)	1998	1999	2000
Cuba	11 139,9	11 180,1	11 217,1
Pinar del Rio	731,3	734,9	737,3
Havana	696,2	701,8	707,8
Havana City	2 192,3	2 189,7	2 186,7
Matanzas	654,5	658,1	661,9
Villa Clara	833,4	834,9	836,3
Cienfuegos	392,4	395,1	396,7
Sancti Spiritus	458,8	460,6	462,3
Ciego de Avila	403,9	407,4	410,7
Camaguey	782,2	785,8	789,9
Las Tunas	525,0	527,9	530,3
Holguin	1 024,9	1 029,6	1 032,7
Granma	827,6	830,0	832,6
Santiago de Cuba	1 027,9	1 032,5	1 037,7

Guantanamo	510,8	512,3	514,1
Isle of Youth	78,7	79,5	80,1

FOREIGN INVESTMENT LAW

The Aim of the Law is to Promote and Provide Incentives for Foreign Investment within our National Territory
This Law Confirms the Seriousness with which Cuba is Pursuing its Policy of Opening Up to Foreign Investment

I, RICARDO ALARCON DE QUESADA, President of the Republic of Cuba's National Assembly of the People's Power,

LET IT BE KNOWN: That the Republic of Cuba's National Assembly of the People's Power, in session on September 5th, 1995, during the Fifth Regular Session of the Fourth Legislature, has approved the following:

WHEREAS: In today's world, without the existence of the socialist bloc, with a globalizing world economy and strong hegemonistic tendencies in the economic, political and military fields, Cuba, in order to preserve its accomplishments despite the fierce blockade to which it is subjected; lacking capital, certain kinds of technology and often markets and in need of restructuring its industry, can benefit from foreign investment on the basis of the strictest respect for national independence and sovereignty, given that such investment can usher in the introduction of innovative and advanced technology, the modernization of its industries, greater efficiency in production, the creation of new jobs, improvement in the quality of the products and services it offers, cost reduction, greater competitiveness abroad, and access to certain markets, which as a whole would reinforce the efforts the country must undertake for its economic and social development.

WHEREAS: The Constitution of the Republic, as it was modified in 1992, recognizes among other forms of property, joint ventures, companies and economic associations which are established in conformity with the law and, in regard to state property and in exceptional cases, when such action is deemed useful and necessary for the country, provides for the partial or total transference of ownership of economic objectives with the goal of developing them.

WHEREAS: The changes taking place in the national economy, aimed at actively promoting and boosting the investment of foreign capital in Cuba and broadening the possibilities in terms of the forms and areas of investment, among other essential factors, surpass the legal possibilities offered until now by Decree-Law No. 50, «On Economic Association among Cuban and Foreign Entities,» approved on February 15, 1982.

WHEREAS: In order to broaden and facilitate foreign participation in the nation's economy, it is convenient to adopt new legislation that may provide greater security and guarantees to the foreign investor and allow the country to obtain financial resources, technology and new markets in any productive sector and in the service sector in which mutual interests have been identified, for the fundamental purpose of achieving sustainable development in the country and recovery of the national economy.

THEREFORE: The National Assembly of the People's Power, making use of the authority conferred upon it by Article 75, paragraph b) of the Constitution of the Republic, resolves to issue the following

CHAPTER I PURPOSE AND CONTENT

ARTICLE 1.

1. This Act has the purpose of promoting and encouraging foreign investment in the territory of the Republic of Cuba in order to carry out profitable activities that contribute to the country's economic capacity and sustainable development, on the basis of respect for the country's sovereignty and independence and the protection and rational use of natural resources, and of establishing, for that purpose, the basic legal regulations under which this should be realized.

2. The norms contained in this Act comprise, among other elements, the guarantees granted to investors, the sectors of the economy which can receive foreign investments, the forms that these may adopt, the various types of investments, the procedure for their authorization, the regulations for these investments relating to banking, taxation, and labor, and the norms related to protection of the environment and the rational use of natural resources.

CHAPTER II GLOSSARY

Article 2.
In this Act, the following terms are used with the definitions indicated in each case:

a) International economic association:

Joint action by one or more national investors and one or more foreign investors within the national territory for the production of goods, the offering of services, or both, for profit, in its two forms, which consist of joint ventures and international economic-association contracts.

b) Authorization:

Document issued by the Executive Committee of the Council of Ministers or a Government Commission, for the realization of one of the forms of foreign investment authorized by this Act, for a specified period.

c) Foreign capital:

Capital originating outside the country, as well as the part of profits or dividends belonging to the foreign investor that may be reinvested in accordance with this Act.

d) Top management posts:

Positions corresponding to person responsible for the direction and administration of the joint ventures and of the company with totally foreign capital as well as the representatives of the parties to international economic-association contracts and the management personnel of companies with totally foreign capital.

e) Government Commission:

Commission designated by the Executive Committee of the Council of Ministers with the authority to approve foreign capital investments in its area of competence in correspondence with what is stipulated in this Act.

f) Administrative concession:

Unilateral action on the part of the Government of the Republic, whereby an entity is granted the right to exploit a public service or a natural resource, or to execute a public work under terms and conditions to be determined.

g) International economic-association contract:

Pact or agreement among one or more national investors and one or more foreign investors, for the joint realization of actions appropriate to an international economic association, without the establishment of a legal entity distinct from each of the parties.

h) Company with totally foreign capital:

Commercial entity with foreign capital, without the involvement of any national investor. **i) Joint venture:**

Cuban commercial company which adopts the form of a registered-share corporation, in which one or more national investors and one or more foreign investors participate as stockholders.

j) Employing entity:

Cuban organization with legal status, authorized to establish a contract with a joint venture or a company with totally foreign capital, through which it supplies, at the company's request, the workers of various skills needed by the company, who will be employed by that organization.

k) Assets:

Salaries, income and other remuneration, as well as increases, compensations and other additional payments received by Cuban and foreign workers, with the exception of those stemming from the economic stimulation fund, should this exist.

l) Foreign investment:

Capital input by foreign investors, in any of the forms stipulated by this Act.

m) Foreign investor:

The natural or juridical person, with a foreign domicile and foreign capital, that becomes a shareholder in a joint venture or participates in a company with totally foreign capital, or that is party to an international economic-association contract.

n) National investor:

State company or entity with legal status, a corporation or other Cuban national entity domiciled in the national territory and which becomes a shareholder of a joint venture or is party to an international economic-association contract.

CHAPTER III GUARANTEES FOR INVESTORS

ARTICLE 3.

The foreign investors within Cuban national territory enjoy full protection and security and their assets cannot be expropriated, except for reasons of the public good or in the interest of society, as declared by the Government, in accordance with the Constitution of the Republic, current legislation, and international agreements covering the mutual promotion and protection of investments undertaken in Cuba. In the case of expropriation, indemnification is made in freely convertible currency and is equal to the commercial value established by mutual agreement.

If an agreement is not reached, the price is set by an organization with internationally recognized prestige in the assessment of business assets, authorized by the Ministry of Finance and Prices and contracted for that purpose with the assent of all parties, or of the foreign investor and the Ministry of Foreign Investment and Economic Cooperation, if the affected party is a company with totally foreign capital.

ARTICLE 4.

1. The period of time granted for the development of operations by a joint venture, the parties to an international economic-association contract or a company with totally foreign capital, can be extended by the same authority that authorized the entities, as long as it is requested by the interested parties before the end of the period.

2. If the period is not extended, at the time of its expiration the joint venture, international economic-association contract or company with totally foreign capital shall be liquidated, as stipulated in the constituent documents and existing legislation, and the portion due to the foreign investor shall be paid in freely convertible currency, except in the case of an express agreement to the contrary.

ARTICLE 5.

Foreign investments are equally protected against third party reclamations which comply with the law and are in accordance with Cuban laws and rulings of national courts of justice.

ARTICLE 6.

1. At any moment, subject to the consent of all parties, the foreign investor in an international economic association can sell or transfer its total or partial share of the company to the State or a third party, subject to government authorization, receiving the corresponding price in freely convertible currency, except in the case of an express agreement to the contrary.

2. The foreign investor in a company with totally foreign capital can at any moment sell or transfer, in any form, to the State or a third party and subject to authorization by the Government, its total or partial share of the company, receiving the corresponding price in freely convertible currency, except in the case of an express agreement to the contrary.

ARTICLE 7.

The corresponding price to be paid to the foreign investor, in the cases discussed in Articles 4 and 6 of this Act, is set with the consent of both parties or, when that is not feasible, by an organization with internationally recognized prestige in the assessment of businesses and authorized by the Ministry of Finances and Prices to operate in national territory, and contracted for that purpose jointly by all parties, or by agreement of the foreign investor in a company with totally foreign capital and the Ministry of Foreign Investment and Economic Cooperation.

ARTICLE 8.

The State guarantees the foreign investor the free transference abroad, in freely convertible currency, free from taxes or any fee related to such transference, of:

a) Net profits or dividends obtained as a result of the investment; and

b) The moneys due him or her in the cases discussed in Articles 3, 4 and 6 of this Act.

2. Foreign citizens working in a joint venture, for the parties in any other form of international economic associations or in a company with totally foreign capital, as long as they are not permanent residents in Cuba, have the right to transfer abroad the income they receive, within stipulated amounts and according to the other regulations issued by the National Bank of Cuba.

ARTICLE 9.

Joint ventures and the parties to international economic-association contracts are obliged to pay taxes in line with the special regulations stipulated by this Act, until the expiration of the period for which they were authorized.

The stipulations made in the previous paragraph are not applicable to the rates, contributions (with the exception of social security contributions) and formal duties established in current legislation, nor to the payment obligations included in the Mining Act of December 21, 1994, or other legal provisions which may be issued in regard to natural resources, which shall be observed in the manner and extent stipulated in those laws.

CHAPTER IV SECTORS OPEN TO FOREIGN INVESTMENT

ARTICLE 10.

Foreign investments may be authorized in all sectors, excluding health and education services for the population and the armed forces institutions, with the exception of the latter's commercial system.

CHAPTER V FOREIGN INVESTMENTS

MANIFESTATIONS AND FORMS OF FOREIGN INVESTMENT

ARTICLE 11.

For the purposes of this Act, foreign investments are defined as:

a) Direct investments, through which the foreign investor participates in an effective manner in the management of the joint venture or company with totally foreign capital, and through which the foreign investor makes his or her own contributions in international economic-association contracts; and

b) Investments in stocks or other securities or bonds, either public or private, which do not fit the definition of direct investments.

ARTICLE 12.

Foreign investments shall adopt one of the following forms:

a) Joint venture;

b) International economic-association contract; or

c) Company with totally foreign capital.

JOINT VENTURES

ARTICLE 13.

1. Joint ventures imply the establishment of a legal status distinct from that of any one of the parties. They adopt the form of registered-share corporations and current legislation in this field applies to them.

2. The proportions of capital stock which should be contributed by the foreign investor and the national investor are agreed upon by both partners and defined as part of the authorization.

3. The establishment of a joint venture must take the form of a public document, and annexes to this notarized document include the agreement of economic association, the bylaws governing the company and the authorization.

The agreement of economic association contains the fundamental pacts between the partners for the realization and development of the joint venture's operations, and for the achievement of its objectives, among them the guarantees of Cuban participation in the administration or joint administration of the company and the assurances of a market for the company's products or services; the bases of its accounting system and the estimate and distribution of profits.

The joint venture's bylaws shall include provisions related to the corporation's organization and operation, which must cover the general shareholder's meeting, its characteristics and organization; the necessary quorum and the requirements for exercising the right to vote at the general shareholders' meeting; the structure and characteristics of the management and administrative body; the method by which these bodies make their decisions, both in the general shareholders' meeting and within the management and administrative body, which could range from a simple majority to unanimity; provisions for dissolution and the procedure for liquidating the company; as well as other stipulations resulting from the current legislation in the field, this Act and the agreements between the parties.

4. If the public document does not designate the person or persons who shall administer the joint venture, the first general shareholders' meeting can be held and the members of the management and administrative body can be designated, in line with the bylaws.

5. Once the joint venture is created, the partners cannot be changed except with the consent of the parties and the approval of the authority that granted the authorization.

A change of partners is defined as the substitution of the foreign partner by another person or company, or of the Cuban partner by another person or company.

6. Joint ventures can establish offices, representations, branch offices and affiliates, in national territory and abroad, as well as participating in entities abroad.

7. A joint enterprise acquires legal status when it is included in the Registry maintained by the Republic of Cuba's Chamber of Commerce regarding these activities.

INTERNATIONAL ECONOMIC- ASSOCIATION CONTRACTS

ARTICLE 14.

1. International economic-association contracts have the following characteristics, among others:
a) They do not imply a legal entity separate from those of the contracting parties.

b) They may have the objective of carrying out any activity authorized by the contracting parties.

c) The contracting parties are free to stipulate all the pacts and clauses that they deem to be in accordance with their interests, as long as they do not infringe on the authorized objective, the conditions of the authorization or current legislation.

d) Each contracting party makes separate contributions, which constitute a cumulative amount which they own at all times, and even though they do not constitute capital stock, it is in their interest to establish a common fund, as long as the portion of ownership belonging to each of the parties is well defined.

2. The text of the contract states the proportion of taxes to be paid by each party and the times of the year in which profits are distributed among them, after meeting their fiscal obligations, as well as the responsibility for losses, if there are any.

3. In an international economic-association contract, the party which carries out an act of management which benefits all parties is fully responsible to third parties, but among the parties each one is responsible to the extent or proportion stipulated in the contract.

4. Once an international economic-association contract is granted, the participants cannot be changed, except with the agreement of the parties and the approval of the authority that granted the authorization.

5. An international economic-association contract must be presented in the form of a public document in order to be approved and goes into effect the moment it is included in the Registry maintained by the Republic of Cuba's Chamber of Commerce regarding these activities.

TOTALLY FOREIGN COMPANY

Article 15.

1. In the company with totally foreign capital, the foreign investor manages the company, enjoys all the rights pertinent to it and is responsible for all the obligations described in the authorization.

2. The foreign investor involved in a company with totally foreign capital may act as an individual or a corporation within Cuban national territory:

a) Through the creation of a foreign entity of which the investor is the owner, within the form of a stock corporation and by being included in the Registry of the Republic of Cuba's Chamber of Commerce; or

b) By being included in the Republic of Cuba's Chamber of Commerce and acting independently.

CHAPTER VI REAL ESTATE INVESTMENTS

ARTICLE 16.

1. Under the authorization of this Act, investments can be made in real estate and acquire ownership and other property rights over that real estate.

2. The investments in real estate discussed in the previous paragraph can be utilized for:

a) Housing and other structures destined for private residence or tourism activities of persons who are not permanent residents in Cuba;

b) Housing or offices of foreign companies;

c) Real estate development for use in tourism.

ARTICLE 17.

Investments consisting of the purchase of real estate which constitute corporate activity are considered direct investments.

ARTICLE 18.

The conditions and terms under which the purchase and transfer of real estate discussed in Article 16 of this Act are determined in the authorization and must be in accord with current legislation.

CHAPTER VII CONTRIBUTIONS AND THEIR VALUATION

ARTICLE 19.

1. For the purposes of this Act, contributions are defined as the following:

a) Freely convertible currency;

b) Machinery, equipment or other physical or tangible goods;

c) Intellectual property rights and other rights over intangible goods;

d) Property rights over personal items and real estate, and other rights over these, including usufruct and surface rights; and

e) Other goods and rights.

The contributions which do not consist of freely convertible currency shall be assessed in that currency.

2. Transfer in favor of national investors of property and other rights over state property, for the purposes of contributions by them, shall be carried out under the principles established in the Constitution of the Republic, and under the prior certification of the Ministry of Finance and Prices, in consultation with the corresponding agency and with the approval of the Executive Committee of the Council of Ministers.

The payments of intellectual property rights and other rights over intangible goods shall be covered by current legislation on the matter.

3. Payments in freely convertible currency are set according to their value on the international market and conversion into the national currency, for accounting purposes, shall be realized according to the National Bank of Cuba's exchange rates. The freely convertible currency which constitutes payment of foreign capital should enter the country through the authorized banking entity for use in operations in the national territory.

4. The payments which are not made in freely convertible currency, except those consisting of intellectual property rights and other rights over intangible goods, and which are destined for the capital stock of joint enterprises, or which constitute payments in international economic-association contracts, are valued according to the methods freely agreed upon by the investors. Their value can be determined with the aid of the corresponding expert certifications drawn up by entities under the authority of the Ministry of Finance and Prices.

5. The evaluation of the contributions that are not made in freely convertible currency, except for those in payment for intellectual property rights and other rights over intangible goods, is always made with the aid of expert certifications drawn up by entities under the authority of the Ministry of Finance and Prices.

6. Payments consisting of intellectual property and other rights over intangible goods shall be assessed by methods freely agreed upon by all the national and international investors and between the foreign investor and the Ministry of Foreign Investment and Economic Cooperation, in the case of payments to a totally foreign capital enterprise

CHAPTER VIII NEGOTIATIONS AND AUTHORIZATION OF FOREIGN INVESTMENT

ARTICLE 20.

1. For the creation of an international economic association, the national investor must negotiate with the foreign investor every aspect of the investment, including its economic feasibility, the respective payments, the association's form of management and administration, as well as the legal document needed for its formalization.

2. In the case of a company with totally foreign capital, the Ministry of Foreign Investment and Economic Cooperation indicates to the investor the responsible Cuban entity in the sector, subsector or economic activity for which the investment is planned, and the investor must analyze its proposition with that entity and obtain the corresponding written approval.

ARTICLE 21. 1. Authorization for foreign investments in national territory is granted by the Executive Committee of the Council of Ministers, or by a commission designated for that purpose.

2. The Executive Committee of the Council of Ministers has the exclusive power to authorize foreign investments in any of the sectors listed below or those with the following characteristics:

a) When the total sum of payments made by foreign and national investors is greater than the equivalent of ten (10) million U.S. dollars in freely convertible currency;

b) In the case of totally foreign capital companies;

c) Investments made in public services such as transportation, communications, aqueducts, electricity, or for the construction or exploitation of a public work;

d) When a foreign company with capital shares owned by a foreign state is involved;

e) When the investment involves the exploitation of a natural resource, in accordance with legislation for the protection of the environment and rational use of natural resources;

f) Investments which include the transference of state property or of a real right which is the property of the State; and

g) In the case of the armed forces' commercial system.

3. The Government Commission has the power to authorize foreign investments not mentioned in the previous paragraph.

ARTICLE 22.

The foreign investor who expects to obtain authorization for a company with totally foreign capital shall present its request, jointly with the corresponding Cuban entity, to the Ministry of Foreign Investment and Economic Cooperation.

ARTICLE 23.

1. To set up a joint venture or establish an international economic-association contract, the written request should be presented jointly to the Ministry of Foreign Investment and Economic Cooperation by the foreign investor and the national investor.

2. The investment request is presented along with the following documents.

a) For the establishment of joint ventures and the granting of international economic-association contracts: draft versions of the economic association agreement and the bylaws of the proposed joint venture or the contract to be granted, as well as an economic feasibility study, in both cases.

b) In regard to the foreign investor: documentation attesting to his or her identity and solvency, as well as proof that he or she is a legitimate representative of the corporation, when applicable.

c) In regard to the national investor, in the case of a state enterprise or entity: express written acceptance granted by the maximum authority in the sector, subsector or economic activity in which the foreign investment is being made; in the case of a commercial association or civilian service organization based on totally Cuban capital, express authorization of the general shareholders' meeting, which grants the specific authority to sign the corresponding documents with the foreign investor.

d) When the foreign investor proposes the constitution of a company with totally foreign capital: acceptance by the maximum authority of the sector, subsector or economic activity for which the investment is planned, the text of the bylaws, an economic feasibility study, documentation attesting to the foreign investor's identity and solvency, and in the case of a juridical person, proof that the foreign investor is a legitimate representative authorized to make the specific investment.

e) The documents accompanying the investment request must be duly authenticated, when pertinent.

3. In order for the Ministry of Foreign Investment and Economic Cooperation to accept the request, it must be presented with the formalities described in the present Article.

4. Once the request is accepted by the Ministry of Foreign Investment and Economic Cooperation, it shall be submitted for consultation to all the corresponding agencies and institutions, in order to obtain their report on matters pertinent to them.

5. Once the above procedures are completed, the Ministry of Foreign Investment and Economic Cooperation shall refer the accumulated documentation and its evaluation to the Executive Committee of the Council of Ministers or the Government Commission, as the case may be, so that it may make the pertinent decision.

6. The decision denying or approving the foreign investment is handed down within a period of sixty (60) days from the date on which the request was presented, and it must be notified to the applicants.

ARTICLE 24.

1. The authorization contains the conditions under which it is granted and the objective and time period of the form of investment in question.

2. If the objective of the approved investment is the exploitation of a public service or a natural resource, or the construction and exploitation of a public work, the Executive Committee of the Council of Ministers may grant the corresponding administrative concession, under the terms and conditions established by said Committee.

ARTICLE 25.

The conditions established in the authorization can be clarified through the Ministry of Foreign Investment and Economic Cooperation, at the request of the parties.

CHAPTER IX BANKING SYSTEM

ARTICLE 26.

1. Joint ventures, foreign investors and national investors which are party to international economic-association contracts, jointly or individually, and totally foreign capital companies shall open accounts in freely convertible currency in any bank in the National Banking System, through which they shall receive and make payments related to their operations.

2. Joint ventures and national investors who are parties to international economic-association contracts may open and operate accounts in freely convertible currency in banks located abroad, with the authorization of the National Bank of Cuba.

ARTICLE 27.

Joint ventures, parties to international economic-association contracts and totally foreign capital companies can be authorized on an exceptional basis by the Executive Committee of the Council of Ministers to effect certain charges and payments in nonconvertible national currency.

ARTICLE 28.

Joint ventures, foreign investors and national investors who are parties to international economic-association contracts, and totally foreign capital companies can arrange loans in foreign currency:

a) With a bank in the National Banking System or a financial entity approved by the National Bank of Cuba;

b) With banks or financial entities abroad, in accordance with existing legal regulations covering this matter.

CHAPTER X EXPORT AND IMPORT SYSTEM

ARTICLE 29.

Joint ventures, national and foreign investors who are parties to international economic-association contracts, and totally foreign capital companies have the right, in accordance with established legislation in the field, to export their products directly and to import, also directly, whatever is needed for their purposes.

CHAPTER XI LABOR SYSTEM

ARTICLE 30.

Foreign investment activities must observe the labor and social security legislation in effect in Cuba, with the adjustments included in this Act.

ARTICLE 31.

1. The workers in activities corresponding to foreign investments shall be, as a rule, Cubans or foreigners permanently residing in Cuba.

2. However, the management and administrative bodies of joint ventures or totally foreign capital companies, or the parties to international economic-association contracts, may determine that certain top administrative positions or some posts of a technical nature shall be filled by persons who are not permanent residents in the country and, in those cases, determine the labor conditions to be applied and the rights and obligations of those workers. Nonpermanent residents in the country who are contracted are subject to the country's current legislation covering immigration and foreigners.

ARTICLE 32.

1. Joint ventures, the parties to international economic-association contracts and totally foreign capital companies may be authorized to create an economic stimulus fund for Cubans or permanent residents in Cuba who are working in activities corresponding to foreign investments.

2. The contributions to the economic stimulus fund shall be made out of earned profits. The amount of these contributions shall be agreed upon between the joint ventures, foreign investors and national investors who are party to international economic-association contracts, and totally foreign capital companies, on the one hand, and the Ministry of Foreign Investment and Economic Cooperation, on the other hand.

ARTICLE 33.

1. The workers in joint ventures who are Cuban or permanent residents in Cuba, with the exception of the members of the management or administration, are contracted by an employing entity proposed by the Ministry of Foreign Investment and Economic Cooperation, and authorized by the Ministry of Labor and Social Security.

The members of the management or administration of a joint venture are designated by the general shareholders' meeting and hired directly by the joint venture.

Only in exceptional cases, with the proper authorization, may a joint venture directly employ all the persons who work in that company, and always in accordance with current legal provisions in the field of hiring.

2. The persons working for the parties to international economic-association contracts are contracted by the Cuban party, in accordance with current legal provisions in the field of employment.

3. In totally foreign capital companies, the services of Cuban workers and foreign workers residing permanently in Cuba, with the exception of the members of the management and administrative body, shall be hired through a contract between the company and an employing entity proposed by the Ministry of Foreign Investment and Economic Cooperation, and authorized by the Ministry of Labor and Social Security.

The members of the management and administration of the company with totally foreign capital are designated by the company and directly hired by it.

4. Payments to Cuban workers and foreign workers residing permanently in Cuba are made in national currency which must be obtained beforehand from convertible foreign currency, except in the case described in Article 27 of this Act.

ARTICLE 34. 1. The employing entity discussed in the previous Article individually contracts and directly hires Cuban workers and permanent residents. This employing entity pays those workers their wages.

2. When a joint venture or company with totally foreign capital considers that a specific worker does not meet the requirements of the job, it can request that the employing entity replace that worker with another. Any labor dispute is settled with the employing entity, which pays the worker, at its own expense, the indemnification to which he or she is entitled, determined by the competent authorities. In pertinent cases, the joint venture or company with totally foreign capital compensates the employing entity for such payments, in accordance with the procedure established, and always in compliance with existing legislation.

ARTICLE 35.

Notwithstanding what is stipulated in the preceding articles of this Chapter, the authorization approving the foreign investment can in exceptional cases establish special labor regulations.

ARTICLE 36.

The technological advances consisting of innovations and other tangible goods which are covered by intellectual property law and which are developed within the framework of an international economic association or by Cuban workers in a foreign capital company are covered under current legislation in the field.

ARTICLE 37.

The Ministry of Labor and Social Security is empowered to issue as many complementary legal provisions as it considers necessary for the best application of what is described in this Chapter, especially in the fields of hiring and labor discipline.

CHAPTER XII SPECIAL TAXATION AND DUTIES SYSTEM

ARTICLE 38.

Joint ventures, foreign investors and national investors who are parties to an international economic-association contract are subject to the following fiscal obligations:

a) Income tax;

b) Tax covering the utilization of the labor force and contributions to social security;

c) Customs duties and other payments;

d) Land transportation tax, covering the ownership or possession of land motor vehicles; and

e) Documents tax, which covers rates and payments when applying for, obtaining or renewing certain documents.

ARTICLE 39.

For the purpose of this Act, the payment of taxes by the persons and companies mentioned in the previous Article carries the following characteristics:

a) Income taxes are levied at a rate of thirty percent (30%) of net taxable income. In cases considered in the nation's interest, the Executive Committee of the Council of Ministers can exempt all or part of the tax on net income that is reinvested in the country.

b) When the exploitation of renewable or nonrenewable natural resources is involved, the income tax rate can be raised by decision of the Executive Committee of the Council of Ministers. In that case, the taxation rate can be raised as high as fifty percent (50%).

c) In regard to the tax on utilization of the labor force and social security contributions, the following is established:

1. For utilization of the labor force, a discount is granted in the current taxation rate, to a rate of eleven percent (11%).

2. Social security contributions are covered by a taxation rate of fourteen percent (14%).

3. The taxation rates expressed in the two previous clauses are applied on the total wages and other income from any source received by the workers, except what is turned over to them as economic stimulus.

d) Foreign investors who are partners in joint ventures or parties to international economic association contacts are exempted from paying taxes on personal income obtained from the businesses' profits.

ARTICLE 40.

The company with totally foreign capital is obliged throughout the duration of its operations to pay taxes in accordance with the current tax legislation.

Article 41.
For the purposes of this Act, persons and companies discussed in the present Chapter may be granted special customs dispensations, in accordance with existing legislation.

ARTICLE 42.

The payment of customs tariffs, duties and other fees shall be realized in freely convertible currency, even in those cases in which the amount is expressed in national currency, discounting the exceptional cases which may be established by the Executive Committee of the Council of Ministers.

ARTICLE 43.

The Ministry of Finance and Prices, after consulting with the Ministry of Foreign Investment and Economic Cooperation and taking into account the benefits and size of the investment, the recovery of capital and the indications made by the Executive Committee of the Council of Ministers for priority sectors of the economy and the benefits that could be accrued by the national economy, may grant total or partial exemptions, on a temporary basis, or grant the benefits within its jurisdiction, in relation to the special taxation system.

ARTICLE 44.

Joint ventures, the parties to international economic-association contracts and totally foreign capital companies are subject to the «Norms for Assessing the Most Significant Assets and Liabilities» issued by the Ministry of Finance and Prices. Such persons can freely determine the accounting system which most suits them, as long as the adopted system conforms to universally accepted accounting principles and meets fiscal demands.

CHAPTER XIII RESERVES AND INSURANCE

ARTICLE 45.

1. Joint ventures, foreign and national investors party to international economic-association contracts and totally foreign capital companies are obliged to establish reserves, charged to profits, to cover contingencies that may arise in their operations.

2. The procedure for establishing, utilizing and liquidating the reserves foreseen in the previous clause is regulated by the Ministry of Finance and Prices.

ARTICLE 46.

Without detriment to the reserves discussed in the previous Article, joint ventures, foreign and national investors party to international economic-association contracts, and totally foreign capital companies may establish other reserves on a voluntary basis, in accordance with the regulations of the Ministry of Finance and Prices.

ARTICLE 47.

1. Joint ventures, foreign and national investors who are parties to international economic-association contracts, and totally foreign capital companies should contract for insurance policies, with companies authorized by the Ministry of Finance and Prices to operate in the country, for the protection of goods, properties, operations and any other activities or against any risks as necessary, on the basis of premiums and other contractual conditions which are competitive internationally.

2. Industrial, tourism or other installations or lands leased by state enterprises or other national organizations are insured by the leasee in favor of the leasor, in accordance with the conditions foreseen in the previous clause.

CHAPTER XIV REGISTRY AND FINANCIAL INFORMATION

ARTICLE 48.

Joint ventures, national and foreign investors party to international economic-association contracts, and totally foreign capital companies before commencing their operations, shall be inscribed in the Registry maintained on these activities by the Republic of Cuba's Chamber of Commerce, within a period of thirty (30) days following the date of authorization.

ARTICLE 49.

1. Persons and companies mentioned in the present Chapter shall present to the Ministry of Foreign Investment and Economic Cooperation, within a period of ninety (90) days following the end of their fiscal year, an annual report of their operations in that period.

2. The presentation of an annual report by the persons and companies covered by the present Chapter is independent from their obligations to provide information to the Ministry of Finance and Prices, the corresponding tax administration and any others that may be established for statistical purposes.

CHAPTER XV DUTY-FREE ZONES AND INDUSTRIAL PARKS

ARTICLE 50.

With the goal of stimulating exports and international trade, the Executive Committee of the Council of Ministers may authorize the establishment of duty-free zones and industrial parks, in delimited areas of national territory.

ARTICLE 51.

1. Duty-free zones are defined as areas in which, by decision of the Executive Committee of the Council of Ministers, a special system can be established covering customs duties, exchange rates, taxation, labor, migration, public order, capital investment and foreign trade, and in which foreign investors can participate for the purposes of financial operations, importing, exporting, storage, productive activities or reexporting.

2. Industrial parks are defined as areas in which, by decision of the Executive Committee of the Council of Ministers, a special system can be established covering customs duties, taxation, labor, capital investment and foreign trade, for the development of productive activities with the participation of foreign capital.

ARTICLE 52.

The authorizations of foreign investments, if pertinent, may consign particular facilities and incentives offered to foreign investors in the duty-free zones and industrial parks.

ARTICLE 53.

The establishment and norms related to the operation of duty-free zones and industrial parks shall be regulated by special legislation issued for that purpose.

CHAPTER XVI ENVIRONMENTAL PROTECTION

ARTICLE 54.

Foreign investment is conceived and stimulated in the context of the country's sustainable development, which implies that during the course of the investment, environmental conservation and the rational use of natural resources shall be carefully undertaken.

ARTICLE 55.

The Ministry of Foreign Investment and Economic Cooperation, in pertinent cases, submits the investment proposals it receives for the consideration of the Ministry of Science, Technology and the Environment, so that the latter may evaluate the investment's suitability from the environmental point of view and determine whether an environmental impact evaluation is required, as well as the suitability of granting the pertinent environmental licenses and establishing a control and inspection program in accordance with current legislation.

ARTICLE 56.

1. The Ministry of Science, Technology and the Environment institutes the measures which may be required to properly control situations that could lead to damage, dangers or risks for the environment and the rational use of natural resources.

2. The person or company responsible for the damage or harm is obliged to reestablish the previous environmental situation, repair the material damage and indemnify the injured parties.

CHAPTER XVII RESOLUTION OF CONFLICTS

ARTICLE 57.

1. The conflicts which may arise in relations between partners of a joint venture, or between foreign investors and national investors party to an international economic-association contract, or between partners in a company with totally foreign capital in the form of a nominal share corporation shall be resolved in accordance with the founding documents.

2. The same rule applies when the conflict arises between one or more of the foreign partners and the joint venture or company with totally foreign capital to which the partner or partners belong.

ARTICLE 58.

Litigation over the execution of economic contracts between joint ventures, foreign investors and national investors party to international economic-association contracts or totally foreign capital companies, on the one hand, and state enterprises or other national entities are the jurisdiction of the economic division of the People's Courts established by the Governing Council of the People's Supreme Court.

BASIC TITLES ON CU

BA

IMPORTANT!
All publications are updated annually!
Please contact IBP, Inc. at ibpusa3@gmail.com for the latest ISBNs and additional information

TITLE
Cuba A "Spy" Guide - Strategic Information and Developments
Cuba A Spy" Guide"
Cuba Air Force Handbook
Cuba Air Force Handbook
Cuba Army Defense Policy and National Security Handbook
Cuba Army Defense Policy and National Security Handbook
Cuba Army Weapon Systems Handbook
Cuba Army Weapon Systems Handbook
Cuba Army Weapon Systems Handbook
Cuba Banking & Financial Market Handbook
Cuba Banking & Financial Market Handbook
Cuba Business and Investment Opportunities Yearbook
Cuba Business and Investment Opportunities Yearbook
Cuba Business and Investment Opportunities Yearbook Volume 1 Strategic Information and Opportunities
Cuba Business Intelligence Report - Practical Information, Opportunities, Contacts
Cuba Business Intelligence Report - Practical Information, Opportunities, Contacts
Cuba Business Law Handbook - Strategic Information and Basic Laws
Cuba Business Law Handbook - Strategic Information and Basic Laws
Cuba Business Law Handbook - Strategic Information and Basic Laws
Cuba Business Law Handbook - Strategic Information and Basic Laws
Cuba Business Success Guide - Basic Practical Information and Contacts
Cuba Clothing & Textile Industry Handbook
Cuba Clothing & Textile Industry Handbook
Cuba Company Laws and Regulations Handbook
Cuba Constitution and Citizenship Laws Handbook - Strategic Information and Basic Laws
Cuba Country Study Guide - Strategic Information and Developments
Cuba Country Study Guide - Strategic Information and Developments Volume 1 Strategic Information and Developments
Cuba Criminal Laws, Regulations and Procedures Handbook - Strategic Information, Regulations, Procedures
Cuba Customs, Trade Regulations and Procedures Handbook
Cuba Customs, Trade Regulations and Procedures Handbook
Cuba Diplomatic Handbook - Strategic Information and Developments
Cuba Diplomatic Handbook - Strategic Information and Developments
Cuba Ecology & Nature Protection Handbook
Cuba Ecology & Nature Protection Handbook
Cuba Ecology & Nature Protection Laws and Regulation Handbook

TITLE
Cuba Economic & Development Strategy Handbook
Cuba Economic & Development Strategy Handbook
Cuba Education System and Policy Handbook
Cuba Electoral, Political Parties Laws and Regulations Handbook - Strategic Information, Regulations, Procedures
Cuba Energy Policy, Laws and Regulation Handbook
Cuba Export-Import and Business Directory
Cuba Export-Import and Business Directory
Cuba Export-Import Trade and Business Directory
Cuba Export-Import Trade and Business Directory
Cuba Fishing and Aquaculture Industry Handbook - Strategic Information, Regulations, Opportunities
Cuba Foreign Policy and Government Guide
Cuba Foreign Policy and Government Guide
Cuba Healthcare Sector Organization, Management and Payment Systems Handbook - Strategic Information, Programs and Regulations
Cuba Immigration Laws and Regulations Handbook - Strategic Information and Basic Laws
Cuba Industrial and Business Directory
Cuba Industrial and Business Directory
Cuba Internet and E-Commerce Investment and Business Guide - Strategic and Practical Information: Regulations and Opportunities
Cuba Internet and E-Commerce Investment and Business Guide - Strategic and Practical Information: Regulations and Opportunities
Cuba Investment and Business Guide - Strategic and Practical Information
Cuba Investment and Business Guide - Strategic and Practical Information
Cuba Investment and Business Guide - Strategic and Practical Information
Cuba Investment and Business Guide - Strategic and Practical Information
Cuba Investment and Business Profile - Basic Information and Contacts for Succesful investment and Business Activity
Cuba Investment and Trade Laws and Regulations Handbook
Cuba Investment, Trade Strategy and Agreements Handbook - Strategic Information and Basic Agreements
Cuba Justice System and National Police Handbook
Cuba Justice System and National Police Handbook
Cuba Labor Laws and Regulations Handbook - Strategic Information and Basic Laws
Cuba Land Ownership and Agriculture Laws Handbook
Cuba Medical & Pharmaceutical Industry Handbook
Cuba Medical & Pharmaceutical Industry Handbook
Cuba Medical and Healthcare System and Regulations Directory
Cuba Mineral & Mining Sector Investment and Business Guide - Strategic and Practical Information
Cuba Mineral & Mining Sector Investment and Business Guide - Strategic and Practical Information
Cuba Mining Laws and Regulations Handbook
Cuba President Fidel Castro Handbook

TITLE
Cuba President Fidel Castro Handbook
Cuba Recent Economic and Political Developments Yearbook
Cuba Recent Economic and Political Developments Yearbook
Cuba Recent Economic and Political Developments Yearbook
Cuba Research & Development Policy Handbook
Cuba Research & Development Policy Handbook
Cuba Research & Development Policy Handbook
Cuba Starting Business (Incorporating) in....Guide
Cuba Tax Guide Volume 1 Strategic Information and Basic Regulations
Cuba Taxation Laws and Regulations Handbook
Cuba Telecom Laws and Regulations Handbook
Cuba Telecommunication Industry Business Opportunities Handbook
Cuba Telecommunication Industry Business Opportunities Handbook
Cuba: How to Invest, Start and Run Profitable Business in Cuba Guide - Practical Information, Opportunities, Contacts

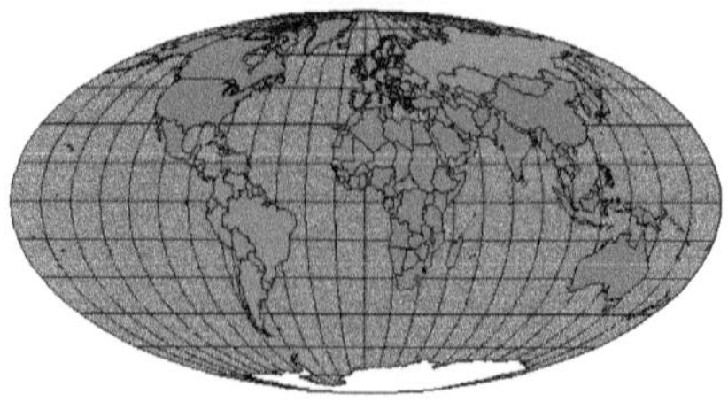

WORLD MINING LAWS AND REGULATIONS HANDBOOK LIBRARY

Price: $149.95 Each

Title
1. Afghanistan Mining Laws and Regulations Handbook
2. Albania Mining Laws and Regulations Handbook
3. Algeria Mining Laws and Regulations Handbook
4. Angola Mining Laws and Regulations Handbook
5. Argentina Mining Laws and Regulations Handbook
6. Armenia Mining Laws and Regulations Handbook
7. Australia Mining Laws and Regulations Handbook
8. Austria Mining Laws and Regulations Handbook
9. Azerbaijan Mining Laws and Regulations Handbook
10. Bahrain Mining Laws and Regulations Handbook
11. Bangladesh Mining Laws and Regulations Handbook
12. Belarus Mining Laws and Regulations Handbook
13. Belgium Mining Laws and Regulations Handbook
14. Benin Mining Laws and Regulations Handbook
15. Bolivia Mining Laws and Regulations Handbook
16. Bosnia and Herzegovina Mining Laws and Regulations Handbook
17. Botswana Mining Laws and Regulations Handbook
18. Brazil Mining Laws and Regulations Handbook
19. Brunei Mining Laws and Regulations Handbook
20. Bulgaria Mining Laws and Regulations Handbook
21. Burkina Faso Mining Laws and Regulations Handbook
22. Burundi Mining Laws and Regulations Handbook
23. Cambodia Mining Laws and Regulations Handbook
24. Cameroon Mining Laws and Regulations Handbook
25. Canada Mining Laws and Regulations Handbook
26. Cape Verde Mining Laws and Regulations Handbook
27. Cayman Islands Mining Laws and Regulations Handbook
28. Central African Republic Mining Laws and Regulations Handbook
29. Chad Mining Laws and Regulations Handbook
30. Chile Mining Laws and Regulations Handbook
31. China Mining Laws and Regulations Handbook
32. Colombia Mining Laws and Regulations Handbook
33. Comoros Mining Laws and Regulations Handbook
34. Congo Mining Laws and Regulations Handbook
35. Congo, Dem. Republic Mining Laws and Regulations Handbook
36. Cook Islands Mining Laws and Regulations Handbook
37. Costa Rica Mining Laws and Regulations Handbook
38. Cote d'Ivoire Mining Laws and Regulations Handbook
39. Croatia Mining Laws and Regulations Handbook
40. Cuba Mining Laws and Regulations Handbook
41. Czech Republic Mining Laws and Regulations Handbook
42. Denmark Mining Laws and Regulations Handbook
43. Djibouti Mining Laws and Regulations Handbook
44. Dominican Republic Mining Laws and Regulations Handbook
45. Dubai Mining Laws and Regulations Handbook
46. Ecuador Mining Laws and Regulations Handbook
47. Egypt Mining Laws and Regulations Handbook

For additional analytical, business and investment opportunities information, please contact Global Investment & Business Center, USA at (202) 546-2103. Fax: (202) 546-3275. E-mail: rusric@erols.com

Title
48. El Salvador Mining Laws and Regulations Handbook
49. Equatorial Guinea Mining Laws and Regulations Handbook
50. Eritrea Mining Laws and Regulations Handbook
51. Estonia Mining Laws and Regulations Handbook
52. Ethiopia Mining Laws and Regulations Handbook
53. Fiji Mining Laws and Regulations Handbook
54. Finland Mining Laws and Regulations Handbook
55. France Mining Laws and Regulations Handbook
56. Gabon Mining Laws and Regulations Handbook
57. Gambia Mining Laws and Regulations Handbook
58. Georgia Mining Laws and Regulations Handbook
59. Germany Mining Laws and Regulations Handbook
60. Ghana Mining Laws and Regulations Handbook
61. Greece Mining Laws and Regulations Handbook
62. Guatemala Mining Laws and Regulations Handbook
63. Guinea Mining Laws and Regulations Handbook
64. Guinea-Bissau Mining Laws and Regulations Handbook
65. Guyana Mining Laws and Regulations Handbook
66. Haiti Mining Laws and Regulations Handbook
67. Honduras Mining Laws and Regulations Handbook
68. Hungary Mining Laws and Regulations Handbook
69. Iceland Mining Laws and Regulations Handbook
70. India Mining Laws and Regulations Handbook
71. Indonesia Mining Laws and Regulations Handbook
72. Iran Mining Laws and Regulations Handbook
73. Iraq Mining Laws and Regulations Handbook
74. Ireland Mining Laws and Regulations Handbook
75. Israel Mining Laws and Regulations Handbook
76. Italy Mining Laws and Regulations Handbook
77. Jamaica Mining Laws and Regulations Handbook
78. Japan Mining Laws and Regulations Handbook
79. Jordan Mining Laws and Regulations Handbook
80. Kazakhstan Mining Laws and Regulations Handbook
81. Kenya Mining Laws and Regulations Handbook
82. Korea, North Mining Laws and Regulations Handbook
83. Korea, South Mining Laws and Regulations

Title
Handbook
84. Kuwait Mining Laws and Regulations Handbook
85. Kyrgyzstan Mining Laws and Regulations Handbook
86. Laos Mining Laws and Regulations Handbook
87. Latvia Mining Laws and Regulations Handbook
88. Lesotho Mining Laws and Regulations Handbook
89. Liberia Mining Laws and Regulations Handbook
90. Libya Mining Laws and Regulations Handbook
91. Lithuania Mining Laws and Regulations Handbook
92. Macedonia Republic Mining Laws and Regulations Handbook
93. Madagascar Mining Laws and Regulations Handbook
94. Malawi Mining Laws and Regulations Handbook
95. Malaysia Mining Laws and Regulations Handbook
96. Mali Mining Laws and Regulations Handbook
97. Mauritania Mining Laws and Regulations Handbook
98. Mauritius Mining Laws and Regulations Handbook
99. Mayotte Mining Laws and Regulations Handbook
100. Mexico Mining Laws and Regulations Handbook
101. Micronesia Mining Laws and Regulations Handbook
102. Moldova Mining Laws and Regulations Handbook
103. Mongolia Mining Laws and Regulations Handbook
104. Morocco Mining Laws and Regulations Handbook
105. Mozambique Mining Laws and Regulations Handbook
106. Myanmar Mining Laws and Regulations Handbook
107. Namibia Mining Laws and Regulations Handbook
108. Nepal Mining Laws and Regulations Handbook
109. Netherlands Mining Laws and Regulations Handbook
110. New Zealand Mining Laws and Regulations Handbook
111. Nicaragua Mining Laws and Regulations Handbook
112. Niger Mining Laws and Regulations Handbook
113. Nigeria Mining Laws and Regulations Handbook
114. Norway Mining Laws and Regulations Handbook
115. Oman Mining Laws and Regulations Handbook

Title
116. Pakistan Mining Laws and Regulations Handbook
117. Papua New Guinea Mining Laws and Regulations Handbook
118. Paraguay Mining Laws and Regulations Handbook
119. Peru Mining Laws and Regulations Handbook
120. Philippines Mining Laws and Regulations Handbook
121. Poland Mining Laws and Regulations Handbook
122. Portugal Mining Laws and Regulations Handbook
123. Qatar Mining Laws and Regulations Handbook
124. Romania Mining Laws and Regulations Handbook
125. Russia Mining Laws and Regulations Handbook
126. Rwanda Mining Laws and Regulations Handbook
127. Sao Tome and Principe Mining Laws and Regulations Handbook
128. Saudi Arabia Mining Laws and Regulations Handbook
129. Scotland Mining Laws and Regulations Handbook
130. Senegal Mining Laws and Regulations Handbook
131. Serbia Mining Laws and Regulations Handbook
132. Sierra Leone Mining Laws and Regulations Handbook
133. Slovakia Mining Laws and Regulations Handbook
134. Slovenia Mining Laws and Regulations Handbook
135. Somalia Mining Laws and Regulations Handbook
136. South Africa Mining Laws and Regulations Handbook
137. Spain Mining Laws and Regulations Handbook
138. Sri Lanka Mining Laws and Regulations Handbook
139. Sudan Mining Laws and Regulations Handbook
140. Suriname Mining Laws and Regulations Handbook
141. Swaziland Mining Laws and Regulations

Title
Handbook
142. Sweden Mining Laws and Regulations Handbook
143. Syria Mining Laws and Regulations Handbook
144. Taiwan Mining Laws and Regulations Handbook
145. Tajikistan Mining Laws and Regulations Handbook
146. Tanzania Mining Laws and Regulations Handbook
147. Thailand Mining Laws and Regulations Handbook
148. Togo Mining Laws and Regulations Handbook
149. Trinidad and Tobago Mining Laws and Regulations Handbook
150. Tunisia Mining Laws and Regulations Handbook
151. Turkey Mining Laws and Regulations Handbook
152. Turkmenistan Mining Laws and Regulations Handbook
153. Uganda Mining Laws and Regulations Handbook
154. Ukraine Mining Laws and Regulations Handbook
155. United Arab Emirates Mining Laws and Regulations Handbook
156. United Kingdom Mining Laws and Regulations Handbook
157. United States Mining Laws and Regulations Handbook
158. Uruguay Mining Laws and Regulations Handbook
159. Uzbekistan Mining Laws and Regulations Handbook
160. Venezuela Mining Laws and Regulations Handbook
161. Vietnam Mining Laws and Regulations Handbook
162. Yemen Mining Laws and Regulations Handbook
163. Zambia Mining Laws and Regulations Handbook
164. Zimbabwe Mining Laws and Regulations Handbook

www.ingramcontent.com/pod-product-compliance
Ingram Content Group UK Ltd.
Pitfield, Milton Keynes, MK11 3LW, UK
UKHW051458290926
15471UKWH00008B/1285

9 781433 077265